THE ORIENTAL INSTITUTE
2012-2013 ANNUAL REPORT

The Oriental Institute, Chicago

ISBN-13: 978-1-61491-016-9
ISBN-10: 1614910162

Editor: Gil J. Stein

Cover and title page illustration: "Birds in an Acacia Tree." Nina de Garis Davies, 1932. Tempera on paper. 46.36 × 55.90 cm. Collection of the Oriental Institute. Oriental Institute digital image D. 17882. *Between Heaven & Earth* Catalog No. 11.

The pages that divide the sections of this year's report feature images from last year's special exhibit Between Heaven & Earth: Birds in Ancient Egypt.

Printed through Four Colour Print Group, by Lifetouch, Loves Park, Illinois

CONTENTS

CONTENTS

INTRODUCTION

INTRODUCTION

Gil J. Stein

My colleagues and I are honored to present you with this year's *Oriental Institute Annual Report 2012–2013*. Over the past year our faculty and staff have been extremely active in our mission of exploring the civilizations of the ancient Near East and communicating our discoveries to both scholars and the broader community through our museum, our public programs, Oriental Institute membership, and our internationally recognized publications.

Although our archaeological fieldwork in Syria has been suspended indefinitely due to the uprising and horrific civil war in that country, our Hamoukar and Zeidan projects continue in the analysis and publication of their excavation results from the seasons up through 2010. Our ongoing excavations in Egypt (Edfu, Giza), Israel (Marj Rabba), Jordan (Maitland's Mesa), the Palestinian Territories (Khirbat al-Mafjar/Jericho), and Turkey (Kerkenes, Zincirli) continue to make important discoveries that are reshaping our understanding of ancient developments in the Near East. The success of our excavations depends on the combined efforts of trained professionals working closely with students and volunteers. In that respect, I am especially happy that Yorke Rowan and Morag Kersel's excavations at Marj Rabba in Northern Israel brought along five intrepid high-school students from the Rowe-Clark Math & Science Academy in Chicago to give them a rare opportunity — first-hand exposure to the excitement (and hard work) of exploring the Chalcolithic civilization of this region in the fifth millennium BC.

Ray Johnson and his team continue the important research of the Epigraphic Survey at Chicago House, recording and restoring the unique monuments of Medinet Habu and the UNESCO World Heritage Site of Luxor.

The Chicago Hittite Dictionary (CHD), edited by Theo van den Hout and Harry Hoffner, published the third fascicle of the letter Š volume in print form, while the digital version was readied for the web as part of the *e*CHD. At the same time it should come as no surprise that our premier Egyptian Lexicography Project — the Chicago Demotic Dictionary CHD) — is entering the (electronic) afterlife as editor Jan Johnson works with Brian Muhs, François Gaudard, and an international team of advisors to begin converting the PDF version of this dictionary into a highly flexible and more accessible digital form. The Persepolis Fortification Archive Project under Matt Stolper's leadership continues to make major strides in analyzing and documenting the thousands of texts and seal impressions that comprise this unique 2,500-year-old administrative archive of King Darius the Great and the Persian empire. We are nearing completion of this innovative project, and our plan is to make these priceless records accessible in digital form to researchers worldwide.

We continue to move forward in implementing our ambitious Integrated Database (IDB) project, which seeks to unite all the main data archives within the Oriental Institute into a single searchable structure that will be accessible to scholars and the public through the Internet. We crossed a major threshold this past year in linking the nearly half a million records in our Research Archives (library) with the 300,000 objects in our museum, and in making this trove of searchable data available to the public through the Oriental Institute's website. This is the culmination of years of effort by IT Department head John Sanders, whose retirement this past year marks another major change for the Oriental Institute. Happily, John's successor, Paul Ruffin, has leaped into the breach and is working closely with Angela Spinozzi, Foy Scalf, Scott Branting, Jack Green, and Helen McDonald to continue expanding and improving the IDB.

The Oriental Institute has increased the scope of its long-standing commitment to the preservation of cultural heritage. We have now completed the first year of our partnership with the National Museum of Afghanistan in Kabul. This program, sponsored by the U.S. Department of State, is a three-year effort to develop a database and complete digital inventory of the holdings of the National Museum. The project is proceeding rapidly, and our Kabul team, led by field director Michael Fisher, has now inventoried more than 17,000 of the Museum's estimated 60,000 objects.

Within the Oriental Institute's museum, our special exhibit Between Heaven & Earth: Birds in Ancient Egypt, developed and curated by Rozenn Bailleul-LeSuer, delighted and educated thousands of visitors by showing the ways that birds bridged the natural and cultural worlds to permeate virtually every aspect of Egyptian society, from economy to art to religion, and even played a key role in the hieroglyphic writing system.

Our Public Education and Outreach Section is embarking on an ambitious set of improvements under its new department head, Catherine Kenyon, and new staff members such as Carol Ng-He. Working with volunteer coordinator Terry Friedman and other key staff members such as Sue Geshwender and Moriah Grooms-Garcia, we are reinventing our Docent Program, developing online public education courses, implementing joint programs with the University of Chicago Lab School, and expanding our programming for children, families, and K-12 educators.

The above is just a thumbnail sketch of the numerous exciting developments across the board in our research and public communication programs over the past year. This work is only possible due to the dedicated efforts of our faculty and staff, and through the support of the thousands of members, donors, our Visiting Committee, and numerous other supporters of the Oriental Institute. To all of you I extend my deepest thanks.

————————

IN MEMORIAM

Deborah Aliber

On December 5, the Oriental Institute lost a dear friend and dedicated volunteer when Deborah Aliber passed away. Debbie served as a member of the Oriental Institute Visiting Committee for six years and was recognized as an Emeritus Docent. She began volunteering with the Oriental Institute while her husband, Bob, held a faculty position at the University of Chicago Booth School of Business. Among her many accomplishments, Debbie played a critical role in the formation of the Docent Library and served as its first librarian. Under her visionary leadership, the Docent Library has become an important resource for the Oriental Institute that is used daily by docents as they prepare for tours and expand their knowledge of the ancient world. Debbie and Bob were also generous donors to the Oriental Institute, and the Persian Gallery is named in honor of their contributions of time and talent.

Debbie's enthusiasm for the history and cultures of the ancient Near East led to numerous study trips to Egypt, Syria, Turkey, Iran, India, and around the Eastern Mediterranean Sea. Along with her warm and outgoing personality, Debbie was intellectually engaged in a wide variety of issues and was a passionate student of history and film. She was also culturally active and enjoyed visits to a wide variety of museums and theater performances.

The faculty, staff, and volunteers of the Oriental Institute count themselves as fortunate to have known and worked with Debbie. A special memorial service was held in the Robert and Deborah Aliber Persian Gallery in March. Debbie will be remembered for her dedication to advancing knowledge of the ancient world, her commitment to lifelong education, as well as her easy smile, infectious laughter, and welcoming demeanor.

Nina Longley

In June we mourned the loss of Nina Longley. A great friend to the Oriental Institute, Nina dedicated more than twenty-five years of service through the volunteer program. Nina's lifelong interest in world cultures and archaeology led her to join the Institute as a member and a volunteer. Along with her work with us, Nina was actively engaged with South Suburban Archaeological Society and facilitated numerous programs featuring Oriental Institute faculty and researchers. A passionate advocate for the Oriental Institute, Nina recruited and mentored countless volunteers who remain actively engaged with the program today.

A pioneer resident of Park Forest, Nina enjoyed a very successful career as a public-health nurse. Her involvement with the Oriental Institute began upon her retirement. Her passion for travel dovetailed with her intellectual interests and Nina explored a wide range of fascinating destinations, ranging from Egypt, Turkey, Syria, and Jordan to China and Tibet, Papua New Guinea, Italy, and Greece. Friend and fellow Oriental Institute volunteer Debbie Aliber accompanied Nina on an especially memorable trip to Iran in 1998, where Nina was photographed by *National Geographic* magazine.

Nina will long be remembered by her many friends and fellow volunteers at the Oriental Institute. All of us at the OI are thankful for her many contributions and are grateful to have had the chance to share an important part of Nina's life.

Barbara Mertz

Egyptologists and mystery lovers throughout the world joined the Oriental Institute in marking the passing of Barbara Mertz in August 2013. Barbara was the author of two nonfiction books on Egyptology, *Temples, Tombs, and Hieroglyphs: A Popular History of Ancient Egypt* and *Red Land, Black Land: Daily Life in Ancient Egypt*, which have remained in print for more than thirty years. Writing as Elizabeth Peters, Barbara was the author of the beloved Amelia Peabody series of thirty-seven mystery-suspense novels, many set in Egypt. Under her Barbara Michaels pseudonym, she produced an additional twenty-nine suspense novels.

Barbara was born in Canton, Illinois, and moved to the Chicago suburbs as a schoolgirl. At thirteen, she was introduced to the Oriental Institute on a visit with an aunt. She attended the University of Chicago and recalled that she was "supposed to be preparing myself

to teach …. I took two education courses before I stopped kidding myself and headed for the Oriental Institute." She earned her bachelor of arts, master of arts, and doctorate from the University of Chicago, specializing in Egyptology. Positions in academia were highly competitive and Barbara did not receive appropriate encouragement to enter that job market. Instead, she married, raised children, and began writing, incorporating her vast knowledge of Egyptology into her many books.

Barbara was a frequent visitor to Chicago House in Luxor, where she conducted research for her novels in the library and at various archaeological sites. She is remembered fondly by the generations of Chicago House staff as a valued friend, a dedicated supporter, and an insightful colleague. Her zest for life, sense of humor, and passion for adventure made her a most welcome house -guest. A long-time member of the James Henry Breasted Society, Barbara provided generous support for a number of Oriental Institute initiatives in Egyptology including the Epigraphic Survey, archaeological fieldwork, and climate-control improvements for the Oriental Institute Museum.

It would be difficult to measure the impact that Barbara Mertz has had raising awareness of ancient Egyptian civilization and on popular interest in Egyptology. Her nonfiction works and novels have promoted an accurate understanding and appreciation of ancient Egypt among lay audiences, and she has likely inspired many of her readers to continue learning about this fascinating civilization and to visit modern Egypt. Barbara Mertz will long be remembered as an alumna and dear friend, an author committed to historical accuracy, a steadfast scholar, and a dedicated advocate for Egyptology. All of us at the Oriental Institute are proud of our association with this remarkable woman.

Janet Russell

Last October, the Oriental Institute was saddened by the loss of Janet Russell, a longtime friend and dedicated Oriental Institute volunteer. Janet was a resident of Concord, California. As a child, she was happiest when she was exploring the library. Her passion for learning brought her first to Reed College and then to the University of Chicago, where she earned a master's degree in library sciences. According to her obituary, Janet "became a librarian so that she could help others find answers to their questions, bring order out of chaos." Her career path led her to focus on indexing books and reference works, and her work on indexing the Anglo-American Cataloguing Rules, known as the "bible" of the library world, earned her recognition worldwide. In 2004, she was presented with the H. W. Wilson Award, one of her profession's highest honors.

Her volunteer work with the Oriental Institute was especially meaningful to Janet as it offered her the opportunity to explore and deepen her knowledge of Near Eastern history and culture, which was a lifelong interest. Participation with the volunteer program also brought intellectual stimulation and the company of like-minded friends and colleagues. Janet served as a docent, which allowed her to share her knowledge with countless Oriental Institute visitors of all ages. Janet's passion for the Oriental Institute and its volunteer program was beautifully demonstrated in her creation of a significant endowment fund through her estate, which will benefit the Oriental Institute's volunteer program and outreach efforts. Janet's gift to the Oriental Institute has created a living legacy of her dedication to the pursuit of knowledge as well as her commitment to serving others. We extend our deep sympathies to her family as well as our gratitude for her many contributions to the Oriental Institute.

Mari Terman

Mari Terman passed away in January 2013. A longtime docent and dedicated member of the Oriental Institute Visiting Committee, Mari will be dearly missed by the Institute faculty, staff, and volunteers. Mari grew up in Hyde Park and her lifelong fascination with archaeology and the Middle East began with dinner-table conversations and visits to the Oriental Institute. She studied at the University of Chicago Laboratory School, the College of the University of Chicago, and Radcliffe College.

In 1998, Mari began volunteering as a docent with the Oriental Institute. Visiting Committee member Deborah Halpern remembers, "I immediately recognized Mari as being one of the most inquisitive and curious people I ever have known. There was never a lecture presented where she did not offer a poignant question. And while we all learned new information from the OI, Mari taught us all to be more thoughtful learners, and that may be the greatest lesson of all."

Mari will be remembered as a true champion of the Oriental Institute; for her bright, energetic, innovative mind and her deep commitment to improving her community and the lives of those around her. The faculty, staff, and volunteers of the Oriental Institute are particularly grateful to the Terman family for designating the Institute as a recipient of philanthropic contributions in memory of Mari. The outpouring of support received is a testament to the positive impact Mari had on so many lives.

———————————

RESEARCH

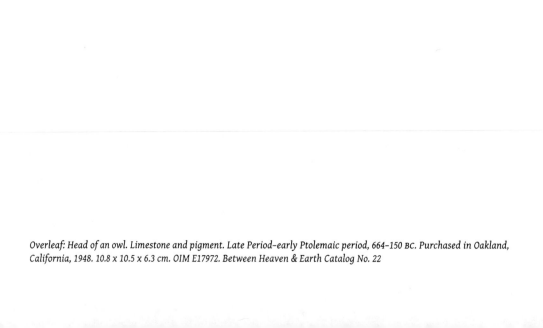

Overleaf: Head of an owl. Limestone and pigment. Late Period–early Ptolemaic period, 664–150 BC. Purchased in Oakland, California, 1948. 10.8 x 10.5 x 6.3 cm. OIM E17972. Between Heaven & Earth Catalog No. 22

PROJECT REPORTS

ARCHAEOLOGY OF ISLAMIC CITIES

Donald Whitcomb

Fustat, in modern-day Cairo, has a unique role in the archaeology of Islamic cities. It was one of the first capital cities founded after the Muslim conquest and, like Basra, Kufa, and other foundations, this settlement was a new location and not the modification of an older classical city (e.g., Alexandria). Descriptions from medieval geographers suggest an urban core called the Ahl al-Raya, around which the *khittat* or tribal districts were laid out.

A series of articles on the archaeology of Islamic cities within previous *Oriental Institute Annual Reports* have examined the principles behind early urban organization at Fustat. In the 2004–2005 *Annual Report*, a model was explored in light of al-Muqaddasi's urban terminology from the tenth century (pp. 15–16). In the 2005–2006 *Annual Report*, this model was expanded with information from the extensive excavations to explain what George Scanlon, one of its most prominent archaeologists, called the "riddle" of the earliest foundation. In addition, the new landscape methodology of Tony Wilkinson was employed to address subsequent urban development (p. 23). This series of articles also examined the city of Rayy, medieval Teheran, and its beautiful glazed sherds recovered during Oriental Institute excavations, then being studied by Tanya Treptow. Soon afterwards, Tanya organized these artifacts and their story into a fine temporary exhibit and catalog in the Oriental Institute Museum.

Just a few months ago, Tanya defended her doctoral dissertation on "Evolving Excavations," describing the origins of the practice of Islamic archaeology in Egypt from

Figure 1. Aly Bahgat sitting in the ruins of a house at Fustat, Old Cairo

the 1880s to the 1980s. This is a fascinating examination of personalities and institutions involved with the recognition of an Islamic past and the stages of employment of excavation methodologies. The fundamental example for this "pre-history" of Islamic archaeology was the site of Fustat. The mounds of Fustat were the archaeological setting where Aly Bahgat devised a method for recovering artifacts, especially fine glazed ceramics, and architectural monuments, particularly large houses, on behalf of the Museum of Arab Art from 1914 to 1924. This presentation of archaeological remains led contemporary scholars to speak of the resurrection of the early Islamic city.

Some forty years later, George Scanlon regenerated interest in these ruins, which were under threat from urban development in modern Cairo. He benefited from the new currents of archaeology being employed in the Nubian salvage campaigns. The whole neighborhoods he uncovered became valued in terms of the cultural heritage of Egypt. The most recent campaigns for the recovery

Figure 2. Solomon Schechter studying documents from the Cairo Geniza

of the city of Fustat have been conducted by Roland-Pierre Gayraud on behalf of the French Archaeological Institute (IFAO). He concentrated on a fringe of the city called Istabl ʿAntar, where he discovered a stratified sequence of early Islamic houses, as well as a Fatimid-period cemetery with magnificent Islamic works of art. Perhaps as important, he revealed another aspect of the urban planning and development. Regrettably, these areas were slated for modern housing developments and are now threatened to be entirely destroyed.

The history revealed in Tanya's dissertation is another example of the magic of Egypt, even extended into its more recent archaeological periods. This suggests a need for new archaeological models, ones focusing on urban social structures available through medieval documents from the Cairo Geniza, as studied first by Solomon Schechter and then by S. D. Goitein. The heritage of Fustat has been under threat for over a century, and yet, with increasingly clear goals, methods, and practices, new models may enrich the experience of Egypt and the modern world.

References

Goitein, S. D.

1967–1993   *A Mediterranean Society: The Jewish Communities of the Arab World as Portrayed in the Documents of the Cairo Geniza.* 6 volumes. Berkeley: University of California.

Treptow, Tanya

2007   *Daily Life Ornamented: The Medieval Persian City of Rayy.* Oriental Institute Museum Publications 26. Chicago: The Oriental Institute.

2013   Evolving Excavations: The Origins of a Practice of Islamic Archaeology in Egypt. PhD dissertation, Department of Near Eastern Languages and Civilizations, University of Chicago.

Whitcomb, Donald

2010   "An Umayyad Legacy for the Early Islamic City: Fustat and the Experience of Egypt." In *Umayyad Legacies: Medieval Memories from Syria to Spain*, edited by Antoine Borrut and Paul M. Cobb, pp. 403–16. Islamic History and Civilization, Studies and Texts 80. Leiden: Brill.

CAMEL
CENTER FOR ANCIENT MIDDLE EASTERN LANDSCAPES

http://oi.uchicago.edu/research/camel

Scott Branting

Central to CAMEL's mission at the Oriental Institute is the support that we provide to researchers, both in the Institute and around the world, with interests in using geospatial data, such as maps or satellite images, in their research. We do this by acquiring and storing geospatial data sets that will be of use to researchers, adding value to the some of the data sets through processes like digitization or georectification, and making them available as needed to support various avenues of research. In addition, CAMEL seeks to find new ways to engage interested individuals through outreach programs and to use our data to teach and train students at all levels of education, from sixth graders to university students and beyond. This past year at CAMEL, we touched on all of these various facets of the CAMEL mission.

As profiled in last year's annual report, researchers come to CAMEL in order to receive additional training and to make use of our expertise, resources, and collections. This past year we were very pleased to host Stephanie Rost, an advanced doctoral student in the Anthropology Department at Stony Brook University. Her Wenner-Gren Foundation-funded doctoral research project is examining irrigation management and state involvement in the Umma province of the Ur III state (ca. 2100–2004 B.C.), located in present-day Iraq. This work, which touches on several areas of expertise at the Oriental Institute, uses satellite and map data as a geospatial framework within which to analyze Ur III administrative records alongside more recent, historically attested irrigation systems in this area. Spatially situated models of labor input and administration of irrigation systems, derived from historical attestations overseen by both local and more regional powers, allow for a more nuanced reading of the Ur III records pertaining to irrigation administration. The results of Stephanie's work so far clearly demonstrate a correlation between the layout of irrigation systems and the historically situated social organization of its management. Particular spatial patterning of systems can be linked to labor inputs, strength of state oversight, and long-term sustainability. We all very much look forward to the completion of this research and the variety of contributions that it may make to water management in both the past and present.

Stephanie wasn't the only researcher making use of CAMEL during this past year. Well over one hundred requests were received and facilitated by CAMEL. This volume is in keeping with the past several years, and will hopefully dramatically increase even further in the years ahead as we strive to bring the wealth of our collections online within the framework of the Institute's online Integrated Database. We also received word from several scholars over the past year, including Stephen Moshier, who was highlighted last year in the *Annual*

Figure 1. This declassified US spy satellite image in the CAMEL collections was taken in 1969 and shows the town of Apamea in Syria, indicated by the arrow, an important city under the Seleucids and Romans. Reports from the field as well as modern satellite imagery have revealed recent widespread looting of this ancient city (cf. traffickingculture.org/data/looting-at-apamea-recorded-via-google-earth)

Report, of recent or impending publications that make use of CAMEL data or resources. It is always wonderful to see the fruits of research that CAMEL's work helped facilitate.

CAMEL received a number of new data sets during the year. Donations of data from individuals, research projects, and institutions are always welcome. The United States Geological Survey (USGS) provided us with a complete set of the 22,702 tiles of the ASTER satellite GDEM Version 2 digital elevation model data. This data set, which provides topographic information on the entire land surface of the globe between 83° N and 83° S (fig. 2), including the entire Middle East, was jointly released by the Ministry of Economy, Trade, and Industry (METI) of Japan and the United States National Aeronautics and Space Administration (NASA). Additional satellite data was donated to CAMEL by Stephen Moshier and our own Susan Penacho and Joshua Cannon. Some of these donations added to the impressive number of declassified US spy satellite images in our collections, a number that is currently at just over 2,300 and

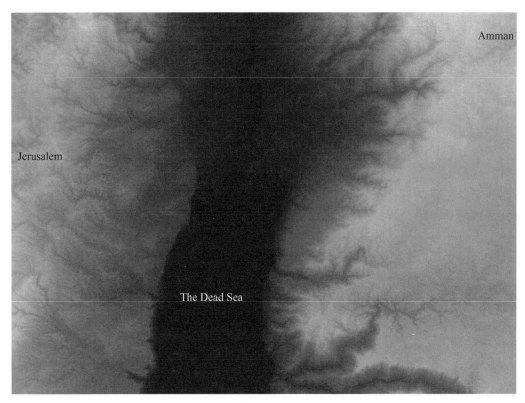

Amman

Jerusalem

The Dead Sea

Figure 2. A portion of one of the GDEM Version 2 tiles that CAMEL received from the USGS this year. It shows the topography of the area around the Dead Sea, including the area of the cities of Jerusalem and Amman. Digital Elevation Models are a very useful way to bring elevation information into Geographic Information Systems (GIS) software programs for generating viewsheds, least-cost paths, or 3-D models

Figure 3. The new Contex HD Ultra i4250s large-format scanner in action within the CAMEL Laboratory

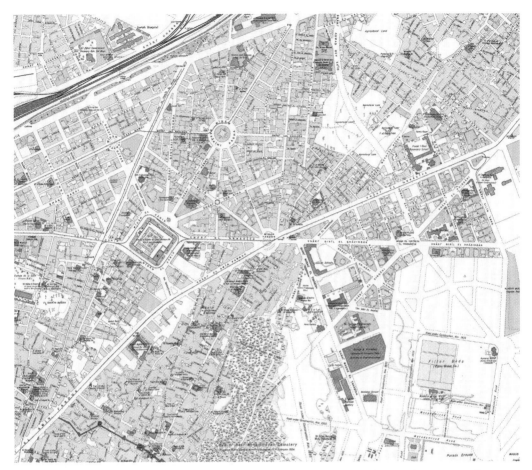

Figure 4. A portion of one of the Survey of Egypt Town Series maps that can be found in the CAMEL collections. It shows a neighborhood of Cairo in 1937. Although the names of certain streets and landmarks have changed, many of the features, such as mosques, are still present in the modern landscape

that is expected to increase markedly over the next year. Included in this number are images georectified by the CORONA Atlas of the Middle East project (corona.cast.uark.edu), which were provided to the project by CAMEL as part of a cooperative agreement. Our own work of georectifying declassified US spy satellite images by hand continued during this year with several hundred more images being georectified by CAMEL staff and volunteers.

CAMEL also received a brand-new Contex HD Ultra i4250s large-format scanner this year (fig. 3). The previous Contex large-format scanner, purchased in 2005 through a generous University of Chicago Provost's Program for Academic Technology Innovation (ATI) grant, finally ceased working after a long life of scanning thousands of maps, plans, and illustrations. The new scanner, funded by the Oriental Institute, will continue our mission of digitization. Already it has been put to good use scanning numerous large-format documents for the Diyala Project.

Finally, CAMEL continued to participate in outreach efforts this past year. The ACCESS sixth-grade program that we engaged in with the Chicago Public Schools the past several years has ended, but we expanded upon that outreach in January with a lecture to sixth-grade students at Coretta Scott King Magnet School in University Park, Illinois. In addition, not to neglect adults, a public lecture jointly sponsored by the Chicago Council on Science

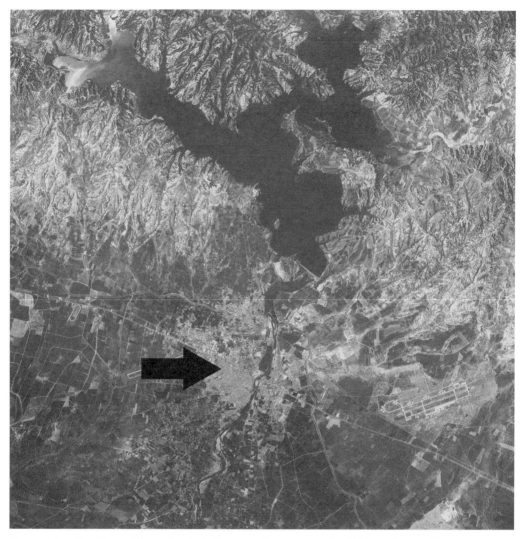

Figure 5. A portion of one of the declassified US spy satellite images in the CAMEL collection that was georectified by the CORONA Atlas of the Middle East project. It shows the city of Adana in Turkey, marked by the arrow, as well as the Seyhan Dam and reservoir to the north of the city as they appeared in 1969

& Technology (C²ST) and the Oriental Institute was presented in March. Titled "Spies, Satellites, and Archaeology: Mapping the Ancient Middle East," this lecture showcased much of the data and technologies that CAMEL employs to further research and monitoring of cultural heritage across the Middle East.

CAMEL is dependent on its dedicated staff and volunteers to provide the effort necessary to undertake this work. Elise MacArthur and Susan Penacho served as associate directors of CAMEL again this year, while Aleksandr Altskan, Hannah Loftus, Sunameeka Panigrahy, Patrick Thevenow, and Catherine Yeager were student assistants. CAMEL volunteers for this year were Josh Cannon, Alexander Elwyn, Larry Lissak, Giulia De Nobili, and Paige Paulsen. Together with all those listed above who provided contributions of geospatial data and the financial support of the Oriental Institute, they are the driving force that allows the work of CAMEL to grow and flourish.

CHICAGO DEMOTIC DICTIONARY (CDD)

François Gaudard and Janet H. Johnson

This year's great achievement was the completion of the Chicago Demotic Dictionary original plan, that is, to provide an updated lexicographical tool of the stage of the ancient Egyptian language known as Demotic. The Dictionary staff consisted of Janet Johnson, François Gaudard, and graduate students Brittany Hayden, Jonathan Winnerman, and Kate Lockhart, who joined our team last summer. In the winter, Brittany left us after working for about five years on the project. We thank her for her excellent contributions and wish her much success for the future.

As always, Janet Johnson and François Gaudard worked on the letter files, while Jonathan Winnerman and Kate Lockhart continued checking our Text Information, Abbreviation Authors, and Bibliographical Information files. Letter file T (329 pages) has been posted online, and François finished checking and completing the last letter, namely, S (542 pages), adding about 150 new pages to the final file. It will be posted online after a final style check. We have been assisted by Oriental Institute docent Larry Lissak, who scanned photographs of various Demotic texts and also part of Wilhelm Spiegelberg's *Nachlasse*. In its present state, the Dictionary consists of over 4,500 pages including about 45,000 scans.

On August 29, 2012, Jan, our new colleague Brian Muhs, and François organized a public roundtable on "Digital Demotic," hosted by the Franke Institute for the Humanities of the University of Chicago. This meeting brought together several American and European Demotists, classicists, as well as various University of Chicago affiliates actively involved in "digital humanities" projects. Two of our European colleagues, namely, Mark Depauw and Friedhelm Hoffmann, who are editors of websites concerned with Demotic, were kind enough to accept to take part in the discussion via Skype. Other Demotists worldwide, who were not able to attend, had been invited to send us their comments and suggestions before the meeting. The goal of this conference was to discuss the future of the CDD and, more precisely, to help us determine how we should now use and present our data in order to satisfy the digital needs of the CDD users in the most effective way. With general consensus, it was decided that our next step should be to turn the current PDF files into a searchable database housed on the Oriental Institute's website. At the beginning of the roundtable, Sandy Schloen and Miller Prosser from OCHRE Data Services gave a presentation on possible adaptations of this project to our Dictionary. We would like to extend our thanks to the Franke Institute, the Oriental Institute, and the Department of Near Eastern Languages and Civilizations for hosting and providing the funding for the roundtable, as well as all the meeting participants for their useful comments and suggestions.

On June 6, 2013, Jan and François participated in the University of Chicago "Knowledge Fair: A Celebration of Leaders in Philanthropy," which was an event to recognize the generous support of University donors and to give them the opportunity to interact and learn more about research and projects at our University (fig. 1). Jan presented a PowerPoint about the various steps involved in the creation of scans and hand copies of single words for dictionary entries, while François prepared a detailed handout and poster explaining the place of Demotic in the development of the ancient Egyptian language and writing systems.

We are grateful to our colleagues who regularly give us their input on the Dictionary, in particular, Eugene Cruz-Uribe, Friedhelm Hoffmann, and Joachim Friedrich Quack, and we would like to thank Willy Clarysse, Richard Jasnow, Mark Smith, Robert Ritner, and Karl-Theodor Zauzich for answering some of our bibliographical and lexicographical questions. Special thanks also go to Veena Elizabeth Frank Jørgenssen for providing us with various references from the Erichsen files in Copenhagen, and to Brittany Mullins for her help in preparing for the "Knowledge Fair." There are also several people we would like to thank for their invaluable help and support over the years, namely, Thomas Urban and Leslie Schramer for helping us with font issues and preparing letter files before their posting online, John Sanders and Paul Ruffin for their technical

Figure 1. The Oriental Institute table at the University of Chicago "Knowledge Fair," with informational material about the Chicago Demotic Dictionary

support, and, of course, Larry Lissak for his dedication and the excellent work he has been doing for us since 2007. Moreover, we would like to take this opportunity to announce the formal appointment of François Gaudard as Associate Editor of the CDD and Brian Muhs as Associate Director.

Among the various categories of words included in the CDD, it will be no surprise that insults are some of the least talked about in Egyptian literature. They are nonetheless an integral part of ancient Egyptian culture. Indeed, they give us insight into daily expressions and the creativity of the colloquial language.

When one thinks of insults in Demotic, one of the first texts that comes to mind is the so-called Harper's Song.[1] Composed in the second century AD, this work is not related to earlier Egyptian harper's songs found in tombs of the New Kingdom.[2] In the latter, "the injunction to live happily in the face of death and an uncertain afterlife is addressed to the living man."[3] Instead, the Demotic text is an invective against a harper named Hor-udja (Ḥr-wḏꜣ) "May Horus be sound!"[4] The role of a harper was to enliven both private parties and religious festivals, but, in this text, Hor-udja is said to be a terrible musician, who sings out of key and is only concerned with overindulging in food and alcohol. Wherever there is meat, he comes with his harp, being "faster than a fly on blood or a vulture which has seen a donkey."[5] He mixes up everything, playing joyful songs at funerals and sad ones at festivals. His audience is so stupefied that they are not able to insult him, and even the gods are mad at him. The anonymous author provides us with an anthology of Demotic insults and derogatory expressions, which happens to be a goldmine for linguists and lexicographers. Among others, the harper in question is called ḥnš "stinker,"[6] ḥrš n lḫ "ponderous fool" (lit., "burden of foolishness"),[7] sg "idiot,"[8] and rmṯ iw=f sꜣf r pꜣy=f iry "defiler of his companion."[9] However, nothing can top the epithet ḫnt nq,[10] literally, "foremost of fornicators," rendered as "arch fornicator" in the CDD, and which, according to the ancient author, would be a more appropriate name than Hor-udja for our notorious harper. It has been argued that the inspiration for this text could have been the works of Greek iambic poets such as Archilochus.[11] However, as noted by Dieleman and Moyer, "the newly discovered 'Songs for the Bastet Festival' make it more plausible to associate the genre with the drinking festivals described by Herodotus (2.60) and known from other Egyptian sources."[12]

Although used less commonly, insults also appear in Demotic tales. In the first story of Setna Khaemuas, for example, the enigmatic Tabubu, whom Setna is crazy about, refers to her maidservant as *tꜣy ḫnšṱ.t n ẖl* "this stinking servant-girl."[13] As one would expect, stories set in a military context, such as those of the Inaros-Petubastis cycle, are also likely to include a variety of insults. In the story known as "Egyptians and Amazons,"[14] Prince Petekhons, a son of Inaros, attacks with his Egyptian and Assyrian troops the so-called "Land of the Women," ruled by Queen Serpot. Throughout the fighting between Petekhons' troops and the Amazons, the narrator tells us that the soldiers "called out curses and taunts, the speech of warriors."[15] Unfortunately, this time the author was very stingy with details and did not give us any of these belligerent insults. In another story, called the "Battle for the Prebend of Amon,"[16] Prince Petekhons, when reading a letter asking him to come to the help of Pharaoh Petubastis, who usually ignored him, calls the latter a *ḥm ḫlte rmṱ n Tꜥne* "canal-fish fisherman, man from Tanis,"[17] in order to belittle him. In the same text, one of the Asian supporters of the high priest of Horus in Buto, who fights Petubastis to recover the prebend of Amun, calls an ally of the king, namely, Minnebmaat, a *Nḥs ꜣIgš wnm qmꜣ n rmṱ Yb* "Nubian from Kush, gum-eater (and ?) man of Elephantine."[18] This derogatory epithet, designating Nubian people, is also used in the second story of Setna Khaemuas, in which the hero refers to the *tš n wnm qmy* "district of gum-eaters."[19] In the "Battle for the Armour of Inaros,"[20] yet another story of the Inaros-Petubastis cycle, Pami, Inaros' son, wants to recover his father's magnificent piece of armor stolen by General Wertiamenniut, his enemy, and calls him a *ṯ-dꜣdꜣy wnm ⌈ꜣ⌉w⌈š⌉ [n P]r-bttⸯy⌉* "curly-haired resin-eater of Mendes."[21] Invectives focusing on the insulted person's region of origin were not unusual and could be particularly offensive. In fact, such a phenomenon was very common in ancient Egypt to the point that some enemy countries were almost systematically mentioned with an insult, especially in official royal texts. As we have already seen, such was the case with the kingdom of Kush,[22] which was often referred to as "wretched Kush"; likewise, this is seen with other foes like "that wretched enemy of Kadesh."[23] Nowadays, in our daily language, we still commonly use expressions that attribute to foreigners character traits seen as negative, rude, or inappropriate. In English, the idiom "to take French leave" means that someone has left a gathering without announcing his departure to the host. Ironically, the equivalent expression in French, namely, "filer à l'anglaise," attributes this bad conduct to the English. Likewise, the ancient Greeks, at least in Alexandria, could use the expression Αἰγυπτιστί "in Egyptian fashion," in the sense of "craftily," in order to disapprove of the native Egyptians' behavior, as attested in Theocritus' Idyll 15/47–48:

οὐδεὶς κακοεργὸς δαλεῖται τὸν ἰόντα παρέρπων Αἰγυπτιστί
No evildoer molests the passer-by, sneaking up in the Egyptian fashion.

In turn, the Egyptian name of Alexandria, namely, *Rꜥ-qt* (Rakotis) "building yard" (or "under construction") was possibly a way for the natives to make fun of the new city of the Macedonian rulers.[24]

Even the gods could be scorned. From the Late Period onwards, the god Seth was regularly insulted and humiliated for having betrayed and killed his brother Osiris. In P. Berlin 8278b,[25] for example, he is called *ꞽwšꜣ p3 why* "the failed one,"[26] while being depicted as an inebriated and lustful donkey.

Naturally, wisdom literature always suggests moderation in one's actions and speech. Therefore being offensive is considered unbalanced and undesirable behavior. So we will conclude with the wise words of ancient Egyptian sages who used to say: "Do not slander lest you be slandered!"[27] as well as, "It is better to bless someone than to do harm to one who has insulted you."[28]

Notes

[1] P. Harper (= P. Vienna KM 3877). See Thissen 1992.

[2] See, e.g., Lichtheim 1945.

[3] See Wente 1962, p. 118.

[4] Note that this name was also used as an epithet by the Roman emperor Claudius. On Roman imperial epithets in Demotic, see Gaudard and Johnson 2011.

[5] P. Harper, 3/17.

[6] P. Harper, 2/2.

[7] P. Harper, 2/8.

[8] P. Harper, 3/13.

[9] P. Harper, 3/20.

[10] P. Harper, 3/3.

[11] See Thissen 1992, pp. 13–15.

[12] See Dieleman and Moyer 2010, p. 440. See also Depauw and Smith 2004, and Hoffmann and Quack 2007, pp. 305–11.

[13] P. Cairo 30646, 5/6; Ptolemaic (dated year 15 [Ptolemy III (?) = 232 BC]).

[14] P. Serpot (= P. Vienna 6165 + 6165A)(ca. AD 200). See Hoffmann 1995. For a discussion on the Amazons and another passage of P. Serpot, see Gaudard and Johnson 2008, p. 27.

[15] P. Serpot, 3/4–5 and 3/48.

[16] P. Spiegelberg (Late Ptolemaic period). See Spiegelberg 1910.

[17] P. Spiegelberg, 13/14. Note that Hoffmann in Hoffmann and Quack 2007, p. 102, translated: "Kanalfisch(?)-Fisher von einem Mann von Tanis," which one could render as "fisher of canal(?)-fish of a man from Tanis." Or translate: "Tanite hunter of ichneumon" as Jasnow 2001, p. 71 n. 59. N.B.: The ichneumon is also more commonly known as an Egyptian mongoose.

[18] P. Spiegelberg, 15/20–21.

[19] P. BM 604 vo, 3/5 (Roman, dated year [7 Claudius I = AD 46/47]).

[20] P. Krall (= P. Vienna 6521–6609 + fragments) (Roman, dated year ⌐2⌐2 Had[rian] = AD 137/38). See Hoffmann 1996.

[21] P. Krall, 5/2. Since the text is damaged, we do not give a hand copy of this example.

[22] Kush was situated in what is now Sudan.

[23] See, e.g., Epstein 1963.

[24] For discussion, see, e.g., Chauveau 1999, pp. 3–6; Depauw 2000.

[25] Ptolemaic (dated year 35 [Ptole]my VI = 147 BC). See Gaudard 2005 and 2012.

[26] P. Berlin 8278b, x+11. See Gaudard 2005, pp. 169, 183 n. 81, 202.

[27] P. Louvre 2414b, 2/1 (Ptolemaic, dated year 23 Ptolemy VI = 159 BC). Translation: Hughes 1982, p. 53.

[28] P. Insinger, 23/6 (Late Ptolemaic). Translation: Lichtheim 1980, p. 203.

References

Chauveau, Michel

1999   "Alexandrie et Rhakôtis: le point de vue des Égyptiens." In *Alexandrie: une mégapole cosmopolite* (Actes du 9ème colloque de la Villa Kérylos à Beaulieu-sur-Mer les 2 & 3 octobre 1998), edited by Jean Leclant, pp. 1–10. Cahiers de la Villa "Kérylos" 9. Paris: Académie des Inscriptions et Belles Lettres.

Depauw, Mark

2000   "Alexandria, the Building Yard." *Chronique d'Égypte* 75: 64–65.

Depauw, Mark, and Mark Smith

2004   "Visions of Ecstasy: Cultic Revelry before the Goddess Ai/Nehemanit." In *Res severa verum gaudium: Festschrift für Karl-Theodor Zauzich zum 65. Geburtstag am 8. Juni 2004*, edited by Friedhelm Hoffmann and Heinz-Josef Thissen, pp. 67–93. Studia Demotica 6. Leuven, Paris, Dudley: Peeters.

Dieleman, Jacco, and Ian S. Moyer

2010   "Egyptian Literature." In *A Companion to Hellenistic Literature*, edited by James J. Clauss and Martine Cuypers, pp. 429–47. Chichester and Malden: Wiley-Blackwell.

Epstein, Claire

1963   "That Wretched Enemy of Kadesh." *Journal of Near Eastern Studies* 22: 242–46.

Gaudard, François

2005   The Demotic Drama of Horus and Seth (P. Berlin 8278a, b, c; 15662; 15677; 15818; 23536; 23537a, b, c, d, e, f, g). Ph.D. dissertation, University of Chicago.

2012   "Pap. Berlin P. 8278 and Its Fragments: Testimony of the Osirian Khoiak Festival Celebration during the Ptolemaic Period." In *Forschung in der Papyrussammlung: Eine Festgabe für das Neue Museum*, edited by Verena M. Lepper, pp. 269–86. Ägyptische und Orientalische Papyri und Handschriften des Ägyptischen Museums und Papyrussammlung Berlin 1. Berlin: Akademie Verlag.

Gaudard, François, and Janet H. Johnson

2008   "Chicago Demotic Dictionary (CDD)." In *The Oriental Institute 2007–2008 Annual Report*, edited by Gil Stein, pp. 25–27. Chicago: The Oriental Institute of the University of Chicago.

2011   "Chicago Demotic Dictionary (CDD)." In *The Oriental Institute 2010–2011 Annual Report*, edited by Gil Stein, pp. 27–31. Chicago: The Oriental Institute of the University of Chicago.

Hoffmann, Friedhelm

1995   *Ägypter und Amazonen: Neuebearbeitung zweier demotischer Papyri, P. Vindob. D 6165 und P. Vindob. D 6165 A*. Mitteilungen aus der Papyrussammlung der Österreichischen Nationalbiliothek (Papyrus Erzherzog Rainer), Neue Serie, 24. Vienna: Verlag Brüder Hollinek.

1996   *Der Kampf um den Panzer des Inaros: Studien zum P. Krall und seiner Stellung innerhalb des Inaros-Petubastis-Zyklus*. Mitteilungen aus der Papyrussammlung der Österreichischen Nationalbiliothek (Papyrus Erzherzog Rainer), Neue Serie, 26. Vienna: Verlag Brüder Hollinek.

Hoffmann, Friedhelm, and Joachim Friedrich Quack

2007   *Anthologie der demotischen Literatur.* Einführungen und Quellentexte zur Ägyptologie 4. Berlin: Lit Verlag.

Hughes, George R.

1982   "The Blunders of an Inept Scribe (Demotic Papyrus Louvre 2414)." In *Studies in Philology in Honour of Ronald James Williams: A Festschrift,* edited by Gerald E. Kadish and Geoffrey E. Freeman, pp. 51–67. Society for the Study of Egyptian Antiquities Publications 3. Toronto: The Society for the Study of Egyptian Antiquities by Benben Publications.

Jasnow, Richard

2001   "'And Pharaoh Laughed ...': Reflections on Humor in Setne 1 and Late Period Egyptian Literature." *Enchoria* 27: 62–81.

Lichtheim, Miriam

1945   "The Songs of the Harpers." *Journal of Near Eastern Studies* 4: 178–212.

1980   *Ancient Egyptian Literature: A Book of Readings,* Volume 3: *The Late Period.* Berkeley: University of California Press.

Spiegelberg, Wilhelm

1910   *Der Sagenkreis des Königs Petubastis nach dem Strassburger demotischen Papyrus sowie den Wiener und Pariser Bruchstücken.* Demotische Studien 3. Leipzig: J. C. Hinrichs.

Thissen, Heinz-Josef

1992   *Der verkommene Harfenspieler: Eine altägyptische Invektive (P. Wien KM 3877).* Demotische Studien 11. Sommerhausen: Gisela Zauzich Verlag.

Wente, Edward F.

1962   "Egyptian 'Make Merry' Songs Reconsidered." *Journal of Near Eastern Studies* 21: 118–28.

CHICAGO HITTITE DICTIONARY AND ELECTRONIC HITTITE DICTIONARY (CHD AND eCHD)

Theo van den Hout

On July 31, the third fascicle of the Š-volume rolled off the press: close to two hundred densely printed pages covering the entire stretch of Hittite words starting in *ši-*, from *šia-* "one" to ᴸᵁ*šizišalla-*, a word of unknown meaning, possibly denoting some kind of profession. As usual, we are deeply grateful to Tom Urban and Leslie Schramer of our Publications Office for shepherding it so professionally through the several phases toward the final printed version. Much of last year was spent on proofreading all the material. It is quite amazing how many very small and bigger errors there are in the proofs, and one always dreads the very first look in the freshly printed product: one glance and you might spot a period in the wrong place, a misspelling (or something worse!), and there is no longer anything you can do about it! On the other hand, it is encouraging to see how every reader sees different errors, so we are fairly confident that between the four proofreaders (Richard Beal, Petra Goedegebuure, Oğuz Soysal, and Theo van den Hout) we have caught most of them. Having this fascicle out we are all the more determined to resume work on the final installment of the current volume.

Meanwhile, Sandra Schloen and Dennis Campbell have continued their work to convert the completed articles of the Š-volume into a format appropriate for the electronic version (*e*CHD) delivered via the Online Cultural and Historical Research Environment (OCHRE). The techniques used for converting the original volumes L, M, N, and P are no longer valid, given the progression of technology. The Dictionary articles, now being written, edited, and formatted in newer versions of Microsoft Word and Adobe InDesign, are much more complex documents than previously and pose a number of challenges that complicate the task of parsing the structure of the documents for appropriate representation in database format. Nonetheless, the technology is stabilizing around newer XML-based document formats and we are moving forward in such a way that we will also be poised to handle new content being produced for future volumes. The first step is to convert all existing CHD content not yet in the online version from representation in the non-Unicode Hittite Dictionary font, to representation in a new Unicode-based font. We have developed a utility to batch-convert folders full of documents, appropriately substituting character code points and fonts while retaining all document formatting. We are also creating a powerful document transformation (XSLT) that exploits the XML-based formats of Word and InDesign, identifies the inherent structure in the documents — the hierarchy of sub-meanings within meanings, links to textual sources, cross-references to bibliography and other articles, etc. — and creates appropriate database content for the electronic version.

Another important step in our electronic efforts was the creation by Campbell of a User Manual with lots of illustrations in the form of screenshots, diagrams, etc. that explain the intricate and very powerful query system. This will eventually be posted online and hopefully help our "consumers." Finally, continuing coverage of our Turkish-language online dictionary, Soysal prepared the Turkish version of the words *šaptamenzu-* to *-ši-* that were already published in CHD *Volume Š, fascicle 2* (Chicago: The Oriental Institute, 2005).

This year our efforts to keep the lexical file database of the Dictionary up-to-date continued with work on *Keilschrifttexte aus Boghazköi* (KBo) volume 47 under the supervision of graduate student Oya Topçuoğlu. We have benefited greatly from Groddek's transliterations in DBH 33 (Detlev Groddek, *Hethitische Texte in Transkription KBo 47*. Dresdner Beiträge zur Hethitologie 33. Wiesbaden: Harrassowitz, 2011) and our senior research associate Oğuz Soysal's extensive review of the publication. Soysal also spent much of his time preparing the transliterations of the recent cuneiform editions, Keilschrifttexte aus Boghazköi volumes 51, 55, 56, 58, and 60 for the CHD files. Van den Hout has started transliterating KBo 61 for inclusion in our files.

In spring we went through a change in our staff, where Joanna Derman, our graduating student, left her post at the CHD and her duties were taken over by Joshua Cannon, a graduate student specializing in Anatolian studies. Oya and Josh expect to finalize work on KBo 47 and proceed with new volumes by this winter. Besides Josh, we also gratefully welcomed Shirlee Hoffman, who will help us systematize our numerous offprints and xeroxes. Shirlee comes to us as a volunteer from the Oriental Institute's Public Education Office, and we very much hope to keep her busy in the CHD office!

On a sadder note, we had to say good-bye to Joanna and Dennis. Joanna graduated from the College and has been awarded a Fulbright to teach English in Turkey. While doing so, she will consider her options for grad school; her interests go in the direction of international studies/law and the modern Middle East with a focus perhaps on Turkey. We are all grateful for the work she did for the Dictionary and we will miss the enthusiasm and passion with which she approached everything. Dennis has finally obtained what he deserves: he will start the new academic year as an assistant professor of ancient Near Eastern history at San Francisco State University. Dennis defended his dissertation several years ago now and all that time he has been our go-to person for anything *e*CHD related. In those same years he has become one of the world's leading experts on Hurrian and we are very happy he has agreed to remain one of our consultants on Hurrian texts and entries. We will miss his cheerfulness in the Dictionary room and his everlasting willingness to help out and step in where needed. We wish both Dennis and Joanna the very best in their careers!

We had several visitors to our Dictionary room on the third floor. First of all, there was Dr. Matteo Vigo, a PhD in Hittitology from the University of Pavia in northern Italy. He came to us through an Ambassadorial Rotary Fellowship. He worked on transforming his dissertation into several articles, as well as on some research projects, but he also helped out with the Dictionary, writing some articles for the future T-volume. It was wonderful to have Matteo and his wife Benedetta around. She is also a PhD from Pavia, but in ancient Near Eastern art history. She spent a lot of time in the Research Archives and in the Museum basement working on a specific collection that, among other things, includes some seals from Anatolia. At the end of the year Dr. Fatma Sevinç Erbası came to us for a month. She is assistant professor for ancient Near Eastern history at Eskişehir Osmangazi University in Turkey and does a lot of work on Hittite. Prof. Herrman Genz from the American University of Beirut paid us a brief visit. He was here as a committee member for a dissertation defense dealing with the archaeology of Lebanon, but Dr. Genz used to be involved in the excavations at Boğazköy, the site of the former Hittite capital, and he still publishes on the topic. Finally, Mr. Tayfun Bilgin, a student of Prof. Gary Beckman at Ann Arbor, used our files for his dissertation on Hittite bureaucracy.

A final and more permanent visitor you can see on the west wall of our Dictionary room: the Hittite king Tudhaliya IV in the warm embrace of his patron deity Sarruma. In the 1970s or 1980s, Prof. Hans Güterbock with Harry Hoffner, one of the two founders of the CHD, was able to buy from the Pergamon Museum in Berlin a cast of one of the reliefs of the rock sanctuary called in Turkish Yazılıkaya, just outside the Hittite capital Hattusa. This was made possible through a generous gift of Visiting Committee member Mr. Albert ("Bud") Haas. The originals were made in 1882(!) by Karl Humann. He was on a mission from the Prussian Academy to make casts of the *Monumentum Ancyranum*, the temple of the Roman emperor Augustus in Ankara. At the request of the Berlin Museums, however, he traveled on to Boğazköy to make squeezes of the Yazılıkaya reliefs. Having been made so early our cast has actual historical value preserving a very early state of the relief, less than sixty years after its discovery. Güterbock had hoped to display it in the Oriental Institute Museum

Figure 1. Cast of Tudhaliya IV in the office of the Hittite Dictionary

but casts did not fit the philosophy of the Museum at the time and so it stayed in the basement. At some point it was even moved to off-site storage, where it simply gathered dust. After several years of lobbying, however, and thanks to the support of Jack Green, the Oriental Institute's new chief curator, we were able to get it upstairs. Museum preparators Erik Lindahl and Brian Zimerle made a beautiful plinth and installed it, as you can see in figure 1 (see also fig. 3 in Erik Lindahl's *Prep Shop* report).

EASTERN BADIA ARCHAEOLOGICAL PROJECT: MAITLAND'S MESA, JORDAN

Yorke M. Rowan

The Eastern Badia Archaeological Project examines late prehistoric land and water use in two study areas in the eastern desert of Jordan, referred to as the *badia* (badlands), or the Black Desert. These two study areas are situated along the edge of the *harra*, the rugged extensive series of lava flows from Damascus to the northern edge of the Nafud Desert in Saudi Arabia. Co-directed with Gary Rollefson (Whitman College), the project focuses on Wisad Pools and the Wadi al-Qattafi/Maitland's Mesa (fig. 1). Both areas include remarkable concentrations of basalt structures in the hundreds, most collapsed and unidentifiable to function or period, and both unexamined archaeologically.

Wadi al-Qattafi is a broad, shallow drainage running roughly north–south, about 60 kilometers east of Azraq (fig. 2). On either side of the wadi approximately thirty mesas capped by basalt rise about 40–60 meters above the drainage bottom, creating dramatic vistas. The mesas, remnants of eroded Miocene flood basalts, range in size from 60 × 75 meters to about 1.2 × 0.4 kilometers. One of these, Maitland's Mesa (M-4), was first noted in 1927 and photographed by RAF pilot Percy Maitland while flying the Cairo-Baghdad airmail route. From the air, the mesa reminded Maitland of an Iron Age fort in Wales, drawing a parallel between the basalt structures along the southern edge of the mesa and a crenellated parapet (the site thus

Figure 1. Location of Wisad Pools and Maitland's Mesa in eastern Jordan (courtesy of Google)

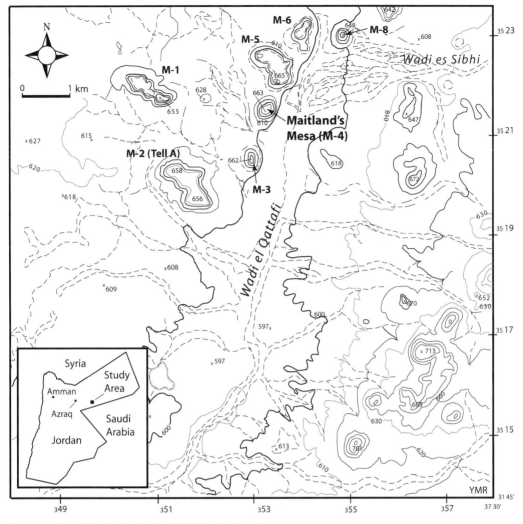

Figure 2. Map of Wadi al-Qattafi with Maitland's Mesa (M-4)

became known as Maitland's Hillfort). The site was largely unremarked until Alison Betts mentioned visiting the site in the 1980s.

Starting in 2008, several exploratory seasons of survey and documentation in the area revealed that most mesas have at least one basalt tower tomb on top (most looted), with perhaps a few collapsed structures atop the mesa and a few animal pens on the lower slopes. Maitland's Mesa, however, stands out among the mesas due to the large number of structures on top, ranging from animal corrals to small basalt elliptical or circular cells. The most strik- ing feature is the long, linear feature along the southern edge of the mesa noted by Maitland, which consists of over fifty rectangular to oval chambered cairns, many collapsed or looted (fig. 3). These seem linked to a large tower tomb, repeatedly looted. Similar features, known from our research at Wisad Pools, and on the Arabian Peninsula, are known as "tomb tails" in some publications.

During these seasons, nearly 500 structures and features were identified on the summit and slopes of Maitland's Mesa. Atop the oval-shaped mesa, approximately 200 structures are

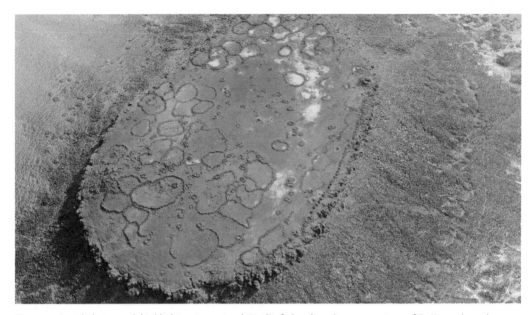

Figure 3. Aerial photograph highlighting tower tomb "tail" of chambers (image courtesy of D. Kennedy and APAAME)

documented, including not only the cairn chain, but also corrals, single- and double-celled structures, and a few U-shaped features, all constructed of the locally available basalt cobbles, boulders, and slabs (fig. 4). In addition, ten flint tool and debitage concentrations dated to the early Epipaleolithic, pre-pottery Neolithic, and Late Neolithic were recorded along the slopes. Also along the southern slope is a concentration of collapsed structures similar in appearance to the *nawamis*, the fourth-millennium BC roofed, stone-masonry form of burial structure known from the Sinai and the Arabian Peninsula.

Dating any of these structures is extremely difficult. Parallels are rare, and the contours of many structures are obscured by the collapse. Material culture is limited, with only a few non-diagnostic pottery fragments. Stone tools primarily represent two different techno-logical complexes, Lower/Middle Paleolithic Levallois and late prehistoric flake and blade technologies. As surface finds, these artifacts cannot definitively date the structures, but Late Neolithic, Chalcolithic, or Early Bronze seemed most likely.

In 2012 we excavated two small, circular stone features atop the mesa. One was a single-cell structure (165) and the other a double-cell structure (14). Basalt cobbles, haphazardly piled on each other, form low circular to oval walls only a few courses high; these were not intended to be walls that stood very much more than a few courses in height. Possibly these served to hold down roofing of skins or some other material as basic sheltering huts. Struc-ture 165, for instance, was oval (1.7 × 1.3 m) with two standing stones defining the threshold on the southeast. Excavation revealed very little depth (10–15 cm) in sediment before the basalt bedrock was found. In the double hut (14), one cell with a broad opening and possible paving (B) leads into a second cell (A) with more constricted entrance (fig. 5). Both cells had low walls ranging between 30 and 40 centimeters in height; cell A (1.8 × 1.4 m) was smaller than cell B (1.95 × 1.70 m). The only material culture found were non-diagnostic lithics on the surface of Cell A. Similar to many other cells atop the mesa, many cells are connected

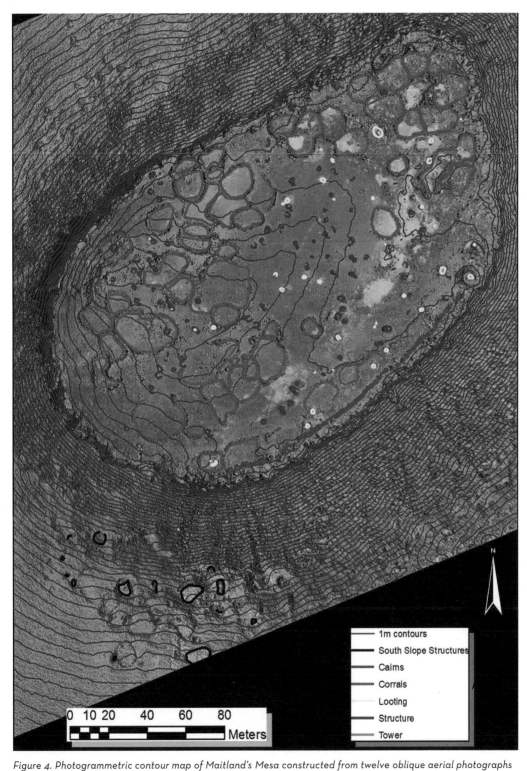

	1m contours
	South Slope Structures
	Cairns
	Corrals
	Looting
	Structure
	Tower

Figure 4. Photogrammetric contour map of Maitland's Mesa constructed from twelve oblique aerial photographs and a series of ground-control points collected with a total station on the ground. Aerial photographs were converted to a digital elevation model (DEM) in PhotoscanPro software and the resulting model was converted to a 1-meter contour interval map in ArcGIS. The underlying image of the site is an orthomosaic also constructed in Photoscan and output to ArcGIS (image by A. C. Hill)

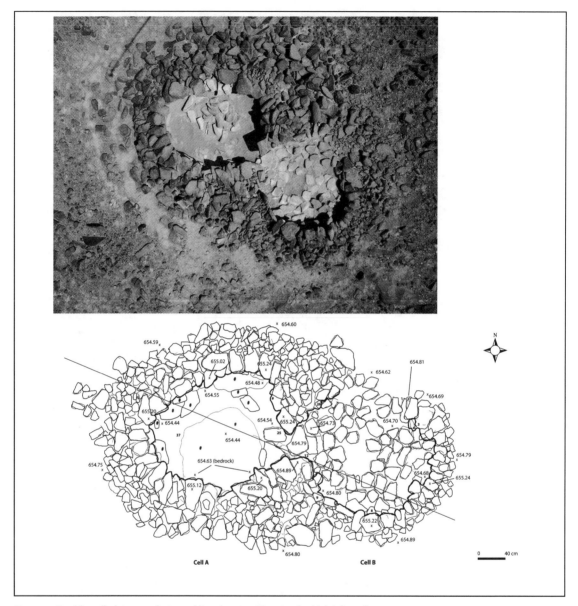

Figure 5. Double-cell ghura 14, photo and line drawing (drawing by M. M. Kersel)

features, often with one cell apparently paved with flat basalt cobbles, leading to another cell with an entrance denoted by two larger upright basalt slabs.

The lack of material culture associated with these structures was disappointing but not surprising, given the lack of sediment and rarity of artifacts on the top of the mesa. Without this crucial link we cannot date the cells, but the poverty in material culture suggests that these were largely temporary structures, not intended for long-term use. Perhaps these were the huts of visitors to the top, possibly watching over flocks. But why bring flocks to the top of a mesa? The particular contours of the mesa surface may be the answer; rainwater collects on the eastern side during wet months, an attractive reason for pastoralists to corral animals on top, possibly providing greater protection.

Nearly thirty structures are visible on the southern slope. Most are circular, probably around a single interior space, although one large two-roomed rectilinear structure (7.0 × 3.5 m) is distinct from the others. Although a few of the round cells are large (up to 10 m in diameter), many range between 2 and 3 meters in diameter. One of these collapsed round structures (SS-11) was selected for excavation because it was apparently undisturbed by looting, and the entrance was preserved. The assumption that this might be a mortuary structure similar to the *nawamis* of the Sinai was quickly discarded with clearance of the collapsed basalt slabs. Their removal exposed an oval plan and a second entrance on the eastern side of the structure. The dry masonry basalt slabs that also seemed similar to construction techniques used for the *nawamis* were not used in the interior.

Two building phases were recognized. In the first, the building interior was built on the slope with a fill layer to level the small (ca. 2 × 3 m) space (fig. 6). A long, shaped basalt slab found in the fill probably acted as the roof support for a very low ceiling that necessitated crouching inside the structure. Hearths were found above this lowest level, suggesting repeated use. Unlike the exterior, interior wall construction includes large flat slabs vertically erected and supported by smaller stones wedged into gaps and crevices. A second doorway opened on the northeast; both doorways had vertical slabs supporting a lintel just under a meter in height.

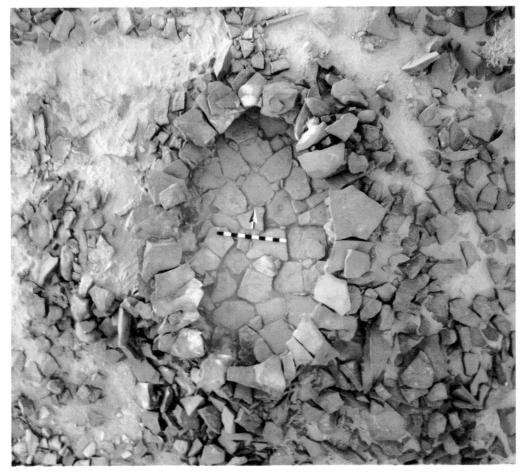

Figure 6. Plan view of SS-11

Figure 7. Photograph showing entrance to SS-11, with openings to exterior storage areas

The second doorway opened on to a courtyard (fig. 7), which included a small stone-lined hearth with ashy sediment. An ash dump was found in the courtyard, near the northeast entrance, below a later enclosure wall. Also in this area of the southeastern edge was found a low corbeled space (1.90 × 1.45 m) with single central pillar in situ standing about 45 centimeters high, presumably a storage room (L.018). A smaller triangular storage space (L.020) also opened onto the courtyard; the larger storage room may also have had an opening on the southern aspect.

In the second phase, the eastern entrance was blocked and the courtyard walls added. The building's interior was reconfigured by leveling the floor and paving it with flat basalt slabs (ca. 30–40 × 50 cm); small stones were wedged between the slabs. A small gap in the center may have acted as a socket for the long, shaped pillar for additional roof support. These changes raised the floor further, possibly leaving so little clearance that crawling into the space was necessary.

Unlike the virtually empty cells excavated on the top of the mesa, artifacts were plentiful in SS-11. In addition to a few handstones and limited animal bone, flint artifacts were found that included tabular knives, unifacial and bifacial knives, scrapers, notches, and denticulates. A few arrowheads, diagnostic of the Late Neolithic (Yarmouk, Haparsa) suggest dates between 6500 and 6000 BC (fig. 8).

Although this structure proved not to be a mortuary structure, these exciting results allow us new insights into the occupation and use of the eastern desert. The many other similar structures ringing Maitland's Mesa, and possibly at a few other mesas along the Wadi al-Qattafi, suggest much denser, longer-term occupation than assumed for this arid region. The ability to date with confidence structure SS-11 to the Late Neolithic dramatically alters our understanding of the region, and the permanence with which people lived in the area. Despite the current arid and virtually unpopulated environment, such investment

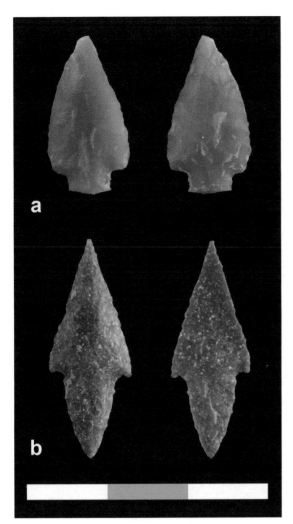

Figure 8. Projectile points from SS-11: (a) Yarmouk point, (b) Haparsa point (photo by G. O. Rollefson)

in substantial structures indicates much more than a nomadic existence with little long-term habitation. Instead, small groups of people may have lived a large portion of the year here, only leaving during the driest months. Clearly, one excavated structure at Maitland's Mesa, and another Late Neolithic structure at Wisad Pools, precludes conclusive statements, but in each case these Late Neolithic structures suggest residential occupation with some permanence, albeit seasonally constrained. Like the structure at Wisad Pools, this corbelled structure highlights a previously unknown phenomenon for the eastern badia.

The construction of these buildings required labor investment that anticipated repeat visits, presumably during the wetter months. Despite the need for much more research than these limited investigations, these initial results cause a reconsideration of the late prehistoric use and habitation of the area. Combined with other research initiatives in the area, the eastern badia of Jordan seems less empty during the late prehistoric periods.

EPIGRAPHIC SURVEY

W. Raymond Johnson

On April 15, 2013, the Epigraphic Survey, in cooperation with the Egyptian Supreme Council of Antiquities/Ministry of State for Antiquities Affairs, completed its eighty-ninth six-month field season in Luxor; Chicago House's activities ran from October 15, 2012, through April 15, 2013. Projects included epigraphic documentation, conservation, and restoration work at Medinet Habu (funded by a grant from the United States Agency for International Development [USAID] Egypt); the continuation of our documentation program at the Theban Tomb 107 of Nefersekheru; a month of salvage documentation work at Khonsu Temple at Karnak (in cooperation with the American Research Center in Egypt [ARCE]); and conservation, restoration, and maintenance of the blockyard open-air museum at Luxor Temple (partly funded by the World Monuments Fund [WMF]), as well as documentation of blocks from the Basilica of St. Thecla in front of the Ramesses II eastern pylon.

Medinet Habu

Epigraphy

Documentation continued this year in the Small Temple of Amun, focusing on the recording of materials in the ambulatory and on the facade, destined for publication in *Medinet Habu X*. Our work was supervised by Ministry of State for Antiquities (MSA) inspectors Mr. Atito Mohamed Hassan, Mr. Mahmoud Ahmed Hussein Gad, Miss Eman Haggag Yousef, Mr. Mohamed Ahmed Selim, Mr. Mahmoud Mohamed el-Azab, and Mr. Hosny Mohamed Abd el-Wahab. Egyptian Documentation Center observers of our epigraphic techniques this season at Medinet Habu, Theban Tomb (TT) 107, and Khonsu Temple were Mr. Mohamed Rizq Ibrahim Rageb, Mr. Ali Sayid Ali, and Mr. Ahmed Hussein Khali. Epigraphers included senior epigraper Brett McClain, and epigrapher Jen Kimpton; artists included senior artists Margaret De Jong and Sue Osgood, artist/Egyptologist Krisztián Vértes, and artist Keli Alberts. The artists' and epigraphers' efforts this season were concentrated mainly on work in the ambulatory and facade of the Small Temple, with priority given to material for *Medinet Habu X*. Significantly, all enlargements destined for publication in *Medinet Habu X* have now passed the inking stage, with only two collations pending completion in 2013–14. Considerable numbers of drawings are also in progress for *Medinet Habu XI, XII*, and the follow-

Figure 1. Margaret De Jong focusing raking light on Pinudjem inscription, small Amun Temple (photo by Yarko Kobylecky)

Figure 2. Sue Osgood with historic inked and digital drawing. February 22, 2013 (photo by Ray Johnson)

ing volumes. All publications will include facsimile drawings and translations (where appropriate) of all the late-period graffiti found on the walls, documented by Tina Di Cerbo and Richard Jasnow. Work on facsimile drawings at Medinet Habu, continued this year by the full staff, is proceeding at an encouraging rate, allowing the completion of all fieldwork for *Medinet Habu X* by spring 2015.

Although the amount of epigraphic work completed by the Epigraphic Survey during a season at Medinet Habu cannot be quantified strictly in terms of numbers of scenes drawn and collated, especially given the increasingly heterogeneous nature of our other projects at the site, we may nevertheless form a general impression of this year's progress by noting the drawings that have passed through the following stages of the Chicago House process:

Penciling completed this season: 19
Inking completed (including summer 2012): 31
Collation completed: 9
Transfer Check completed: 14
Director Check completed: 11

Figure 4. Tina Di Cerbo recording Christian graffiti digitally, Medinet Habu. March 2013 (photo by Ray Johnson)

Figure 3. Jen Kimpton "at the wall" in the Medinet Habu small Amun temple, February 22, 2013 (photo by Ray Johnson)

Medinet Habu Blockyard

The conservation team, supervised by senior conservator Lotfi Khaled Hassan and assisted by Nahed Samir Andraos, continued conservation, consolidation, and display of fragmentary material in the new, protected blockyard built by Chicago House against the southern Ramesses III enclosure wall. An additional component of the recording work at Medinet Habu has been the ongoing documentation and processing of this fragmentary material from the precinct, now securely stored in the blockyard. The focus of much of blockyard epigrapher Julia Schmied's effort during fall 2012 was the continued recording and analysis of a corpus of approximately 300 fragments coming from the houses and other monuments of the late Ramesside and early Third Intermediate Period, which were situated within the Medinet Habu enclosure. All are now documented in digital photographs, and some are being reconstructed by Lotfi and the conservation team. In addition, photographer Yarko Kobylecky, assisted by Ellie Smith, has provided film photographs of over 200 of the fragments in this corpus to date, and Juli has scanned these photographs for inclusion in her study. She also made scale perspective drawings of approximately 150 of the fragments, mostly doorjambs, as aids to the reconstruction of fragment groups, along with hand copies of all of the texts in this corpus. Juli has created, in addition to the main Medinet Habu fragment database, another fragment database specific to the Late Ramesside/Third Intermediate Period corpus, and a reference database for collecting stylistic parallels and published references and aids for the analysis of the collection.

To date, over 4,000 fragments from Medinet Habu have been registered and entered into the Medinet Habu database, and the sorting, labeling, and study of various parts of the collection continued throughout the first half of the season. Registration, transfer,

Figure 5. Architectural joining of Ramesses III doorjamb blocks, Medinet Habu, March 2013, Brett McClain, Nahed Andraos, and Lotfi Hassan (photo by Ray Johnson)

Figure 6. Juli Schmied and reassembled doorjamb, 2012 (photo by Ray Johnson)

Figure 7. Medinet Habu conservation and stone team, February 13, 2013. Nahed, Hamada, Frank, Lotfi, Mustafa, Ahmed, and Mohamed (photo by Ray Johnson)

labeling, and analysis of the Medinet Habu fragments is envisioned to be a long-term project, with the goal of continuing to sort and register the remaining unclassified blocks, and to continue the assembly of the open-air museum in front of the new blockyard (under Lotfi's supervision). Perhaps we may even reconstruct elements of the Ramesses III palace in situ. Also planned is the registration and moving into the new blockyard of remaining loose fragments scattered in the area of the western fortified gate.

The Domitian Gate

This season marks the third season in our Medinet Habu Domitian Gate restoration work. Three years ago we noted that the first-century AD sandstone gate of the Roman emperor Domitian, reassembled by Georges Daressy from scattered blocks in the late nineteenth century behind the small Amun temple, was in danger of collapse due to groundwater-salt decay of its foundations. After consultation with the MSA/SCA, conservator Lotfi, master mason Frank Helmholz, and our structural engineer Conor Power, it was decided that the gate had to be completely dismantled in order to properly replace the foundations with new sandstone, specially damp-coursed against any future groundwater problems. Permission was granted by the MSA/SCA to begin that work in 2011, and dismantling began then.

This season Frank and the Chicago House workmen cut and shaped seven new replacement blocks for the lowest courses of the gate, and put into place the bottom-most course on a new rein-

Figure 8. Mahmoud Abdel Haris cutting stone, January 2013 (photo by Frank Helmholz)

Figure 10. Claudius Gate cleanup, December 3, 2012 (photo by Frank Helmholz)

Figure 9. Frank and new Domitian Gate footing March, 2013 (photo by Ray Johnson)

forced concrete footing, installed last year. One partially preserved old block and one new stone were joined, and all new stones were bolted to the new damp-coursed foundation with steel pins. The remaining blocks from the gate are stored on platforms to the north of the gate and are awaiting additional documentation and consolidation next season before reconstruction. Frank will continue cutting and shaping new stone blocks that will replace some of the missing and decayed blocks next season.

Another Roman-period gate from the time of the Roman emperor Claudius outside the Medinet Habu eastern enclosure is in bad condition due to groundwater salt decay and will be dismantled for restoration next season. This season it was cleaned and roped off to protect it from further damage.

The ground around the Medinet Habu precinct continues to dry out, thanks to the USAID-funded, west bank dewatering program that was inaugurated two years ago September (in 2010). The water level in the sacred lake to the north of the small Amun temple has stayed down, back to levels recorded during our first work at Medinet Habu in the 1930s. Re-erection of the gate is scheduled to be finished in 2014.

TT 107, Theban Tomb of Nefersekheru

This winter the Survey continued its documentation work at the Theban Tomb of Nefersekheru (TT 107). Our work was facilitated by MSA Inspector Miss Fatma Ahmed Salem. Work was undertaken at the site from January 12 through February 12, 2013. Our Australian collaborators, Boyo and Susanne Ockinga, first undertook a brief architectural survey of the facade of the tomb (January 12–14), focusing on the damaged entrance to the tomb and the later mudbrick structures built into it.

After the architectural survey, Sue resumed and finished her drawing on the site, and at the end of the four-week period of work, Margaret completed her enlargement penciling as well. As a result of this season's work, all the enlargements for TT 107 have now been penciled, and the inking of these will be completed by the end of summer 2013. It is hoped that the epigraphers can begin collation during the 2013–2014 field season, and that it will be possible to continue the archaeological work, architectural study, and conservation work on the site as well.

Figure 11. Inspector Fatma, Margaret, and Brett review drawings at TT 107, February 12, 2013 (photo by Ray Johnson)

Khonsu Temple, Karnak

This year's season at Khonsu Temple began on March 14, 2013, and ran until April 11, 2013. The focus of the work was the documentation of reused blocks embedded in the walls of Khonsu Temple. The team consisted of Keli Alberts and Jen Kimpton, with Yarko Kobylecky as photographer; Brett McClain consulted on epigraphic questions when needed, and final checks were provided by the field director. Our work was supervised by MSA Inspector Miss Salwa Fathalla Gassan.

Despite the brevity of the season, and the presence of only one artist, five new drawings were completed, all drawn by Keli Alberts. These include: KhF0332A and B, a two-sided reused block employed in the southwest corner of the Hypostyle Hall that bears an inscription of Ramesses II (based on style) and a later inscription of Ramesses III; KhF0333, another Rames-side block adjacent to KhF0332AB; KhF0315, a very large architrave block belonging to the reign of Horemheb, located above the eastern door of the Hypostyle Hall; and KhF0327 in the east wall of Room V, a block bearing Eighteenth Dynasty raised decoration that also featured a cartouche frieze added in sunk relief by Ramesses II. In addition to these new drawings, KhF1248, a reused *talatat* discovered in the SCA excavation in the court, was revisited and prepared for director-check. Also in progress is a drawing of a newly discovered architrave block adjacent to KhF0315; it is the 371st in situ reused block that we have noted at Khonsu Temple.

All five of the new drawings were collated by Jen Kimpton, discussed, and prepared for director check. In addition, Jen recollated the loose fragment KhF1248 and began the collation of KhF0317, an architrave block belonging to the reign of Thutmose IV. Besides collation, Jen also reexamined several blocks from past seasons to measure (or remeasure) their dimensions for the purpose of isometric renderings. Finally, over the course of the Chicago House 2012--2013 season, Jen completed the database entries for all the blocks of the past seasons; the Khonsu database now contains 427 records and provides for each block its photographs, preliminary and final drawings, digital isometric drawings, collation sheets, dimensions, architectural elements, dating criteria, etc.

Four new blocks were photographed by Yarko Kobylecky this season. These include: KhF0316 and KhF0321 in Room I; KhF0322 in Room III; and KhF0327 in Room V.

Figure 12. Yarko photographing ceiling block at Khonsu Temple, March 25, 2013 (photo by Pia Kobylecky)

Figure 13. Keli and Jen collating at Khonsu Temple, April 1, 2013 (photo by Yarko Kobylecky)

2013 Season Totals

Total new drawings: 5 complete, 1 in progress
Total new collations: 6 complete, 1 in progress
Total new director-checks: 21

2008–2013 Khonsu Temple Totals

Total in situ blocks mapped so far: 371
Drawings of in situ blocks director checked: 219
Total loose fragments registered: 268
Total loose fragments requiring drawing: 144
Total loose fragments drawn: 144
Total loose fragments director-checked: 136

Luxor Temple

Documentation

Imperial Cult Chamber Facsimile Drawing

This season a significant new project was begun at Luxor Temple, the purpose of which is to produce full facsimile documentation of the Late Roman fresco paintings in the Imperial Chamber (Room V). Using the digital drawing equipment acquired this season, Krisztián Vértes developed a method for capturing the details of the paintings by penciling on an enlargement, which is then scanned, and then bleached, the pencil drawing then serving as the basis for a version that is inked digitally. The experimental stage and on-site development of this method, followed by the penciling of a complete sample enlargement (taken from CH neg. no. 20115) occupied Krisztián for the last three weeks of January.

The goal of this new initiative is the definitive publication of the frescos added to this chamber during the First Tetrarchy. In addition to the facsimile drawings of the paintings, which will be presented alongside our high-quality color photographs of same, the publication is envisioned to integrate the detailed study of the architectural components of the chamber and the surrounding rooms, which were extensively modified at the end of the third century AD, when the temple came to serve as the center of the Roman legionary encampment. These have over the past several years been the subject of an in-depth investigation by Chicago

Figure 14. Krisztián Vértes penciling Roman frescos, Imperial Cult chamber, Luxor Temple, January 2013 (photo by Yarko Kobylecky)

House architect Jay Heidel. Presenting the paintings in facsimile and the architectural study at the maximum level of detail will provide a fully integrated and complete publication of this terminal stage of the temple's use as a temple. It is intended that Krisztián and Jay will devote a considerable portion of the next few field seasons to the completion of this project.

Our work at Luxor Temple this year was supervised by MSA inspectors Mr. Gamal Amin Ebaid, Mr. Omar Yousef Mohamed, Mr. Ahmed Abd el-Nazeer Abd el-Wareth, and Mr. Ashraf Abdou Mohamed.

Thecla Church Project

The primary focus of work this season was the continued drawing of Thecla Church Arch 2 material by architect Jay Heidel. (Arch 2 is the arch fronting the apse of the church.)

AutoCAD drawings were completed for two blocks, resulting in four drawings. Sixteen drawings were also collated for correction transfer during the summer of 2013. There are currently fifty-seven collated drawings awaiting correction transfer. The decision has been made that, rather than make the correction transfers in AutoCAD (which has unresolved issues with sun/shadow conventions), the collated drawings will be redrawn with sun/shadow convention in Photoshop using the Wacom tablet. The AutoCAD drawings will be used in the architectural reconstruction drawings (with single-weight lines). Jay began the digital inking of the granite engaged columns of Arch 2 (an inscribed, reused monument of Thutmose III) using the Wacom drawing tablet.

Luxor Temple Educational Signage

Another focus of work this season was the continuation of work on educational signage for the Luxor temple precinct. An additional copy of the previously completed orientation sign was erected to the northwest of the Ramesses II pylon for the orientation of groups arriving to the precinct, and three additional signs were completed in layout form by Jay and edited by the senior epigrapher and the director. They include: the "Ancient Luxor" orientation sign, the "Pylons of Ramesses II" sign, and the "Ramesses II Court" sign. The final corrections will be transferred during the summer of 2013.

Figure 15. Shelving for storage of small blocks, Luxor Temple, Hiroko and Mohamed (photo by Ray Johnson)

Luxor Temple Conservation

Between January 19 and March 20, 2013, conservator Hiroko Kariya continued her annual conservation monitoring, condition-surveying, and treatment in the Luxor Temple block-yards, open-air museum, and Thecla Church blocks, all recorded in the block-yard database.

The Luxor Temple Fragment Project was begun in the 1995–1996 season by conservator John Stewart. The project's original focus on approximately 2,000 registered fragments quickly evolved to include the roughly 50,000 inscribed fragments in the Luxor Temple blockyards and open-air museum. For the last five years the project focused on the reconstruction of the Sun Court wall, the creation and upgrading of the open-air museum, and annual blockyard maintenance. Some fragments were moved and dispersed on mastabas and storage shelves, and the fragments' location on the database updated. The current work has been funded by a

Figure 16. Digital lesson on the Wacom drawing tablet, supervised by Krisztián (at right), December 2012 (photo by Jen Kimpton)

grant from the World Monuments Fund (WMF) and Robert W. Wilson, completed this season, for which we are very grateful.

Some talatat blocks and fragments unearthed during the mastaba construction exhibited severe, active deterioration even after chemical treatment and/or protection, and it was determined best to keep them underground. The buried fragments are located along the east wall of Colonnade Hall and in the north–south pathway in the northern blockyard. During the 2011–2012 season, the blocks were reburied using fired-brick walls and clean sand. This season, additional brick walls were built around the buried blocks to keep the sand from sliding. It was then filled with clean sand to cover the fragments.

Luxor Temple Structural Condition Study

Structural engineer Conor Power continued his condition study of the Luxor Temple structure from March 30 to April 2, 2013, and he found that the temple continues to be stable. He found no movement or destabilization of the Ramesses II pylons or great Colonnade Hall columns. Based on a comparison with photographs taken in the year 2000, Conor found that there continues to be a noticeable reduction of overall moisture levels in the temple, and that there is no sign of moisture in lower walls. His conclusion is that the USAID-funded east-bank groundwater lowering engineering project, activated in 2006, continues to have a positive effect on Luxor Temple with a reduction of salt efflorescence and moisture levels in the structure, and is a great success.

Chicago House

Digital Inking Program

Thanks to special grants from the Women's Board of the University of Chicago and our friend and Oriental Institute Visiting Committee member Dr. Marjorie M. Fisher, the Epigraphic Survey was pleased to inaugurate an exciting new digital epigraphy training program this past

Figure 17. Jay digitally "inking" an inscribed granite block from Luxor Temple, March 2013 (photo by Ray Johnson)

winter. During the first three weeks of December artist/Egyptologist Krisztián Vértes inducted the entire epigraphic team into the mysteries of digital inking and collating utilizing Wacom drawing tablets, Photoshop software, and a whole host of tricks. These new tools and techniques will now allow our recording to go faster and more accurately. Tina Di Cerbo and Richard Jasnow have been utilizing similar techniques and technology for years in the documentation of graffiti at Medinet Habu, but this is our first foray into digital facsimile drawing, and we are all extremely pleased with the results so far. You will be hearing much more about this new chapter in our recording history in reports to come.

The Marjorie M. Fisher Library, Chicago House

The Chicago House Marjorie M. Fisher Library opened for the season on October 24, 2012, and closed on April 10, 2013, under the direction of librarian Marie Bryan assisted by assistant librarian Anait Helmholz. Added to the collection were 213 titles (222 volumes), of which 80 were monographs/books, 105 were journals, 19 were series volumes, 4 were pamphlets, and 5 were parts of sets. Of these, 109 were gifts, including a complete run of *Papyrus*, fifty-eight issues in all, a gift from Lisa Manniche. Fifty-eight other gifts were made from thirty-five different individuals and institutions. Anait repaired 120 volumes during the season.

Physical conversion of records from the old Chicago House system to the Library of Congress classification system continued this season, kindly assisted in January by Oriental Institute Visiting Committee member Andrea Dudek. During her three-week stay, Andrea managed to finish converting 238 titles/300 volumes, God bless her. A grand total of 444 titles/513 volumes were completely converted this season, and 186 titles remain to be converted next season. We are almost there!

The Tom and Linda Heagy Photographic Archives

This season Chicago House Tom and Linda Heagy Photographic Archives registrar Ellie Smith, in addition to assisting photographer Yarko Kobylecky with the field photography, registered 107 new large-format negatives taken by Yarko at Medinet Habu, Luxor Temple, and Khonsu Temple (nos. 21397–21568). Ellie also sleeved 800 Jacquet 35-mm slides, and while she was at it, reorganized all of the Medinet Habu small Amun temple and Luxor Temple slides. She scanned 1326 archival photographs of Philae Temple, 470 "hand copies" of Medinet Habu small Amun temple inscriptions, and 582 35-mm slides. Tina Di Cerbo continued to supervise the Photo Archives data storage and backup systems. Archivist Sue Lezon worked with Tina on data storage, and with Krisztián and Brett on computer equipment procurement neces-

Figure 18. Chicago House visit of Ambassador Anne Patterson and David Patterson November 23, 2012 (photo by Yarko Kobylecky)

sary for the new digital epigraphy program. Special thanks must go to Professor and Mrs. John Shelton Reed and Mrs. Lisa Alther for the gift of a large-format scanner that already forms a crucial component in our digital program, and to Ambassador and David Patterson, US Embassy Cairo, and to USAID director Mary Ott, and project manager Sylvia Atalla for helping get it to Luxor before the end of our season. At the request of the local MSA, Sue took a series of digital reference photographs and general views at Medinet Habu for the Inspectorate's use. Yarko Kobylecky photographed loose blocks at Medinet Habu and Luxor Temple, and in situ reused blocks at Khonsu Temple this season. He also produced photographic drawing enlargements for the art team; bleached finished, inked drawings for collation; and coordinated the blueprinting process. He scanned thirty-one deteriorating nitrate negatives for digital backup. At the request of the MSA, Yarko also photographed the newly cleaned paintings and reliefs of Ptolemy VIII at the Qasr el-Aguz temple near Medinet Habu. From March 16 to 30, Alain and Emmanuelle Arnaudies worked in the Photo Archives with Tina and Sue on the Jacquet database, and continued to enter data on the master database from Medinet Habu and Luxor Temple, and record missing negatives for duplication back in Chicago. Special thanks must go to John Larson, Oriental Institute Museum Archivist, for sending partial scans of archaeological field notebooks of Uvo Hölscher.

Chicago House

Tina Di Cerbo opened and closed the house as usual this season, but during the opening found that much of the library plumbing had given up the ghost, requiring a *lot* of extra, unexpected work. She and our workmen rose to the challenge, and both house and library wings were fully operational by the time the staff arrived in mid-October 2012 to resume work. Thank you, Tina! This season was eventful in many ways. When we arrived, senior accountant Essam el-Sayed and his wife Nidaa were on the Hajj, a joyous occasion for them. While Essam was away, administrator Samir Guindy assisted by Samwell Maher kept the finance office running smoothly. We finished up the remaining funds of our World Monuments Fund Grant (a Robert W. Wilson Challenge to Conserve Our Heritage Grant) at Luxor Temple, for which we are tremendously grateful. In March we received an extension of our USAID-Egypt grant that will help cover work at Medinet Habu and Luxor Temple for the next couple of years. We were very pleased to host the Minister of State for Antiquities Dr. Mohamed Ibrahim to a site visit and review of our work at Medinet Habu in November. US Ambassador to Egypt Anne Patterson and David Patterson came by several times to see our site work and Chicago House, as did new USAID director Mary Ott and project manager Sylvia Atalla. And there were some surprises. At the beginning of December I had a small "cardiac episode" that required an operation in Cairo and some rest and physical therapy in Chicago during the month of January. During that time Chicago House was skillfully managed by senior epigrapher Brett McClain, aided by the entire Chicago House team; not a single day of work was missed. I am greatly indebted to Brett, but also to Tina, Jay, and Lotfi, who accompanied me to Cairo, and to Jay who made sure I followed doctors' orders during my recovery at home. It was very weird being back in Chicago over the Christmas and New Year holidays; my last Christmas in Chicago was in 1977, and things had changed a lot! But all went well, and I returned to Luxor at the beginning of February a "new man."

It has been a time of transitions, of many kinds. After the end of our season in April and when we were all back home, Egypt's government changed again, and is now in the midst of trying to work out a system where everyone is represented, not just a few. On a happy note, we have a new addition to our Chicago House "family," little David Vértes, who was born on April 9, 2013. Mother Juli and father Krisztián are deliriously happy and doing well, despite the sleep deprivation.

But there have been losses as well. Former Chicago House artist Richard Turner passed away in Britain on January 11, 2013. Richard, a talented figurative painter, photographer, and poet, worked at Chicago House from 1968 until 1973, and again from 1976 until 1980. His imagination and spirit were infectious.

And, sadly, our dear friend Helen Jacquet passed away on April 25, husband Jean by her side, in Carouge, Switzerland. After a career spanning more than forty years spent working on sites from Nubia to Memphis, including their excavations of the Treasury of Thutmose I at North Karnak, Helen and Jean resided with the Epigraphic Survey team at Chicago House from 1997 until 2007. While

Figure 19. Krisztián and David digitally inking Roman fresco drawings (photo by Juli Schmied)

with us Helen finished and published her groundbreaking *The Graffiti on the Khonsu Temple Roof at Karnak: A Manifestation of Personal Piety* (Oriental Institute Publication 123. Chicago: The Oriental Institute, 2003), the third volume in the Epigraphic Survey's Khonsu Temple series. In this volume she compiled, mapped, drew, translated, analyzed, and presented 334 rooftop texts in hieroglyphic, hieratic, and Demotic scripts, a real labor of love begun as an ARCE Fellow and finished forty-five years later. She and Jean consulted with the Chicago House team on many aspects of the Survey's work at Luxor Temple and Medinet Habu, and it was a real joy to have them with us for that decade. Helen represented everything we will always aspire to be as scholars, Egyptologists, and human beings. She was ninety-five years old, yet her largest publication (two huge volumes on the pottery of their North Karnak excavations) came out only last year, and her latest book on the Nubian site of Tabo is still in press at the Institut Français d'Archéologie Orientale du Caire (IFAO). She raised the bar high, and we will miss her.

* * *

The Epigraphic Survey professional staff this season, besides the director, consisted of J. Brett McClain as senior epigrapher, Jen Kimpton and Christina Di Cerbo as epigraphers; Boyo

Figure 20. Helen Jacquet-Gordon at Arminna West, March 1961 (photo no. JHJ 3070)

Ockinga and Susanne Binder as archaeologist/epigraphers; Margaret De Jong and Susan Osgood as senior artists, Krisztián Vértes and Keli Alberts as artists; Julia Schmied as block-yard supervisor; Jay Heidel as architect/artist; Yarko Kobylecky as staff photographer; Susan Lezon as photo archivist and photographer; Elinor Smith as photo archives registrar and photography assistant; Carlotta Maher as assistant to the director; Essam El Sayed as senior accountant; Samir Guindy as administrator; Samwell Maher as administrative assistant; Marie Bryan as librarian; Anait Helmholz as librarian assistant; Frank Helmholz as master mason; Lotfi K. Hassan as conservation supervisor, Nahed Samir Andraus as conservator at Medinet Habu, and Hiroko Kariya as conservation supervisor at Luxor Temple. Alain and Emmanuelle Arnaudiès worked on the Chicago House Digital Archives database, Louis Elia Louis Hanna worked as database architect, Conor Power worked as structural engineer, Helen Jacquet-Gordon and Jean Jacquet continued to consult with us from Switzerland, and Girgis Samwell worked with us as chief engineer.

To the Egyptian Ministry of State for Antiquities and Supreme Council of Antiquities we owe sincerest thanks for another productive collaboration this season, especially to Dr. Mohamed Ibrahim, Minister of State for Antiquities; Dr. Ahmed Eissa, former Minister of

Chicago House professional staff, 2012–2013. Top row, left to right: Samir Guindy (administrator); Essam el-Sayed (senior accountant); Samwell Maher (assistant administrator); Girgis Samwell (chief engineer). Second row from top, left to right: Melinda Hartwig (visiting scholar); Tina Di Cerbo (epigrapher/artist); Jen Kimpton (epigrapher); J. Brett McClain (senior epigrapher); Krisztián Vértes (egyptologist/artist); Keli Alberts (artist). Second row from bottom, left to right: Marie Bryan (librarian); Anait Helmholz (librarian assistant); Frank Helmholz (stone mason); Margaret De Jong (senior artist); Ellie Smith (photo archives registrar); Lotfi Hassan (conservator); Joia Samir Andraos; Nahed Samir Andraos (conservator); Jay Heidel (architect/artist); Ray Johnson (director); Hiroko Kariya (conservator); Yarko Kobylecky (photographer). Photo by Sue Lezon

State for Antiquities; Dr. Mustafa Amin, Chairman of the SCA, and Dr. Abdel Satar, former SCA Chairman; Dr. Mohamed Ismail, General Director of Foreign Missions; Dr. Adel Hosein, Head of the Pharaonic Sector for the SCA; and Dr. Mohamed el-Bially, former Head of the Pharaonic Sector; Dr. Mansour Boraik, General Director of Luxor and southern Upper Egypt; Dr. Mohamed Abdel Azziz, General Director for the West Bank of Luxor; Mr. Ibrahim Suleiman, Director of Karnak Temple; Mr. Sultan Eid, Director of Luxor Temple; and Mme. Sanaa Ahmed Ali, Director of the Luxor Museum. Special thanks must go to the MSA inspectors with whom we worked so well this season, all noted above.

It is another pleasure to acknowledge the many friends of the Oriental Institute whose generous support allows Chicago House to maintain its documentation, conservation, and restoration programs in Luxor. Special thanks must go to the American Ambassador to Egypt, the Honorable Anne Patterson and David Patterson; former American Ambassador to Egypt Margaret Scobey; Cynthia Whittlesey and Andrew Mitchell, Cultural Affairs Office of the US Embassy; Mary Ott, director of the United States Agency for International Development in Egypt and Walter North, former director of USAID Egypt, and former directors Jim Bever, Hilda (Bambi) Arellano, Ken Ellis, and Bill Pearson; Dr. Marjorie M. Fisher; David and Carlotta Maher; O. J. and Angie Sopranos; Misty and Lewis Gruber; Nassef Sawiris; Mark Rudkin; Dr. Barbara Mertz; Daniel Lindley and Lucia Woods Lindley; Eric and Andrea Colombel; Piers and Jenny Litherland; Kitty Picken; Dr. Fred Giles; Tom Van Eynde; Helen and Jean Jacquet; Marjorie B. Kiewit; Nancy N. Lassalle; Tom and Linda Heagy; Curt and Lisa Ferguson; Shafik Gabr, ARTOC Group, Cairo; Judge Warren Siegel and Janet Siegel; Barbara Breasted Whitesides and George Whitesides; Miriam Reitz Baer; Andrea Dudek; Beth Noujaim; James Lichtenstein; Jack Josephson and Magda Saleh; Priscilla (Peppy) Bath; The Secchia Family; Emily Fine; Nan Ray; Anna White; Janet and Karim Mostafa; Waheeb and Christine Kamil; Caroline Lynch; Polly Kelly; Howard and Diane Zumsteg; Louise Grunwald; Lowri Lee Sprung; Andrew Nourse and Patty Hardy, Kate Pitcairn; Drs. Francis and Lorna Straus; Dr. William Kelly Simpson; Dr. Ben Harer; Dr. Roxie Walker; Stephen Lash; John Barbie; Nan Ray; Tony and Lawrie Dean; Mr. Charles L. Michod, Jr; Dr. Gerry Scott, Kathleen Scott, Mary Sadek, Amira Khattab, and Jane Smythe of the American Research Center in Egypt; Dr. Michael Jones of the Egyptian Antiquities Conservation Project; and all of our friends and colleagues at the Oriental Institute. I must also express our special gratitude to the Egyptian Ministry of State for Antiquities (MSA); USAID Egypt, British Petroleum Egypt, the Getty Grant Program of the J. Paul Getty Trust, LaSalle National Bank, Mobil Oil, Coca-Cola Egypt (Atlantic Industries), Vodafone Egypt, and the World Monuments Fund (and especially Robert W. Wilson) for their support of our work. Sincerest thanks to you all!

* * * * * * * * * *

ADDRESSES OF THE EPIGRAPHIC SURVEY

October through March:	**April through September:**
Chicago House	The Oriental Institute
Luxor	1155 East 58th Street
Arab Republic of Egypt	Chicago, IL 60637
tel. (011) (20) (95) 237-2525	tel. (773) 702-9524
fax (011) (20) (95) 238-1620	fax (773) 702-9853

HOUSEHOLD STUDIES IN COMPLEX SOCIETIES

Miriam Müller

The ninth annual University of Chicago Oriental Institute Post-doctoral Seminar, with the title "Household Studies in Complex Societies: (Micro) Archaeological and Textual Approaches," organized by Miriam Müller, was held on Friday, March 15, and Saturday, March 16, 2013, in Breasted Hall. Over two days, the papers and discussions focused on household archaeology, a topic that has generated considerable interest in recent years, particularly for the region of the Near East. Well implemented in New World archaeology, the subdiscipline still lacks the recognition and definition in Near Eastern archaeology. With an equal integration of texts and new scientific analyses, so-called microarchaeology, the Oriental Institute with its wide range of research interests covering the entire Near East seemed to be the best place for tackling household archaeology in an interdisciplinary approach. Since a major part of research in this field is currently being undertaken in Europe, this year's conference had an exceptionally high number of international scholars, from Austria, Egypt, England, Germany, Italy, and the United States.

Household archaeology is a relatively recent development that was introduced in the 1970s as a potentially new subfield in archaeology. With the advent of processual archaeology in the late 1950s, an integration of cultural anthropology and archaeology, and a stronger

Pictured, from bottom, left to right: (row 1) Miriam Müller, Felix Arnold, Lynn Rainville, Cynthia Robin, Paolo Brusasco, David Schloen; (row 2): Peter Miglus, Peter Pfälzner, Kristin De Lucia, Nicholas Picardo, Aaron Brody; (row 3) Kate Spence, Lisa Nevett, Nadine Moeller, Heather Baker, Elizabeth Stone, Jens-Arne Dickmann; (row 4) Adelheid Otto, Neal Spencer

emphasis on the individual and individual behavior, scholarly interest consequently turned toward the concept of households. This new bottom-up approach promised to serve as a link between theories of social change and material culture and could thus also have the potential to lead to a better understanding of wider social processes. Mesoamerican scholars led the field in the 1970s and defined first principles in the 1980s. Over the past three decades, various theories, models, and techniques have been introduced to explore households, such as the use of ethnographic data, economic models, gender theory, and microarchaeology. By initiating the Oriental Institute seminar on (micro) archaeological and textual approaches toward households, it was hoped that an integrated interdisciplinary exchange would lead to a better understanding of households in the ancient Near East and beyond.

The conference was structured in six sessions thematically divided into the topics "Method and Theory," "Activity-area Analysis," "Social Stratification," "Ethnicity and Identity," "Private and Political Economy," and "Urban–Rural and Core–Periphery Relations." Scholars of different disciplines, dealing with different time periods and regions, were thus encouraged to discuss their various approaches to the topics, critically reflect methodologies, and find inspiration in each other's research strategies. Each session was followed by a podium discussion with the speakers. In an assessment of all the papers, three respondents summarized important points and presented their own research and perspective on household archaeology. The conference was concluded with a roundtable discussion.

After a preamble by Christopher Woods and my own introduction to the topic, we started off the first day of the conference with an overview on theoretical and methodological discussions in household archaeology. The first and second sessions were chaired by Yorke Rowan. Our first speaker, Adelheid Otto (University of Mainz), presented in an exemplary approach what can be done by the integration of archaeological, historical, and scientific sources for the interpretation of households at Tall Bazi, a site of the second millennium BC in northern Syria. She was able to not only show different activity areas in the typical houses and give an insight in the inhabitants' diet, but also draw conclusions on the societal structure. Her examination was based on the differentiation of inventory types following Michael Schiffer's seminal work on site formation processes. However, Tall Bazi presents a very favorable example, since the city was burnt in a violent attack. Otto's discussion of the influences of pre- and post-abandonment processes on the archaeological record and in particular artifact assemblages in the houses led over to the second paper of the morning session, by Kate Spence (University of Cambridge, UK). Spence's presentation of ancient Egyptian architecture at the New Kingdom site Amarna, its conceptualization, and interpretation revealed the striking patterning of ancient Egyptian houses focused on the head of the household and his interaction with visitors and family members. Spence advocated a close examination of the household's physical frame, the house, and challenged the idea of functional spaces as the primary conceptual structure of a house. The last speaker of this session, Paolo Brusasco (University of Genoa), addressed the interaction of texts and archaeology in the definition of family composition in second-millennium BC Mesopotamia. He analyzed family archives from Ur and Nippur and compared changes in the family structure to alterations in the house layout. Brusasco could convincingly show that households' life cycles are reflected in the houses' networks and thus underline the importance of text studies for understanding households.

After a brief coffee break we returned for the second session of the day, which was devoted to activity-area analysis. Peter Pfälzner (University of Tübingen) started the session with a detailed introduction into possibilities and constraints of activity-area research based on the important work by Susan Kent. He used two examples of third-millennium BC household contexts at Tell Bderi and tomb contexts at Qatna, both in Syria, to clarify different types of deposits and artifact assemblages. He proposed an integrated approach of a functional, economic, social, diachronic, symbolic, and architectural analysis. The second speaker of this session, Lynn Rainville (Sweet Briar College), then gave a presentation on her meticulous work at the Assyrian site Ziyaret Tepe in southeastern Turkey, using so-called micro debris or micro refuse analysis. By taking samples of floor levels and midden deposits and floating them to retrieve miniscule objects, a more reliable picture can be gained about the objects that were used in the city's houses. Rainville was able to show that it is essential to compare macro and micro artifacts and also use ethnographic data to infer activities that were carried out at a certain place. Felix Arnold (German Archaeological Institute, Cairo) then looked at second-millennium BC and first-millennium BC houses on the island of Elephantine in southern Egypt to investigate the specific aspect of waste disposal in a diachronic perspective. He concisely traced the development from a less obvious distinction between clean and unclean space in the Middle Kingdom houses to a growing separation in the Late Period houses. He was able to show a clear partition between inside and outside space, maybe depicting a greater distinction of public and private space. The wish for cleanness and purity as an ideal state of comfort is also reflected in contemporaneous texts. Lisa Nevett (University of Michigan) completed the session with an assessment of the current state of household archaeology in classical antiquity and outlined that especially classical archaeology in Greece is considerably behind the developments in neighboring disciplines. While the abundance of available texts has always played a major role in understanding households, the investigation of artifact assemblages significantly lags behind, also as a result of the available data-sets. First steps in the direction of a less architecturally and text based approach have already revised a number of aspects that seemed to be overtly dominant household themes, such as a strong gendered perspective. Nevett advocated the integration of micro archaeological techniques such as micromorphology and microartifact studies to open up new perspectives on Greek domestic contexts.

After the lunch break, everyone reconvened for the third session of the day, on social stratification. Both afternoon sessions were chaired by Jack Green. My own contribution dealt with a residential area of the second-millennium BC site of Tell el-Dabʿa in the eastern Nile delta in an attempt to characterize the population and possibly determine class. This was achieved by a multiscalar approach combining data from estate, house, and tomb contexts, by analyzing architecture, artifact assemblages, skeletal material, and texts. The example could shed light on the so far only poorly attested part of the ancient Egyptian society that I would like to call a *middle class*. Since the considerable wealth that is displayed in the neighborhood under investigation does not seem to come as a state reward for fulfilling a governmental position, the term *elite* does not seem to apply for the inhabitants of this neighborhood. The session was concluded with a presentation by Heather Baker (University of Vienna) determining household cycles in first-millennium BC Mesopotamia. By tracing the development and changes of a family over four generations, Baker was able to show how difficult it is to understand internal modifications in a house without the help of texts.

After the last coffee break of the day, the final session dealt with the concepts of identity and ethnicity. Nicholas Picardo (Harvard University) presented the example of a highly institutionalized household model in Middle Kingdom Egypt. As part of one of the typical pyramid or temple settlements, rigidly state-planned cities with an orthogonal grid and standardized houses, Picardo discussed one of the large mansions that feature private quarters, but also official suites and a highly controlled access network. By analyzing seal impressions from the house, he tried to demonstrate shifting identities related to changing masters of the household with their specific positions in the bureaucratic landscape. Aaron Brody (Pacific School of Religion, and Badè Museum of Biblical Archaeology Berkeley), our last speaker of the day, then concluded with a paper on ethnic markers in the archaeological record of Iron Age Tell en-Nasbeh in Israel. He investigated modes of diet, ritual, language, dress, and habitation as well as the effects of empire on local identity constructions and the notions of boundaries. Brody was able to show how, for example, local Judean traditions persist in the domestic realm, particularly in the food-preparing process. Drinking sets, and thus objects used for representation, however, depict the influence of the Assyrian empire by their imitated form. We ended the day with a very welcome reception in the museum galleries. Afterwards, the conference participants enjoyed a school-bus ride to Chinatown, where we were rewarded with excellent food and drinks.

The second day of the conference comprised two sessions chaired by Donald Whitcomb. Two speakers presented their research in the first session of the day on private and political economy. Jens-Arne Dickmann (University of Freiburg) started with a presentation of the organization and economy of the Casa del Menandro at Pompeii. It became immediately clear how well defined a Roman house is already on the basis of the textual evidence and specific installations designating different room types and associated activities. Since the Casa del Menandro is the largest urban household at Pompeii, it is possible to distinguish several subunits that belonged to different members of the household — slave families, the porter, the majordomos, and the master and his family — that essentially formed separate households within the large mansion. Dickmann stressed the difficulty in assigning objects to specific activities and instead used written evidence, graffiti on the walls, as one example to locate areas where servants fulfilled their daily duties. Kristin De Lucia (University of Wisconsin) focused in her paper on household economy in pre-Aztec Xaltocan in Mexico. By using microartifact and soil chemistry analyses combined with ethnographic data, she was able to show how much information can be gained with these methods when houses bear literally no installations or macroartifacts to determine activities therein. De Lucia could not only demonstrate multicrafting households, but also labor division and market exchange.

The final session of the conference was devoted to urban–rural and core–periphery relations. Peter Miglus (University of Heidelberg) documented in his paper how a household on the periphery of the Mesopotamian heartland in Bakr Awa in northern Iraq retained traditional expressions in architecture, symbolisms, and ideology of the Mesopotamian kingship and thus outward reflections, but displayed a very local character in the private sphere, for example, in the use of local pottery types. Neal Spencer's (British Museum, London) contribution on households in Egyptian occupied Amara West in Nubia concluded the conference. He contrasted the development of a densely built neighborhood within the city walls with spaciously arranged villas outside the city's enclosure. By combining architectural, functional, economic, symbolic, and diachronic analyses with an investigation of plant remains and skeletal material in the adjacent cemeteries, and also considering the third dimension — an upper floor, lighting and ventilation — Spencer was able to convey a picture of the ancient living conditions. Mircomorphological analyses will in the future add even more information. He furthermore traced cultural entanglement in different styles of Nubian and Egyptian architecture, pottery types, and burial customs and related this development to a long history of Nubian-Egyptian coresidence where the boundaries were naturally blurred after a certain time.

After the final coffee break of the day, three respondents commented on the different papers and provided an insight into their own research and involvement with household archaeology. Nadine Moeller (Oriental Institute) focused her response on the contributions on ancient Egyptian households. She summarized the different papers and raised a number of important aspects. Moeller highlighted the difficulty in distinguishing class and moreover ethnicity via household analysis. She furthermore gave an insight in the domestic archaeological record of the Old Kingdom, a period that was not covered in the papers, and the difficulty even discerning households at that time. Elizabeth Stone (Stony Brook University) expressed a rather critical attitude toward the state of an integrated approach in Near Eastern archaeology. From her perspective, the lack of data from old excavations and the limitations of today's archaeological research in terms of exposure were to be held responsible for the current and, in her view, very backward state of household archaeology in the Near East. Cynthia Robin (Northwestern University), on the other hand, stressed the progress in Mesoamerican archaeology in recent years in bringing together the historical and scientific approach that can help to reveal the hidden transcripts of past societies. In the attempt to determine and locate specific household tasks within the architectural frame by the presenters, she emphasized the overall multifunctionality of household space that was exhibited in almost all the papers.

All eighteen conference participants reconvened on the stage for the roundtable discussion led by David Schloen (Oriental Institute). The discussion started with a provocative comment by Schloen, who proclaimed the limits of archaeology to determine certain social concepts and behavior in past societies. He made a strong case for the integration of texts that was seconded by other participants over the course of the discussion. Following up on that, the use of ethnoarchaeology was emphasized and contrary to earlier developments that had discredited the application of ethnographic data, it was even advocated to not only use ethnoarchaeological analogies for a specific area, but to look for parallels in other societies, periods, and regions. Furthermore, the aspect of landscape reconstruction was highlighted, which has a direct effect on households and which needs to be included in the analysis. The participants generally disagreed with Stone's critical attitude toward the state of Near Eastern archaeology and agreed upon the necessity to combine all lines of evidence without giving priority to any of the available data-sets that were mentioned in the different papers. Realizing this challenge requires the integration of all the different specialists providing these types of data-sets in the research agendas from the start. And even if for certain places and periods not all of the different techniques and data-sets are available, one should take it as strength, think creatively, and explore different ways to come to a better understanding of households in the past. The proceedings of this seminar will be published as part of the Oriental Institute Seminar (OIS) series during the coming academic year (2013–2014).

The seminar definitely fulfilled its proposed goal of bringing together specialists from all different regions and periods. The participants were able to exchange ideas and further the development of the discipline by applying an integrated approach with the promise to come to a more reliable picture of households in past societies. I would like to thank the Oriental Institute at this point for supporting my idea and helping me by all available means to organize a successful conference. My thanks goes to Gil Stein for the encouragement and advice in finding a great panel of speakers, to Christopher Woods for his guidance, and to

Steve Camp for the exceptional financial funding of this conference. Bringing together specialists from all over the world would not have been possible without the financial support of Arthur and Lee Herbst, the German Archaeological Institute, and the University of Freiburg. Mariana Perlinac and Brittany Mullins were responsible for the great atmosphere and accommodation that made this conference such an enjoyable event. I thank John Sanders and Paul Ruffin as well as Hannah Van Vels and Ted Good for their expertise and help with the IT and audio-visual equipment; Foy Scalf, Akemi Horii, Monica Velez, and Amy Weber for their great job in announcing the conference; and Emily Teeter and Jack Green for the wonderful gallery tour. Finally, I would like to express my gratitude to Tom Urban and Leslie Schramer for editing the texts and providing the beautiful programs and conference posters.

JERICHO MAFJAR PROJECT

Donald Whitcomb

In the course of the third season of excavation, our familiarity tends to replace the site name of Khirbat al-Mafjar with the common Palestinian designation of Qasr Hisham. As we removed the last of the backdirt from earlier excavations, some seventy truckloads, the Northern Area seemed a fresh field for research. What was a puzzle of walls, platforms, cisterns, and other features of several different periods has become a clear pattern of aspects of an agricultural estate. This was attached to the famed palatial complex of Qasr Hisham and clearly operated as its economic infrastructure.

The excavations at Qasr Hisham have developed, as was intended from the beginning in 2011, as a joint project of the Palestinian Department of Antiquities and the Oriental Institute at the University of Chicago under the direction of Dr. Donald Whitcomb and Dr. Hamdan Taha. The project was assisted by Jehad Yasin as field supervisor with Awni Shawamra, Michael Jennings, Muhammad Ghayyada, and other staff members. Our team of Palestinian and foreign archaeologists was augmented by a group of Palestinian graduate students, bringing a new excitement to the excavations.

Outside the Audience Hall and Bath

During the first two seasons we discovered a new gateway (Area 1) and monumental stairway (Area 2) (see *Oriental Institute Annual Reports* for 2010–2011 and 2011–2012). Muhammad Gayyada, our most experienced archaeologist of the Jericho region, continued these peripheral areas during the 2013 season. Area 1 moved beyond the gateway to the north end of the portico in front of the Audience Hall. This area had been cleared in the 1940s and promised to be little more than clearance of blocks and fill, but it had never been properly recorded (fig. 1). There were five column bases for a long portico. East of the northernmost base was a raised platform made of stone fragments similar to one next to the North Gate, suggesting the inner area along the enclosure wall may have had a series of shops.

The portico was tied to a north–south wall with four walls of fine masonry. These formed four rooms, which may have been market areas separated by low partitions. The southern room had a low bench against the back (west) wall. The next room was axial to the entrance to the Audience Hall; some pavers suggest a formal entrance though this room. The wall between the first two rooms had been removed and a deep pool inserted in this area, carefully plastered with a set of stairs in the southeast

Figure 1. John Whitcomb, the Jericho Mafjar Project photographer, helps move stones in Area 1

corner. The pool was found full of refuse debris, a fine collection of glazed and molded wares of the Abbasid period, when this was part of the Abbasid town.

Area 2 held the double stairway discovered in 2011 and an underground doorway opening to the west, found the following year. This area was excavated by Hamdan Taha in 2006 as two deep trenches; this year the baulk between these trenches was removed. The stratigraphy showed an upper stone construction of the late Abbasid period with abundant Abbasid ceramics, including fine glazes and sgraffiato wares. Below this was a massive collapse of rubble debris and, beneath this, a double arch of fine masonry. This arch seems to have belonged to a large ceremonial hall attached to the Audience Hall, into which a bath was later inserted. Once again, Qasr Hisham reveals an unexpected monument, a mysterious Umayyad structure without apparent parallels.

The Grape Press

Area 6, or the Grape Press, was the finest building in the northern area, indicating the importance of wine, dibs, and other products for which Jericho was famous in the Byzantine and Islamic periods. It is the largest and best-planned press discovered in the entire region.

One remaining element was the north wall and presumed entryway. Excavations revealed a rectangular space where edging suggested the mosaics ceased. Below floor level were large slabs of stone; this would have been the base for a lever press or perhaps a large basin for foot-washing. Our archaeological architect, Ignacio Arce, literally dove into the large vat on the eastern side; with infinite care he cleaned the fallen fragments of brick vaulting and the massive stone arch that had fallen into the vat. Ignacio's skill, and the quality of the Umayyad builders, have revealed the first evidence of roofing above such vats. As he delights

Figure 2. General photo of Northern Area looking east. The grape press is in the right foreground, mosque in left center, and stables behind it

in explaining, the entire building was covered by arches and vaulting, making this the most deluxe example of such presses, in this case for the Umayyad rulers.

The Original Residence or Red Building

During the 2011 season, Michael Jennings and Enrico Cirelli planned and tested the Red Building as Area 3. This building was contemporary with the Grape Press and thus Umayyad in date. Clearance of backdirt from the 1960s excavations gave Tony Lauricella and Sufian ed-Dess an opportunity to study fine stone foundations set into the red, bricky clay that gives the Red Building its name. This was extraordinarily difficult as the finely cut stone had been removed in recent times, leaving only robber trenches where walls once stood. These robber trenches revealed the expected system of rooms: a long room (10 × 4 m) on the interior, east side, behind which was a suite of three rooms on the outer, west side. Two rooms had undisturbed floors with pits and two tabuns built on a packed earth floor, upon which was ash with many artifacts, notably, several complete painted "Abbasid fine ware" vessels, a sphero-conical "grenade," and an anomalous glass bauble. There were also several cakes of charred seeds and extensive glass and metal fragments. The walls of the north edge of this Red Building need further excavation, but it seems that this may have been intended as a "palace" but later abandoned for the structure to the south.

The Stables and Earlier Structures

The stables were a series of long rooms excavated in the 1960s; the function was assumed by the line of feeding troughs or mangers with bases made of a fine limestone called Nabi Musa stone preserved on two of the interior walls (fig. 3). The main passage was paved with cobbled stones, as one might expect in stables; the main entry was clearly on the eastern side, possibly opening onto the *hayr*, a large enclosure some 2 kilometers long. The straightforward delineation of features of stables devolved into what the excavator, Michael Jennings, describes as "perhaps the most complicated square we have opened during the three years of the Jericho Mafjar Project so far."

South of the paved passage were two rooms with mangers and accumulations of ash and organic soil. The wall north of the paved passage held a surprise: this appears to have been a columned portico, later filled in with rubble walling. The columns were square monoliths and the bases were denticulate moldings, spolia taken from an earlier Umayyad or even Hellenistic building!

Figure 3. Muhammad Shalalda excavating in the stables building of Area 3

Moreover, beneath this portico and the other interior walls were two massive walls running north–south. Jennings makes a case for an Umayyad date for this first phase and suggests that it aligns with and may be part of the original Red Building. True, it does not have the finely cut stones, but perhaps this might not be necessary for earlier stables. Architectural drawings and stratified materials from the old baulks will suggest areas for further digging to solve this conundrum.

The Abbasid Mosque

The most important discovery of this season was a mosque belonging to the Abbasid town, excavated by Gregory Williams. The mosque had brick flooring and a deep plastered *mihrab* or prayer niche. An external structure on the western side was probably the foundation for a staircase minaret, an early Abbasid form. The northeast corner had not been excavated in the 1960s and revealed a set of fine bowls, small storage jars, and basins of the same early

Figure 4. Abdullah Daraghmeh (digging), with Greg Williams (in blue shirt) and Don looking at the beginnings of the mosque

Abbasid period. Located near the center of the Northern Area, the mosque was not large, but was sufficient for the small community inside the walls.

In front of the mosque was a large yard and a deep, vaulted cistern with a plastered pool, possibly for ablutions before prayer. East of the mosque was a paved walk leading to an entryway (7200); the entry itself had two benches on either side and paving with fine Nabi Musa limestones. To the south of the entry was a small *hammam* or bath, a cooking area, and many other rooms excavated by Awni Shawamra; this part of Area 8 is not complete and must await further excavations.

An Umayyad Estate and Abbasid Town

Though there is more excavation remaining to be done in the Northern Area, the 2013 season of excavations may present the following interpretations. This part of Khirbet al-Mafjar was established in the Umayyad period as a fine residence (the Red Building) associated with a Grape Press of superb architecture. Together these structures suggest the establishment of an agricultural estate, a *day'a*, as the economic foundation for the Umayyad palace complex to the south (fig. 5).

The removal of the Umayyad caliphate from this region seems to have encouraged an expansion of this settlement with a walled center in the northern area, with its own mosque and residence; housing eventually spread around the Audience Hall and within the palace. This enlarged settlement may be considered a town in its own right, which lasted into the tenth century. The result is an entirely new dimension in understanding the dynamic change

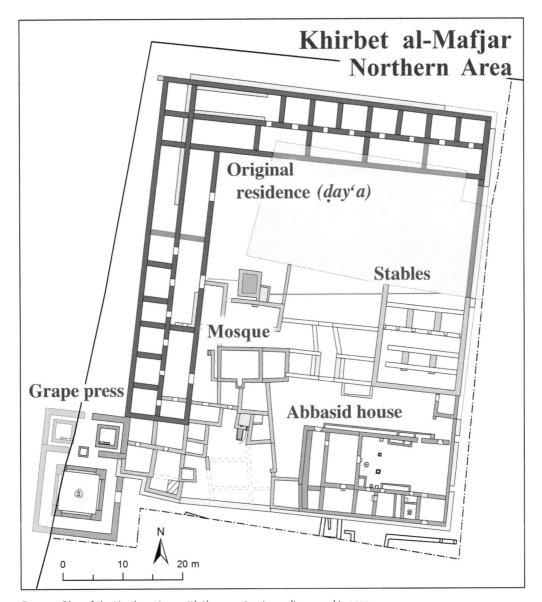

Figure 5. Plan of the Northern Area with the new structures discovered in 2013

from Qasr Hisham into what might be called part of the Madinat al-Ariha (the Islamic city of Jericho). Further excavations promise increasing understanding of new complexities at this archaeological monument.

Hamdan Taha and the author have agreed to assemble a report of these results of the Jericho Mafjar Project. As a first step we have written a general introduction in a new journal, the *Journal of Eastern Mediterranean Archaeology and Heritage Studies*. The article may be downloaded from the JMP website (www.jerichomafjarproject.org), courtesy of the Pennsylvania State University.

KERKENES DAĞ PROJECT

Scott Branting

http://www.kerkenes.metu.edu.tr/

The 2012 season at Kerkenes Dağ was the twentieth season of research at this important late Iron Age site. This milestone was set to be marked by a brief study season, the last under the directorship of Dr. Geoffrey Summers. This would allow work to be completed in advance of final publication of the results of excavations in the Palatial Complex and the Cappadocia Gate. However, plans sometimes change. Instead of a final study season, the time line for the planned shift of the permit from Dr. Summers to me, which had been discussed for years with the General Directorate of Cultural Property and Museums, was accelerated. An abbreviated study season was followed by an opportunity presented to me by the General Directorate to put a team in the field and undertake limited excavations under a permit issued to the local Yozgat Museum. As will be seen in the report that follows, despite the short time frame for assembling a team we were able to take advantage of this opportunity.

Geophysical Investigations

The range of remote sensing that has been applied on a large scale to the work at Kerkenes Dağ since the 1993 season, as well as the results of those surveys, are a key reason why the site has risen from obscurity to being known around the world. For the 2012 season, only a small amount of resistivity survey was planned in order to finish the large area in the northern portion of the site that was surveyed in 2011. Unfortunately, with the permit not being issued in May, when the soil is wet enough to allow resistivity survey, no geophysical work was able to be accomplished. We look forward to resuming this important work next season.

Shortened Study Season and Publication

The planned study season was also cut short by permit decisions. Work on final drawings and photography was accomplished in a shorter than anticipated span of time, while the final inventory list was completed. Only a very small team consisting of Geoffrey and Françoise Summers, Ben Claasz Coockson, and Yasemin Özarslan was allowed to participate. The final monographs for the publication of the excavations from the Cappadocia Gate and the publication of the transportation simulations and test excavations have subsequently been submitted to the Oriental Institute Publications Office. Meanwhile, the final publication of the excavations in the Palatial Complex should be completed by early 2014.

Excavation in Urban Block 8

After receiving word from the General Directorate that I might be able to undertake excavations at Kerkenes Dağ in 2012, we began preparations for that endeavor in June (fig. 1). How-

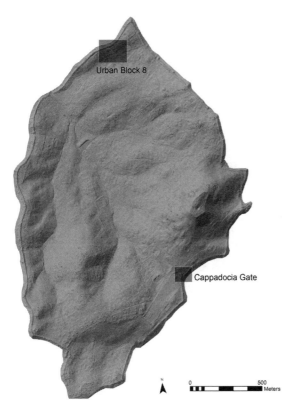

Figure 1. Locations of research at Kerkenes Dağ in 2012

ever, delays in issuing the museum permit, as well as in issuing the necessary research visas, pushed the start of this mini-season well into late August. When the permit and visas were finally issued, only a brief span of just over ten days remained available to us. The museum permit was officially overseen by Necip Becene of the Yozgat Museum, and Yrd. Doç Dr. Abdulkadir Baran, of Muğla Sıtkı Koçman University, was appointed as scientific advisor on the permit. Dr. Baran brought with him a small team to work on uncovering a portion of the top of the city wall along the northeastern side of the city. Unfortunately, the money from the Ministry for their excavations was delayed. We were able to assist them by providing enough funding to allow them to start that work and to cover their room and board, thereby allowing ourselves to continue our own excavation in Urban Block 8 in the northern portion of the city. We also did our best to assist them by providing their team with expertise that they were lacking in order to interpret objects they uncovered in terms of broader Phrygian material, the regional late Iron Age material, and the unique corpus of Kerkenes Dağ material and construction.

Meanwhile, our own excavations within Urban Block 8 have exposed a total area of over 230 sq. m (figs. 2–3). This includes large portions of a multi-roomed structure situated behind a very large columned building within the urban block. It also includes a broad stretch of stone pavement in front of the columned building. This work is part of a multi-year program to clear the full 6,000 sq. m extent of Urban Block 8. It will allow us to get a first glimpse of the range of households that once inhabited the city, as a start to understanding the social organization of the city. It will also provide an impressive example of what one of the 757 urban blocks within the city looked like in the Iron Age.

Trench 31 was a ca. 6 × 7 meter extension of Trench 29. It revealed the entranceway to Room 3 as well as two additional rooms (4 and 5) farther down the slope. A stone staircase comprising six broad steps was found in the northern end of the trench leading from a central stone-paved surface to the entranceway to Room 3. Evidence from postholes suggests that most of this pavement was sheltered by a timber roof. The stone-paved surface comprised two distinct areas of paving stones of different sizes, suggesting phasing in the use of this area. This interpretation was reinforced by a drain within the pavement that originally drew water away from one of the walls. The wall was subsequently altered and the drain filled up to the level of the stone surface in a succeeding phase of use.

The complete exposure of Rooms 4 and 5 awaits excavation in future years when the area can be expanded. However, some interesting finds already suggest some possible uses for at

Figure 2. Annotated photograph of the area of Urban Block 8, outlined in white

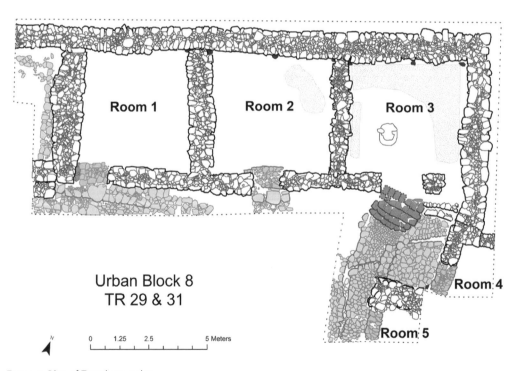

Room 1

Room 2

Room 3

Urban Block 8
TR 29 & 31

Room 4

Room 5

N

0   1.25   2.5   5 Meters

Figure 3. Plan of Trench 29 and 31

least Room 5. Small finds included an iron needle within Room 4, a broken piece of a type XII Phrygian fibula from the southern extent of the stone-paved surface (fig. 4), and fragments of worked ivory from outside the threshold to Room 5 (fig. 5). This latter find is particularly interesting given the unique carved ivory plaque that was found within Room 1 of this struc-

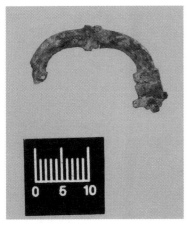

Figure 4. The Phrygian type XII fibula from Trench 31

Figure 5. Fragment of carved ivory from in front of Room 5

ture. Could Room 5 perhaps contain an ivory-working area? Or could it be another room to store more prestigious goods? The answers to this puzzle will have to await future excavation.

Trench 33, meanwhile, was 5 × 8 m in size and located at a distance of 25 m to the south of Trenches 29 and 31. It was situated to reveal 40 sq. m of the area directly in front of the large columned building in Urban Block 8 (fig. 6). A sloping stone paving was uncovered across the entire area, and six potential postholes in the southern end of the pavement hint that portions of the pavement may have been covered. While there were very few small finds recovered on the pavement, a bent iron nail was found lying in the middle portion of the pavement and a very fragmentary corner of a bronze plaque was found closer to where the doorway of the building would have been (fig. 7).

Figure 6. Susan Penacho and Yasemin Özarslan working on photo-recording and planning Trench 33 on the tablet PC

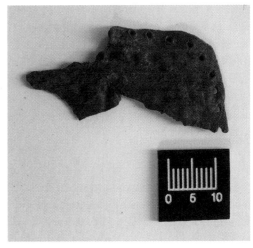

Figure 7. Corner of a bronze plaque found in Trench 33

Following these brief excavations all the finds from the two trenches were cleaned and conserved. The walls in Trench 31 were also conserved and capped with new stone. The surfaces of the room as well as the staircase were covered in geotextile and a layer of clean soil. We then constructed a fence around the entire area of the exposed trenches.

Paleoenvironmental Research

During the 2012 excavations we also systematically collected soil samples for the ongoing scientific analysis of localized activity areas in Urban Block 8. This is part of a larger program to understand who lived in the city, what their connections were to other households in and beyond the city, and what activities they engaged in. It will also allow us to explore the impact that their activities had on their environment, and to compare the results to similar research at the Phrygian capital of Gordion. The very brief season did not allow us to process the over 100 soil samples collected this year. However, next year we will be able to start right away on processing and analyzing these important scientific samples that will offer us new insights into the people who once lived in this place.

Conservation

In the excavation depot, in addition to conservation and processing of current finds, a major rehousing project for stabilizing iron bands excavated in 2003 was undertaken. The bands were carefully cleaned and then encased in specialized conservation material, tested in earlier seasons (fig. 8). The material is formed into a bag and completely encloses the iron, cutting off the oxygen that can continue to corrode the remaining iron. This effort will help preserve the iron bands for years to come. Continued conservation and maintenance work like this is needed every year in order to preserve previously excavated material. Work was also undertaken to find joining pieces of the statue uncovered last year. Two more significant joins were found during this abbreviated season.

Figure 8. Noël Siver conserving and stabilizing the iron bands in the excavation depot

Site Management

Our brief season required that we scale back our program of restoration and ongoing maintenance in the Cappadocia Gate from past years. We did purchase and install permanent fencing around the entire gate area and did minor maintenance to the restored sections (fig. 9). The fencing will help ensure the safety of those visiting this important monument. We look forward to getting back to restoration work within the gate next year during a longer planned season.

Figure 9. New fencing erected around the Cappadocia Gate

Figure 10. One of the new road signs directing people to Kerkenes Dağ

In addition, we paid to have new directional signs constructed and installed at intersections along the road from Sorgun to replace older signs that had been installed years ago (fig. 10). We also paid to have new signs constructed and installed at the excavation house and at the entrance to the site (fig. 11). These will help welcome visitors to the site and will give them a basic orientation to our past twenty years of work here.

Community Outreach and Ethnographic Studies

Yrd. Doç Dr. Sevil Baltalı Tırpan of Istanbul Technical University (ITU), the project's assistant director, not only took part in the excavations but was also able to undertake additional ethnographic interviews during our brief season. As described in last year's report, this work is a critical component of our public outreach and allows us to better understand how we impact the community. It also provides an avenue for integrating memories and knowledge from the local community into understandings of the site as a living place in the modern world.

Figure 11. New welcome sign installed at Kerkenes Dağ. This sign highlights our past twenty years of research and excavation

Future Research

Continued wide-area excavations within Urban Block 8 are planned for the next several years. This will provide us with critical data about the social organization of this ancient city as well as its connections to the wider world that once existed around it, including Persia and Lydia. In addition, continued conservation and site-management work will progress in the years ahead, with more restoration work planned in the important Cappadocia Gate. Complementing and undergirding this work in important ways will be the continued community outreach and ethonographic research.

Permit applications to the Turkish government have, in recent years, been taking two years to complete. While we have already applied for the permit for next year, and are awaiting the decision of the Ministry, it may well require a second application for work to commence in 2014. Hopefully, we can be back excavating and conserving the site in 2013, but with twenty years of work invested in this site we will see the process through to completion no matter how long it takes.

Acknowledgments

Our thanks for an unexpected and yet successful short 2012 season go to the General Director, Murat Süslü, and staff of the General Directorate of Cultural Property and Museums. The work could not have been accomplished were it not for the museum permit issued to the Yozgat Museum, so a very special thank-you goes to the Museum Director Hasan Şenyurt for facilitating this and for appointing Museum staff archaeologist Necip Becene to oversee the permit. Our thanks also go to the Yozgat Director of Culture and Tourism Lütfi İbiş, and to Abdulkadir Baran, of Muğla Sıtkı Koçman University, for serving as scientific advisor on the permit. We are grateful to the Governor of Yozgat Abdulkadir Yazıcı, Yozgat Mayor Yusuf Başer, the Sorgun District Governor Levent Kılıç, and Sorgun Mayor Ahmet Şimşek, who along with their staffs provided continued critical support for aspects of the project. Finally, we are very grateful to the Turkish Consul General in Chicago Fatih Yıldız and his remarkable staff, who greatly facilitated the rapid issuance of the research visas for the team and have provided critical support to the project over the past years.

The team that assembled upon a moment's notice in order to undertake this research was comprised of myself, Assistant Director Sevil Baltalı Tırpan, Yasemin Özarslan, Dominique Langis-Barsetti, Susan Penacho, Noël Siver, and Sümeyye Açıkgöz. We are also very thankful to Emine Sökmen and Tony Lauricella for invaluable assistance that they provided in support of the team.

Principal sponsors of Kerkenes Dağ in 2012 were the Oriental Institute, the Archaeocommunity Foundation, Catherine Novotny Brehm, an anonymous US donor, Hazel Bertz, Andrea Dudek, and Virginia O'Neill. A full list of past sponsors of the project can be found on our web site.

————————————

MARJ RABBA

Yorke M. Rowan and Morag M. Kersel

The Galilee Prehistory Project (GPP) focuses on two broad research themes: the definition and characterization of Galilean sites during the fifth to early fourth millennium BC, and the role of this site and region within the poorly understood late prehistoric sequence from the Late Neolithic to Chalcolithic transition in the southern Levant. Within this approach, our first objective was to identify and excavate a settlement site dating to the Chalcolithic period, generally dated approximately 4500–3600 BC. For this first phase in the Galilee Prehistory Project, we selected a site in the lower Galilee in an area known as Marj Rabba, now the name of the site (also referred to as Har ha-Shaʾavi West). Our goals are to record and document the material culture of the site, establish the period of time the site was occupied, and achieve a detailed understanding of the economy of this formative period. Ultimately, our aim is to examine life in the Galilee during a period that witnesses the first evidence for the development of copper metallurgy, dramatic new burial practices, and rich iconographic elaboration in material culture. Evidence for these elements exists in other Chalcolithic sites in the Negev, the Golan, and the Jordan valley, but thus far we have little or no indication of these characteristics in the Galilee.

After four seasons of survey and excavation at Marj Rabba, a glimpse of a substantial agricultural village is beginning to emerge with notable differences to other roughly contemporaneous sites in more intensively investigated regions such as the Golan, the Jordan valley, and the northern Negev. The pottery, flint, and ground-stone artifacts establish the contemporaneity of the site in general to the Chalcolithic, but the ceramic styles and manufacturing techniques argue for local production of most pottery; the same seems likely for the flint. In the final season and post-excavation analysis we will select pottery samples for petrographic examination in the hopes of distinguishing vessels produced from locally sourced clays versus those originating from farther away. We know that some limited exchange occurs at the site for several reasons. First, some pottery has basalt inclusions (identifiable with the naked eye), a rock type not found locally but common in the eastern Galilee and the Golan. Accordingly, we can conclude that a small percentage of the pottery found at Marj Rabba came from areas to the east. In addition, ground-stone fragments of basalt, both coarse grinding implements and finer bowls recovered on survey and in the excavations, probably derive from the basalt outcrops in the Galilee or Golan. Local resources were largely sufficient for the inhabitants of Marj Rabba, but these examples indicate contact with others living in the larger intra-regional areas of the Golan and Galilee.

During our fourth excavation season at Marj Rabba, conducted from July 10 to August 17, 2012, we brought together a team of students, interns, volunteers, and professionals for the fieldwork. Students from the University of Chicago, DePaul University, Johns Hopkins University, and other institutions worked diligently for five weeks, sometimes under very hot sun. Supported by a Jeff Metcalf internship through the Jewish Studies Center at the University of Chicago, Eleanor Shoshanny Anderson and Andrew Billingsley contributed a new element to the fieldwork, and continued their labors in Jerusalem long after the excavation season ended, helping to process the heavy fraction from flotation, to enter data, and

Figure 1. Rowe-Clark Math & Science Academy students and their teacher Ms. Davis (in glasses) at Marj Rabba

to digitize the plans, notes, and drawings from the field season. In a groundbreaking (pun intended) initiative, we included five high-school students from the Rowe-Clark Math & Science Academy in Chicago. These students, most of whom had to apply for their first passport in order to join the field team, arrived with Bridgette Davis, the intrepid dean of college preparation and persistence at Rowe-Clark (fig. 1). The students and Ms. Davis proved capable, flexible, and energetic, contributing to the project with good humor and hard work. Within a day of arriving in Karmi'el, the students had explored the city and had found the closest New York Pizza venue and the best place to buy their favorite brand of potato chips, bringing them the comforts of home.

In the spring, as part of the efforts to prepare them for the excavation program in Israel, Gil Stein, Yorke, and Morag met with the Rowe-Clark students and Ms. Davis on Saturdays to discuss the Middle East, archaeology, survey, faunal remains, lithics, and pottery. During their summer experience, the Rowe-Clark group visited Akko (the modern city of Acre, on of the oldest continuously inhabited sites in the region), Tel Aviv, Rujm el-Hiri (an enigmatic Chalcolithic site in the Golan), Haifa, and ended their trip with a three-day visit to Jerusalem, the Dead Sea, and Masada. In the fall, the students presented a synopsis of their summer experiences to their classmates, which included a critique of hummus, an explanation of the finer points of using a trowel, and the need to drink water and wear a hat. The summer program was a great success, one we will repeat in the 2013 season with a new group of students and another courageous mentor from Rowe-Clark.

During the 2012 season, we focused the energies of our team on three primary objectives. In Areas AA and BB (fig. 2) we explored the earlier building phases and associated strata; in some cases, this required the removal of the circular stone features exposed in earlier seasons, which are associated with the latest preserved architectural phase. In Area CC we expanded the area to the east in the hopes of exposing architectural elements and associated strata, floors, and features. Finally, we opened a small test excavation in Area DD in order to test the results of our surface survey, which suggested that the site extends to the southwest.

Excavations

In 2012, Area AA consisted of four 5.0 × 5.0-meter squares, and four 2.5 × 5.0-meter squares. The three previous seasons of excavation in Area AA exposed a large area of architecture throughout the area, including numerous large stone circles near the ground surface. Since this and the related later phase architecture had been carefully exposed, drawn, and photographed, a goal of the 2012 season was to remove these later architectural elements in

Figure 2. Aerial view of Areas AA and BB, taken from the quadcopter

order to expose the earlier strata of architecture and hopefully contemporaneous features and surfaces.

Area AA sustained more damage than in previous seasons due to heavy winter rains. Despite barbed-wire fencing, some damage by animals was also evident, both to the ancient features and the section walls of the excavation areas. After extensive cleaning, we began to remove some of the stone circles in order to expose earlier layers. Our first priority was the excavation of circles L.215 and L.226 (see *Oriental Institute Annual Reports* for 2010–2011 and 2011–2012), which each filled nearly one-half of a square. This allowed us to bring squares E2 and F2 to the same excavation level, more equivalent to those reached in 2011. These circles lacked additional layers of stone construction, confirming our earlier tests that suggested we have only the base of these structures.

In 2011, we sectioned an additional stone circular feature (L.207), removing half down to the floor level of the earlier room in squares F1 and E1. This season we carefully removed the other half, which suggested that there was mudbrick deposited below the feature before the stone circle was constructed. In several excavation steps, we eventually lowered this area to the associated room floor (fig. 3), indicated by the pottery found lying flat in the surface.

Figure 3. Aerial view of room and floor in Area AA, after removal of circular stone features

Finally, we removed the two other original, largest circles in Area AA, L.23 and L.225. Circle 23 was the largest of the stone circles, measuring nearly 5 meters in diameter. Like other circles, the edges were carefully laid by creating a double row of larger cobbles, while the interior was filled with a rubble of small cobbles. We took a number of soil samples from on top and within the matrix of these circles. Despite the generally poor preservation of botanicals in the region, we hope that careful sampling and flotation by our archaeobotanist Philip Graham will allow for the identification of cereals or weeds.

New Architecture

This season we concentrated on deeper excavation in one portion of Area AA in an attempt to understand earlier phases of occupation and construction. We selected square D2, since it was already clear of other later architecture. Very soon we uncovered large blocks that were apparently part of a wall that matched wall w.7, one of the first walls uncovered in squares C1 and D1. This new wall is made of regular and nicely faced large boulders on one side, and more regularly utilized field stones on the other side. Since this feature appeared to be parallel to wall L.7 and disappeared into the unexcavated section of square D2/C2, we opened this area to define another architectural unit in Area AA. Unfortunately, a tidy corner connecting this wall was not easily identified because a large pit cut the wall (fig. 3). A large stone-lined pit cuts wall w.6 along the eastern edge in square C2; two V-shaped bowls in the pit suggest that it was a later intrusion that can be dated to the Chalcolithic period. Wall w.6 does not form a corner in the middle of square C2, instead continuing into the southern excavation section. We know from the geophysical work (ground-penetrating radar) conducted in 2011 by Thomas Urban of Oxford University that dense architecture continues into the adjacent field to the south. Additional wall segments in this area will need to be explored during 2013 in order to make sense of architecture. In terms of recovered finds, most artifacts were domestic refuse — pottery, flint tools and debitage, and a few decorative items. A single mace-head was discovered in the southwest, immediately adjacent to pit L.136A.

In Area BB, a number of different walls appear to be built at a different orientation than those of Area AA (fig. 4). In the middle of Area BB (squares G1/H1), walls w.904, w.925, w.922, and w.315B establish the most complete room exposed at Marj Rabba. Excavation of the room interior removed a great deal of rock rubble, suggesting that the walls were constructed entirely of stone (rather than stone foundations with a mudbrick superstructure). The room is not yet fully excavated and will be further excavated in 2013. By the end of the season, a stone pavement (L.329B) was found in the northwest

Figure 4. Area BB, overhead view of room and associated features

corner of the room, and a possible living surface (L.336B) was found in the room. We do not seem to have the base of the walls yet, however, so this may be only the latest preserved floor in the room, with other earlier floors below. Walls w.904 and w.922, running roughly north-west–southeast, abut the south face of wall w.925, a long wall running across the northern edge of Area BB. On the southern end of the room, cross wall w.315B was partly obscured by a later stone circle (L.316B), built around and atop the corner formed by the juncture of walls w.922 and w.315B. Another possible stone circle (L.308B), partly destroyed or rebuilt, was exposed farther to the east in Area BB.

In Area CC, some of the most substantial architecture exposed at Marj Rabba appears notably different from that found in Areas AA and BB (fig. 5). In previous seasons, the exposure of walls, pavement, a pit, and other features indicate the possibility of better preservation and multiple building phases and well-preserved mudbricks. For the 2013 season, we hope to further expose walls to the east, in squares N1 and N20. Below a number of highly disturbed sediments, a new, incomplete wall (w.507C) appears to run approximately 2.5 meters from squares M1/M20, roughly perpendicular to wall w.606. Unfortunately, the juncture between these walls is missing, although further excavation in 2013 may reveal some connection.

To the north of wall w.507C, the mottled matrix seemed to include mudbrick material, possibly the superstructure from this wall. A hard-packed mudbrick feature extended from the wall's end, continuing into the eastern section of the square, at the approximate base of wall w.507C. This suggests a mudbrick surface or foundation on which the wall was built.

To the north of this wall and mudbrick feature was a surface (L.516C) associated with "paving" stones (L.513C) and a hearth (L.512C). The hearth, a tightly packed series of small stones approximately 1 meter in diameter, included fire-cracked rock. The entire matrix was collected for flotation.

The "paving" stones, a small concentration of flat stones, continue into the eastern baulk. These apparently overlay very hard mudbrick, similar to that described below wall w.507C. Given the limited areal extent (ca. 32 × 25 cm), this feature could easily be the remains of a platform, work surface or some other installation. The remains of a poorly preserved floor beneath the paving stones may have extended to the west; pieces of the floor were laminated, suggesting multiple phases of re-use.

The preservation of these features near the ground surface slowed excavation in Area CC, but also hinted at the potential for greater preservation at deeper levels. We will focus on this area during the 2013 season in the hopes of gaining an understanding of the architectural features and their stratigraphic relationships.

Figure 5. Area CC, end-of-season overhead view

Survey and Area DD

Preliminary analysis of the 2011 site survey results demonstrated areas with high concentrations of surface material. As part of the project strategy to determine the extent of the site, a test area was designated as Area DD. The highest density of surface artifacts was in a privately owned olive grove, so we placed a 5 × 5-meter square immediately south of that area, about 130 meters south and 10 meters west of the current excavation areas. Initial artifact collection from the 5 × 5-meter square yielded three buckets of lithics, ceramics, and ground stone.

The ground in this area is unlike the main areas of excavation. Dense, clay-rich sediment is tightly compacted and difficult to break up; sieving was virtually impossible. After a few days of digging, we narrowed the excavation area to only one quadrant (2.5 × 2.5 m), the northeast corner of the square. One meter below the ground surface, the dark, packed clay sediment exhibited no stratigraphy and very few artifacts. At 1.05 meters below the surface, a rim fragment of a Chalcolithic basalt vessel was recovered, and some limestone appeared at about the same depth. A slight change in matrix was also visible, lighter in color with small chalk inclusions, corresponding to smaller cobbles. A crude or possibly damaged wall (L.701D) running northeast–southwest, was exposed at this level in the sondage (fig. 6) and we suspect that the change in matrix may mark the original topsoil level buried later by 1 meter of overburden; this may have been an intentional fill brought in to level out the area. The top of the wall, about 1 meter below the ground surface, was apparently built on the bedrock. Very few artifacts were recovered from this depth, although a few Chalcolithic sherds and a basalt fragment confirm the dating of the wall. This supports the suggestion that the site extended at least this far, as suggested by our surface survey analysis.

Future Directions

Excavations carried out during summer 2013 will mark the end of investigations at the site of Marj Rabba. There are still a number of questions that we need to answer, and these will be the focus of our inquiry during July and August of 2013. We will focus efforts in Areas AA, BB, and CC on clarifying stratigraphic relationships and phasing of the site. In addition, we hope to excavate the site to bedrock, at least in some places, in order to understand a full stratigraphic development of the preserved strata. Our program of intensive recovery of paleobotanical remains and flotation will continue in the hopes of more conclusive evidence for the types of plants being exploited in the area. We will also complete the extensive survey of the area, intensively field-walking two areas skipped in the 2011 pedestrian survey.

Figure 6. Area DD, view of wall w.701D

Acknowledgments

On behalf of the Marj Rabba team, we wish to thank the many institutions and individuals who helped make this a successful season. Excavations at Marj Rabba and the Galilee Prehistory Project were made possible through the generous support of the Oriental Institute of the University of Chicago, Oriental Institute director Gil Stein, and many private donors — Andrea Dudek, Kerry Eason, Margaret Foorman, Joan Fortune, Sue Geshwender, Tracey Giddings, Bob and Janet Helman, Arthur and Lee Herbst, Roger Isaacs, Mhairi Kersel and Blake Lyon, Carlotta Maher, Frances Rowan, Roberta Schaffner, Toni Smith, Nancy Stockmeyer, and Annette and Walter Vandaele. David Ilan and Levana Zias of the Hebrew Union College, Nelson Glueck School of Biblical Archaeology, Jerusalem, continued to offer their advice, logistical support, and equipment, for which we are very appreciative. The Israel Antiquities Authority provided efficient logistical and in-field support. We would also like to thank the staff at ORT Braude College, particularly Maxine Noam and Ora Dahan. At the Oriental Institute, critical administrative support from Steven Camp, D'Ann Condes, Adam Lubin, Tracy Tajbl, and Mariana Perlinac was fundamental to this successful season. Special thanks to our invaluable staff: Andrea Dudek, Phil Graham, Austin Hill, Brittany Jackson, Max Price, Dina Shalem, and the volunteers, students, and local workers, for their dedication, hard work, and boundless energy.

———————————

MUMMY LABEL DATABASE (MLD)

François Gaudard*

The highlight of the past year was the launching of both a Consejo Superior de Investigaciones Científicas (CSIC) website (fig.1) and an Oriental Institute webpage (fig. 2) dedicated to the Mummy Label Database:

http://www.proyectos.cchs.csic.es/death/node/1

http://oi.uchicago.edu/research/projects/mld/

Figure 1. The homepage of the CSIC website dedicated to the project Death on the Nile, hosting the Mummy Label Database

The CSIC website, appropriately named "Death on the Nile," is dedicated to the study of all aspects of death in Greco-Roman Egypt. At the center of this project is the Mummy Label Database. We have included downloadable instructions that will help the user navigate through the database efficiently:

http://www.proyectos.cchs.csic.es/death/sites/default/files/INSTRUCTIONS%20MLD_0.pdf

The website also includes a description of the project, a list of collaborators, a general bibliography and a bibliography organized by country, links to relevant institutions, and an online library providing free downloadable PDF documents of scholarly works by the editors of the project and team members. This library already includes a survey of Greek, Greek/ Demotic, and Demotic mummy labels by K. A. Worp, as the first volume of the series Death on the Nile Online Publications:

http://www.proyectos.cchs.csic.es/death/node/15

In addition, a list of past and future events will inform the users about conferences and meetings related to the project.

As for the Oriental Institute MLD webpage, it includes a description of the project as well as downloadable PDF documents of all the MLD annual reports since 2008–2009. Both websites and the database will be updated on an ongoing basis. Moreover, our aim is to have a preliminary version of the database, with approximately five hundred items, uploaded by the end of October 2013.

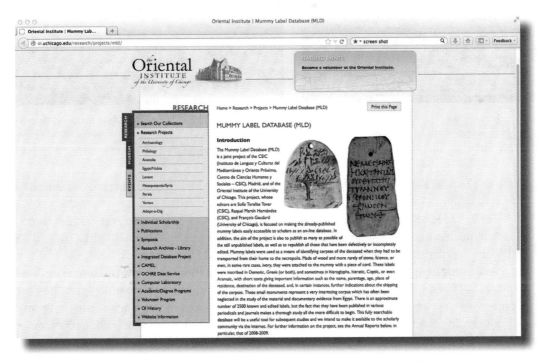

Figure 2. The homepage of the Oriental Institute website dedicated to the Mummy Label Database

This year, the staff of the project consisted of the editors of the Mummy Label Database, namely, Sofía Torallas Tovar (CSIC, Madrid), Raquel Martín Hernández (Universidad Complutense, Madrid), Klaas A. Worp (Leiden University), and François Gaudard (University of Chicago), as well as Sergio Carro (CSIC, Madrid), Marina Escolano Poveda (Johns Hopkins University, Baltimore), Alba de Frutos García (CSIC, Madrid), Alberto Nodar (Universitat Pompeu Fabra, Barcelona), María Jesús Albarrán Martínez (IRHT and CNRS, Paris), and Irene Pajón Leyra (CSIC, Madrid).

As always, team members convened on several occasions: at the Oriental Institute, Sofía, Maria Jesús, and François met in November 2012, and Sofía, Raquel, and François met again in February 2013. In order to clarify technical issues and discuss the interface of the data-

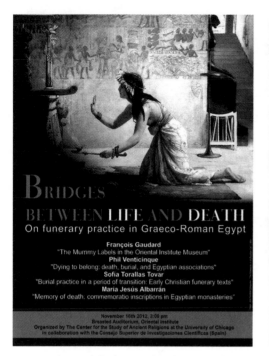

Figure 3. Poster of the first "Bridges between Life and Death" conference, hosted by the Oriental Institute on November 16, 2012

Figure 4. Participants in the first "Bridges between Life and Death" conference (left to right): Maria Jesús Albarrán Martínez, François Gaudard, Phil Venticinque, and Sofía Torallas Tovar

base on the internet, Raquel and Sergio met with the website programmers of Pompeu Fabra University in June 2013.

Sofía, Raquel, Klaas, and Sergio worked on the CSIC website, while François developed the Oriental Institute MLD webpage. At the beginning of April 2013, Raquel visited the British Museum in order to study unpublished Greek mummy labels.

As an ongoing part of the project, we have launched a new series of conferences entitled Bridges between Life and Death: On Funerary Practice in Graeco-Roman Egypt.[1] The first conference was organized by the Center for the Study of Ancient Religions at the University of Chicago, in collaboration with the CSIC, and hosted by the Oriental Institute on November 16, 2012 (figs. 3 and 4). Papers were presented in the following order:

- François Gaudard (University of Chicago), "The Mummy Labels in the Oriental Institute Museum"

- Phil Venticinque (Cornell College), "Dying to Belong: Death, Burial, and Egyptian Associations"

- Sofía Torallas Tovar (CSIC), "Burial Practice in a Period of Transition: Early Christian Funerary Texts"

- María Jesús Albarrán Martínez (CSIC), "Memory of Death: Commemoratio Inscriptions in Egyptian Monasteries"

The second conference, namely, Bridges between Life and Death: On Funerary Practice in Graeco-Roman Egypt II, was hosted by the Centro de Ciencias Humanas y Sociales in Madrid, on February 25, 2013 (fig. 5). Papers were given as follows:

- José Manuel Galán (CSIC): "Re-use of Tomb Chapels in the Ptolemaic Period in Dra Abu el-Naga (Luxor)"

- Raquel Martín Hernández (Universidad Complutense, Madrid): "Material, Text, and Context of Mummy Labels"

- Alba de Frutos García (CSIC): "Organisation of Necropoleis-Workers in Ptolemaic Egypt"

- Phil Venticinque (Cornell College), "Dying to Belong: Death, Burial, and Egyptian Associations"

- Irene Pajón Leyra (CSIC): "Funerary Practice of Barbarian Peoples in a Roman Papyrus"

Figure 5. Participants in the second Bridges between Life and Death conference (left to right): Phil Venticinque, Raquel Martín Hernández, José Manuel Galán, Alba de Frutos García, Sofía Torallas Tovar, and Irene Pajón Leyra

- Sofía Torallas Tovar (CSIC): "Funerary Practice in Transition: On Embalming in Late Roman Egypt"

Sofía also delivered a paper entitled "Egyptian Burial Practice and the First Christians in Egypt" at the conference Cultural Transfer in Late Antiquity and the Middle Ages, held in Córdoba, from November 29 to 30, 2012.

The following publications by team members, which are related to the project, have been published, are in press, or are forthcoming:

- François Gaudard, "A Demotic-Hieratic Mummy Label in the Museu de Montserrat," which will be published in a Festschrift honoring a colleague

- Sofía Torallas Tovar, "Egyptian Burial Practices in Late Antiquity: The Case of Christian Mummy Labels," in *Cultures in Contact: Transfer of Knowledge in the Mediterranean Context; Selected Papers*, edited by Sofía Torallas Tovar and Juan Pedro Monferrer-Sala, pp. 13–24. Series Syro-Arabica 1. Córdoba: Oriens Academic, 2013

- Sofía Torallas Tovar and Klaas A. Worp, "An Interesting Mummy Label in Leiden," *Zeitschrift für Papyrologie und Epigraphik* (2013) (forthcoming)

- Sofía Torallas Tovar and Klaas A. Worp, "New Wooden Labels from Various Collections," *Zeitschrift für Papyrologie und Epigraphik* 184 (2012): 257–70

- Klaas A. Worp and Raquel Martín Hernández, "'Goldfinger' on a Leiden Mummy Label?" *Bulletin of the American Society of Papyrologists* (2013) (in press)

- Klaas A. Worp, "Some Mummy Labels Identified," *Zeitschrift für Papyrologie und Epigraphik* 182 (2012): 273–74

- Klaas A. Worp, *A Survey of Greek, Greek/Demotic and Demotic Mummy Labels Texts*. Death on the Nile Online Publications. Version 1.0 (September 2012), Madrid. Available online at http://www.proyectos.cchs.csic.es/death/sites/default/files/Greek%2C%20GreekDemotic%20and%20Demotic%20Mummy%20Labels%20A%20Survey.%20K.%20WORP_0.pdf

The editors of the MLD would also like to take this opportunity to thank the Spanish Ministry of Science and Innovation (MICINN) for awarding them a grant,[3] Chris Faraone for his help in organizing the first Bridges between Life and Death conference, as well as John Sanders and Paul Ruffin for their technical support.

Notes

[8] For details on this joint project of the Instituto de Lenguas y Culturas del Mediterráneo y Oriente Próximo, Centro de Ciencias Humanas y Sociales — CSIC, Madrid, and of the Oriental Institute of the University of Chicago, readers can consult the *2008–2009 Annual Report*, available online in Adobe Portable Document Format (PDF) at: http://oi.uchicago.edu/pdf/08-09_MLD.pdf

[1] On April 23–24, 2009, we had already organized a first related conference, entitled Bridges between Life and Death: Dionysus, Mysteries, and Magic in the Ancient Greek and Roman World, which was held at the University of Chicago, in the Department of Classics.

[3] Grant ACI-PRO-2011-1132.

NIPPUR

McGuire Gibson

Resting on the drafting table in my office is a very large manuscript for the Inanna Temple publication. Richard L. Zettler, Karen Wilson, and Jean Evans have spent much of the past three years bringing about this long-awaited result. Zettler has been at it since the early-1970s, after Carl Haines turned over the responsibility to me to see his work through to publication a month before his death. Richard derived from the records a magnificent dissertation and later a book on the Ur III level (ca. 2100 BC) of the temple, and then began to work on the earlier levels with Donald Hansen, who had been the chief archaeologist responsible for the digging under Haines in the 1950s and 1960s. Hansen's death in 2007 led us all to rethink the Inanna publication project. Karen and Jean, both of whom had been Hansen's students, were research associates of the Oriental Institute and were available to work on the publication. Robert Biggs, who had been the cuneiform specialist for the Inanna excavations, was also here and ready to work. The technology now existed that would allow us not only to set up a database of all the records and object catalogs but also to make them available to all the members of the team on an interactive basis, and we could digitize and easily manipulate the plans and also share those, especially with Richard at the University of Pennsylvania. With all that coming together, I successfully applied for a National Endowment for the Humanities (NEH) grant that allowed us to do all the computer work and pay at least partial salaries to the research associates. We could pay artists who made great drawings of objects that did not photograph and as well as architects for revised plans.

I have just begun reading the manuscript, but I already know that it is a very fine presentation of one of the most eagerly awaited publications in our field. It reflects not only the work of Carl Haines in the architecture and the overall strategy of excavation and the expert digging and the keen eye for detail that characterized Hansen, but also the great gifts for analysis and interpretation of Zettler, Wilson, Evans, and Biggs. The publication has been long-awaited because the excavations ended in 1962, and although there were a few preliminary reports and important articles on specific types of objects and on chronology derived from the Inanna Temple sequence, there was nothing definitive on paper.

The Inanna Temple took on great importance because it was one of the very few examples of an excavation that traced the history of one institution from the Uruk period (ca. 3200 BC) to the Parthian period (ca. AD 100). Here we had a temple to Inanna, the goddess of love and war and one of the most important of all the gods, that began as a small building in the late fourth millennium and was knocked down and a new larger version built on it, again and again, until the Ur III period, when a very formally-laid-out rectangular building the size of a football field set the standard for all later versions. The size of the Ur III structure could be calculated even though about a third of it had been removed in excavations for the foundation of the uppermost, Parthian, version of the temple. The Parthian builders, with a tradition from the mountains of western Iran, built with huge mudbricks as if they were stones, and they therefore needed to make deep foundations, often as much as five or more meters. Their digging not only damaged the Ur III temple, but also took away almost

Inanna Temple excavations from the surface to Level XVII, from the northwest

*Inanna Temple, (right) Tomb 7 B
7, and (below) its contents*

all traces of the levels between it and the Parthian. There exist only bits of the front walls of some of these later buildings.

The Parthian Inanna temple is remarkable in being built in traditional Babylonian style, attesting to the fact that the powerful Mesopotamian religious and cultural tradition still lived in that time after the coming of Alexander and the Seleucid kings. The Parthian period in Mesopotamia, even with its heavy overlay of Hellenistic and Roman artistic themes and much imported or adapted material culture, still had a Babylonian basis, and there were still some texts written on clay tablets in cuneiform. With the following period, the Sasanian (AD 224–642), the grand Babylonian tradition ended and no more tablets were written, although in some of the folk traditions it lived on, and echoes are still heard in modern Iraq.

Besides the good news on the Inanna Temple, I can also report that we are editing Judith Franke's dissertation for publication. This important work reflects her very detailed excavation and recording of an area called WB on the West Mound at Nippur in 1973. We had opened the area in the previous year, before she joined the team, and had found that although the area looked undisturbed, it had in fact been very extensively excavated by the old Pennsylvania expedition of the 1890s, and to make matters worse, it had also been cut up by Seleucid diggers at about 250 BC. We did establish, however, that one house of the Old Babylonian period (ca. 1750 BC) had been abandoned suddenly, with its courtyard having more than fifty objects left on the floor. It looked as if the occupants had decided to go for a visit somewhere, and never came back. Working with Saleh Hameda, one of the few really expert Sherqati pickmen, who were the grandsons of men who had begun a tradition of excavating going back to the days of the Germans at Assur in the early 1900s, Judith took on the expansion and clarification of WB. In the upper levels, she and Saleh exposed an archive of about a hundred clay tablets used to fill a grave. These tablets turned out to be records of an early Neo-Babylonian governor (ca. 750 BC) and were important as evidence of the reoccupation and revival of southern Iraq after a period of abandonment. They were also able to find bits and pieces of walls and corners of rooms that allowed them to map rooms of a large palace of the governors of Nippur in the Kassite period (ca. 1250 BC). Under it, she exposed the entire Old Babylonian house that we had touched the previous season, and by collecting all the potsherds as well as whole vessels, seeds, bones, and soil samples, she was able to test theories of how the house functioned. This was one of the first uses of such scientific sampling in historical context in Mesopotamia, although since Braidwood's pioneering work or the Oriental Institute at Jarmo in northern Iraq from 1948 to 1950, it had become standard in prehistoric digs. We hope to see this book on its way to the editors in about a year.

In summary, it has been a good year for Nippur in terms of publication. We are still unable to go back to work at the site, but it is safe, guarded, and still as full of potential as ever.

ORIENTAL INSTITUTE-NATIONAL MUSEUM OF AFGHANISTAN PARTNERSHIP AND CULTURAL HERITAGE PROTECTION WORK

Gil J. Stein

The Partnership and Its Goals

The Oriental Institute-National Museum of Afghanistan (OI-NMA) Partnership is a three year project funded by the US Department of State as part of its broader commitment to protect the rich but fragile cultural heritage of Afghanistan. Over the course of more than three decades of unremitting warfare, the National Museum of Afghanistan had been devastated, with an estimated 70 percent of its collections either looted or destroyed, and 90% of its object records lost in the period from 1989 to 2001. In the years since 2001, the US and other international partners have physically rebuilt the museum, and its galleries are once again open to the public. Now, in the second phase of reconstruction, the OI-NMA Partnership seeks to take stock of the museum's surviving collections and develop a long-term, sustainable infrastructure of object curation for the National Museum. Our partnership has five main goals:

1. Develop a secure, easy-to-use, and sustainable Dari-English computer database for the holdings of the National Museum (NMA).
2. Develop the first complete computer-based inventory of the estimated 60,000 objects remaining in the NMA after the looting or destruction of an estimated 70 percent of the museum's holdings during the Afghan civil war and subsequent Taliban rule.
3. Make preliminary conservation assessments of the objects in the NMA's collections as part of the inventory process.
4. Re-house the objects in the NMA's collections in acid-free, archival-quality containers in preparation for a possible move of the collections to a new museum building (if the decision is made to construct a new museum building)
5. Train the NMA staff in international standards of database, recording, and artifact management procedures.

Overall, we want to develop these systems and train the staff of the National Museum to the point where they will be able to use, and add to, the inventory database on their own, with little or no foreign assistance, by the end of the three-year grant period.

As described in last year's *Oriental Institute Annual Report* for 2011–2012, we began the actual work of the partnership at the end of May 2012. The OI component of the partnership consists of the "Chicago team" (Gil Stein, Steve Camp, Jack Green, and Laura D'Alessandro), and the "Kabul team" led by Field Director Michael Fisher, Registrar Catherine Heim,

Figure 1. Oriental Institute team in Kabul, March 2013: Left to right: Steve Camp, Catherine Heim, Mike Fisher, Gil Stein, Hakim, Sattar, and Bilal

Figure 2. Director of the National Museum of Afghanistan Dr. Omara Khan Masoudi

and other registrars and conservators who have been participating in the project for shorter terms (fig. 1). We also periodically work with an international team of consultants who specialize in different aspects of Afghan archaeology and art and can assist us in the inventorying of individual periods or collections. At the US State Department, our key partner is Dr. Laura Tedesco, the Cultural Heritage Program Manager at the Office of Press and Public Diplomacy, responsible for Afghanistan and Pakistan. In Kabul, our principal partner is Dr. Omara Khan Masoudi, Director of the National Museum (fig. 2), along with his staff, notably Chief Curator Fahim Rahimi.

One of the most important aspects of the project is the fact that Oriental Institute staff, led by Field Director Mike Fisher, are living in Kabul and working six days a week in the museum alongside their Afghan colleagues. The ongoing presence of our staff in Kabul creates an atmosphere of real cooperation that gives us every reason to believe that we will conclude the project successfully. We have been fortunate to be able to stay in the guest house of DAFA, the French Archaeological Mission in Afghanistan. DAFA Director Philippe Marquis and Assistant Director Nicholas Engel have been extremely welcoming and helped us greatly throughout the past year. During the past year, OI Executive Director Steve Camp and I have made four trips to Kabul to deliver supplies, coordinate with the OI "Kabul team," and to deal with the administrative aspects of working with the National Museum, the Ministry of Information and Culture, the US Embassy, and ACHCO (the Kabul-based non-governmental organization that handles local logistics for our project).

Progress of the OI-NMA Inventory, 2012–2013

In late May 2012, we began our work in Kabul. National Museum Director Dr. Masoudi allocated office space to our group, and we got to work. Mike Fisher began the task of making our prototype database fully bilingual in both English and Dari (one of Afghanistan's two official languages). The rest of us started to work with the NMA conservation and curatorial staff to get their advice and suggestions on how they would like us to customize the database to best serve the needs of the museum. OI Head Conservator Laura D'Alessandro met extensively with the conservation staff of the National Museum to understand current conditions in the museum and the role that the museum's conservation staff can play in assessing the condition of the museum's ob-

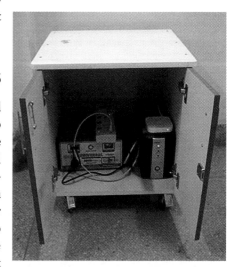

Figure 3. Router extender in a cabinet on wheels — our two "rolling routers" enable the Kabul team to extend our wireless network to reach every gallery and storeroom in the National Museum so that we can carry out the data entry for the museum inventory

Figure 4. Catherine Heim and members of the National Museum staff inventorying objects in the museum storerooms

Figure 5. Screen shot showing the digital image of one of the textiles in the National Museum's ethnographic collection entered into a bilingual inventory record

jects and in re-housing them in archival-quality boxes as part of the inventory process. Laura also asked what kinds of conservation-related information they would like to see included in the database. OI Chief Curator Jack Green organized a workshop for the National Museum staff to discuss the value of databases in collections management, and the ways in which the database we are developing might be especially useful for the needs of the National Museum.

The NMA staff had already done a tremendous amount of the foundational work for the database part of the OI-NMA partnership. Over the last five years, the NMA curators had already completed and scanned thousands of paper inventory forms in both Dari and English. We started the task of transferring the scanned inventory sheets and the several thousand objects from earlier pilot efforts at database development into a single integrated data structure in FileMaker Pro to which all of the objects in the museum will be added as we inventory them.

We examined all the galleries and were able to make an initial assessment of all the museum storage rooms, to give us our first direct view of the number of objects, what sites and periods are represented, what kinds of materials are present, and overall storage conditions as they relate to conservation. Mike Fisher set up our secure local area network and worked with OI Exhibit Preparator Erik Lindahl to develop an ingenious system of router extenders in cabinets on wheels that enabled our wireless network for inventory coding to reach every storeroom in the museum (fig. 3). By September 2012, Mike had developed the database to the point where it was ready to use, and the museum staff had been trained in inventory procedures.

Each inventory team consists of an OI staff person and a staff member of the National Museum, who enter the description of each object in both English and Dari (figs. 4–5). The objects are measured, labeled with an inventory number, and photographed. The digital photos are linked to each inventory record, along with any older paper documentation (if present). Our system is "scalable" in the sense that the more inventory teams we have working, the more storerooms we can cover, and the more objects we can record. We have now expanded our efforts to the point where on any given day two or three teams are working in tandem in different storerooms within the museum. Best of all, our Afghan colleagues have now gained enough hands-on experience that they are working as independent teams to inventory, describe, measure, and photograph the objects in the storerooms. This is ex-

Figure 6. Mike Fisher inside the 40-foot shipping container with archival quality object housing materials shipped from the US to Kabul for the OI-NMA Partnership

actly what we had hoped to achieve: our plan all along has been to provide enough hands-on training that the NMA staff will be able to take over the inventory and be totally comfortable continuing these procedures when the three-year partnership is completed and the OI staff return home in 2015.

By July 2013 the OI-NMA partnership had inventoried 13,000 objects. This is an extremely impressive achievement. As we bring in additional foreign registrars and have additional Afghan staff working on the inventory teams, we hope to double this rate of work in the coming year.

Artifact conservation also plays a key role in the OI-NMA partnership. As we inventory the objects, conservators are providing initial assessments of the condition of the objects in a triage system where we flag those objects most in need of conservation. As part of this process, we are re-housing the objects in archival-quality, acid-free packing materials, bags, and boxes — both to protect them and to prepare them for a possible move to a new museum facility, if this is approved by the Ministry of Information and Culture, and if funding can be obtained.

In planning the project, we knew that acid-free, archival-quality artifact housing materials are impossible to obtain in Kabul, and that they would have to be shipped over 8,000 miles from the US. Laura D'Alessandro and the OI Conservation department worked tirelessly to navigate the tremendously complex labyrinth of Kafka-esque shipping and customs regulations, and in the end achieved something amazing — we were able to ship a 40-foot container by sea to Pakistan, where (after being delayed for weeks by a teamsters' strike in Karachi) it was then trucked overland to the Afghan border, and finally delivered to the National Museum safe and sound in the spring of 2013 (fig. 6). We now know how to do this and are in the process of preparing a second container filled with steel shelving supplies for shipment to Kabul.

As the inventory has progressed, we have made wonderful discoveries — locating and recording objects that had been misplaced during the years of civil war and Taliban rule. My personal favorite is a large, third-millennium BC ceramic mouse-trap from the French excavations at the site of Mundigak in southern Afghanistan. But perhaps the most important re-discovery was a fragment of an Achaemenid administrative tablet initially unearthed in the 1970s by the British excavations at Old Kandahar. The tablet had been moved from its original location and had been presumed to be lost. This is one of the only known examples of Achaemenid tablets written in the Elamite language to have been recovered by archaeological excavations in Afghanistan. Its very presence attests to the scale and effectiveness of the administration of the Persian empire in its eastern satrapies or provinces. In January 2014 we plan to bring Prof. Matthew Stolper, the Head of the OI's Persepolis Fortification Archive Project, out to Kabul to conduct a close examination of the tablet and to prepare a joint publication of this artifact with Mike Fisher. Re-discoveries of this type show the tremendous potential of the NMA collections not only for gallery display, but also as a research resource. We hope that there will be many more surprises like this in the future, and that the museum collections will attract not only visitors from the public, but also researchers from all over the world.

Cultural Heritage Projects in Afghanistan

The OI-NMA Partnership is not alone in its efforts. Over the course of the last year, we have been deeply impressed to learn about and see for ourselves the tremendous range of ongoing projects aimed at preserving different aspects of cultural heritage in Afghanistan. These efforts are being designed and implemented by Afghan organizations, by foreign governments, by private foundations, and by dedicated individuals. There are many different types of cultural heritage in Afghanistan, and they are all at risk. Although they generally receive little or no attention in the world media, there are in fact numerous successful projects of heritage preservation. Most important, it is heartening to see that many of these projects are being done by Afghans, and not just by the international community.

The preservation of archaeological sites is one of the most important single areas of endangered cultural heritage. Looting of sites and the connected illicit antiquities trade are an enormous ongoing problem throughout Afghanistan. Large amounts of looted artifacts have been confiscated by customs officials in London and other centers and have been returned to the National Museum in Kabul. But the illicit trade is ubiquitous. On our trip to Herat in northwest Afghanistan this spring, the OI project team saw antiquities (both genuine artifacts and fakes) openly on sale in the bazaar (fig. 7). To monitor this ongoing problem, a number of groups have been using sequences of dated satellite imagery to develop Geographic Information Systems (GIS) databases of sites and looting in the different regions of the country. And on the ground, several teams of archaeologists have been conducting rescue excavations at key sites under threat of destruction by either looting or economic development.

Perhaps the most important of these efforts is the large-scale collaboration between Afghanistan and the international community to conduct rescue excavations at Mes Aynak.

Figure 7. Looted artifacts along with modern fakes on sale in the Herat bazaar. Extensive looting of sites across Afghanistan continues to be a major threat to Afghan cultural heritage

Figure 8. View of the salvage excavations in the upper town of Mes Aynak in Logar province, Afghanistan. The compound of the mining camp is visible in the background. An international team of archaeologists is racing the clock to complete rescue excavations in the core of Mes Aynak before large-scale mining operations begin

Figure 9. Buddhist stupa at the site of Tepe Narinj on the outskirts of Kabul. Archaeologists from the Afghan Institute of Archaeology excavated and stabilized the architectural remains and constructed a protective fence around the site

Figure 10. Afghan site guards at Tepe Narinj, standing in front of the barred storeroom constructed at the site by the Afghan Institute of Archaeology to protect the large-scale sculpture and other architectural ornaments

Located in Logar province, about 45 km southwest of Kabul, Mes Aynak was an enormous 1,000-hectare Buddhist city, trade entrepôt, and monastic center that flourished especially in the third to seventh centuries AD. The name "Mes Aynak" means "Copper Spring," and the site is located on top of what may be the world's largest known copper deposit. This was the source of the wealth of the ancient city, and it is the source of the threat to its future. The difficult balance between economic development and heritage preservation means that there is only a limited window of opportunity to excavate and document the artistic and architectural treasures of Mes Aynak before it is largely destroyed by modern copper mining activities (fig. 8). Former Deputy Minister for Information and Culture Mr. Omar Sultan has been working extensively with Philippe Marquis of the French Archaeological Mission in Afghanistan and an international excavation team to explore much of the urban core of Mes Aynak and the string of Buddhist monasteries that surround it. Some of the finest sculpture and other artifacts from Mes Aynak are now on display in the National Museum.

On the outskirts of Kabul, at the site of Tepe Narinj, researchers from the Afghan Institute of Archaeology have conducted rescue excavations of a Buddhist monastery complex. When our OI team visited the site in March 2013 and met the Afghan archaeologists who had conducted the rescue project, we were extremely impressed to see that they had stabilized and partially restored the remains of the Buddhist stupas at the site (fig. 9). They had also built secure locked storerooms on site to protect the larger sculptural remains, constructed a fence around the site, and even arranged for paramilitary police to patrol the site and discourage looters (fig. 10). The Afghan archaeologists did all this completely on their own. The Tepe Narinj excavations had the added value of producing numismatic evidence to prove that Buddhism was still thriving in the Kabul area as late as the ninth century AD, more than 100 years later than had been previously thought.

Historical monuments of all periods are at risk in Afghanistan, and a number of different groups have gone to enormous efforts to preserve them. Much of this work has focused on monuments and architecture of the Islamic period. The US State department has supported work to document the minarets of Ghazni and is working to preserve one of the earliest known mosques in Afghanistan, located in the region of Balkh (ancient Bactra, near the modern city of Mazar-i-Sharif). Local Afghan groups in the northwest city of Herat have

Figure 11. The fourteenth-century Timurid Masjid-i-Jami (Friday Mosque) in the city of Herat, northwest Afghanistan — considered one of the most important surviving Islamic monuments in Central Asia. Note Steve Camp in front of the central iwan for scale. Local civil and religious authorities in Herat have supported the long-term restoration of the magnificent glazed tile work that covers the mosque

Figure 12. Detail of some of the glazed tile work on the Masjid-i-Jami in Herat

spent decades working to restore the magnificent tile work of the fourteenth-century Masjid-i-Jami, or "Friday mosque" — one of the most important and beautiful surviving Islamic monuments of Central Asia (figs. 11–12).

Some of the most effective efforts to preserve and restore Islamic monuments in Afghanistan have been sponsored by the Aga Khan Trust for Culture (AKTC). The country director for the AKTC, Ajmal Maiwandi, was kind enough to show us some of these treasures, most notably in Kabul at the sixteenth-century Bagh-i-Babur — the Gardens of Babur, founder of the Mughal dynasty that ruled both Afghanistan and most of India from the sixteenth to the nineteenth century (fig. 13). The beautifully and accurately restored garden is an oasis for picnics, walks, and relaxation in the heart of Kabul, and it forms the largest green space

Figure 13. Bagh-i-Babur (Gardens of Babur) in the heart of Kabul, constructed in the sixteenth century by Babur, the founder of the Mughal dynasty. Restoration of Babur's Garden was funded and carried out by the Aga Khan Trust for Culture (AKTC)

Figure 14. Bagh-i-Babur: restored small royal mosque constructed in the Garden by Shah Jahan, the fifth Mughal emperor. Shah Jahan is best known as the builder of the Taj Mahal

Figure 15. Qalat Ihtiyardin, the massive citadel of Herat. Restoration of the citadel was carried out by the Aga Khan Trust for Culture, while archaeological excavations at the Citadel and the reorganization of the Citadel Museum were carried out by Dr. Ute Franke on behalf of the German Archaeological Institute (DAI)

Figure 16. Nancy Hatch Dupree and Gil Stein in front of the newly completed Afghanistan Center at Kabul University (ACKU). With over 70,000 books, magazines, newspapers, and other documents, the center is the world's largest archive of historical documentation on Afghanistan. Construction of the center was funded by the Afghan government as a key project in cultural heritage preservation

in the city. Nestled in the garden is an architectural gem — the small royal mosque (fig. 14) established by the fifth Mughal emperor, Shah Jahan, best known as the builder of the Taj Mahal. The AKTC has also restored the imposing Qalat Ihtiyardin citadel of Herat (fig. 15) and numerous historic houses in the Old City.

Cultural heritage is not just sites and monuments; it also encompasses literature, history, music, and traditional arts and handicrafts. Often called "intangible heritage," these aspects of Afghan culture have been deeply battered and nearly destroyed by decades of war, refugee displacement, and the near total disruption of Afghan society. We were able to see two especially impressive initiatives that have been preserving these aspects of Afghan cultural heritage. The first of these is the Afghanistan Center at Kabul University (ACKU). This center was founded by Nancy Hatch Dupree, one of the leading and most effective advocates for the preservation of Afghan heritage. Built with funding from the Afghan government, the center is the largest and most comprehensive archive of books, manuscripts, newspapers, and magazines relating to Afghanistan (fig. 16). The center's location on the campus of Kabul University makes this unique collection accessible to the students and faculty, in addition to foreign researchers.

Finally, we were deeply impressed to see the work of the Turquoise Mountain Foundation in the heart of Kabul. This Anglo-Afghan cooperative venture focuses on preserving and revitalizing traditional Afghan arts and craft specialties such as woodworking, ceramics, gem cutting, and jewelry production. The instructors at Turquoise Mountain are some of the last surviving Afghan masters of these crafts, and they are committed to passing along their knowledge (fig. 17). Instead of simply reviving traditional crafts in a static fossilized form, Turquoise Mountain encourages its students to develop new forms of artistic expression and gives them the business training to be successful economically once they have finished their training apprenticeships.

This is only a sampling of the different heritage protection programs that are being implemented with great success in Afghanistan. The main point is that despite extremely difficult conditions, committed efforts like the ones mentioned above are taking place at all, and they are actually succeeding. We are proud that the Oriental Institute's partnership with the National Museum forms a part of this set of initiatives. From everything we have seen over the past year, we are more hopeful than ever that Afghanistan can preserve its heritage as the cultural core for the country's future; we are honored to be able to help in this endeavor.

Figure 17. Master woodworker at the Turquoise Mountain Foundation, in a restored traditional house compound in the Old City of Kabul. Turquoise Mountain supports the revitalization of traditional Afghan crafts such as woodworking inlay, gem cutting, ceramics, and jewelry making. These are key elements of Afghanistan's "intangible heritage"

ORIENTAL INSTITUTE NUBIAN EXPEDITION (OINE)

Bruce Williams with Katarzyna Danys-Lasek, Lisa Heidorn,
Artur Obluski, Joanna Then-Obluska, Nadejda Reshetnikova,
Alexandros Tsakos, and Dobrochna Zielińska

Last year, we reported on the revival of the Oriental Institute Nubian Expedition publication project with four specific publication objectives: the Middle Kingdom fortress of Serra East (1850–1750 BC), the Napatan-period fortress-town of Dorginarti (720–550 BC), the Early and Classic Christian monastery of Qasr el-Wizz (AD 550–900), and the Late Christian-period town at Cerre Matto (Serra East, AD 1000–1200). There are other pieces being worked on elsewhere, but these tasks make up the major part of the work left outstanding from the great 1960s rescue. With five concessions in two countries and a couple dozen sites, depending on how you count them, this was the largest institutional campaign in Nubia, and it is no surprise that publication requires a major commitment from the participants and will span many volumes. It may come as a surprise to some, however, when they read here the assertion that there is no such thing as a final report. Standards of publication change, as do costs, which in some areas actually go down — making another surprise — and the Internet has revolutionized our opportunities for delivering data. So, this year, we added a fifth objective. For over a year Joanna Then-Obluska has been systematically studying and photographing the beads from the OINE with spectacular results that have inspired us to incorporate her work as volumes in the series. With by far the largest truly archaeological collection on this continent (and possibly any continent) from the 1960s rescue, and the superb curatorial work that has been devoted to it, the Oriental Institute offers a unique opportunity to update, expand, and correct our older publications.

Dorginarti and Serra East

With the award of a grant from the Shelby White and Leon Levy Program for Archaeological Publications, we have completed the major part of fund-raising needed to provide services for the project, primarily drafting, architecture, and photography. Work on Serra fortress has been supported by the Michela Schiff Giorgini Foundation, while the White-Levy grant will be joined with a grant awarded last year by the American Research Center in Egypt/ Antiquities Endowment Fund to support work on Dorginarti and Cerre Matto. Using these resources, the architect Nadejda Reshetnikova has been joined on the project staff by Carol Meyer and Natasha Ayers, artists, and Elise MacArthur, photographer.

One other task affected both operations. The Sudan National Museum in Khartoum was assigned the objects retained by Sudan during the rescue. Documentation of these in the field was limited, so we had somehow to go there to see what we could find, draw, and photograph. Fortunately, Prof. Stuart Tyson Smith of the University of California Santa Barbara led a field season to Tumbos at the Third Cataract in Sudan with Bruce Williams as a participant, and the architect for the operation (and for OINE), Nadejda Reshetnikova, agreed to travel with Bruce to Khartoum two weeks early for a brief "study season." Although Nadejda and Bruce were not able to find many of the objects — some were never registered — they found the ones most critical to the current publication effort, including a remarkable early Christian sculpted door jamb. Earlier, Alexandros Tsakos paid a study visit to the museum, and, after considerable research, he found a number of documents that came from the Christian town of Cerre Matto. The project owes thanks to many in the National Corporation for Antiquities and Museums of Sudan, but especially Director General Dr. Abdelrahman Ali and National Museum Director Dr. Ghalia Gar el-Nabi.

Dorginarti

In addition to working on the pottery fabrics, the ceramic material from the fortress, and the architectural details, Lisa Heidorn studied the pottery fragments that indicate metallurgical activities were taking place during the main Level III and IV activities at the fort. Most of the fragments are crucibles, some with thick deposits on their interiors (fig. 1). There are also remains of various types of slag, tuyeres (fig. 2), and pottery equipment used in melting or smelting processes. It is of great interest, therefore, to study a sample of the Dorginarti crucibles and their interior deposits to analyze the crucible fabric and the interior deposits.

Correspondence with Drs. Edgar Pusch and Thilo Rehren, both of University College London, has led to an interest in their testing some of the crucibles and the most heavily slagged deposits, cutting thin sections to analyze the materials. The issues to be addressed by such testing will establish the nature of the metalworking at the site and the relationship of this small-time metallurgical concern with earlier, contemporary, and later industries in Egypt, Nubia, and the Near East.

The Middle Kingdom Fortress at Serra East (Khesef-Medjay)

The major effort in the publication of Serra East this year has been architecture, reconstructing the survey by James E. Knudstad based on his theodolite data by converting angles and distances to coordinates, then using these to construct a new plan. All published plans for the Nubian forts, as well as other large structures in the ancient world, are summary, leaving

Figure 1. Fragment of a crucible from Dorginarti showing layers of deposit on the interior, from locus D 119 (1)

Figure 2. Fragments of tuyeres from Dorginarti locus D 218 (1). These tubular clay objects would have been attached to pot bellows to force air into a fire

out details in favor of presenting a pleasing and easy-to-understand picture of a building. An archaeologist who is trying to understand how a building was built, used, repaired, and even reused needs more than that, and text descriptions alone do not solve the problem. For Serra, we have adopted a presentation approach that involves a very large-scale printed plan — over a meter in length — that shows every detail Jim Knudstad so lovingly put on his survey pages so long ago. A second plan the same size will add his explanatory notes and elevations.

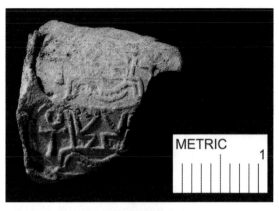

Figure 3. Seal 137 from Quarry Dump II at Serra East. It shows two impressions made by a scarab-seal carved with two ankh-signs flanking opposed Red Crowns on the nub-sign (gold)

Our efforts began with the coordinate conversion, a fairly arduous task undertaken by a devoted volunteer, Lawrence Lissak, assisted by Bruce Williams. The second part, even larger, has been the creation of a new plan using Jim Knudstad's wonderful survey pages, done entirely by Nadejda Reshetnikova, architect for the OINE publication of Serra East and Dorginarti. The draft plan, built in AutoCAD and Adobe Illustrator, is largely finished, and will soon be transferred to a final base plan with annotations. Since the entire plan is vectorized, the online Adobe portable document format (PDF) versions will be scalable by the user in ways not possible for print versions.

A second major effort this year has been a review of the seal impressions. In recent years, the Oriental Institute expedition to Tell Edfu has acquired major experience dealing with late Middle Kingdom sealings and this circumstance provided an invaluable opportunity to cross-check the old identifications, drawings, and classifications. Susan Penacho and Kathryn Bandy have kindly undertaken this work for some months, making a very substantial contribution. In addition, Elise MacArthur is making color photographs of key pieces, which will greatly enhance the publication (fig. 3).

The Late Christian Town of Cerre Matto (Serra East)

We will begin direct preparation of a manuscript for the Christian period at Serra East by the fall. In the meantime, certain events have established an essential foundation, especially in funding. The visit to Khartoum made truly major pieces available for publication. The most important of these is a large sandstone doorjamb of the early Christian period (Khartoum National Museum 14350) found at Serra East north, which was probably intended for use as spolia (reused decorated block) in one of the churches (fig. 4). It now has three panels, originally more, each depicting what is probably a phoenix, wings spread, with a cross on or above its head, which is turned to the side. In front of each bird is a tripod supporting a conical vessel, possibly an incense burner. Adopted as a symbol of Christ and the resurrection, the phoenix appears in Christian art in the Mediterranean, including Egypt as well as Nubia. We have later fragments of phoenix reliefs, actually pierced, from Serra itself and datable to the town, and the motif of the phoenix with wings spread is a significant feature of Christian Nubian art.

Alexandros Tsakos' work in Khartoum recovered manuscripts found at Cerre Matto but registered from Attiri, a site farther upstream. Clarifying the origin of these manuscripts

Figure 4. Photograph and drawing of the central panel from the Serra East doorjamb carved with a phoenix in relief in front of a tripod, possibly with an incense burner. The jamb is now in the Khartoum National Museum, Sudan (drawing by Nadejda Reshetnikova)

will not only enhance the OINE publication of a site that was famous for its manuscripts, but the Khartoum museum's collection.

The architectural work on the building of Serra Fortress has also helped this phase, for important features of the town were reused from the fortress phase and some Christian buildings and features had to be planned because Jim Knudstad used them in his measurements, so we will begin this aspect at a more advanced stage. We have also begun the drawing and photography — arduous work, but a most essential part of any archaeological report. This is particularly true in Christian-period Nubia, where so much of the pottery had painted decoration that could mix Christian, Byzantine, and African elements, even in the same design (fig. 5).

Qasr el-Wizz

The year 2012 brought reinforcements to studies on records and artifacts from the Oriental Institute's excavations at Qasr el-Wizz monastery. Artur Obluski and Alexandros Tsakos were joined by Dobrochna Zielińska (wall paintings) and Katarzyna Danys-Lasek (pottery) in their efforts to publish remains of the sole excavated monastery in Nubia. It allowed expanding analysis to wall paintings and pottery recovered by Harry Smith and George Scanlon in 1961 and 1965 respectively. In the first half of the year, studies on archaeological material recovered from Qasr el-Wizz focused on cemeteries and digital tracing of tomb's drawings. A preliminary version of the section of the volume on Wizz cemeteries has been produced, including their detailed description and information on

Figure 5. Drawing of bowl OIM 24776 from the late Christian period at Serra East. The bowl, of a fine, deep orange (red) pottery, was decorated with black paint. It was part of a foundation deposit under a house (drawing by Carol Meyer)

the artifacts found at the site. It includes a separate chapter on funerary customs at Qasr el-Wizz from the perspective of Christian tradition in Nubia and in other regions of Christian koine in the Mediterranean (fig. 6). The preliminary version also contains some new observations on the distribution of Nubian cemeteries and on possible sources of inspiration for various types of tomb superstructure. While the first seem to derive from certain biblical narratives, which Artur Obluski discusses in a forthcoming work, tomb superstructures seem to be patterned on sacred architecture. Finally, there will be discussions of burials in churches and pilgrimage in medieval Christian Nubia.

Figure 6. An eight-pointed star used as an apotropaic symbol on a tomb superstructure at Qasr el-Wizz

The team also started working on the artifacts that were found in the monastery. The dossiers of documentation from the Egypt Exploration Society and the Coptic Museum in Cairo have been compiled and spurred research on the textual finds from Wizz. The identifications of several texts found in the monastery have been improved thanks to photos taken in the Coptic Museum in Cairo. The majority of the preserved texts from Qasr el-Wizz is of literary character. Text 65-11-105 is the only documentary text in Coptic from Wizz. It seems to be a list of the possessions of the monastery, and it can be dated to around the eighth century AD.

Wall paintings in the monastery were preserved very fragmentarily. Both the few fragments of paintings found in situ and the numerous fragments of plaster that were found in the debris were investigated according to their

Figure 7. Floral decoration from the synthronon in the apse of the church at Qasr el-Wizz

Figure 8. Doorway in a monk's cell at Qasr el-Wizz with reconstructed painted decoration

location. On the basis of the analysis of the photos, we will learn more about the decoration of the monastic church, refectory, and gallery. One can find patterns of a highly original character — ones so far not found in other examples of the Nubian wall painting — such as the floral decoration of the *synthronon* (fig. 7). On the other hand, the paintings/compositions in the western part of the church are very close to examples of paintings from the nearby Paulos Cathedral in Faras, showing both a style and iconography typical for the eighth century. The painted decoration in the block of monks' cells includes two examples where the doorway was decorated with shapes that resemble horns bent downward (fig. 8). It could be interpreted as symbolic *akroterion*. Such elements appear also in the decoration on funerary stelae in Nubia and in painted decoration in the niches in the Faras Cathedral.

This year also brought commencement of the studies of about 3,000 pottery sherds and small finds. The vast ceramic assemblage spans a period of almost one thousand years and can be dated between the fourth and thirteenth centuries AD. Some finds may mark the foundation of the monastery (sixth/seventh–eighth centuries; fig. 9). The better part of the collected material was produced between the ninth and the eleventh centuries and is richly painted with splendid decoration (fig. 7). Then there is a decline in the number of pottery finds that may also mark the changes taking place in the monastery (twelfth–beginning of

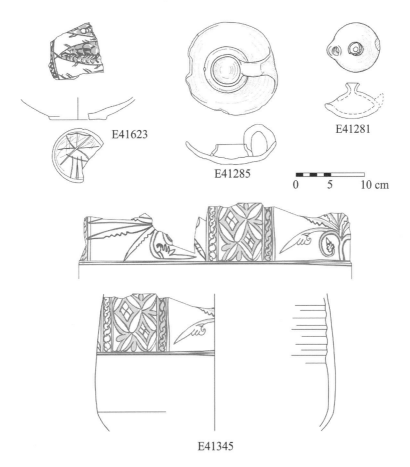

E41623

E41281

E41285

0   5   10 cm

E41345

Figure 9. Selected pottery vessels from Qasr el-Wizz monastery: E41623, a plate (eleventh–twelfth centuries AD); E41345, a vase (twelfth century AD); E41285 and E41281, lamps (sixth and seventh centuries AD) (drawings by Katarzyna Danys-Lasek)

thirteenth century). The pottery collected from the site sheds some light on the movement of bulk goods in the Nile valley. There are objects from workshops all along the Nile valley, from Mareotis, through Fayum, Middle Egypt, Faras, and upriver as far as the kingdom of Alwa (Alodia).

The project has been promoted on three different occasions: in a lecture during the annual General Meeting of the Norwegian Archaeological Society, where the Shenoutian character of the monastery was highlighted on the basis of manuscripts 65-10-62 and 65-11-120 in the Coptic Museum, Cairo; in a contribution to the panel on Old Nubian at the Nilo-Saharan Linguistics Colloquium, where the Nubian linguistic identity of the author of the texts preserved in manuscripts 65-10-59 and 65-11-99 was demonstrated; and in a seminar at the University of Warsaw's Institute of Archaeology.

The implementation of the project so far was possible thanks to the grants from the Foundation for Polish Science, Poland, and the Institute of Comparative Cultural Research in Oslo, Norway. If we find a funding source, mortar, plaster and pigment analyses of the pieces of wall painting collected by Keith Seele and George Scanlon and radiocarbon dating of organic material found in the graves associated with the earliest phase of occupation at the site are scheduled for the next year. They are of crucial importance not only for the history of the site but also for the history of Christianization of Nubia since Qasr el-Wizz church seems to be one of the earliest churches in Nubia, and archaeometric analyses can provide decisive body of evidence.

An Interdisciplinary Study of Beads from the Oriental Institute Nubian Expedition

The main objective of the bead publication project is to create a vast, high-quality illustrated corpus of beads found in the Lower Nubia by the OINE. Since April 2012 more than 100,000 beads, covering the period from roughly 3500 BC to AD 1900, have been photographed and recorded in a comprehensive database. Results of interdisciplinary analysis will be published in two separate volumes of Oriental Institute Nubian Expedition series. So far, the preliminary outcome is very promising: Nubian beads seem to reflect the age and gender of individuals, their social status, ethnic and religious identity, as well as ritual behavior. Last but not least, they tell stories of short-distance and overseas trade contacts, whether transit or terminal in character. On the other hand, beads from the OINE collection have already proved to be excellent chronological indicators that can be used in studies on the North-East Africa and its relations with the Indo-Pacific region.

PERSEPOLIS FORTIFICATION ARCHIVE (PFA) PROJECT

Matthew W. Stolper

In mid-May 2013, Persepolis Fortification Archive Project editors Mark Garrison and Wouter Henkelman were crossing Germany on an intercity train after delivering a joint presentation at the Free University of Berlin. Their lecture, a survey of the religious landscape of early Achaemenid Persia, drew on their years of collaborative work on texts and images preserved in the Persepolis Fortification Archive (http://persepolistablets.blogspot.com/2013/05/from-humban-to-auramazda-image-and-text.html). They were bound for Castelen, near Basel, Switzerland, to discuss the administration of the Achaemenid Persian empire at a conference co-sponsored by the University of Basel and the Oriental Institute. The conference would commemorate the eightieth anniversary of the discovery of the PFA by Ernst Herzfeld (1879–1948), who is buried nearby (http://persepolistablets.blogspot.com/2013/05/celebratory-conference-on-occasion-of.html). The proceedings were to focus on the PFA as the most detailed known manifestation of an "imperial signature" that is traceable across the breadth of the continent that the Achaemenid empire once governed.

On the train, Garrison and Henkelman were discussing Garrison's recent discovery among the fragments of Fortification tablets a few months earlier: a seal impression that links the PFA with the Arshama correspondence. This corpus of Aramaic letters from the Achaemenid satrap who governed Egypt about a hundred years after the time of the PFA had been the

topic of a series of workshops at Oxford University (http://arshama.classics.ox.ac.uk/workshops/index.html), in which Garrison and Henkelman had taken part. The text that accompanied the related seal impression in the PFA was lost, but now, as they conversed on the train, they realized that another fragmentary impression of the same seal might accompany the text on one of the Elamite documents that Henkelman was editing as part of the PFA Project.

Was a Wi-Fi connection possible on the train? It was. Laptops came out. Garrison and Henkelman connected to the PFA Project's dedicated server in Chicago. They located the digital images of Henkelman's document made by student Project workers. They found an image of the impression on the damaged edge of the tablet. Was it made by the same seal? It was. Now the seal, already tied to later circumstances in Achaemenid Egypt, was also tied securely to a name, a person,

Figure 1. Wouter Henkelman at the Berlin train station

a situation in the dense social and institutional fabric that the PFA reveals.

A few months earlier, in Kabul, NELC graduate student Michael Fisher e-mailed Oriental Institute director Gil Stein about a surprising find in the collections of the National Museum of Afghanistan. Fisher was working there as part of the Institute's collaborative cataloging project (http://www.youtube.com/watch?v=GdSt7LVmZH8, and see elsewhere in this *Annual Report*) when he found a fragment of a cuneiform tablet. But when had Afghanistan been in the sphere of

Figure 2. Achaemenid Elamite tablet fragment from Old Kandahar. Photograph by Michael Fisher, by permission of the National Museum of Afghanistan

cuneiform recording? Stein surmised that the fragment might be Achaemenid. I suggested it might be a fragment excavated at Old Kandahar in 1977.[1] We sent Fisher scans of the original excavation photos. Fisher sent back new high-resolution digital images. It was the same object. It preserves only a few cuneiform signs, representing only a few complete words, but comparison with the PFA makes it instantly recognizable as part of a larger record compiled at a regional administrative hub. This unprepossessing relic of a vanished archive is strong testimony to the Achaemenid imperial signature in the eastern territories of the Empire—but only because of what we have learned from the PFA.

Eighty years ago, Ernst Herzfeld sent a telegram from Iran to James Henry Breasted in Egypt, to announce the discovery of the PFA. Breasted wrote to Henri Frankfort in Iraq with a mixture of enthusiasm and reserve:

> This is a demonstration that [the] Persepolis Terrace contains cuneiform tablets and gives us just ground for hoping, or even expecting, that tablet documents from the

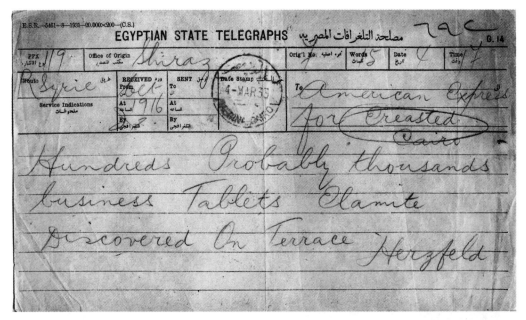

Figure 3. Herzfeld's telegram to Breasted, March 4, 1933, terser than a Tweet: "Hundreds Probably thousands business Tablets Elamite Discovered On Terrace. Herzfeld"

State Archives of the Persian Kings are still lying under the rubbish of the Terrace. If so a new period in the history of the East has begun. Even these <u>business</u> tablets should contribute essentially to a full understanding of the Elamite language.[2]

Richard Hallock was more reserved than enthusiastic when he wrote, after thirty-five years of painstaking study of the PFA, that "The Achaemenid Elamite texts found at Persepolis add a little flesh to the picked-over bones of early Achaemenid history."[3] But today these mere "business tablets" call for more enthusiasm than reserve as they add much more than a little historical flesh, surpassing Breasted's hopes in unexpected ways. Because the PFA Project is building a comprehensive record that represents the Archive's combination of complexity and integrity, because it is distributing the record in forms that can support ongoing research, because it engenders collaborative contributions of specialists, and because it relies on digital methods and media, it has been possible for investigators in Germany and Afghanistan to document the PFA's implications for organization, society and history across the continent-wide reach of the Achaemenid empire, from Memphis to Kandahar (fig. 4). If a legal crisis sparked the PFA Project, consequences like these kindle its ongoing efforts.

During the past year, PFA Project editor Mark Garrison (Trinity University, San Antonio, Texas) and summer worker Erin Daly (Notre Dame University) finished surveying the uninscribed, sealed tablets (PFUT) in the ca. 2,600 boxes of PFA tablets and fragments. They resurveyed about 350 boxes that Garrison had gone over at the beginning of the Project, looking now with more practiced eyes. Garrison and Daly selected 450 more PFUTs for recording. The cumulative sample of PFUTs now exceeds 3,500, between a quarter and a third of the entire sample that the Project expects to record. More than 600 previously unknown seals have been identified so far from impressions on these uninscribed tablets. Daly returned to the Project during the summer of 2013 to join other student workers supported by a grant from Roshan Cultural Heritage Institute, to continue cataloging and recording the PFUTs and the new seals.

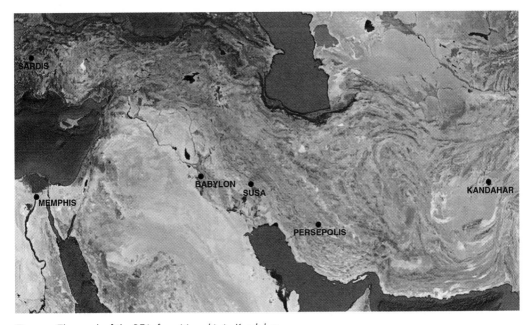

Figure 4. The reach of the PFA, from Memphis to Kandahar

Along with Daly and graduate students Tytus Mikołajczak (NELC) and Emily Wilson (Classics), Garrison checked seal identifications on more than 650 of the unpublished Elamite documents first edited by the late Richard Hallock (PF-NN) and being revised for final publication by PFA Project editor Wouter Henkelman (École Pratique des Hautes Études, Paris). They cataloged more than 180 new seals and recorded them with preliminary sketches. More than a thousand previously unidentified seals have been identified until now from impressions in this sub-corpus.

Figure 5. Mark Garrison oversees student workers recording uninscribed, sealed Fortification tablets; left: Christine Chandler (University of Colorado), right: Erin Daly (Notre Dame University)

Garrison also reorganized the classification of thematic seal types in the burgeoning record of the PFA in the Online Cultural Heritage Resource Environment (OCHRE, see elsewhere in this *Annual Report*), enlarging the number of categories and differentiating them in greater detail. Student worker Megan Kruse (Trinity University) began to populate the entries of the new scheme with data on published seals and new seals.

PFA Project editors Annalisa Azzoni (Vanderbilt University) and Elspeth Dusinberre (University of Colorado) continued to record the Aramaic component of the Archive. Azzoni selected PFATs recorded at the beginning of the PFA Project for new high-resolution scanning with improved techniques. She reviewed and updated the OCHRE public view of monolingual Aramaic documents (PFAT) and the Aramaic epigraphs on Elamite documents (PFAE), set up OCHRE entries for about fifty newly identified PFATs (for a cumulative total of 817), and added draft editions of forty PFATs to pending content in OCHRE, to be processed, glossed, linked, and made public soon. Dusinberre examined and recorded seals on about eighty monolingual Aramaic tablets (PFATS), including the fifty new items. She completed final pencil drawings of about 200 and final inked drawings of more than 180 seals on Aramaic tablets, for a cumulative total of more than 450 final drawings of almost 600 such seals identified until now.

PFA Project editor Henkelman re-collated about 400 of the 2,600 texts in the Hallock *Nachlass* (PF-NN), bringing to about 1,200 the running total of near-final editions entered in OCHRE. I resurveyed more than 500 boxes of Fortification tablets and fragments and selected almost 500 more Elamite tablets and fragments for conservation, image capture, cataloging, and editing. I made draft editions of more than 250 new Elamite texts, bringing the running total over 1,300.

When these and Henkelman's editions of the PF-NN texts are brought to final form they will almost triple the published sample of Achaemenid Elamite Fortification texts. Azzoni's editions of monolingual Aramaic texts will enlarge the unpublished corpus that the late Raymond Bowman studied by almost half. The texts will be intimately linked with a corpus of more than 3,000 seal impressions, nearly double what was known from published tablets, and opening what Albert T. Olmstead foretold as "a whole museum to present a new Achaemenid art."[4]

Dedicated PFA Project conservator Robyn Haynie treated another 100 PFA tablets and fragments before leaving the Project in November for a permanent museum post. When the PARSA Community Foundation agreed to extend its grant to support a full-time conservator, Simona Cristanetti joined the Project in May.

Staff turnover also continues on other phases of the Project. After student photographers Dan Whittington (Classics) and Matt Susnow (NELC) left in 2012, Ami Huang (NELC) continued to make and edit conventional digital images of Elamite Fortification tablets, and then trained undergraduates Taylor Coplen (Philosophy), Rachel Jackson (Visual Arts), and Naomi Harris (Common Year) to carry on the work. In the high-resolution imaging lab, graduate student workers Tate Paulette, Ben Thomas (both NELC), and Jason Herrmann (University of Arkansas) all left for other opportunities. Graduate students Vincent van Exel and Kate Grossman (both NELC) came on the production line. Thomas, with a new PhD, returned to the Project as a postdoctoral researcher, but Grossman, also with a new PhD, will soon leave for a tenure-track academic appointment.[5] The lab made about 3,700 high-resolution flat scans with the BetterLight apparatus, mostly reshoots of Aramaic documents, and about 3,600 Polynomial Texture Mapping (PTM) batches, mostly of sealed, uninscribed tablets. At the University of Southern California, student workers Bekir Gurdil, Claire Shriver, and Kristin Butler processed BetterLight and PTM images of about 650 objects, and at the Oriental Institute, student workers Amee Genova (History) and Naomi Camp (University of Illinois) processed images of almost 100 more. At InscriptiFact (http://www.inscriptifact.com), Marilyn Lundberg and Leta Hunt uploaded images of more than 700 objects to public or staging servers.

Altogether, more than 4,150 PFA tablets and fragments have been recorded with one or both kinds of high-quality images since the beginning of the Project, and high-quality images of more than half of them are public on InscriptiFact and OCHRE, complementing conventional images of about 3,000 more. Looking ahead to the time when the PFA Project winds

Figure 6. PFA Project myrmidons at work. Left: Taylor Coplen (Philosophy) processes photographs of new Elamite tablets. Right: Amee Genova (History) and Naomi Camp (University of Illinois) process PTM sets, while Tytus Mikołajczak (NELC) records seal impressions on new Elamite tablets

down and the imaging lab becomes part of the Oriental Institute's research-support armory, the lab also produces occasional images of other materials (seals and impressions, Sumerian and Akkadian cuneiform tablets, Egyptian mummy labels, fossils, etc.) as a service to colleagues.

Postdoctoral project manager Dennis Campbell, assisted by student workers Özgun Sak (History) and Seunghee Yie (NELC), formatted, parsed, glossed, and linked about 500 new and about 350 published Elamite texts in OCHRE, editing the Elamite glossary and correcting previously entered texts. Undergraduate worker Douglas Graebner (Art His-

Figure 7. OCHRE whisperer Dennis Campbell works on the PFA Project instruction manual

tory) tagged conventional photographs of Elamite texts to make sign-by-sign links between transliterations and images. Currently entered in OCHRE are more than 5,000 of the ca. 6,100 Elamite documents recorded until now, about 4,500 of them public, almost all glossed, parsed, and with attached images (including about 500 with images that are tagged and linked sign-by-sign to transliterations); about 195 Aramaic epigraphs (PFAE) on Elamite tablets (of about 245 identified to date), all public; 815 Aramaic documents (PFAT), about 30 of them public; about 1,000 PFUT, about 900 of them public with linked photos, about 200 with editorial information. The glossaries now include about 3,200 Elamite lemmas and about 150 Aramaic lemmas.

Campbell also began to prepare a manual for managing PFA Project contents, to be used by Project workers who will succeed him when he departs for a tenure-track position at San Francisco State University in the coming academic year. He expects to continue collaborating with the Project, and to draw on Project data in his own research and publication, but his departure will require drastic adjustment, for he has been an integral part of the PFA Project since it began and every element of the OCHRE record reflects his touch.

Under the auspices of Charles Blair, director of the Digital Library Development Center, the University of Chicago Library made more than 70 TB available on its ODS server for PFA Project use. Sandra Schloen and Miller Prosser of the OCHRE Data Service (https://ochre.sites.uchicago.edu/ and see elsewhere in this *Annual Report*), continue to reorganize and rationalize Project files for short-term access and for long-term archival preservation, alleviating the constant pressure on the Project's aging server maintained by Humanities Division Computing.

A historic connection with the Persepolis Fortification Archive (see http://persepolistablets.blogspot.com/2010/06/persepolis-chicago-blackhawks-and.html), may have contributed to the Chicago Blackhawks' dramatic capture of the Stanley Cup in June 2010.

The PFA Project weblog, maintained by Charles Jones (New York University), was viewed more than 7,500 times by more than 5,400 visitors in the last year (about 67,000 pageviews since inception). The newsfeed has seventy-eight subscribers. PFA Project members gave more than twenty-five public lectures and presentations at academic meetings during the last year, including presentations at the annual meetings of the American Schools of Oriental Research (Azzoni, Campbell, Mikołajczak, Prosser, and Stolper) and the American Oriental

Figure 8. Wouter Henkelman and Annalisa Azzoni at Castelen, Switzerland, during a break in the conference marking the 80th anniversary of the discovery of the PFA

Society (Mikołajczak and Stolper), and at the anniversary conference in Switzerland mentioned above (Azzoni, Garrison, Henkelman, and Stolper): lectures by Henkelman in Berlin, Brussels, London, Oxford, Paris, and Tehran; by Garrison at the University of Minnesota, UCLA, and the Metropolitan Museum of Art; by Dusinberre at the Boulder, Colorado, society of the Archaeological Institute of America; and by Stolper in Philadelphia, San Francisco and at Humanities Day in Chicago. Notable among eight more articles and monographs by PFA Project members based substantially on Project results is the forthcoming publication of Garrison's invited lectures at the Collège de France, *The Ritual Landscape at Persepolis: The Glyptic Imagery from the Persepolis Fortification and Treasury Archives* (Persika 17), on the same topic that he and Henkelman had lectured about before they boarded their train from Berlin.

Notes

[1] See Helms 1997, p. 101; Kuhrt 2007, pp. 814f., no. 58.

[2] Breasted to Frankfort, March 8, 1933 (emphasis original). He wrote to Herzfeld on the same day in the same vein: "The fact that you found such documents ... even though they are business tablets ... justifies the hope that we may now look for state documents in the same form" (Breasted to Herzfeld, March 8, 1933). I am indebted to John Larson for making these letters available.

[3] Hallock 1985, p. 588 (published separately in 1971).

[4] Olmstead 1948, p. 178.

[5] Among the Project's collateral results, Grossman and Thomas are the seventh and eighth PFA imaging lab workers to complete doctorates while partially supported by Project work; undergraduate alumni of the Project are nearing completion of doctorates at Michigan, Yale, and elsewhere.

References

Hallock, Richard

1971   *The Evidence of the Persepolis Tablets.* Cambridge: Middle East Centre, University of Cambridge.

1985   "The Evidence of the Persepolis Tablets," in *The Cambridge History of Iran,* Vol. 2: *The Median and Achaemenian Periods,* edited by Ilya Gershevitch, pp. 588–609. Cambridge: Cambridge University Press.

Helms, Svend

1997   *Excavations at Old Kandahar in Afghanistan 1976–78.* Society for South Asian Studies Monograph 2, BAR International Series 636. Oxford: Archaeopress.

Kuhrt, Amélie

2007   *The Persian Empire.* London and New York: Routledge.

Olmstead, Albert T.

1948   *History of the Persian Empire.* Chicago: University of Chicago Press.

———————————

TELL EDFU

Nadine Moeller and Gregory Marouard

The 2012 season at Tell Edfu, Upper Egypt, including work at the Edfu South Pyramid at the village of el-Ghonameya, took place from October 8 to November 25. The Edfu team was Nadine Moeller (director, University of Chicago), Gregory Marouard (co-director, research associate at the Oriental Institute), Natasha Ayers (pottery, PhD candidate, University of Chicago), Kathryn Bandy (small finds, PhD candidate, University of Chicago), Georges Demidoff (archaeology assistant), Clara Jeuthe (flint tools, post-doc French Institute for Oriental Archaeology in Cairo [IFAO]), Valérie le Provost (pottery, post-doc IFAO), Aurelie Schenk (archaeology, Roman Museum of Avenches, Switzerland), Aaron de Souza (pottery assistant, PhD candidate, Macquarie University), Janelle Wade (epigraphy and pottery assistant, PhD candidate, University of Chicago), Lindsey Miller-Weglarz (archaeology assistant, PhD candidate, University of Chicago), and Jonathan Winnerman (epigraphy, PhD candidate, University of Chicago).

This season, the archaeological fieldwork at the site of Edfu focused on two principal areas that are new to the project's research program. The first area, Zone 2, is situated along the eastern side of the archaeological tell, close to the Ptolemaic temple (fig. 1), where Old Kingdom (ca. 2500–2200 BC) settlement remains have been found. This new excavation area is particularly important because settlement remains dating to the third millennium BC are quite rare outside the Memphite region with its prominent pyramids and royal cemeteries that were the focus of the ancient Egyptian elite during this period. These urban archaeological levels are also the oldest ones ever excavated at Edfu.

The other excavation area, Zone 3, lies at the northern edge of the site, which is characterized by the presence of a massive town wall that runs in an east–west direction, turning south where it disappears under later settlement remains. Remains of several round silos, square magazines, and smaller mudbrick buildings have been excavated in this zone. All these had been built against the interior face of the town wall, often making use of it as a rear wall. Preliminary analysis of the pottery assemblages from the associated occupation layers indicates that this part of the settlement dates to end of the third millennium BC, which encompasses the First Intermediate Period and the early Middle Kingdom (ca. 2200–1985 BC).

In addition to the excavation at the tell, our work also focused on the construction of several brick benches or mastabas to serve as platforms for the large number of decorated and inscribed stone blocks in our concession area, which had been placed along the base of the tell several decades ago (fig. 2). The benches will serve to protect the blocks from future groundwater damage as we start to study them and perform conservation work on them. This site-management and "open-air museum" program has been made possible with the very generous support of Bob and Janet Helman.

Work also continued at the Edfu South Pyramid, situated near the village of el-Ghonameya, with the aim to complete the cleaning of the western side of this small step pyramid. The final objective of the 2012 season was the construction of a low brick wall around this pyramid, which is the first step in a plan for the long-term protection of this site. This work also contributes to an increased awareness of the importance of this pharaonic

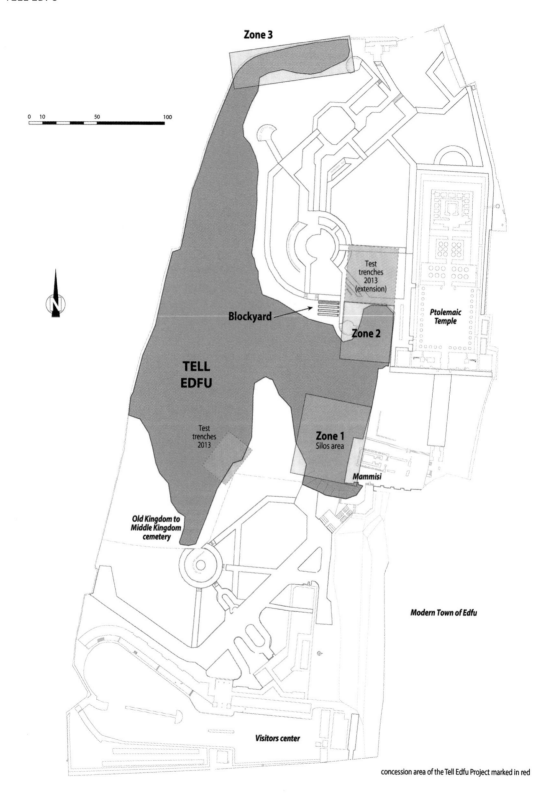

Figure 1. General plan of the site of Tell Edfu showing excavations zones

Figure 2. The Tell Edfu blockyard at the end of the 2012 season

monument among the locals from the surrounding areas. This project has been supported by a grant awarded to Gregory Marouard by the Antiquities Endowment Fund of the American Research Center in Egypt (ARCE).

Zone 2: The Old Kingdom Settlement Remains along the Eastern Side of the Tell

This season it has finally been possible to start excavations of the Old Kingdom settlement remains in Zone 2, which had been prepared for fieldwork over the past two years by removing several meters of *sebakh* debris that had been covering the ancient walls (fig. 3).[1] The excavations have focused so far on the upper layers of the preserved settlement remains, which were quite damaged by *sebakh* diggers who have left many deep holes — several up to two meters deep. The diggers cut through the ancient walls and floor levels in order to extract nitrogen-rich soil

Figure 3. Zone 2, Old Kingdom area (top) in 2009 and (bottom) in 2012

for agriculture. Nevertheless, it was possible to excavate the disturbed areas down to the better-preserved archaeological layers that were still largely intact. The uppermost settlement layers, which were quite fragmentary in their state of preservation, consist of domestic units and small, round or sometimes oval underground grain silos that have been found in a very good state of preservation (fig. 4). According to the associated pottery, they date to the very end of the Old Kingdom (late Sixth Dynasty and possibly the early First Intermediate Period). Some of these grain silos have well-built vaulted mudbrick tops and small openings for filling them from the corresponding floor level above (fig. 4). Our ceramicist Valérie le Provost will study the ceramic assemblages in detail next season.

Farther below these domestic settlement remains, several very thick mudbrick walls were discovered that belong to a sequence of three successive enclosure walls with sloping exterior sides (fig. 5). The oldest enclosure wall seems to have fallen into disrepair at some point prior to the end of the early Sixth Dynasty and was reinforced by a new mudbrick wall that had been built against its exterior face with an inclined foundation made of several layers of sandstone blocks of medium size. The exterior face of this restoration shows the remains of small, square buttresses and, particularly rare, traces of exterior plaster, which might indicate that this secondary repair had a primarily decorative function. These details clearly underline the importance of this wall and its permanence in the urban landscape in this part of town. Much later a new wall, 1.70 meters wide, was built on the exterior of the older enclosure and its restoration. This latest wall addition was separated from the older ones by a small gap, produced by the relatively steep inclination of the outer face of the first set of walls, into which several small transverse walls forming small compartments were inserted that were then filled with rubble (fig. 5). This sequence of three consecutive phases of walls in fact represents the same sequence of Old Kingdom enclosure walls already known from the

Figure 4. The newly discovered Old Kingdom enclosure walls and domestic silos

Figure 5. The sequence of successive enclosure walls excavated in Zone 2

western side of Zone 2 (fig. 6). Based on the orientation and architectural details, there must have been an angle in the area that is now under the modern paved pathways of the "open-air museum," where they would have turned toward the east. This angle was certainly destroyed by *sebakh* digging and, despite archaeological diagnostic works conducted prior the construction of the benches of the new blockyard, it has not been possible to identify any traces of these walls here. The enclosure walls seem to have had rather shallow foundations, which were completely removed when the *sebbakhin* used this area as a quarry to dig for fertilizer at the turn of last century. However, the newly exposed town walls in Zone 2 provide new evidence about where the possible northern limit of the Old Kingdom town had been during the Fifth and Sixth Dynasties. This newly discov-

Figure 6. The Old Kingdom enclosure walls visible in the vertical cuts left by the sebbakhin to the west of Zone 2

ered sequence of walls, if they had functioned indeed as town walls, runs in an east–west direction but forms a right angle in the area close to the later Ptolemaic temple enclosure wall. It is possible that this angle was once part of a large gate area.

To the south of these enclosure walls were excavated several unusually thick mudbrick walls (between 2.30 m and 2.70 m wide) that belong to some large building complex (fig. 7). On the western side of one of these walls was discovered a small doorway that still had its wooden lintel and parts of the actual door were preserved in situ (fig. 8). This doorway seems to have provided access to a larger open space or courtyard toward the east. The precise function of this building remains unknown and will be investigated further in the next season. The objects that have been discovered in relation to this building and the surrounding

Figure 7. Remains of a large Old Kingdom building complex (ca. Fifth Dynasty)

Figure 8. Wooden lintel and door remains on the Old Kingdom building complex

Figure 9. Bread mold, pot stand, and complete potteries found in the upper, abandonment layers of the Old Kingdom building

area show numerous traces of metallurgic activity (fragments of crucibles and some pieces of slag) as well as an interesting ceramic assemblage with a large quantity of bread molds and beer jars. One of the complete bread molds that was excavated here was an unfired one with the hieroglyphic sign for bread attached to the outside of the vessel as if it had served as a sample mold (fig. 9). The pottery assemblage as well as the other finds from this area are not really characteristic for a purely domestic settlement context but indicates either the presence of an official type of building linked to the elite such as a palatial complex or it might have been part of a sanctuary or temple complex.

Zone 3: The First Intermediate Period Remains on the Northern Edge of the Settlement

Zone 3, the second area where this season's work focused, lies at the northern side of Tell Edfu. Last year we cleaned a sequence of two large town walls in this area, including some settlement remains that had been spared from destruction by the earlier *sebakh* extraction. The aim of this season was to excavate the mudbrick structures that had been built against the interior face of the first town wall in order to establish the chronology of the enclosure walls and the function of the various buildings and storage installations in this part of the ancient town (fig. 10).

Three principal phases of mudbrick structures have been excavated which include numerous mudbrick walls forming small rooms and square storage magazines. Most of these walls are relatively thin, with a thickness of about 30–40 centimeters. Some of them were built with the same size bricks as the enclosure wall. In two cases it has been possible to note that bricks of the structures that were built against the enclosure wall were linked directly to the bricks of the wall while other constructions were simply leaning against it. This strongly suggests that the construction phase of the town enclosure and these buildings occurred at the same time, indicating that this settlement area was subject to some larger planning effort within the town.

In one of the rooms excavated in this area, just south of where the wall curves, more than forty clay sealings stamped with button and scarab seals were found in the occupation layer covering the mud floor. A large storage jar had been sunk into the southern part of this room (fig. 11). Remains of a small doorway with its stone threshold and door socket in situ were found leading into another room, much of which has disappeared due to *sebbakh* digging. An additional room was excavated a few meters northeast of the previous one, and here the remains of a burnt and collapsed roof of wooden beams, smaller wooden branches, twigs, and pieces of matting have been excavated (fig. 10). The collapsed roof lay directly on the mud floor of the room, sealing occupational remains under multiple wooden beams, which had been quite well preserved. The wood and related organic material was collected for further analysis.

The second phase of buildings in this area consists of several small, square silos or magazines used for grain storage. They were constructed of thin mudbrick walls, which were only one brick thick (ca. 13–14 cm). Most of them had been built into rooms of the earlier building phase (fig. 10). All these square grain silos had a fill of gray ash on their outsides in order to protect the stored grain from insect infestation and rodents. On the floor of one of these silos a thin deposit of grain was found which has been collected for an archaeobotanical analysis.

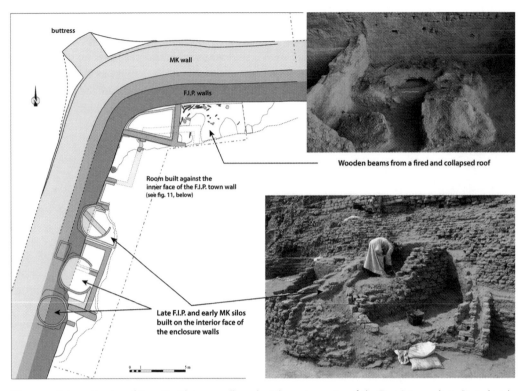

Figure 10. *Schematic plan of Zone 3 with town walls and settlement remains of the First Intermediate Period and early Middle Kingdom*

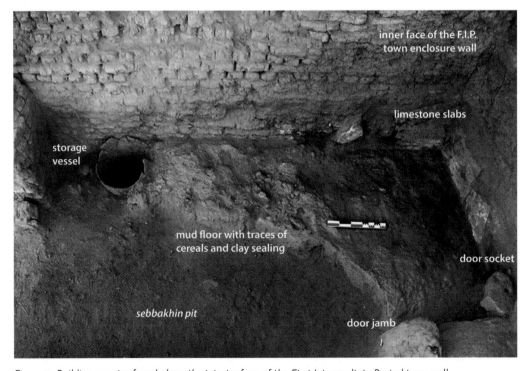

Figure 11. *Building remains found along the interior face of the First Intermediate Period town wall*

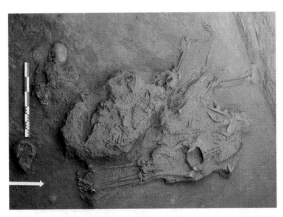

Figure 12. Human and dog skeletons found inside a silo (late First Intermediate Period -early Middle Kingdom)

While excavating the remains of a larger grain silo built against the round curve of the town wall at the northwestern side of Zone 3 an unexpected discovery was made. On the floor of this silo three human skeletons were discovered together with the remains of at least two dogs (fig. 12). No signs for a proper burial were found and it seems that the three individuals were simply thrown into the silo, which is also confirmed by the fact they lay partially on top of each other with different orientations. On the arm of the uppermost skeleton pieces of a small bracelet made with faience beads and a faience stamp seal together with a scarab seal were found. This could be an indication that one of these individuals had been an administrator, a supposition that is further corroborated by the signs of heavy use on these two seals.

The last phase of occupation in this area consists of round grain silos (fig. 10) that were built on a higher level and already cutting into the oldest phase of the town wall, which by then must have fallen out of use and into disrepair. By that time, the first enclosure wall had been replaced by a second town wall, which was built with much larger bricks against the exterior face of the first wall and partially above it. The associated pottery assemblage recovered during the excavations in this area spans the early First Intermediate Period (abbreviated F.I.P. in the figures) into the first half of the Middle Kingdom (abbreviated MK). This provides an excellent opportunity to investigate the evolution of pottery dating to one of the lesser-known periods of ancient Egyptian history.

The Edfu Blockyard Project

Another aim of the 2012 season was to construct four large brick benches to be used as low platforms for the more than 300 decorated and inscribed stone blocks lying at the base of the tell (fig. 13). These blocks originate from various different locations, some of them having been excavated in 1984 beneath the first court of the Ptolemaic temple, others having been found to the east of the temple, in the modern town of Edfu, which still covers part of the ancient settlement. A large number of the stone blocks come from the French and Franco-Polish excavations at Tell Edfu, which took place in the 1920s and 1930s.

One of the tasks has been to clean the blocks as carefully as possible and to record them in detail in our Filemaker database on an iPad (fig. 14). This was done on site by NELC students Janelle Wade and Jonathan Winnerman, who were in charge of the epigraphic study. This work follows the guidelines of the Chicago House Epigraphic Survey (Luxor), and in October Epigraphic Survey senior epigrapher Brett McClain together with Chicago House staff members Krisztián Vértes, Jen Kimpton, and Keli Alberts joined the Edfu team for a site visit in order to provide advice to Jonathan and Janelle about the best methods to record the blocks.

By the end of the season, four large benches (mastabas) were constructed from red bricks with two waterproof layers of black tar (bitumen) between the brick layers, which will pro-

Figure 13. General view of blockyard project area with Zone 2 and Ptolemaic temple in the background

Figure 14. Graduate student Jonathan Winnerman copying a hieroglyphic inscription on a sandstone block

tect the stone from any groundwater and dampness in the future. The blocks were carefully placed on these mastabas and can now be easily seen by interested visitors (see fig. 2).

Work at the Pyramid of El-Ghonameya

Work also continued this season at the small step pyramid near the village of el-Ghonameya, which lies to the southwest of the modern town of Edfu (fig. 15). The main aim of the Edfu-South Pyramid Project has been to continue the work of cleaning the western side of the monument, which is the only side that had not been cleared last season (see *Oriental Institute News & Notes* 213 [2012] for details). The lower courses of stones were freed from sand and rubble, exposing a small graffito, which post-dates the pyramid and probably belongs to the New Kingdom. On the eastern side of the pyramid, more cleaning work was done to complete the work from last year (fig. 16). The stone foundation of a small shrine or offering chapel that once had stood here is now clearly visible (fig. 17). It might have been used for the royal cult of the late Third Dynasty king Huni, to whom this pyramid has been attributed. This clearly emphasizes a cultic purpose of these pyramids, which were not royal funerary monuments but had a more symbolic function, one perhaps linked to the cult of the living king. The results from the Edfu-South Pyramid have finally laid to rest any theory relating to administrative buildings being part of these monuments. Some additional survey work was also carried out in the neighboring quarry areas north of the pyramid.

Another objective of last season at the pyramid had been to build a wall around the site in order to protect it from the growing cemetery on the northern side as well as the main street and expanding village on the southern side of the pyramid (fig. 15). With support from an Antiquities Endowment Fund grant from ARCE, it was possible to construct a low brick wall 250 meters (820 feet) in length around the site employing as much as possible local workers in order to support the village community (fig. 18). The red bricks used for construction were produced in the vicinity of el-Ghonameya in traditional brick kilns, which also reduced the problems with the timely supply of building materials. This protective wall is one meter high and encloses the archaeological site on the northern, southern, and eastern sides (figs.

Figure 15. Google Earth© view of the small pyramid site at el-Ghonameya in 2005 (top) and 2013 (bottom), showing the encroachment of the modern cemetery and village

Figure 16. East face of the small step pyramid showing remains of a shrine or chapel

Figure 17. Details of the foundation and the negative of a small shrine-chapel on the eastern side of the pyramid

Figure 18. The Edfu-South Pyramid team

Figure 19. The new wall protecting the pyramid site, view to the southeast

Figure 20. Backfilling operation in progress to protect the chapel remains, with the new protective wall in the foreground; view to the southwest

19–20). In negotiation with the local mayor, two entrances were left open to allow people to walk through the site in direction to and from the cemetery, but no vehicles can pass here anymore (fig. 20). This wall should also reduce the deposition of modern waste, which has been an ongoing problem at the site.

Acknowledgments

The directors would like to thank the Edfu Project team for their excellent contributions and efforts during the excavation as well as the local inspectorate at Edfu, foremost Ahmed Saadi, Susi Samir Labib, and our inspectors Afrah Mahmoud (Tell Edfu) and Mustafa (Edfu-South Pyramid) for their collaboration and support. A big thank-you also goes to Ramadan Hassan Ahmed and Amal Abdullah Ahmed for providing access to work in the magazine of Elkab.

We would also like to express our sincere gratitude to many of our Oriental Institute members, foremost Bob and Janet Helman, who have made the blockyard project possible, Andrea Dudek, Daniel and Annette Youngberg, Stephen and Patricia Holst, Joan S. Fortune, Steven and Heidi Camp, and Rosemary Ferrand. Additionally, we would like to thank the Oriental Institute and the National Endowment for the Humanities for their generous financial contribution to the Tell Edfu Project.

Notes

[1] For details on the practices and effects of *sebakh* extraction, see Bailey 1999.

Reference

Bailey, D. B.

1999   "Sebakh, Sherds and Survey." *Journal of Egyptian Archaeology* 85: 211–18.

WRITING IN EARLY MESOPOTAMIA PROJECT

Christopher Woods and Massimo Maiocchi

Overview. *Christopher Woods*

The Writing in Early Mesopotamia (WEM) project endeavors to provide a comprehensive description of how the technology of cuneiform writing represented language. The project will investigate early cuneiform writing from the perspective of both language — how sound and meaning are systematically expressed diachronically and synchronically — and semiotics — the graphic organization and history of the symbols that comprise the system. The scope of the project is the cuneiform written record from the invention of writing in the late fourth millennium BC (ca. 3300 BC) through the Old Babylonian period (ca. 1600 BC). While Sumerian writing is at the center of the project — Sumerian being in all likelihood the language for which writing was invented in Mesopotamia — the adaptation of the script to express Semitic (Akkadian and Eblaite) and the long-term interplay between these writing systems are major concerns.

The following brief report introduces this new Oriental Institute endeavor, initiated the past academic year and supported generously by the Andrew W. Mellon Foundation, the Linda Noe Laine Foundation, and the Oriental Institute's Erica Reiner Fund. Below, we provide an overview of the WEM project and conclude with a description of our database work, which has been our primary occupation for the 2012–13 academic year. The project is currently staffed by Christopher Woods and Massimo Maiocchi (Mellon Postdoctoral Fellow), Howard Farber and Steven George provided part-time assistance, and University of Chicago undergraduate and Metcalf Fellow Abigail Hoskins worked full-time on the project during the summer of 2013. Beginning this upcoming academic year (2013–14), the WEM project will collaborate closely with another new initiative at the University of Chicago concerned with early writing, the Neubauer Collegium's Signs of Writing the Cultural, Social, and Linguistic Contexts of the World's First Writing Systems (described under Christopher Woods's individual research [see separate report]).

1. Rationale

The motivation for this project lies in the fact that to date there has been no rigorous study of cuneiform writing, let alone one that is linguistically oriented, or informed by typological comparisons or interdisciplinary perspectives. In the case of Sumerian, for which our understanding of the writing system is marred by lacunae and misconceptions, this absence is particularly conspicuous. After nearly a century and a half of the decipherment effort, writing remains largely *terra incognita* — a fundamental domain that has yet to be subjected to rigorous investigation. For the philologist, the written record is naturally the point of access for all inquiry, and so the study of the medium that conveys the message stands as a desideratum in its own right. Further, writing and its associated problems are bound up with the higher-level concerns of phonology and morphology. Although not often acknowledged by scholars working on Sumerian grammar, the absence of a coherent theory of Sumerian writing is arguably the greatest obstacle to describing the language. The WEM project will have wide implications for the field of Assyriology, as it will not only provide the basis upon which grammatologically informed theories of Sumerian grammar and lexicography may be built, but will add substantially to our knowledge of early scribal practices and training.

More broadly, writing — often hailed as humankind's greatest technological and cultural achievement — is a fundamental and perennial subject of scholarly inquiry. A comprehensive description of Sumerian writing will make an essential contribution to our understanding of early writing systems and the cognitive processes by which humans first made language visible. Taking its place alongside the nearly contemporaneous Egyptian invention (ca. 3200 BC), as well as the Chinese (ca. 1200 BC) and Mayan (ca. 400 BC) inventions, cuneiform is one of the four "pristine writing systems," the four original writing systems from which all others, directly or indirectly, developed. Cuneiform not only boasts what might very well be the world's oldest writing system, but also stakes claim to the largest corpus of incipient writing and some of the clearest evidence for the cultural and social context out of which writing sprung. As such, cuneiform plays a pivotal role in the story of how humans first made language visible and for the study of writing systems broadly. The WEM project will be of interest not only to cuneiform specialists, but also to those interested in writing systems, literacy, the psycho-linguistics of reading, and cognitive representation more generally.

2. Approach and Goals

At the core of the project are extensive databases of spellings that are meaningful to the description of the writing system. The collection of this data is an endeavor that requires the systematic review, categorization, and analysis of thousands of texts written between the invention of writing and the end of the Old Babylonian period. Of particular interest are syllabaries compiled by the ancients, the temporal and spatial distribution of logographic and syllabic writings, as well as variant spellings, that is, those writings that do not conform to the standard orthography. Writings of these types are particularly revealing of the mechanics and organization of the system as well as the relationship between the written and spoken languages. Differentiating variants that are phonologically or morphologically significant from those that are merely orthographic is a major concern of inquiries of this kind. Taking a typological and interdisciplinary approach, the WEM project considers individual orthographic phenomena and the cuneiform writing system as a whole within the context of writing systems research more generally and of the other early "pristine" writing systems specifically. The particular interest in the Egyptian, Chinese, and Mesoamerican systems lies in the fact that they exhibit striking similarities to — and some notable differences from — Sumerian writing. As an intrinsically interdisciplinary endeavor, the WEM project also draws upon fields allied to the study of writing systems, including linguistics, semiotics, the philosophy of language, as well as information science and cognitive psychology. Considering cuneiform writing from multiple perspectives allows for insights and a broadly based understanding of the system, which would not be possible adhering only to a philological approach.

The end products of the Writing in Early Mesopotamia project will be two-fold, consisting of synthetic print publications on one hand, and, on the other, electronic research tools upon which the former will rely. The ultimate goal of the project will be a comprehensive description of early cuneiform writing in monograph form. Qiu Xigui's monumental *Chinese Writing* (tr. G. L. Mattos and J. Norman, Berkeley, 2000) provides a suitable model for the publication envisioned. In conjunction with the Neubauer Collegium's Signs of Writing endeavor, the WEM project will host short- and long-term visiting scholars as well as three annual interdisciplinary workshops (successively on the University of Chicago campus in 2014, and the University of Chicago centers in Beijing [2015], and Paris [2016]) on topics seminal to the project and writing systems broadly. Project members, collaborators, and other invited speakers will participate in these workshops; the Oriental Institute will publish a selection of the proceedings at the conclusion of the series. The topics covered by these workshops will range from the more technical, such as the role of logography in pristine writing systems, to the more culturally oriented, such as the interaction between bilingualism and writing in antiquity. As described above, the synthetic, published output of the project will rest upon the collection and organization of large data sets that describe the temporal and spatial attestations of written forms and variant spellings (see further below). At the core of this endeavor are the indigenous syllabaries that preserve native scribal understanding of graph-to-sound correlations, and exemplars of the Sumerian literary corpus of the Old Babylonian period, which represent the largest corpus of textual variants. As these sources have broad Assyriological importance beyond their value for writing, the project will make this material available on-line in the form of open-access, searchable databases.

3. Collaborators

Integral to the project is a network of collaborators and partners with expertise in the fields and writing systems that are of central importance. These members include at this time: Cuneiform — Paul Delnero (Johns Hopkins University), Piotr Steinkeller (Harvard University); Chinese — Wolfgang Behr (University of Zurich), Edward Shaughnessy (University of Chicago); Egyptian — Janet Johnson (University of Chicago), Andréas Stauder (University of Basel); Writing Systems and Linguistics — Richard Sproat (Google Labs).

4. 2012–2013 Progress

Our work this year has included compiling a library and bibliography of writing systems research. Our primary focus, however, has been on developing the aforementioned database, which is central to the project, as well as a theoretically suitable and practical method of morphological parsing, which would allow for advanced database queries. In what follows, M. Maiocchi describes our efforts with the database, some of the issues encountered, and some of the protocols developed, with regard to the encoding of text.

4.1. Database Description. *Massimo Maiocchi*

4.1.1. Identification of Textual Corpus

Our first step in creating a database for the analysis of cuneiform writing was to identify an initial test corpus of suitable texts, which is a relatively large collection of tablets that present significant variations in morphology and lexicography. Once the database and search algorithms are sufficiently tested with these initial texts, we will expand the range of documents included in the corpus. The ten Sumerian literary compositions known as the Decad — these were the first ten literary texts apprentice scribes would encounter in the scribal

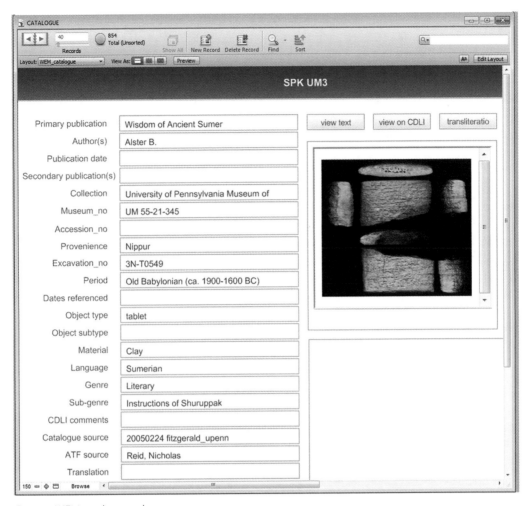

Figure 1. WEM catalog sample

curriculum —seemed an obvious choice, on account of the large number of exemplars preserved and the existence of recent and comprehensive editions compiled by Paul Delnero (Johns Hopkins). That these texts are essentially complete, well attested in multiple copies, and are well understood grammatically are further advantages. Additionally, we included the wisdom text "Instruction of Shuruppak" in this initial group. The long history of this text in the scribal curriculum, spanning from the Early Dynastic III through the Old Babylonian periods (ca. 2600–1600 BC) provides an ideal test case for encoding of diachronic variation.

The relevant information for each text has been entered in a catalog, in which the individual tablets receive an identification number (primary key), as well as bibliographical reference concerning editions, secondary literature, museum number, provenience, dating, physical condition of the text, collection, photos, and copies where available. At present, the catalog of the WEM project includes 853 texts and text fragments, a figure large enough for proper statistical analysis.

From a typological point of view, the test corpus currently contains:

- narrative mythological compositions featuring deities (Enki's journey to Nippur, Inana and Ebih) and heroes (Gilgamesh and Huwawa A);
- royal praise poetry (Shulgi A, Lipit-Ishtar A);

- wisdom literature (Instruction of Shuruppak);
- hymns to deities (Inana B, Enlil A, Nungal A) and temples (Kesh temple hymn);
- scribal training literature (Song of the Hoe).

Care has been taken to assure that our database is easily linkable to other major Assyriological projects, such as the Cuneiform Digital Library Initiative (CDLI), the largest repository of cuneiform documents in digital format available on line; the WEM catalog includes references to the CDLI identification numbers for individual texts.

4.1.2. Normalization of Readings and Coherence Check

As many of the transliterations used for our project stem from various and sundry sources, and so exhibit a wide range of incompatible transliteration conventions, it is necessary to normalize all textual witnesses prior to encoding. This process also includes proper Unicode rendering of the texts (some sources use special non-Unicode fonts to represent special characters commonly used in standard Assyriological transliterations). In addition, the readings of individual signs have been altered to conform to WEM conventions, which include broad transcriptions and the use of long values (so for instance the reading šag$_4$ is preferred to ša$_3$ "heart"). Finally, minor collations to the texts are made, and improved descriptions of the textual breaks found in the documenation are given, during the course of encoding.

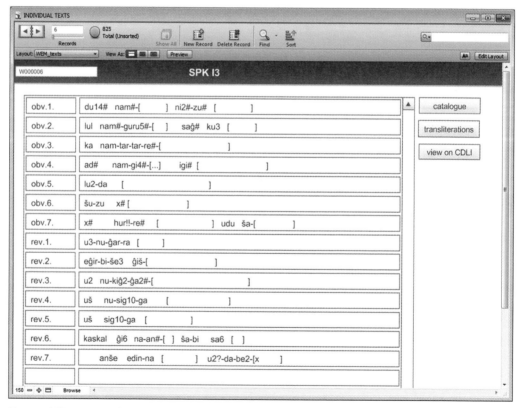

Figure 2. WEM text transliteration

4.1.3. Development of Digital Tools to Process the Texts

To accelerate the process of encoding, as well as to avoid manual mistakes during the delicate step of collecting textual variants, a suite of Perl scripts have been developed. These are small programs, written in a programming language, that makes easy the development of computational methods applied to textual analysis. They take properly formatted transliterations as input, recognize individual words, and search for variants. In order to achieve this goal, the transliterations of the individual exemplars have been formatted and aligned into columns. A side benefit of this process is that the aligned presentation of textual witnesses facilitates the identification of variants at a glance.

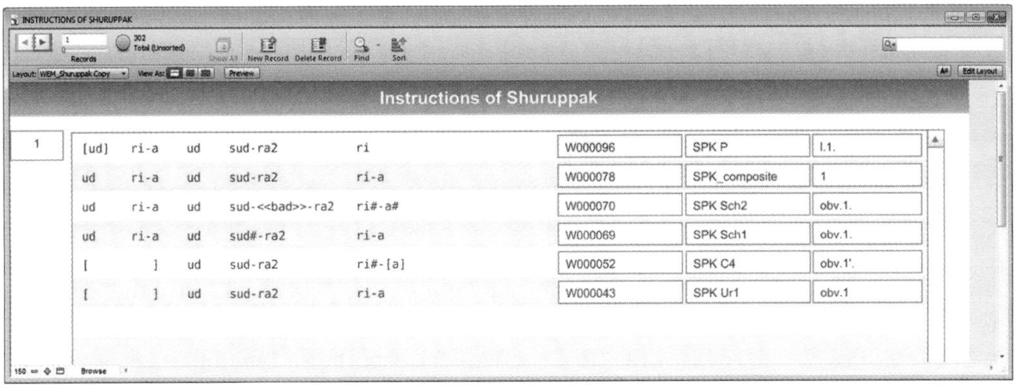

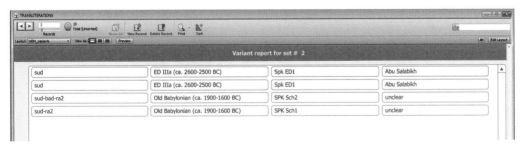

Figure 3. WEM composite view

Specifically, the Perl script parses well-formed transliterations and creates a network of relationships between the individual words of the texts, which are grouped together in bundles of variants. Every lexeme is consequently given a unique identification number, and is linked to all other attestations of the same item. Lexemes can be browsed in the variant report layout, which makes it easy to identify diachronic and regional variations.

4.1.4. Morphological Encoding

Subsequently, individual morphemes are encoded to account for allomorphs. The encoding itself is made on a tabular format related to the one containing the individual lexemes and composed by "unique items" in order to avoid repetitive encoding of identical lexemes in the same context. For instance, in figure 3 one can identify that the word sud-ra$_2$ occurs five times in the same "column." Instead of encoding each instance separately, it is sufficient to do so only once, the information entered being automatically transferred to the other attes-

Figure 4. WEM variant report

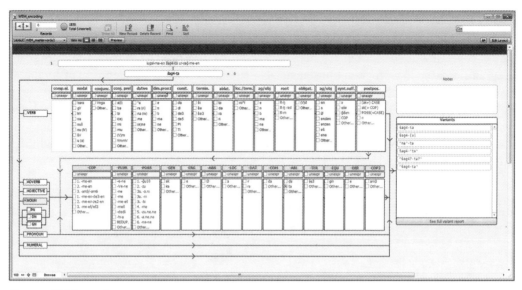

Figure 5. WEM encoding

tations. This reduces by roughly a tenth the amount of work to be done, since the encoding process is manual.

A check-box system reduces the time needed for encoding and minimizes errors introduced by typos. The parsing is broad and avoids controversial aspects of Sumerian verbal morphology. In this way we minimize the potential for forcing interpretation and pre-judging the very grammatical phenomena the database seeks to investigate.

4.1.5. Graphemic Analysis

In the last step of the process every morpheme is analyzed by another Perl script that produces a sign list and syllabary for the individual compositions, and so allows for a statistical analysis based on the distribution of signs and sign values. The list is graphemic in that compound signs are split, when possible, into their individual units. For instance, the word

Figure 6. Graphemic sign list and syllabary

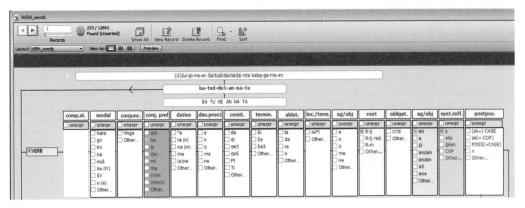

Figure 7. Detail of the encoding of a composite line (first line), the selected word (second line), and the sequence of signs associated in the surrounding context (third line)

for shepherd, sipad in Sumerian, is considered as the union of the PA and UDU signs, and is listed under both. The tool can be fine-tuned to work at the most basic level of sign composition, reaching into the realm of palaeography.

This script also turns standard Assyriological transliterations into sequences of sign names. This is particularly useful for searching the database for signs regardless of their readings in context.

When completed, the database will provide a unique tool for the analysis of writing and grammar, allowing for unprecedented search capabilities on both graphic and morphological levels. It will be possible, for instance, to query the database not only for the presence, but also absence of grammatical morphemes (as for instance in the case of the syntactic cross-referencing between nominal post-positions and verbal infixes). We will also be able to quantitatively describe the relative distribution of morphological elements and generate statistics relating to the frequency of variant spellings, as well as the distribution of signs and sign combinations as a function of period and region.

INDIVIDUAL RESEARCH

Richard H. Beal

Richard H. Beal spent his time updating, reference-checking, and copy editing articles for the third fascicle of the Š volume and the beginning of the T volume of the Hittite Dictionary. After a concentrated period of reading and rereading the final manuscript and page proofs, he collected and collated the corrections made by all the Hittite Dictionary staff and, under the supervision of Leslie Schramer of Oriental Institute Publications, he inputted these into the publications' computer files. Then the third fascicle of the Š volume (words beginning with *ši-*) was finally sent to the printer. Outside of office time he completed a review for the *Journal of the American Oriental Society* of the book *Rêves hittites* (Culture and History of the Ancient Near East 28. Leiden: Brill, 2007) by Alice Mouton, who had been a guest of the Oriental Institute and the Hittite Dictionary for one year and subsequently became a professor at the Université de Strasbourg and a member of the Centre national de la recherche scientifique (CNRS). He also completed a review for our own *Journal of Near Eastern Studies* of Jan de Roos, *Hittite Votive Texts* (Uitgaven van het Nederlands Instituut voor het Nabije Oosten te Leiden [PIHANS] 109; Leiden: Nederlands Instituut voor het Nabije Oosten, 2007). Eating up much time was copy editing and creating an index for *Creation and Chaos: A Reconsideration of Hermann Gunkel's Chaos Kampf Hypothesis* (Eisenbraun's), which he is editing with his wife, Oriental Institute alumna JoAnn Scurlock. He also participated in the reference checking of Scurlock's *Sourcebook for Ancient Mesopotamian Medicine*, to be published in the series Writings from the Ancient World by the Society for Biblical Literature, which will contain transliterations and translations of all types of Mesopotamian diagnostic and therapeutic texts. He and his wife went on a tour and picture-taking spree of Iran. Seeing our first ziggurat in person was probably the high point of many high points. During the tour, our fellow tourists repeatedly remarked on the incredible warmth shown to Americans by the Iranian people we met. While in Iran, Beal gave a lecture on Hittite language, history and culture to a large audience (boys on the right, girls on the left) at the University of Tehran.

Robert Biggs

Robert Biggs completed his work on the cuneiform texts from the Inanna Temple at Nippur (mainly mid-third millennium BC) which he has worked on, mostly at the Iraq Museum in Baghdad, as opportunity and time permitted in the years since 1972. See Karen Wilson's contribution for details of the project.

In the summer of 1972, he received a fellowship from the American Research Institute in Turkey to study and make drawings of mid-third-millennium Sumerian literary and lexical texts from the Iraqi site of Fara, approximately contemporary with the texts excavated by the Oriental Institute at the Iraqi site of Abu Salabikh and which he published in 1974 as *Inscriptions from Tell Abū Ṣalābīkh* (Oriental Institute Publications 99; Chicago: University of Chicago Press). The Fara tablets were excavated at a time when the Ottoman empire included present-day Iraq, so the government's share of the finds were sent to Istanbul. They were published by a French scholar in 1937 and 1957, but in a way that does not meet scholarly needs of today. Because Biggs did not have an opportunity to return to the Turkish capital to recheck his copies against the originals, the copies were never published. Even though he has communicated individual copies to colleagues, he is now preparing to make all his copies publicly accessible. Robert Englund of the University of California, Los Angeles, who heads the Cuneiform Digital Library Initiative, has offered to make scanned copies available on this site.

Biggs has also completed his study of a number of Ur III (late third-millennium BC) documents from a museum in South Dakota.

François Gaudard

The 2012–2013 year has been particularly productive, rewarding, and successful on many levels for **François Gaudard**. He finished checking and completing the last letter of the Chicago Demotic Dictionary (CDD), namely, S (542 pages), adding about 150 new pages to the final file. Moreover, after eighteen years of extensive work on every aspect of the CDD, first as a research assistant and then as an associate editor, Gaudard was particularly pleased and proud to see the completion of the original plan of the project for which he invested so much of his time and career (see separate CDD report).

Another highlight of the year was the official launch of both a Consejo Superior de Investigaciones Científicas (CSIC, Madrid) website and an Oriental Institute webpage dedicated to the Mummy Label Database (MLD). Gaudard, who is the co-founder and co-editor of both the MLD and the "Death on the Nile" project, wrote and developed the MLD webpage for the Oriental Institute website (see separate MLD report).

In July 2012, Gaudard lectured on the various scripts and stages in the development of the ancient Egyptian language for the University of Chicago Egyptology summer class "Ancient Egyptian Language, Culture, and History," taught by Rozenn Bailleul-LeSuer. On August 29, 2012, Gaudard, together with Janet H. Johnson and our new colleague Brian Muhs, organized a public roundtable on "Digital Demotic," hosted by the Franke Institute for the Humanities of the University of Chicago, in order to discuss the future of the CDD (see separate CDD report). On November 16, 2012, he presented a paper entitled "The Mummy Labels in the Oriental Institute Museum" at the first "Bridges between Life and Death: On Funerary Practice in Graeco-Roman Egypt" conference, hosted by the Oriental Institute (see separate MLD report). In April 2013, he was invited as a guest lecturer for the class "Writing Systems and Decipherment," taught by Christopher Woods. On June 6, 2013, Gaudard, together with Janet H. Johnson, participated in the University of Chicago "Knowledge Fair: A Celebration of Leaders in Philanthropy," which was an event to recognize the generous support of University donors and to give them the opportunity to interact and learn more about research and projects at our University (see separate CDD report).

As was the case during the past years, Gaudard served as an editorial consultant for Egyptology articles published in the *Journal of Near Eastern Studies* (JNES) and the *Journal of the Society for the Study of Egyptian Antiquities* (JSSEA). He was also able to attend the sixty-fourth annual meeting of the American Research Center in Egypt (ARCE), held in Cincinnati, Ohio, from April 19 to 21, 2013.

During the year, Gaudard had the following articles published: "Birds in the Ancient Egyptian and Coptic Alphabets," in *Between Heaven and Earth: Birds in Ancient Egypt,* edited by

Rozenn Bailleul-LeSuer, pp. 65–70 (Oriental Institute Museum Publications 35; Chicago: The Oriental Institute, 2012); "Pap. Berlin P. 8278 and Its Fragments: Testimony of the Osirian Khoiak Festival Celebration during the Ptolemaic Period," in *Forschung in der Papyrussammlung: Eine Festgabe für das Neue Museum*, edited by Verena M. Lepper, pp. 269–86 (Ägyptische und Orientalische Papyri und Handschriften des Ägyptischen Museums und Papyrussammlung Berlin 1; Berlin: Akademie-Verlag, 2012).

Other publications by Gaudard are now in press, including: "A Demotic-Hieratic Mummy Label in the Museu de Montserrat," which will be published in a Festschrift honoring a colleague, and "Rosetta Stone," in *Encyclopedia of Ancient Greek Language and Linguistics* (EAGLL), edited by Georgios K. Giannakis (Leiden: Brill). Gaudard has also been working on various new articles, including one focusing on an unknown aspect of the god Seth, which is now ready and will be published in a forthcoming Festschrift honoring a colleague. In addition, he was also invited to contribute an article to another Festschrift, and continued to work on several of his long-term publication projects.

McGuire Gibson

McGuire Gibson has devoted as much time as he could in the last year to finishing off a commitment he made to edit and republish Mr. Muzahim Hussein's book on the Queens' Tombs and related excavations at Nimrud. One result of his trip to Baghdad in May 2003, when he viewed not just the results of the looting of the Iraq National Museum but also the destruction and vandalizing of the offices of the State Board of Antiquity, was to agree with three or four Iraqi colleagues that he and Mark Altaweel, then an advanced graduate student (now on the faculty of University College London), would work with them to reconstruct, translate, and publish important articles that had been destroyed. This work resulted in publications in international journals, with Arabic versions in the Iraqi journal *Sumer*. Toward the end of the project, which was funded initially by a grant from the National Endowment for the Humanities and then a larger grant from the US State Department, they were asked to take on the republication of Muzahim's book. He had been the excavator of the Northwest Palace of Assurnasirpal (ca. 850 BC) in 1988 when the first tomb was discovered, and in 1989–90 he found three more. Later, he discovered a set of vaults that were also probably originally tombs that had been desecrated and looted, but many objects were left behind. He also discovered and emptied a well in a courtyard that had 180 skeletons, some with manacles and shackles, representing probably the personnel of the domestic wing of the palace when it fell to the Medes and Babylonians in 612 BC.

Part of the digging, and all of the analysis and preparation for publication, were done after the 1991 war, when Iraq was in dire economic conditions, with little money for archaeology. Despite the problems, Muzahim completed a text in Arabic and English, with 221 color illustrations. When it was published in Baghdad in 2000, the color printing was not very good and the magnificent finds from the Queens' Tombs did not receive the treatment they deserved.

Altaweel and Gibson took on the job, and after Altaweel retranslated and did a first editing, Gibson began to work on it. Meeting with Muzahim for a couple of weeks each summer in Istanbul for three years, they were able to clarify details and gain much better photographs, new drawings, and elicit much more information on exact findspots of the objects. Of greatest importance was a set of digital photographs that Muzahim took in 2012 of his object registers,

Gold jewelry from Nimrud. Left: Earrings (ND 1989_19a-b, Tomb II, Sarcophagus); center: bracelets (ND 1988_51, tomb I); right: hinge view of anklet (ND_1989_306, Tomb III, Coffin 2). Photos by Donny George

which gave explicit data and in some cases images of objects that otherwise had not been represented. Steven George was invaluable in translating the hand-written Arabic entries and in preparing images of objects for the book. In Chicago, two students, Lindsay Miller and Jessica Henderson, as part of a seminar project, created a database that Gibson found invaluable as he used and expanded it. This database will form the catalog of objects in the publication. Alexandra Witsell and Katharyn Hanson, who worked as Gibson's assistants for several years, were persons on the project.

The result of all this work is that the manuscript of the Queens' Tombs is about to be handed over to the editorial office of the Oriental Institute. To follow, very shortly, are the manuscripts of two shorter reports by Saleh Rmeidh and Hussein Ali Hamza, which will be combined in a book entitled *Iraqi Excavations in the Diyala Region.* Because the Rmeidh manuscript describes work done at Tell Asmar, ancient Eshnunna, where the Oriental Institute excavated in the 1930s, and because the Hamza report is on Tell Muqtadiya, another site in the same region with very similar material, they not only make sense as a combined book but also as one that the Oriental Institute should publish.

In other activities, Gibson still serves as president of The American Academic Research Institute in Iraq (TAARII), and he has been negotiating for permission to set up a center in Baghdad. TAARII maintains its overseas operations in Amman, but looks forward to shifting to Iraq. As president of TAARII, in November he organized for the Iraqi Cultural Center in Washington a symposium on Remote Sensing in Archaeology, showing its potential for research and for monitoring the condition of sites. Almost all of the presenters were either from the Oriental Institute or were former graduates, illustrating the important role that Chicago has played in the development of this field in archaeology. As an adjunct to the meeting, Chris Woods of the Oriental Institute gave a presentation on Gilgamesh, which was a great success.

Gibson also still serves on the boards of the American Institute for Yemeni Studies and the Council of American Overseas Research Centers.

Petra M. Goedegebuure

Petra M. Goedegebuure devoted the majority of her research time this year on finishing and submitting her monograph *The Hittite Demonstratives: Studies in Deixis, Topic and Focus* (accepted for publication in the series Studien zu den Boghazköy-Texten; Harrassowitz).

In order to explain the functions of the Hittite demonstratives and accented pronouns, Petra constructed a descriptive model based on a combination of cognitive-functional and typological approaches to referential expressions. The application of this model not only led to an improved description of the demonstratives *ka-* "this" and *apa-* "that" and the accented pronoun *apa-* (which is the same as the demonstrative but with completely different meanings and use), but also to a reclassification of the pronoun *aši*. The pronoun *aši* does not mean "he, she, it" as previously assumed but is a demonstrative with the meaning "that, yonder." This "new" distal demonstrative required a reappraisal of the hitherto accepted distal semantics of *apa-*, which does not mark remote objects at all but points at objects in the vicinity of the addressee. An analogy that illustrates the relevance of this change is to imagine that the demonstrative system of English was always incorrectly believed to consist of only *this*, with all cases of the non-proximal demonstrative *that* misunderstood as an anaphoric pronoun. *That* in statements like "*this* is my chair and *that* one is his" would be interpreted as only referring to a chair that was mentioned before; it would never be understood as directing the attention to a chair at some distance from the speaker.

As a third-person pronoun, *apa-* expresses emphasis. A detailed analysis showed among other things that *apa-* in preverbal position marks a referent as the Contrastive Focus of its clause (in "the dog (not the cat) chased the horse," *dog* is in Contrastive Focus). Non-contrastive focal *apa-*, on the other hand, always occurs in initial position. This correlation between preverbal position and emphatic contrast had not been noted before, which meant that crucial parts of the ancient author's intention were overlooked. For English this amounts to not being able to detect the difference between contrastive "the dog (not the cat) chased the horse" and non-contrastive "the dog chased the horse."

Petra also published two articles ("Hittite Iconoclasm: Disconnecting the Icon, Disempowering the Referent," in *Iconoclasm and Text Destruction in the Ancient Near East and Beyond*, edited by Natalie Naomi May, pp. 407–52 (Oriental Institute Seminars 8; Chicago, The Oriental Institute, 2012); "Split-ergativity in Hittite," in *Zeitschrift für Assyriologie und vorderasiatische Archäologie* 102/2 (2013): 270–303; and several entries ("Hattic (Language)," "Labarna," "Kashka") for the *Encyclopedia of Ancient History* (www.encyclopediaancienthistory.com).

Petra furthermore participated in the Chicago Hittite Dictionary (CHD) Project, proofreading the third volume of Š (see project report for the CHD). She also initiated the CHD Paleography Project, announced at the Rencontre Assyriologique Internationale in Leiden (2012). For the chronological organization of lexemes the CHD currently relies on a palaeography that was established in the 1970s. In the last years, however, views on the introduction and development of writing in Hittite society have changed, and as a result the field requires a reassessment of the palaeographic dating methods.

Gene Gragg

Gene Gragg's work continues, with Gregg Reynolds of NORC (National Opinion Research Center), on both the structure (linked-data repository) and the interface (for paradigm query and manipulation) of the paradigm database project, AAMA (Afroasiatic Morphological Archive — but still with heavy emphasis on Cushitic-Omotic). Currently, the authoritative data is coded in XML files, from which Turtle RDF is generated (since Turtle is readable), from which RDF/XML is generated (since RDF/XML is not very readable), which is loaded to the triple store. However json-ld (Jason Linked-Data, http://www.w3.org/TR/2013/WD-json-ld-20130411/) is being considered, as in other projects, as a more linked-data friendly alternative to XML.

Work is proceeding, if slower than anticipated, on the front end, which is in the process of being constructed in Cappuccino (http://www.cappuccinoproject.org), a web application framework based on Apple's Cocoa framework. Its language, ObjectiveJ, is an implementation of ObjectiveC (the official Apple development language) in Javascript. Hopefully, we will be able to post a first version of the application in the course of the next academic year.

Reports on the present status of AAMA were made in two talks: "What is a Paradigm Database," at the forty-first North American Conference on Afroasatic Linguistics, Yale University, February 17, 2013; and "The Afroasiatic Morphological Archive: A Paradigm Database," Université Paris Diderot Laboratoire de Linguistique Formelle, May 23, 2013.

Jack Green

There was seldom time for individual research in the past year due to **Jack Green**'s intensive work on multiple museum projects including overseas visits, but progress was made on several levels.

The following contributions to *Oriental Institute News & Notes* appeared over the past year: "Behind the Scenes at the Oriental Institute Museum: Lending the Collections" (no. 217 [2013]: 3–6), "Fulfilling Breasted's Vision: The Oriental Institute Integrated Database Project" (with Scott Branting and Foy Scalf), and "Catastrophe! Ten Years Later: Looting, Destruction, and Preservation in Iraq and the Wider Middle East" (with Katharyn Hanson) (both no. 218 [2013]: 9–13, 18–19).

One volume was submitted for publication: the co-edited and co-authored (with Emily Teeter) Oriental Institute Museum Publication for the special exhibit: *Our Work: Modern Jobs — Ancient Origins* (in press at the time of writing).

Conference presentations, lectures, and seminars included a paper given at the American Schools of Oriental Research annual meeting in Chicago (November 17, 2012), related to research conducted for the Oriental Institute's Picturing the Past exhibit, entitled "Restoring the Past: A Brief History of Imaging and Imagining the Ancient Middle East." In conjunction with the Catastrophe! Ten Years Later exhibit, Jack co-organized (with Katharyn Hanson) and participated as a panelist in a seminar on Catastrophe! Ten Years Later: Looting, Destruction, and Preservation in Iraq and the Wider Middle East, at the Oriental Institute (April 16, 2013). Jack also co-presented at the Theoretical Archaeology Group conference in Chicago with Hamza Walker of the Renaissance Society, on "Curatorial Responses to Danh Vo's 'We The People' at the Oriental Institute Museum" (May 10, 2013), as part of the session "The Way of the Shovel: On the Archaeological Imaginary in Art." Jack also gave a guest lecture for an event organized by the Assyrian Church of the East, in Niles, Illinois, on the topic of the Rediscovery of Ancient Assyria.

Individual research continued to focus on preparations for a research article for "Gender and Sexuality" being prepared for Blackwell's forthcoming *Companion to the Art of the Ancient Near East*, edited by Ann C. Gunter (Northwestern University). Work also progressed on the Oriental Institute Museum 100 Highlights publication with Emily Teeter.

Work in progress continued with the preparation (with Ros Henry) of a volume of letters and photographs of British Near Eastern archaeologist Olga Tufnell. Long-term preparations for publication also continued on the Tell es-Saʿidiyeh Cemetery Publication Project, particularly on the Persian-period burials.

In this past financial year, Jack was also invited to join the Committee on Archaeological Research Policy (CAP) for the American Schools of Oriental Research (Class of 2015).

Rebecca Hasselbach

This academic year has seen the publication of two books by **Rebecca Hasselbach**: *Case in Semitic: Roles, Relations, and Reconstruction* (Oxford Studies in Diachronic and Historical Linguistics 3. Oxford: Oxford University Press, 2013), which investigates the case system attested in various Semitic languages. In this book, which uses the methodologies of historical linguistics and typology, Hasselbach suggests a new reconstruction of the case system and original alignment from which the attested case systems derived. Instead of the commonly assumed accusative system, which faces several problems, she proposes an original marked-nominative system. The book further investigates phenomena related to case systems, such as word order and head- and dependent-marking structures. The second book, *Language and Nature: Papers Presented to John Huehnergard on the Occasion of his 60th Birthday* (Studies in Ancient Oriental Civilization 67. Chicago: The Oriental Institute, 2012) is an edited Festschrift in honor of Hasselbach's dissertation advisor John Huehnergard, which she edited together with another of Huehnergard's former students, Naʿama Pat-El from the University of Texas at Austin. This volume contains twenty-nine scholarly articles on a variety of topics relating to ancient Near Eastern languages and cultures, and art contributions by a friend of the honoree.

The Festschrift for John Huehnergard includes an article by Hasselbach, "The Verbal Endings -*u* and -*a*: A Note on Their Functional Derivation" (pp. 119–36), which investigates the origin of various modal and subordinate markers used on verbs in Semitic. Hasselbach suggests that these verbal markers are derived from original case endings that were grammaticalized into subordinate and modal markers based on cross-linguistically well-known grammaticalization paths.

Hasselbach further gave several scholarly presentations, including a talk on "Agreement and the Development of Gender in Semitic," presented at the Workshop on Semitic and Historical Linguistics (University of Texas at Austin) in October 2012, and "The Reconstruction of the Semitic Case System and the 'Absolute State' of Akkadian: A Historical and Typological Perspective," which she presented in March 2013 at Harvard University.

During the academic year, Hasselbach has further worked on a new book project: the translation and revision of Josef Tropper's *Grammar of Classical Ethiopic* (*Altäthiopisch: Grammatik des Geʿez mit Übungstexten und Glossar*, Münster: Ugarit-Verlag, 2002), which was originally published in German.

Janet Johnson

Janet Johnson spent much of the year working on the Demotic Dictionary (see separate report). She enjoyed the wonderful publicity for the Dictionary which came with the coverage in the *Chicago Tribune* and *New York Times* of the completion of the (letter files of the) Dictionary and the Internet, radio, and television coverage which followed. Having a chance to talk with school groups and other members of the general public about the Dictionary and about life in Egypt in "Demotic" times was fun and made a wider public aware of the Oriental Institute's commitment to long-term basic research. Subsequent participation in the University's "Knowledge Fair" brought visits from some old friends and again spread the word about our work and the work of the Oriental Institute in general. She gave a lecture on the Dictionary for a local church group, lectured on the legal and social status of women for the intensive three-week summer program for high-school students which is offered by one of our graduate students in Egyptology each summer through the Graham School of Continuing Studies, discussed Demotic texts as a source for the study of religion in Late Period Egypt for the Summer Papyrology Institute, and gave a tour of the Egyptian gallery of the Oriental Institute Museum to a class on "Greco-Roman Egypt in the Imagination" from Valparaiso University taught by a former student. She participated in this year's annual meeting, held in Cincinnati, of the American Research Center in Egypt (ARCE), where she serves as the Oriental Institute's representative to the council of (Research) Supporting Institutions and just finished a three-year term as a representative of the council to the ARCE Board of Governors. Administratively, she served on the Council of the University Senate, served on several faculty hiring and review committees, served as a reviewer for the *Journal of Near Eastern Studies* (the journal of the Department of Near Eastern Languages and Civilizations), and participated in tenure reviews for faculty at other universities.

W. Raymond Johnson

This year **W. Raymond Johnson** completed his thirty-fifth year working in Egypt, his thirty-fourth full year working for the Epigraphic Survey in Luxor, and his sixteenth season as Chicago House Field Director. In November, 2012 Ray gave three lectures in Copenhagen at the University of Copenhagen Department of Cross-Cultural and Regional Studies and the Danish Egyptological Society on the current work of the Epigraphic Survey, and on the monument-building activities of Tutankhamun in Thebes. During his stay he had the pleasure of studying the Amarna *talatat* collection of the Ny Carlsberg Glyptotek museum with curator Tine Bagh. Later that month Ray gave a public lecture on the work of the Epigraphic Survey at the Ministry of State for Antiquities in Zamalek, Cairo. In April he studied Amarna blocks in Berlin, Hannover, and Hildesheim. In late June Ray traveled to Turin to study the extensive Amarna *talatat* collection in the Egyptian Museum, thanks to museum director Eleni Vassilika. On July 18, 2013, Ray gave a lecture to the South Suburban Archaeological Society on the work of the Survey in post-Revolution Egypt. In August Ray had the pleasure of studying the largest collection of *talatat* outside of Egypt at the Metropolitan Museum of Art (MMA) in New York, assisted by Jay Heidel and Margie Fisher, thanks to Acting Department Head Diana Craig Patch and the MMA Egyptian Department. Articles appearing in print (or about to) include: "The Epigraphic Survey, Oriental Institute, University of Chicago (Chicago House) in Luxor, Egypt," in the exhibition catalog *Explorations: Egypt in the Art of Susan Osgood*, edited by Rogério Sousa (University of Porto, Portugal, 2013), pp. 29–38; "Same Statues, Different King (Amenhotep IV)," in *KMT: A Modern Journal of Ancient Egypt* (Winter 2012), pp. 49–54; "Sexual Duality and Goddess Iconography on the Amenhotep IV Sandstone Colossi at Karnak," in the Festschrift for Dorothea Arnold, Metropolitan Museum of Art (BES 19, forthcoming); and "Conservation of the Monuments of Amenhotep III at Luxor Temple," in the colloquium proceedings, The

Ministry of State for Antiquities and Colossi of Memnon and Amenhotep III Mortuary Temple Conservation Project, Luxor Museum, March 4, 2012 (forthcoming).

Charles E. Jones

As the year comes to an end, **Charles E. Jones** has been appointed Tombros Librarian for Classics and Humanities in the George and Sherry Middlemas Arts and Humanities Library at Penn State University. In this position, he will oversee collections and materials pertaining to the ancient world and will facilitate digital initiatives in teaching and disseminating information relating to Classics, Near Eastern studies, art and archaeology, and related fields. He and his family will move there in early August. Jones continues his association with the Oriental Institute via the Perseplis Fortification Archive Project, the IraqCrisis Mailing list, and the identification, description, and dissemination of information of digital antiquity by way of Abzu (http://www.etana.org/abzubib) and the Ancient World Online, or AWOL, (http://ancientworldonline.blogspot.com/). In the coming year, Jones will work with a multi-institutional team on The Ancient World Online Accessibility project, which will integrate AWOL's content with library discovery systems and create a new dissemination channel that will improve accessibility and seamlessly create new records and update existing ones. When completed, the proposed project will move us much closer to realizing the shared vision of making accessible to scholars and to the public around the world materials that tell the story of the ancient world.

Walter E. Kaegi

Walter E. Kaegi delivered an invited lecture, "Reassessing Arnold J. Toynbee the Byzantine Historian," on November 28, 2012, at the University of Illinois at Urbana-Champaign, for the Program in Modern Greek Studies and the History Department. On March 1, 2013, he delivered an invited lecture, "Seventh-century North Africa: Military and Political Convergences and Divergences," at the international conference Africa-Ifriqiya: Cultures of Transition in North Africa between Late Antiquity and the Early Middle Ages, held at Rome, Italy, at the Museo Nazionale Romano — Terme di Diocleziano. It was sponsored by the Deutsches Archäologisches Institut, Rome, Italy, and Durham University, Durham, England, UK. He published two papers: (1) "Byzantine Sardinia Threatened: Its Changing Situation in the Seventh Century," in *Atti del convegno di Oristano (22-23 marzo 2003) 'Forme e caratteri della presenza bizantina nel Mediterraneo occidentale: la Sardegna (secoli VI-XI),'* 22-23 March 2003, edited by Paola Corrias, pp. 43–56 (Cagliari, Sardinia: MT, 2013); (2) "The Heraclians and Holy War," in *Byzantine War Ideology between Roman Imperial Concept and Christian Religion: Akten des Internationalen Symposium (Vienna, 19-21 May 2011)*, edited by J. Koder, and I. Stouraitis, pp. 17–26 (Denkschriften, Philosophisch-Historische Klasse, Österreichische Akademie der Wissenschaften 452; Vienna: Verlag Österreichischen Akademie der Wissenschaften, 2012). He prepared a paper "Reassessing Arnold J. Toynbee the Byzantine Historian" for the Bernard Bachrach Festschrift, which Ashgate will publish. He revised and updated "The Byzantine-Arab Frontier: Barrier or Bridge? Reconsiderations after Twenty-five Years" for publication in the proceedings of the international congress Byzantium and the Arab World, Encounter of Civilizations, held at Aristotle University of Thessaloniki, Thessaloniki, Greece. He composed an essay on "Byzantium in the Seventh Century" for the *Oxford Handbook on Maximus the Confessor*, edited by Pauline Allen and Bronwen Neil (Oxford: Oxford University Press). He is revising his 2012 paper entitled "The Islamic Conquest and the Defense of Byzantine Africa: Campaigns and Conquests in Context, Reconsiderations" for publication in a collective volume with Dumbarton Oaks/Harvard. He published a review of Irfan Shahid, *Byzantium and the Arabs in the Sixth Century*, Volume 2, Part 2: *Economic, Social and Cultural History* (Washington, DC: Dumbarton Oaks Research Library and Collection, 2009), in the *Journal of Near Eastern Studies* (71 [2012]: 404–06). He helped to edit volume 31 of the journal *Byzantinische Forschungen*. He was history bibliographer for the journal *Byzantinische Zeitschrift*. He served as co-director of the Workshop on Late Antiquity and Byzantium. He continued to supervise continuing retrieval of audiotaped lectures from his Byzantine History Courses at the University of Chicago from the 1980s and early 1990s, with indispensable assistance from University of Chicago Audio/Visual Services in Stuart 004. He performed editorial work for the *Journal of Near Eastern Studies*. He continued to serve as Ex Officio Member of the Officers, US National Committee for Byzantine Studies. He participated in the new University of Chicago Study Abroad program in Istanbul, teaching a section of Middle East Civilization in Istanbul –2 Byzantium from April 22 through May 9, 2013 (Yildiz Technical University, Beşiktaş). In September 2012 he made his first trip to China. He visited museums and sites in Beijing, Xian (ancient Chang'an), and Shanghai, where he gained comparative insights for the history of the later Roman empire and Byzantine empire.

Morag M. Kersel

During the summer of 2012 **Morag M. Kersel** continued to direct the survey component of the Galilee Prehistory Project (GPP) at the site of Marj Rabba (directed by Yorke Rowan). At the same time Morag also worked on recording the excavations at the site, drawing architectural plans and sections, which are later rendered digitally back in Chicago by Oriental Institute Visiting Committee member Roberta Schaffner. During the 2012 field season, five high school students from the Rowe-Clark Math & Science Academy in Chicago, accompanied by their intrepid mentor, Bridget Davis, spent five weeks excavating alongside undergraduate and graduate students from the US and abroad. Continuing the great success of this initial foray, five additional students and another mentor, Maggie Culhane, will join the GPP excavation team on the project during the summer of 2013. By way of preparation, during spring 2013 Morag, Yorke Rowan, and Gil Stein conducted a series of Saturday morning workshops on the Middle East, archaeology, survey, faunal remains, and the Chalcolithic period with the high-school students. During the mid-morning break they were introduced to foods of the Middle East, although American donuts proved to be a more popular option.

Morag M. Kersel drawing architectural plans at Marj Rabba, Galilee Prehistory Project (photograph by A. C. Hill)

With Yorke Rowan, she presented the results of the 2012 field season at Marj Rabba at the annual meeting of the American Schools of Oriental Research in November 2012. At the same academic meetings one of the GPP summer field-school students, Allen Reinert of DePaul University, presented a poster on excavating Chalcolithic houses. Morag and Yorke continued to work on preliminary artifacts and survey analyses, which will culminate in a comprehensive final publication on the five seasons of excavation and survey at Marj Rabba.

In spring 2013 Morag was a discussant in the Oriental Institute Seminar Catastrophe! Ten Years Later: Looting, Destruction, and Preservation of Cultural Heritage in the Wider Middle East. The seminar examined, assessed, and discussed the state of cultural-heritage protection in the ten years since the ransacking of the Iraq Museum in the aftermath of the coalition forces invasion of Iraq. Morag was also a speaker in the Cultural Diplomacy Seminar hosted by the Cultural Policy Center of the University of Chicago. Her talk discussed aspects of the recently published volume *U.S. Cultural Diplomacy and Archaeology: Hard Heritage, Soft Power* (New York: Routledge, 2013) that she co-authored with Christina Luke. This volume highlights some of the ways archaeologists and archaeology act as unofficial US ambassadors by fostering good relationships (abroad and in the US) through investigations into the past.

Massimo Maiocchi

Massimo Maiocchi joined the Oriental Institute and the Department of Near Eatern Languages and Civilizations on the first of October as a Mellon Postdoctoral Fellow and instructor in Assyriology. Over the last nine months, he extensively worked on the Writing in Early Mesopotamia project, the aim of which is to provide a complete description of the cuneiform writing system, with special focus on the developments that occurred in its early phase, from the end of the fourth to the beginning of second millennium BC. He set up a database for textual analysis of a group of literary texts known as "the Decad." Besides the conceptualization of table relations, the work concerned digitalization of texts, normalization of readings, lemmatization, encoding, and development of Perl and SQL scripting to manage the large amount of data — roughly 850 texts and text fragments are presently included in the catalog. The goal of this database is to provide scholars the possibilities to search for textual variants and morphographic features, which are extremely significant for a better understanding of the corpus.

In addition, Maiocchi focused on the early history of the Tigridian region, as part of the ARCANE Project (Associated Regional Chronologies for the Ancient Near East). This is a large-scale project that aims to synchronize relative and absolute regional chronologies of the ancient Near East as a whole. The results of his studies will be published by the end of the current year in an article titled "A Sketch of Political History of the Early Tigridian Region," in *Associated Regional Chronologies for the Ancient Near East and the Eastern Mediterranean: Tigridian Region*, edited by P. Bieliński and E. Rova (ARCANE 5. Turnhout: Brepols). The contribution provides an in-depth overview of the epigraphic evidence for the reconstruction of third-millennium history of the region roughly extending from Assur (Qalʾat Sherqat) to the Illisu dam area in Turkey, and from the sites on the upper Tharthar River to the Dunkan dam on the lower Zab. The reevaluation of the available material suggests that the region flourished considerably after the fall of the Sargonic empire, in sharp contrast with the contraction of urbanization in the nearby Upper Khabur region. As part of his interest in northern Mesopotamia before the rise of second-millennium Assyria, Maiocchi also prepared a review article of the recent volume edited by H. Weiss, *Seven Generations Since the Fall of Akkad* (Wiesbaden: Harrassowitz, 2012), which will appear in the forthcoming issue of the *Journal of Near Eastern Studies.*

As part of his academic duties, in the Winter 2013 quarter, Maiocchi taught a class on Eblaite (AKKD 40399) for advanced students of Akkadian. The goal of this class was to introduce the students to the language and civilization of Early Dynastic Ebla (ca. 2400–2350 BC), focusing on primary sources unearthed there, including chancellery documents, rituals, administrative, and literary texts. In addition, in the Spring 2013 quarter he was assistant teacher for a class titled "Writing Systems and Decipherment" (NEHC 20355), which provided the students with an overview of various typologies of scripts (syllabic, logo-syllabic, alphabetic), with special reference to the so-called pristine writing systems of ancient Egypt, Mesopotamia, China, and Mesoamerica. He also devoted some of his time to peer review for the *Journal of Near Eastern Studies* and the *Journal of Ancient Near Eastern Religions.*

Gregory Marouard

Gregory Marouard spent the entire summer of 2012 on the processing of field data from the Tell Edfu Project 2011 season in Egypt.

Between early October and late November Gregory joined the Tell Edfu 2012 season as co-director of the project together with Nadine Moeller (see Nadine's individual research). He was in charge of fieldwork in Zone 2, a new area focusing on the Old Kingdom settlement remains occupied between the end of the Fifth Dynasty and the early First Intermediate Period. He also resumed the study of the Old Kingdom enclosure walls located in the same sector (see *Tell Edfu* project report). Another objective of last season has been the conservation program in order to protect more than three hundred inscribed and decorated sandstone blocks that were deposited at the foot of the tell several years ago. Gregory assured the design of the new blockyard and oversaw the technical implementation in form of building several platforms specifically adapted to receive the various kinds of blocks. The inventory in the database and the analysis of the blocks has been assigned to Jonathan Winnerman and Janelle Wade, both graduate students in Egyptology at the Department of Near Eastern Languages and Civilizations.

The excavation at Tell Edfu also included a short mission at the small provincial pyramid at el-Ghonameya. Gregory supervised the end of the cleaning operation at the main monument and the construction of a protective low fence of 250 meters in length, financed with an award from the Antiquities Endowment Fund program of the American Research Center in Egypt. It was the penultimate intervention at this site where most of the protection program has been completed. It should also be noted that the short article published by Gregory and Hratch Papazian in the *Oriental Institute News & Notes* 213 (Spring 2012) has been republished in a Danish version in the December 2012 edition of the journal *Papyrus* ("Edfu-pyramid – projektet," *Papyrus* 32/2 [2012]: 24–37).

In early December, Gregory joined as associate director a survey mission at the small provincial pyramid of Sinki at Abydos (Upper Egypt), a project conducted by Hratch Papazian, visiting associate professor at the University of Copenhagen (see *Egyptian Archaeology* 42 [2013]: p. 27). In two weeks, he completed an extensive statistical survey of the surrounding archaeological area of the step pyramid, which is seriously threatened by the fast growth of modern homes and trash dumps. A systematic localization and collection of the pottery sherds on the surface has confirmed the nearly total disappearance of the archaeological evidence of the Old Kingdom in this area and underlined the possible absence of any worship or administrative installation in relation to the pyramid. These results confirm some of the conclusions made after the cleaning operation at the contemporaneous small pyramid at el-Ghonameya/Edfu.

Gregory at Wadi el-Jarf, Egypt

For two weeks in early January 2013, Gregory participated in a new project at the site of the Dendara temple in Upper Egypt, which is a French Archaeological Institute (IFAO) mission conducted by Pierre Zignani (Centre national de la recherche scientifique [CNRS], architect at the French Center at the Karnak temple). After almost seven years without any mission at this site, the current goal is to rebuild a new collaborative research program on the external part of the Hathor temple. The Predynastic section of the necropolis and the geomorphological study of the ancient environment will be supported by Yann Tristant (Macquarie University, Sydney). Gregory will conduct the study of the enclosure walls and the settlement area, more specifically, the domestic area of the late Old Kingdom and the First Intermediate Period which is situated to the east of the Hathor temple. This fieldwork will provide an important parallel to the ongoing work of the Tell Edfu Project. This is also a unique opportunity for the Oriental Institute to start a new joint project with the IFAO on a major archaeological concession in Egypt and a "sister site" of Edfu.

Emily Teeter has provided significant elements for this project regarding the numerous objects from Dendara preserved in the Oriental Institute Museum collection. Gregory also made the necessary contacts with the Petrie Museum at University College in London and with the University of Pennsylvania museum, which hold the excavation records of the Old Kingdom and Late Old Kingdom cemetery (conducted by W. M. F. Petrie in 1898 and C. Fischer between 1915 and 1917), an area that should be also included in the new program of excavations.

Between March and April 2013, Gregory joined the French mission on the Red Sea coast and the excavation of the oldest Egyptian harbor at Wadi el-Jarf (Paris La Sorbonne University — IFAO). He was in charge of the excavations of the maritime part of the site, which have led to the discovery of a large storage building, 40 meters in length, located along the coast and dating from the beginning of the Fourth Dynasty (ca. 2600–2550 BC). In four of the parallel storage magazines, ninety-nine in situ ship anchors have been excavated. In the area of the storage galleries located three miles from the shore, the excavation uncovered several dozen large fragments of papyrus dating back to the beginning of the Fourth Dynasty. This is an exceptional set of reports and food accounts, and several documents mention King Khufu, builder of the Great Pyramid at Giza. Some of them contain a precise date: the twenty-sixth year of his reign (thirteenth cattle census). This is the largest corpus of papyri known for the entire Old Kingdom and the oldest inscribed papyrus ever discovered in Egypt (see "Possibly World's Oldest Sea Port Found in Egypt," *GMA News Online*, April 15, 2013, http://www.gmanetwork.com/news/story/303946/scitech/science/possibly-world-s-oldest-sea-port-found-in-egypt and http://english.ahram.org.eg/News/69024.aspx).

Two new articles concerning the excavation at this site are currently in press: (1) P. Tallet, G. Marouard, and D. Laisney, "Un port de la IVe Dynastie identifié au ouadi al-Jarf (mer Rouge)," *Bulletin de l'Institut Français d'Archéologie Orientale* 112 [2012]; (2) G. Marouard, "Un nouvel atelier de potiers de la IVe Dynastie au ouadi al-Jarf (Mer Rouge)," in *Studies on Old Kingdom Pottery*, Volume 2, edited by T. Rzeuska and A. Wodzinska, 2013.

Finally, in June 2013, Gregory has completed his season of excavation with a one-month mission at the site of Buto in the western Nile delta. This is a joint project of the University of Poitiers (France) and the German Archaeological Institute in Cairo. He completed an extensive survey of the Kom A area, which had been started in 2012. He also took charge of three new areas of extensive cleaning, which cover a total surface of 1,400 square meters. It has been the aim to better understand the stratigraphic evolution of a large domestic area within the settlement dating from the Saite period (sixth century BC) to the beginning of the Hellenistic period (early third century AD).

In the course of this year, Gregory has also participated in several conferences. In December 2012 he participated in the international workshop The Tower Houses in Egypt during the Late Period, the Ptolemaic and Roman Periods, held at the Paris IV La Sorbonne, France, with a lecture on "Maisons-tours et organisation des quartiers domestiques dans les agglomérations du Delta: l'exemple de Bouto de la Basse Époque aux premiers lagides." In March he presented a paper on the "Recent Works on the Late Periods at Buto (2011–2012)" at the 2013 Egypt Exploration Society (EES) Delta Survey Workshop, held at the British Council in Cairo, Egypt. On April 17, 2013, he gave a joint brown-bag talk (with R. Ritner and B. Muhs) for the mini-series on Household Archaeology at the Oriental Institute. Finally, in April 2013, he presented a joint paper with N. Moeller at the sixty-fourth annual meeting of the American Research Center in Egypt in Cincinnati entitled: "The 3rd Millennium B.C. at Tell Edfu — New Discoveries of the 2012 Season."

Gregory is currently planning a new project for a pottery and geomagnetic survey on a large urban site of the Hellenistic and Roman period discovered by observations of recent satellite images. The site, probably a new Ptolemaic *ex-nihilo* foundation, is situated in a particularly isolated part in the Lake Menzaleh (eastern Nile delta) and has never been surveyed or even visited by any archaeologist since the end of the nineteenth century. This will be a joint project of the Oriental Institute and the Department of Classics at the University of Chicago, with the support of Gil Stein and Alain Bresson. If official authorizations permit and political as well as economic conditions remain stable in Egypt, the first mission will be conducted for a couple of weeks at the end of September 2013.

Carol Meyer

Carol Meyer submitted the third and last volume of the Bir Umm Fawakhir final reports to the Oriental Institute's editorial office in August. It has since been accepted for publication and reviewed; revisions are in progress. With twenty-odd years of research in and about the Eastern Desert of Egypt winding down, Meyer started several new projects. With thanks to Don Whitcomb, she resumed a long-postponed study of the Aqaba glass corpus. This is a large and well-excavated body of early Islamic glass, and to date there are no other published corpora from this time period. The glass has the potential to document archaeologically the transition from Byzantine culture to the emerging Islamic one. For instance, the Byzantine wine goblets declined in numbers and were in time replaced by a series of distinctive cylindrical cups or bowls. This is also the period when the Mediterranean Sea ceased to be *mare nostrum* and its shores and ports were divided between the Byzantine and rising Umayyad powers. For lands under the rule of the caliphs, the focus of trade shifted from the Mediterranean to the Red Sea, Persian Gulf, and the Indian Ocean. Since glass is widely traded, both for its intrinsic value and as containers for perfume, medicines, and other expensive items, the Aqaba corpus will provide an opportunity to follow some of the new trade patterns. To date, all the 1986 material has been sorted and tabulated on a new database table and diagnostic pieces have been drawn. The 1987 material was tabulated and drawn in the 1990s but needs to be incorporated in the new table. There were four seasons of excavation after 1987, so the project is expected to take several years. Secondly, Bruce Williams is resuming publication of the last sites excavated behind the Aswan High Dam in the 1960s (see the report on the *Oriental Institute Nubian Expedition*). Meyer will write the sections on glass found at Dorginarti and Serra East and will assist in preparing the pottery corpus from all the remaining sites. Finally, a project that Meyer worked with in Syria in 1978 at Tell Nebi Mend (ancient Qadesh) under the direction of Peter Parr, is also at long last being published. Meyer will publish the 1978 corpus of Late Hellenistic, Roman, and Byzantine-period glass. The early Roman corpus in particular is valuable as being excavated, which is not true of a surprising amount of the glass of this period, and being close very close in time and space to the presumed place of invention of the first mass-produced glass, the distinctive mold-formed bowls, in Lebanon.

Nadine Moeller

Much of **Nadine Moeller**'s autumn was taken up by directing the fieldwork at the ancient town of Tell Edfu in Egypt, where two new excavation zones have been started, shifting the aim of this project to the exploration of settlement remains dating to the third millennium BC (see *Tell Edfu* report). After the excavation in December, she traveled to Rome for a conference entitled Reading Catastrophes, Methodological Approaches and Historical Interpretation: Earthquakes, Famines, Epidemics, Floods between Egypt and Palestine — 3rd–1st Millennium BC, which was held at the University "La Sapienza." At this occasion she co-presented a paper with Robert Ritner on the "Ahmose Tempest Stela: An Ancient Egyptian Account of a Natural Catastrophe." This lecture has been submitted for publication in form of a joint article to the conference organizers. It is an updated version of a manuscript entitled "The Ahmose 'Tempest Stela,' Thera and Comparative Chronology," which has been submitted by Ritner and Moeller to the *Journal of Near Eastern Studies*.

After the conference in Rome, Moeller traveled to Berlin for the members' preview opening of the new Amarna exhibit at the Neues Museum, which celebrates the 100 years of discovery of the bust of Nefertiti.

In February 2013, Nadine finished her book project entitled *Urban Society in Ancient Egypt — An Archaeological Study of the Egyptian Towns and Cities*, Volume 1: *The Settlements from the Predynastic Period to the End of the Middle Kingdom (ca. 3500–1650 B.C.)*, which has been accepted for publication by Brill publishers. This volume, which brings together the latest archaeological data, presents an entirely new in-depth study setting the parameters for Egypt as an early urban society, an aspect that has frequently been clouded by the repeated comparisons to ancient Mesopotamian city-states. In comparison with settlement archaeology in the ancient Near East, the focus on towns and cities can be considered a relatively recent trend in Egyptian archaeology, a field that has concentrated much on the study of the rich mortuary culture but noticeably less on aspects of urban society. The submitted manuscript fills an important gap in dealing with Egyptian settlements and can be considered a first synthesis of this material.

Furthermore, Moeller gave a lecture at the Archaeological Institute of America Chapter in Toledo at the end of February about the discoveries of the 2012 season at Tell Edfu. In March she was one of the respondents at the international conference on Household Studies and Complex Societies held at the Oriental Institute, and which was organized by the postdoctoral scholar Miriam Müller. At the end of March, Moeller was invited as the guest speaker for the annual ANSHE lecture held at Johns Hopkins University in Baltimore, where she presented her new research on "The Role of Town Planning During the Middle Kingdom: A New Evaluation." In April, Moeller participated at the annual meeting of the American Research Center in Egypt (ARCE) held in Cincinnati, where she presented the new results from the excavations of the Old Kingdom and First Intermediate Period settlement at Tell Edfu. For the remainder of the academic year she focused on preparing a major grant proposal to the National Science Foundation as well as several additional articles.

Brian Muhs

During the academic year 2012–2013, much of **Brian Muhs'** research related to his book project, "The Ancient Egyptian Economy," which explores how social and legal institutions shaped the development of modes of distribution in ancient Egypt. He gave two lectures relating to this research: on March 16, 2013, he participated in the conference Heracleion in Context: The Maritime Economy of the Egyptian Late Period, at The Queen's College, Oxford, where he presented a paper on "Money Taxes and Maritime Trade in Late Period Egypt"; and on April 3, 2013, he gave an Oriental Institute Members' Lecture, co-sponsored by the Archaeological Institute of America, Chicago, on "Death and Taxes in Ancient Egypt."

Muhs also conducted and fostered research involving Demotic sources for ancient Egyptian society and culture. He organized and secured funding for the seventh triennial Demotic Summer School, which was held at the Oriental Institute on August 27–28, 2012, as well as the Roundtable "Digital Demotic," held at the Franke Institute of the University of Chicago on August 29, 2012. The Summer School allowed Demotists to present difficult texts and to discuss them with each other before they were published. Muhs presented two "Loan Accounts from the Archive of Panas Son of Espemetis." The Roundtable discussed the Chicago Demotic Dictionary with many of its users at the Summer School, to determine how it might better serve them in the future. On April 17, 2013, Muhs presented a Brown-bag Lecture at the Oriental Institute, together with Greg Marouard and Robert Ritner, on "Reconstructing Houses and Households of the Late Pharaonic Era (6th–1st Cent. B.C.): Possibilities and Limits," in the Oriental Institute mini-series on Household Archaeology. He discussed how Demotic family archives from Ptolemaic Egypt illustrated household histories and lifecycles that illuminated contemporary archaeological evidence. On July 5, 2012, he gave a guest lecture on "Ptolemaic Demotic Texts and Bilingual Archives" for the annual Summer Institute of Papyrology, which was held at the Regenstein Library of the University of Chicago that year.

Muhs submitted three articles, including "More Papyri from the Archive of Panas Son of Espemetis" for the journal *Enchoria*, based on a paper he presented at Oxford the previous year; "Egyptian Legal Texts," for *The Oxford Encyclopedia of the Bible and Law*; and "Eight Inscribed Stones, the First Chariot Driver of His Majesty, and Tell el-Muqdam in the Ramesside Period," for *Weseretkau "Mighty of Kas": Papers in Memory of Cathleen A. Keller*, based on fieldwork in 1993. He also completed three reviews of books on topics related to his own book project. One of these reviews and two short articles appeared this year, namely "Demotic Orthography in B. H. Stricker's Notebooks," in *Aspects of Demotic Orthography. Acts of an International Colloquium held in Trier, 8 November 2010*, edited by S. P. Vleeming, pp. 63–68 (Studia Demotica 11. Leuven: Peeters, 2013); and "Robert Curzon and His Mummy Labels," *Journal of Egyptian Archaeology* (98 [2012]: 285–91). Muhs also taught courses on Introductory Coptic, Old Egyptian, Egyptian literature and culture, and Second Intermediate Period and Ptolemaic Period history.

Hratch Papazian

During late November and early December of 2012 **Hratch Papazian** carried out an initial season of fieldwork at the Old Kingdom step pyramid in South Abydos (also known as the Sinki pyramid) with Oriental Institute research associate Gregory Marouard; Kathryn Bandy, PhD candidate in Egyptology at the University of Chicago; and Ole Herslund of the University of Copenhagen. A systematic survey and mapping of the entire concession was conducted, supplemented by the collection and analysis of the ceramic material. This project retains parallels with Papazian's and Marouard's work at the Old Kingdom Edfu pyramid (itself part of this Institute's Tell Edfu Project, directed by Nadine Moeller), which is contemporaneous with the Abydos structure and shares multiple features with it. The next phase — and also the urgent focus — of the work at Abydos will consist of safeguarding the site from the ever-expanding agricultural zones that encircle the area and the various ad hoc paths that crisscross it; some fields had already encroached on the archaeological area even prior to this season's work.

Papazian contributed a chapter entitled "The Central Administration of the Resources in the Old Kingdom: Departments, Treasuries, Granaries and Work Centers" for the volume *Ancient Egyptian Administration*, edited by Jaun Carlos Moreno García (Handbuch der Orientalistik I/104. Leiden: Brill, 2013). An article on "The State of Egypt in the Eighth Dynasty" will be published later in the year in the *Journal of Egyptian History*. This study provides new historical perspectives regarding the end of the Old Kingdom and the status of Egyptian kingship in the early phases of the First Intermediate Period; the second installment of that research is forthcoming and will revolve nearly exclusively on the analysis of the inscriptional evidence from the Eighth Dynasty. Separately, he continues work on his next monograph, namely the publication of the Old Kingdom Gebelein papyri.

Robert K. Ritner

During the past academic year **Robert K. Ritner** continued his research on the link between the eruption of the Thera volcano on Santorini and the description of unparalleled climactic events detailed in the "Tempest Stela" of Ahmose, founder of Egypt's Eighteenth Dynasty. In the fall, in conjunction with Nadine Moeller, he submitted to the *Journal of Near Eastern Studies* a manuscript entitled "The Ahmose 'Tempest Stela,' Thera and Comparative Chronology." On December 3, he and Moeller further discussed their results in the lecture "The Ahmose Tempest Stela and the Thera/Santorini Eruption" presented at the international conference Reading Catastrophes: Earthquakes, Famines, Epidemics, Floods, between Egypt and Palestine, 3rd–1st Millennium B.C., sponsored by Rome University "La Sapienza." That report is now in press in Rome as "The Ahmose Tempest Stela: An Egyptian account of a natural catastrophe."

Furthering the theme of chronology, Ritner completed "Egyptian New Kingdom Evidence for the Chronology of Alalakh," to be published in *Alalakh Excavations 2006-2010: The LB II Levels*, edited by K. Aslıhan Yener, Murat Akar, and Mara T. Horowitz (Alalakh Excavations 2. Istanbul: Koç University Press). In association with this work in Turkey, he co-authored with Hasan Peker a catalog, "Hatay Arkeolgi Muzesi —Unprovenienced Seals from the Amuq."

In addition to these studies, Ritner produced a number of publications on Egyptian religion and magic. He completed the proofreading of the new paperback edition of his sold-out volume *The Joseph Smith Egyptian Papyri: A Complete Edition* (Salt Lake City: The Smith Pettit Foundation, 2012). For a forthcoming Festschrift, he produced a study on "The Origin of Evil in Egyptian Theological Speculation." In *Göttinger Miszellen* (236 [2013]: 5–6) he published "Some Errors in a Publication of the Petrie Collection," and "Heka among the Phoenicians" (237 [2013]: 93–95). For the Institute's publication *Iconoclasm and Text Destruction in the Ancient Near East and Beyond*, edited by Natalie Naomi May (Oriental Institute Seminars 8. Chicago: The Oriental Institute, 2012), he published "Killing the Image, Killing the Essence: The Destruction of Text and Figures in Ancient Egyptian Thought, Ritual and 'Ritualized History'" (pp. 395–405). For the Institute's catalog *Between Heaven & Earth: Birds in Ancient Egypt*, edited by Rozenn Bailleul-LeSuer (Oriental Institute Museum Publications 35. Chicago: The Oriental Institute, 2012) he wrote four entries: "Apotropaic Knife," "Thoth Rebus Amulet," "Thoth and Maat Amulet," and "Thoth and Feather Amulet" (pp. 143–46). On a historical, rather than purely religious topic, he wrote "The Statue of Liberty and Its Ties to Egypt," published in the *Oriental Institute News & Notes* (no. 216 [2013]: 13) and online (http://oi.uchicago.edu/pdf/statue_of_liberty_and_its_ties_to_egypt.pdf).

Beyond the talk in Rome noted above, Ritner gave multiple lectures throughout the year. At Akrotiri on the island of Santorini, he provided a keynote address on "Egyptian Examples of the 'Koine' Art Style of the Second Millennium B.C." for the Chrosteres/Paint-Brushes Conference (May 24). For the California Museum of Ancient Art in Los Angeles, he began the annual lecture series with "Magic at the Creation: The Theory and Practice of Egyptian Religious Ritual," followed by a book signing of *The Mechanics of Ancient Egyptian Magical Practice* (April 22). In Chicago, he spoke on "Coptic Magical Texts" for the Summer Papyrological Institute (July 25). He opened the Oriental Institute Mini-Series Medicine and Magic in the Ancient Near East: A Search for the Cure with a lecture on "The Theory and Practice of Medicine and Magic in Ancient Egypt" (October 10). For the Chicago conference Ancient Amulets: Words, Images and Social Contexts, he discussed "'Aggressive Therapy' in Egyptian Amuletic Treatment: Two Case Studies" (February 16). He closed The Oriental Institute Member's Lecture Series with the talk "'Awake in Peace!': Interpreting, Seeking and Combating Dreams in Ancient Egypt" (June 5).

When not writing or lecturing, Ritner taught courses on Middle Egyptian literature, Coptic texts, Demotic texts, and Third Intermediate Period history.

Yorke Rowan

During July–August 2012, **Yorke Rowan** directed the fourth season of excavations at the Chalcolithic (ca. 4500–3600 BC) site in the lower Galilee (see *Marj Rabba* report). As noted in the *2011–2012 Annual Report*, geophysical studies were conducted at Marj Rabba in 2011 by Thomas Urban (Oxford); the initial results of the ground-penetrating radar were presented in *Antiquity* (86/334 [December 2012]; online at http://antiquity.ac.uk/projgall/rowan334). Evidence for extensive architecture supports the survey results indicating that the site extends across the fields to the north and south of the open excavation areas. Yorke presented "Marj Rabba: A Chalcolithic Settlement in the Lower Galilee" (with Kersel, Hill, Price, Shalem, and Jackson) at the annual American School of Oriental Research meetings in Chicago (November 2012).

In the broader context of ancient ritual and the Chalcolithic period in the southern Levant, Yorke published two monograph chapters. One was the published version of his paper, "Sacred Space and Ritual Practice at the End of Prehistory in the Southern Levant" presented at the annual Oriental Institute Seminar, *Heaven on Earth: Temples, Ritual, and Cosmic Symbolism in the Ancient World*, edited by Deena Ragavan, pp. 259–83 (Oriental Institute Seminars 9; Chicago: The Oriental Institute, 2013). The other chapter, "The Subterranean Landscape of the Southern Levant during the Chalcolithic Period," co-authored with David Ilan (Hebrew Union College) and appearing in *Sacred Darkness: A Global Perspective on the Ritual Use of Caves*, edited by Holley Moyes, pp. 87–108 (Boulder: University Press of Colorado, 2013), concerns death and the use of underground space during the Chalcolithic period. At the annual meetings of the Archaeological Institute of America, he presented "Evidence for South Levantine Long-distance Interactions during the Fourth Millennium B.C.E."

The Eastern Badia Project, co-directed with Gary Rollefson (Whitman College), continued survey and excavation work around the black-topped mesa known as Maitland's Mesa (M-4). This included excavation of a structure, previously posited to be similar to a *nawamis* — fourth-millennium BC tombs known from the Sinai. Rather than a mortuary structure, this was apparently for habitation. The corbelled building, constructed of massive basalt slabs and modified at least twice, dates to the Late Neolithic and was published in *Neo-Lithics* (1/12 [2013]), "A 7th Millennium B.C. Late Neolithic Village at Mesa 4 in the Wadi al-Qattafi, Eastern Jordan," with Wasse and Rollefson. Both Eastern Badia projects (Maitland's Mesa and Wisad Pools) were summarized in "Archaeology of Jordan" in the *American Journal of Archaeology* (116/4 [2012]: 711–13). In "Archaeology at the Margins," a session Yorke organized with Jaimie Lovell for the World Archaeology Congress in Jordan (2013), he presented (with Rollefson and Wasse) "Little Houses on the Prairie: Jordan's Eastern Badia in the Late 7th Millennium B.C."

In the journal *Heritage and Society* (5/2 [2012]: 199–220), Yorke published with Morag Kersel (DePaul) "Beautiful, Good, Important and Special: Cultural Heritage, Archaeology, Tourism and the Miniature in the Holy Land," a study of Mini-Israel, a theme park in Israel. Yorke also published reviews of two books; one of *Socio-Economic Aspects of Chalcolithic (4500–3500 B.C.) Societies in the Southern Levant: A Lithic Perspective* by Sorin Hermon (BAR International Series

1744; Oxford: Archaeopress, 2008) in the *Bulletin of the American Schools of Oriental Research* (365 [2012]: 82–84); and the other, for the *Journal of the Economic and Social History of the Orient* (56 [2013]: 107–10) of *Metals, Nomads and Culture Contact: The Middle East and North Africa* (London: Equinox, 2010) by Nils Anfinset.

Seth Sanders

This year's research by **Seth Sanders** for the West Semitic Political Lexicon project produced two conference presentations, two articles accepted for publication, and plans for a conference to be published in the *Journal of Ancient Near Eastern Religions*.

The project's investigation of the historical development of ways of talking and thinking about politics in West Semitic languages such as Amorite, Ugaritic, Phoenician, and Hebrew led to "Naming the Dead: State Formation and Ancestor Formation in the Iron Age Levant" and "How Did Biblical Literature Begin? Epigraphy, Theory and Anachronism," both given at the Chicago Society of Biblical Literature meeting in November. Written versions were accepted as "Naming the Dead: Monumental Writing and Mortuary Politics in Late Iron Age Anatolia and Judah" in *Maarav* and "What Epigraphy Tells Us about Reading Biblical Narrative: The Audience and Politics of Absalom's Stand" in *Literacy and Orality in Ancient Israel*, edited by Brian Schmidt.

A colloquium, planned for the American Oriental Society and a special issue of the *Journal of Ancient Near Eastern Religion*, on "Myths of Justice in the Ancient Mediterranean World" will examine some historical foundations and developments of myth in politics. A West Semitic myth in the second-millennium BC connects the king's role as victorious cosmic warrior to his role as just judge. This myth shaped political concepts of the Hebrew Bible, where God wins sovereignty by defeating Leviathan only to have his own justice questioned, leaving a powerful political legacy for the West. Related topics covered will include Hammurapi's endowment by Shamash: the myth and politics of debt-relief; incantations, divination and judgment by the divine court in Mesopotamian ritual and scholarship; Herodotus' parody of the foundations of the Median empire; and the divine witnesses and sanctions in the plague-prayer of Mursili.

Oğuz Soysal

Oğuz Soysal continued his job with the Chicago Hittite Dictionary (CHD) Project. Much of his time was spent preparing the transliterations of the recent cuneiform editions, *Keilschrifttexte aus Boğazköi* volumes 51, 55, 56, 58, and 60 for the CHD files. He made also the Turkish translation for the electronic CHD (*eCHD*) covering the words *šaptamenzu-* to *-ši-*, which were already published in CHD Š, fascicle 2.

As a personal study Soysal published in the Turkish journal *Colloquium Anatolicum* (11 [2012]: 309–46) an article on the Middle Hittite History, "Kantuzzili: A Regent for Tutḫaliya 'the Younger'?"

In addition, Soysal continued in 2012–2013 his new project involving the unpublished Hittite texts bearing the siglum "Bo," which were transferred from the Staatliches Museum in Berlin to the Museum of Ancient Anatolian Civilizations in Ankara in 1987. As part of his duties in the CHD Project, he prepared transliterations of 170 cuneiform fragments from the range between Bo 9536 and Bo 9736, whereby he noticed a number of joins and duplicates of some important Hittite compositions. The first results are now found online at the *Konkordanz der hethitischen Keilschrifttafeln* (http://www.hethport.uni-wuerzburg.de/hetkonk/) under their relevant text categories; a related article "Joins, Duplicates, and More from the Unpublished Bo 9000-fragments" appeared in the Dutch journal *Anatolica* (38 [2012]: 169–90). The pictures, transliterations, and other textual treatments of the entire material are now ready for the monograph entitled *Unpublished Bo-Fragments in Transliteration (Bo 9536–Bo 9736)*, an upcoming volume of the series Chicago Hittite Dictionary Supplements.

After an agreement with Ms. Başak Yıldız, the curator in the Museum of Ancient Anatolian Civilizations in Ankara, Soysal started in December 2012 to take digital pictures of another group of tablets. These 170 fragments are in the number range from Bo 8695 to Bo 9535 and are being considered for another volume of *Unpublished Bo-fragments in Transliteration* under co-authorship with Ms. Yıldız.

Foy Scalf

On November 17, 2012, **Foy Scalf** presented a paper with Helen McDonald on the Oriental Institute Integrated Database Project at the annual meeting of the American Schools of Oriental Research in Chicago. The panel was organized around the theme of "Topics in Cyberinfrastructure, Digital Humanities, and Near Eastern Archaeology." In addition to hosting a forum for a number of interesting papers, the occasion brought together Magnus Widell, Chuck Jones, and Foy Scalf, the successive librarians for the Oriental Institute for the past thirty years! Foy gave another presentation on the Integrated Database to an enthusiastic delegation from the University of Michigan on May 17, 2013, who visited the Oriental Institute in preparation for their own database migration in the near future.

Despite the time commitments related to work on the Integrated Database Project for the Research Archives, he found time to dedicate toward his research interests in Demotic studies. He has joined Friedhelm Hoffmann, Franziska Naether, and Ghislaine Widmer in compiling the *Demotistische Literaturübersicht*, a biannual annotated bibliography of all work conducted in the field of Demotic studies. *Demotistische Literaturübersicht* 33 was completed in February 2013 and will appear in the next issue of the journal *Enchoria*. In addition, he presented several papers and publications during the course of the year on matters of religion in Late Period Egypt.

At the invitation of guest curator Rozenn Bailleul-LeSuer, Foy presented a paper on "The Organization of the Sacred Animal Cults for the Ibis and the Falcon in Ancient Egypt" for the Birds in Ancient Egypt symposium on November 10, 2012, at the Oriental Institute. That lecture presented an overview of the information found in his chapter "The Role of Birds across the Religious Landscape of Ancient Egypt" that appeared in the Oriental Institute's special exhibit catalog *Between Heaven & Earth: Birds in Ancient Egypt*, edited by Rozenn Bailleul-LeSuer (Oriental Institute Museum Publications 35; Chicago: The Oriental Institute, 2012). He also authored several object entries for the catalog, including an interesting *ba*-statue showing the deceased with falcon body and human head. He and Rozenn plan to co-author an article on the *ba*-statues in the Oriental Institute Museum and compare them with the currently known corpus in the published literature.

In April, Chicago hosted the sixty-fourth annual meeting of the American Research Center in Egypt, where Foy gave a paper based on research from his dissertation entitled "A Reception before Osiris: Illustrating Demotic Funerary Texts." In this paper, he argued that the variation found in the illustrations and texts of a certain class of Demotic funerary manuscripts suggest that they were at times composed from memory, rather than copied in a scriptorium as often supposed. A more detailed account of the philology on which this argument is based will be presented at the upcoming meeting of the American Philological Association.

Gil J. Stein

Gil Stein continued with the work toward publication of his 1992–1997 excavations at the fourth-millennium BC Uruk Mesopotamian colony site of Hacınebi. Working with Dr. Belinda Monahan, the work on the publication of the Late Chalcolithic ceramics from the site has progressed greatly. All the plates have been completed, as have drafts of six chapters of this volume. We hope that the manuscript will be completed and ready for review by the Oriental Institute Publications Department by the end of the coming 2013/14 academic year.

As principal investigator of the Oriental Institute's partnership with the National Museum of Afghanistan (see report in this volume), Gil and Oriental Institute executive director Steve Camp made four trips in 2012–2013 to Afghanistan to assess project progress, coordinate with the National Museum director Dr. Omara Khan Masoudi, and deliver supplies to field director Mike Fisher and the Kabul team of registrars, conservators, and consultants.

Gil traveled to the Kurdistan region of northern Iraq in August 2012 and again in May 2013 to investigate the possibility of starting a new Oriental Institute field project focused on the Late Chalcolithic period in this upland area east of the Tigris River. On the 2012 trip, Gil and Dr. Abbas Alizadeh visited potential sites for excavation and examined survey collections in Dohuk, Suleimaniya, and Erbil provinces (fig. 1). Iraqi Kurdistan has a special resonance for the Oriental Institute since it was here, in Suleimaniya province, that Robert and Linda Braidwood conducted their pioneering excavations at the early Neolithic site of Jarmo from 1948 to 1955. It was a wonderful experience to be able to present Kamal Rashid, the director of antiquities for Suleimaniya province, with the Oriental Institute Publication of the Braidwoods' final report on the Jarmo excavations.

Gil and Abbas also visited sites in Erbil province. This area is best known for the city of Erbil, whose citadel sits on top of the massive mound of the ancient urban center of Arbela (fig. 2). The broad Erbil plain is dotted with numerous mounds and remnants of ancient irrigation systems from Assyrian canals to Achaemenid qanats. Surface ceramics at the 46-hectare site of Surezha, about 20 kilometers south of Erbil, showed that this site had a significant occupation in the fifth–fourth millennium BC Ubaid and Late Chalcolithic 1–2 periods (fig. 3). On this basis, Gil applied for an excavation permit, and plans to start a five-year program of excavation at the site in late summer 2013, co-directed with Abbas Alizadeh.

Figure 1. Gil and Abbas examining Chalcolithic ceramics from site collections in the Suleimaniya Museum, Kurdistan region, Iraq

Figure 2. The citadel of Erbil sits at the top of the massive ancient mound of Arbela and towers over the modern city. The citadel is currently the focus of a major program of preservation and architectural restoration

Figure 3. Fifth-millennium BC Ubaid painted ceramics from surface collections at the 46 ha site of Surezha, 20 km south of Erbil

Gil has given several lectures and presentations during the past year. In February 2013 he presented the keynote lecture "Political Landscapes of Distribution: Power Relations and the Circulation of Value in Ancient Complex Societies" at the University of Michigan Collaborative Archaeology Workgroup's conference Movement in Ancient Economies: Archaeological Approaches to Distribution. On April 16, 2013, he presented a paper on "Cultural Heritage Preservation in Afghanistan Ten Years after the Looting of the National Museum in Baghdad" at the Oriental Institute's Seminar Catastrophe! Ten Years Later: Looting, Destruction, and Preservation of Cultural Heritage in Iraq and the Wider Middle East. On April 25, Gil presented an invited paper, "The Mesopotamian Presence at Hacınebi, Southeast Turkey, and Variation in Modes of Interaction in the Uruk Expansion," in Berlin at the eighth international colloquium of the German Oriental Society, titled Uruk – Ancient Near Eastern Metropolis and Cultural Center.

Gil also published the article "The Development of Indigenous Social Complexity in Late Chalcolithic Upper Mesopotamia in the 5th–4th Millennia BC – An Initial Assessment" in the journal Origini 24 (new series 5): 115–42.

Matthew W. Stolper

In addition to research as part of the Persepolis Fortification Archive Project (described elsewhere in this Annual Report), **Matthew W. Stolper** submitted an article on "Elamite Sources" to A Companion to the Achaemenid Empire, edited by Bruno Jacobs and Robert Rollinger for Wiley-Blackwell; "Three Personal Reflections on Elias Bickerman" to a collection of articles accompanying the publication of the annual Rostovtzeff Lecture that Pierre Briant delivered at Yale in 2011, now being edited by J. G. Manning for publication by Yale Classical Studies; and a revised essay on the Oriental Institute's Persian Expedition of 1931–1939 for a volume on Iranian Studies in America, being edited by Frank Lewis for Eisenbrauns. His paper at the annual meeting of the American Schools of Oriental Research, given jointly with Annalisa Azzoni, dealt with the typology of Aramaic epigraphs on Elamite Persepolis Fortification documents. His paper at the American Oriental Society, "Atossa Re-enters," dealt with new evidence for the presence and status of the Achaemenid queen Atossa, extravagantly prominent in literary works by Aeschylus, Herodotus, and Gore Vidal, but hitherto elusive in the quotidian records of the Persepolis Fortification Archive.

Emily Teeter

When not working on museum special exhibits, **Emily Teeter** continues to do research on objects in the collection of the Oriental Institute Museum. She gave a paper on an embalming cache at the annual meeting of the American Research Center in Egypt, and she is finalizing an article on a stela from Deir el Medina excavated at Medinet Habu. She has resumed the publication project of the Institute's Ptolemaic water clock in collaboration with Marv Bolt of the Adler Planetarium, and she continues to work on finalizing a project of source readings on ancient Egyptian religion.

Emily gave a number of talks in the last year, many of them to chapters of the American Research Center on Egypt (ARCE) in Phoenix, Seattle, Dallas, and Berkeley, and also to the Egypt Exploration Organization of Southern California. In Dallas, she also conducted a full-day seminar on Egyptian architecture. She also spoke on Egyptian religion at the Field Museum, on temple musicians for the Heritage Foundation of the Chrysler Museum in Norfolk, on the birth of consumerism to the South Suburban Archaeological Society, and she presented a Harper Lecture on popular religion in ancient Egypt to University of Chicago alumni in Dallas.

Emily attended several board meetings of ARCE. In April she rotated off the Board, having served in several capacities for the last fifteen years. In April, she attended a board meeting of the Council of Overseas Research Centers (CAORC) as the representative for ARCE. In January, she took part in a video-conference of American museum professions throughout the US with the director of the Grand Museum Project, Cairo, to discuss current issues in the museum world.

Publications for the year include book reviews in the *Journal of Near Eastern Studies* and *KMT: A Modern Journal of Ancient Egypt*, as well as a catalog entry on our mummy of Meresamun that was published by the National Museum in Prague. She also served as an editor for part of the Proceedings of the International Committee of Egyptology (CIPEG/ICOM).

In the fall, Emily was part of a lecture team for an Oriental Institute trip to Egypt, Jordan, and Lebanon.

Theo van den Hout

Last year was the first of **Theo van den Hout**'s second term as chair of the Department of Near Eastern Languages and Civilizations (NELC). This meant very little time for his own research besides the work on the Chicago Hittite Dictionary (CHD; see separate report). Theo was invited to Johns Hopkins University in October and talked about "Scribes and Scholars at Hattusa." In November 2012 he presented at an interdisciplinary symposium on Scale Models, organized by the University of Chicago and Northwestern University. He read a paper on "Kingship and the Hittite Royal Funerary Ritual" at the annual meeting of the Society of Biblical Literature in Chicago in December, and gave two talks at Brown University in April 2013.

Theo submitted for publication a brief history of Dutch Hittitology for a volume (in Dutch) to celebrate the seventy-fifth anniversary of the Nederlands Instituut voor het Nabije Oosten (NINO, Dutch Institute for the Near East) in Leiden, an obituary of his former adviser Philo Houwink ten Cate for the *Archiv für Orientforschung*, and an article for the catalog of the upcoming Oriental Institute special exhibit on the Zincirli excavations.

Since the previous *Annual Report* the following publications appeared in print: "Administration and Writing in Hittite Society," *Archivi, depositi, magazzini presso gli ittiti. Nuovi materiali e nuove ricerche/Archives, Depots and Storehouses in the Hittite World. New Evidence and New Research*, edited by M. E. Balza, M. Giorgieri, and C. Mora, pp. 41–58 (Studia Mediterranea 23; Genova: Italian University Press, 2012); an article in Japanese on the first centenary of Hittitology as a discipline in the *Journal of the Faculty of Letters. History* (Tokyo: Chuo University 58 [2013/03]: 41–64); three entries in the *Reallexikon der Assyriologie* 13 (2011 ff.): 426, 426–27, and 460–63; as well as two reviews in the *Zeitschrift für Assyriologie* 102 (2012): 344–47 and 350–53.

Tasha Vorderstrasse

In the academic year 2012–2013 **Tasha Vorderstrasse** continued to work as a research associate on the catalog of Islamic archaeology at the Oriental Institute Museum as well as on a publication of highlights of the Islamic collection. As a result of this work, she was able to re-discover important material in the Oriental Institute Museum collections, including some fragments that are supposed to be from the medieval Cairo Genizah that had been bought by the museum in the 1930s. In addition to her work in the museum, she spent two weeks in Jerusalem at the Rockefeller Museum working on the inscribed marble objects from the 1930s–1940s excavations at Khirbet al-Mafjar that have never been thoroughly studied. Thanks are due to Ms. Alegre Savariego at the Rockefeller for assisting this work, and the Oriental Institute and the Palestine Exploration Fund for providing financial assistance. She also continued her work on Chinese sources for the Balkh Art and Cultural Heirtage Project (BACH).

Vorderstrasse also gave a variety of lectures, including two at the 2012 annual meeting of the American Society of Oriental Research in November: "Chinese Material Culture from Moščevaja Balka in the North Caucasus," and "Reconstructing a Medieval Tomb at Antioch." The second lecture has been submitted as a pre-conference paper to a symposium at the University of Balamand. An expanded version of the first paper was given at the Late Antique and Byzantine Studies Workshop at the University of Chicago "Texts, Textiles, and Trade in the North Caucasus." She presented two lectures at the University of Chicago Armenian Circle: "Excavating at the Medieval City of Dvin in Armenia" and "Armenians and Armenian Material Culture in Jerusalem" in November and April respectively. In December she gave a lecture at DACOR (Diplomatic and Consular Office Retired) in Washington, DC: "Beyond the Gold: Interpreting the Site of Tillya Tepe in Afghanistan." In January she gave a lecture on "Re-Discovering Alan Wace's Excavations at Alexandria" for the American Research Center in Egypt (ARCE) Chicago chapter, and in April she also participated in the Household Archaeology Oriental Institute mini-series, giving a talk "Reconstructing Houses and Archives in Early Islamic Egypt." In May she presented as part of Connecting with the Caucasus Speaker Series: "Medieval Wall Paintings of Georgia: Iconography of Patronage" by the Center for East European and Russian/Eurasian Studies (CEERES).

She submitted an article "An Overview of the Medieval Pottery from the Antiochene Region Excavated by Mécérian" to the *Mélanges de Université de Saint-Joseph*, and the following articles appeared in print: "Descriptions of the Pharos of Alexandria in Islamic and Chinese Sources: Collective Memory and Textual Transmission," in *The Lineaments of Islam: Studies in Honor of Fred McGraw Donner*, edited by P. M. Cobb, pp. 457–81 (Leiden: Brill, 2012); "Coinage and the Monetary Economy in 7th Century Nubia," in *Arab-Byzantine Coins and History*, edited by T. Goodwin, pp. 169–81 (London: Archetype, 2012); "Medieval Encounters between China, Mongolia, Antioch, and Cilicia," in *East and West in the Medieval Eastern Mediterranean*, Vol. 2: *Antioch from the Byzantine Reconquest until the End of the Crusader Principality* (acts of the congress held at Hernen Castle (the Netherlands) in May 2006), edited by K. Ciggaar and V. van Aalst, pp. 345–66 (Orientalia Lovaniensia Analecta 199; Leuven: Peeters, 2013).

John Z. Wee

John Z. Wee took up his appointment as a Provost's Postdoctoral Scholar and Lecturer in the Department of Near Eastern Languages and Civilizations (NELC) on August 1, 2012. At the Oriental Institute's fall 2012 mini-series on Medicine and Magic in the Ancient World: A Search for the Cure, he presented a lecture on "Mesopotamian Texts and the Knowledge Assumptions of Medical Diagnosis" and participated in the joint panel discussion (October 27, 2012). He is also organizing an international and interdisciplinary symposium on "The Body in Ancient Medicine" (Oriental Institute, May 2–4, 2014), papers from which will be published as a symposium volume (Oriental Institute Seminars). The symposium has already received wide support from co-sponsors such as the Oriental Institute, the Center for the Study of Ancient Religions, the Morris Fishbein Center, the Committee on Conceptual and Historical Studies of Science, Dean Martha Roth of the Humanities Division, and the departments of Classics and NELC. Additional funding from the Franke Institute for the Humanities is currently under consideration.

John has been revising his 2012 dissertation (Yale University) for publication as two separate books. Brill Academic Press has already accepted one book (*Knowledge and Rhetoric in Medical Commentary: Mesopotamian Commentaries on the Diagnostic Series Sa-gig*) for publication in its Culture and History of the Ancient Near East (CHANE) series. Another book (*Medical Diagnosis in Ancient Iraq*) is still under revision and review, but should be released in 2014 or 2015. John's article on "Lugalbanda Under the Night Sky: Scenes of Celestial Healing in Ancient Mesopotamia" will be published in the April 2014 issue of the *Journal of Near Eastern Studies*. From June 29 to July 1, 2012, he participated in a Classics conference on *HOMO PATIENS: Approaches to the Patient in the Ancient World* (Berlin), and his paper on "Case History as Minority Report in the Hippocratic Epidemics I" is forthcoming in Brill's Studies in Ancient Medicine (SAM) series. Another article entitled "Grieving with the Moon: Pantheon and Politics in the Lunar Eclipse" is being reviewed at the *Journal of Ancient Near Eastern Religions*.

At the 223rd meeting of the American Oriental Society (Portland, March 15–18, 2013), John was part of a panel on Empiricism in Mesopotamian Technical Literature and presented a paper on "Medical Signs as Signs: The Immediacy of Experience in the Diagnostic Series Sa-gig." Since the contents of this paper were already to be published in his books, he agreed to contribute another essay to the forthcoming conference volume. John will speak on "Measurements in Babylonian Drawings of Planets and Star Constellations" at the twenty-fourth international congress of History of Science, Technology and Medicine (Manchester, July

22–28, 2013). This presentation builds on an earlier paper presented as a Brown-bag Lunch Talk at the Oriental Institute on January 30, 2013, and it represents John's ongoing research on the micro-zodiac. For his participation in the congress, he received grant assistance from the European Research Council.

John is working with Professor Eckart Frahm from Yale University on a digital project that aims to publish searchable cuneiform editions and translations of commentaries online. John is responsible for commentaries on the Diagnostic Series Sa-gig, which he edited as part of his 2012 dissertation. From June to August 2013 he will be at the British Museum archives working on cuneiform tablets and fragments of *Enūma Anu Enlil* astrological commentaries.

Donald Whitcomb

The academic year began for **Donald Whitcomb** with teaching a very stimulating seminar on Islamic Pottery as Historical Evidence, with students interested in the new discoveries and interpretations from our Khirbet al-Mafjar excavations, balanced by two young archaeologists preparing a corpus of Islamic pottery from Armenia. I was invited to present the Mafjar discoveries to the biennial symposium of the Historians of Islamic Art Association in New York.

In early January, we arrived in Jerusalem during a heavy snowfall, more than we had experienced in Chicago. We descended into the Jordan valley to Jericho, where they had endured heavy rain. Once again our luck held and we lost only two days to rain in the next six weeks. Our third season of excavations for the Jericho Mafjar Project began with some noise; a bulldozer and three large trucks removed the massive mounds of the 1960s excavations and we had literally a new site to dig. The direction of this season was more interesting with the presence of seven Palestinian students, as described in the Jericho Mafjar Project report in this volume. Once again we enjoyed the assistance of Silvia Krapiwko and Alegre Savariego in the Rockefeller Museum in Jerusalem, and as a final treat, we toured similar sites of Sinnabra (Khirbet Karak), Khirbet al-Minya, and Tiberias with Tawfiq Daʾadli, an archaeologist from Jerusalem who also worked with us. In the meantime, I co-wrote an article with Hamdan Taha, "Khirbet al-Mafjar and Its Place in the Archaeological Heritage of Palestine," which appears in the *Journal of Eastern Mediterranean Archaeology and Heritage Studies* 1 (2013): 54–65. The article may be downloaded from the "news" on our website (www.jerichomafjarproject. org), with the permission of the Pennsylvania State University Press.

I returned to Chicago just in time for the Oriental Institute Seminar on Household Archaeology, where I chaired some sessions but really wanted to discuss our Abbasid House at Mafjar. For Spring quarter I offered the course Introduction to Islamic Archaeology, in which I changed the content with new sites and information reflecting the rapid progression of this field. During this time, I slipped away to New York City again, this time to chair a session for the conference on The Archaeology of Sasanian Politics, held at the Institute for the Study of the Ancient World at New York University. One of its unexpected pleasures was meeting an Italian archaeologist working on the Islamic city of Istakhr near Persepolis. She reports that my hypothesis on building behind the mosque has proven correct (it's nice to be right after so many years).

The end of the year saw the completion of Tanya Treptow's dissertation on the development of Islamic archaeology in Egypt. She focuses on the excavations at Fustat, then known as Old Cairo, and has inspired a brief report in the archaeology of Islamic cities in this volume. The celebrations for Tanya were soon followed by the sad news of the death of

Constantine Baramki, the son of the first excavator at Mafjar, whom we visited last year. I am pleased that plans are underway to renew the Hisham's Palace Museum, which means we will install a new panel testifying to Dimitri Baramki's remarkable discovery and his understanding of Qasr Hisham in the 1930s.

Karen L. Wilson

Karen Wilson's book *Bismaya: Recovering the Lost City of Adab* (Oriental Institute Publications 138; Chicago: The Oriental Institute, 2012), arrived at the Institute in July of 2012. This report chronicles the history and presents the results of the University of Chicago's first expedition to Iraq in 1903–1905.

During the past year, Karen continued to work on the final publication of the Oriental Institute excavation of the Inanna temple at the site of Nippur in Iraq during the late 1950s and early 1960s. This project is a joint endeavor undertaken with Robert Biggs, Jean Evans, McGuire Gibson (University of Chicago), and Richard Zettler (University of Pennsylvania). The project has included the preparation of a digital catalog of finds linked with images of the objects plus the scanning of all negatives and drawings as well as the field records generated by work on the site. Michael K. Hannan, of Hannan Architecture and Planning, has prepared final architectural plans for the Inanna temple levels at Nippur using AutoCAD, Angela Altenhoffen has produced final inked drawings of the sealings, and Steven George digitized the drawings of stone vessels. Karen was awarded a fellowship by TAARII (The American Academic Research Institute in Iraq) to support her research on Nippur during the summer of 2012. She is pleased to report that the manuscript for the final publication of the Inanna temple excavations was given to Mac Gibson on May 31, 2013, for review.

Karen also continued to serve as Kish Project Coordinator at the Field Museum, preparing the final publication of the results of the Joint Field Museum and Oxford University Expedition to Kish in 1923–1933. She is extremely pleased that the Oriental Institute Publications Committee has agreed to publish the manuscript as a volume in the Oriental Institute Publications series. The work will include papers presented at a symposium in November 2008 focusing on current research and updated excavations at the site. Contributions include studies of the human remains, textual evidence, lithics, animal figurines, and stucco as well as a catalog of the Field Museum holdings from Kish and Jamdat Nasr.

Karen's manuscript "Ancient Mesopotamia: Highlights from the Collections of the Oriental Institute, University of Chicago," is in progress and, when published, will serve as the gallery guide to the Edgar and Deborah Jannotta Mesopotamian Gallery. It will also provide a much-needed general book that will introduce the reader to the history and culture of ancient Mesopotamia.

Christopher Woods

Chris Woods devoted much of this past year to implementing the Writing in Early Mesopotamia project, continuing work on the proto-literate accounting devices (token envelopes — for details, see *Oriental Institute News & Notes*, no. 215, Fall 2012), completing several publications, and continuing work on long-term projects.

Dr. Massimo Maiocchi joined the Oriental Institute this year as a two-year post-doctoral fellow in connection with the Writing in Early Mesopotamia project. Massimo's position was made possible through a Mellon Foundation grant we were fortunate to win last year through a Humanities- and Social Sciences-wide competition. As detailed in the Writing in Early Mesopotamia project report (see separate report), our efforts this year have focused on designing a database that will facilitate the study of Sumerian writing by capturing and categorizing orthographic variation, and allowing for complex queries. Our work has also centered upon collecting, inputting, and morphologically parsing texts for inclusion in the database. As part of the Mellon fellowship, Chris and Massimo co-taught a course this year on writing systems and decipherments for graduate and undergraduate students.

Complementing the Writing in Early Mesopotamia project, Chris, in collaboration with Edward Shaughnessy (East Asian Languages and Civilizations), launched a new interdisciplinary effort concerned with early writing, Signs of Writing: The Cultural, Social, and Linguistic Contexts of the World's First Writing Systems. The project represents our successful application to the Neubauer Collegium for Culture and Society; Signs of Writing is one of four inaugural large-scale, three-year projects sponsored by the Neubauer Collegium. Signs of Writing is a three-year research project designed to investigate, from a comparative and interdisciplinary perspective, the cultural and social contexts and structural properties of the world's oldest writing. Particular emphasis is placed on the four primary, or pristine, writing systems from Mesopotamia, China, Egypt, and Mesoamerica, looking at the similarities and differences in the archaeological and paleographic records across regions and the psycho-linguistic processes by which humans first made language visible. Annual conferences and short- and long-term visiting scholars will integrate research from a wide range of disciplines — the over-arching goal of which is to make the University of Chicago an international center for the study of early writing. Organized broadly around the linguistic, social, and cultural contexts of early written language, the project will concern itself with a broad range of topics, including the origins and structures of writing systems, the relationship between speech and writing, reading and cognition, the adaptation of writing systems and bilingualism, scribal transmission and education, literacy, the materiality and archaeological contexts of writing, and the rise of written genres.

Chris gave talks on proto-literate administrative devices at the American Schools of Oriental Research meeting in November 2012, which took place in Chicago, and at the American Oriental Society meeting in Portland, Oregon, in March. In December he spoke on "Gilgamesh in Ancient and Modern Context" at the Smithsonian (Washington, DC) for the Iraqi Cultural Center of the Iraqi Diplomatic Mission. Chris also presented on the origins of writing in typological perspective at invited lectures at the University of Pennsylvania in October and at Cornell University in March. The summer of 2013 included a research trip to the Schøyen collection outside of Oslo, Norway, to document the important collection of proto-literate clay envelopes and tokens; these artifacts, which nicely complement those from Chogha Mish in the Oriental Institute's collection, will be published in the CUSAS series. Chris's articles "Mutilation of Text and Image in Sumerian Sources," "Grammar and Context: Enki & Ninhursag ll. 1–3 and a Rare Sumerian Construction," and "Relative Clauses at Garshana" were published this year. Chris continues to edit the *Journal of Near Eastern Studies* and to oversee the Oriental Institute's Post-doctoral Scholars program, which was expanded this year to include two post-docs serving staggered, two-year appointments.

RESEARCH SUPPORT

COMPUTER LABORATORY

John C. Sanders

Two eventualities occurred this past year: (1) the first phase of the Institute's Integrated Database (IDB) was completed and made available via the Institute's website; and (2) I retired at the end of March, forty years after arriving at the Oriental Institute to be the surveyor, field architect, and cartographer for the Nippur Expedition!

I retire from my position with many memories and friendships, but with sadness because I will no longer be directly involved in future Institute endeavors. I pass the IT torch to Paul Ruffin, whose multiple talents in the realm of computing are more than capable of not only continuing what I started but, more importantly, Paul can shepherd the Institute through the next steps in its Information Technology (IT) growth.

Projects

Integrated Database

My work with McGuire Gibson at Nippur and other Mesopotamian archaeological sites continued until July of 1990, when my role changed to IT and computer support for the entire Institute. After one month in my new position, I convened a meeting of all faculty and staff. I suggested that the Institute needed to computerize and integrate the various paper-based recording systems that each separate unit of the Institute maintained on their own (for example, the Museum, Education, Conservation, Research Archives). The idea was well received at the time, but other Institute priorities and developments delayed this eventuality until this past February 1, 2013, when the Oriental Institute's Integrated Database came online, providing scholars, students, and the general public with access to the Institute's Museum Registration and Library catalog records.

I am proud to have played a part in the development of this vital research tool for ancient Near Eastern studies, along with a large list of dedicated Oriental Institute staff members and programmers from the University's Web Services division who, over the past decade, contributed to the launch of the IDB (I acknowledged by name many of these individuals in last year's Computer Laboratory *Annual Report*). At the present time only the earliest stage of the IDB has been completed. Several phases of development remain in order for the IDB to reach all of its intended goals, such as the addition of Museum Conservation records, Museum photographic archives, map collections from the CAMEL Laboratory, several specific archaeological field project records, and the Museum archives. These eventualities will come to pass over the next few years.

Electronic Publications Initiative

The Institute's Electronic Publications Initiative has been virtually completed; the Initiative was our decade-long effort to electronically reproduce all the Institute's past print publications and newsletters. With this year's addition of 123 Oriental Institute publications, *News & Notes* volumes 1–159, along with the most recent additions for Fall 2012 and Winter 2013, and thirty-one Oriental Institute *Annual Reports* going back to the first issue in 1928, the backlog has been cleared and the entire Publications Office catalog is now available for free download in the Adobe Portable Document Format (PDF) from the Institute's website. I congratulate Tom Urban, Leslie Schramer, and the entire Publications Office staff for their tremendous efforts to complete this monumental task. A job well done!

I encourage everyone to read that portion of the Publications Office section of this *Annual Report* regarding the status of the Institute's Electronic Publications Initiative, then visit the Catalog of Publications page on our website where you will be able to download these past and current titles of our publications in electronic form:

http://oi.uchicago.edu/research/pubs/catalog/

The Oriental Institute Website

The Epigraphic Survey added several updates to the project's homepage with notes, photographs, and a significant amount of information about the work from their latest field season that ended in April 2013. Additionally, the July 2012 edition of the *Chicago House Bulletin* is now available for download in PDF format. Information regarding another Egyptian research project, the new Mummy Label Database (MLD) project, is now available on the Institute's website.

Information regarding three Museum exhibits were added: Between Heaven & Earth: Birds In Ancient Egypt, on view from October 16, 2012, to July 28, 2013, was the first American exhibit devoted to birds in the Nile valley. The exhibit explored the impact that birds had on ancient Egyptian religion, design, and the conception of the state; Danh Vo's We the People, which juxtaposes ancient and contemporary art, was a special exhibit at the Oriental Institute Museum from September 11, 2012, to December 16, 2012; another Museum special exhibit, Catastrophe! Ten Years Later: The Looting and Destruction of Iraq's Past, revisited and updated a selection of the panels from the original show first displayed at the Oriental Institute in 2008. Additionally, the Mission Statement of the Oriental Institute Museum and the Department of Public Education and Outreach is now available on the Institute's website

Details about the 2013 Oriental Institute Seminar, Household Studies in Complex Societies, (Micro) Archaeological and Textual Approaches," which took place March 15–16, 2013, were added to the website, and a poster of the event is available for download as a PDF.

The Research Archives added the May 2012 through May 2013 Acquisitions Lists to the website, and the Oriental Institute's *2011–2012 Annual Report* was converted to PDF by the Publications Office and added to the website.

An itinerary for the Membership Office's fall 2013 travel program, to accompany Oriental Institute assistant professor of Egyptian archaeology Nadine Moeller on her tour to "Egypt's Oases: A Journey through the Western Desert," November 22–December 9, 2013, is on the Institute's website. A not-to-be-missed opportunity for all Egyptophiles!

And lastly, several Institute scholars added content to their sections of the Individual Scholarship component of the website: one article by François Gaudard; three articles by

Norman Golb; two articles by Robert Ritner; and two articles Foy Scalf. All these resources are now available as PDFs.

*　*　*

For further information concerning the above-mentioned research projects and other electronic resources in general, refer to the "What's New" page on the Oriental Institute's website, at

http://oi.uchicago.edu/news/

Paul D. Ruffin

I am proud to have taken the position of IT support specialist for the Oriental Institute. John Sanders has done outstanding work for the Oriental Institute and can never be replaced. I originally started my IT career by working at the Apple Store as a mobile technician and a teacher. I use to provide workshops, classes, and repair sessions for multiple customers. Later in my career, I was offered a position at Innerworkings as a helpdesk technician. I have provided end-user support for over 800 users throughout the North American region and was in charge of handling IT support for the sales division. As the new IT support specialist for the Oriental Institute, I will continue to expand the technological growth that is needed for the organization. Throughout this year, I will meet with our faculty and staff to discuss what the needs and concerns are for the upcoming year and create solutions to fit those needs. I also look forward to learning more about the superb research that is done on ancient Near Eastern civilizations.

Windows 7 Migration

Recently, Microsoft announced it will no longer support Windows XP. Due to the high number of viruses, malware, and various other online threats, I have initiated a system upgrade to many of the Windows users. The goal is to have the Windows 7 system upgrade completed by the end of the summer. Windows 7 will provide enhanced security and performance.

Cisco VoIP Phone System Upgrade

The Oriental Institute will have a new phone system installed during the fall of 2013. We will convert our old PBX systems to Cisco VoIP. VoIP means Voice over Internet Protocol, which signifies a phone that is powered through the Internet. One of the major advantages to having a VoIP is lowered phone costs. Another great feature is the new voice to e-mail functionality. Oriental Institute faculty and staff will now be able to receive voicemails in their e-mail inbox. This feature also allows users to check voicemail outside of their office as long as there is access to e-mail.

Solarwinds Web Help Desk

The Oriental Institute will have its first ticketing system called Web Help Desk. This program is provided by Solarwinds, a renowned IT services company. Web Help Desk is an IT support and content-management solution. This new software will provide management for users' requests throughout the Oriental Institute. With the system, users will see increased response times and productivity for IT support. I will be able to keep records of each computer's previous incidents and problems. This is important information because it allows me to track an ongoing problem and see if another solution will be required to fix the issue, such as hardware replacement.

Integrated Database

I am excited to work with the Oriental Institute using the KE EMu Integrated Database. For the past few months, I have been working with John Sanders, Scott Branting, and Foy Scalf on getting up to date. Our goal is to provide public access to information about our research and the object-based collections that are managed by the Oriental Institute. So far I have added new users to the registry, provided access to new assistants, and have worked extensively on learning how to manage permissions for users and new assistants. We are working on the multistage project implementing an image archive into the IDB. I will be working with the web development of the Integrated Database, checking the web statistics to see what can be done to increase the efficiency of IDB online. We will soon enter Phase 2 of the project, which involves setting up an image archive. We have agreed that Phase 2 will involve working with both IT services and KE staff to gain knowledge of a transfer session. I look forward to working with both Museum and Conservation for the upcoming projects.

INTEGRATED DATABASE PROJECT

Scott Branting

Phase one of the Integrated Database Project was successfully completed during this past year. This is quite an achievement that has been eight years in the making. As described in last year's annual report, the Integrated Database Project is designed to provide a more stable, integrated, and web accessible platform for housing the millions of records, photographs, maps, artifacts, and texts that the Oriental Institute has produced or acquired since its inception. An expanding effort over the past decades has digitized a large amount of this information, but it was held in a wide range of different software and did not allow for queries to cross between the different collections. Some of the software was also becoming outdated and unstable, a relic of the early and very forward thinking initiatives of the Oriental Institute in the 1980s and 1990s.

Over the past two years a wide range of different members of the Oriental Institute family have participated in the effort to bring Phase One of this project to a successful conclusion. Foy Scalf, Helen McDonald, and Susan Allison have put in long hours designing templates for accessing the data and testing their implementation within the KE EMu software that powers the new system. Volunteers and students have put in countless hours cleaning up data, testing recently imported data, or adding in completely new data. Faculty, staff, students, and volunteers have graciously participated in focus groups led by Wendy Ennes, to guide

Figure 1. The Search Our Collection webpage (oi.uchicago.edu/idb), which provides the entry point for people to search the over 650,000 records pertaining to the Oriental Institute collections

the design of the new "Search Our Collections" webpages that provide access to this data. John Sanders and I have coordinated this effort together with our external project manager, Angela Spinazze. Jack Green, Chief Curator of the Museum whose units house and maintain much of this data, played a key supportive role in completing Phase One since joining the Oriental Institute. Over the past year, the University's IT Services group, particularly Rose Pezzuti Dyer and Alan Takaoka, brought our ideas to life through their software coding skills. None of this would have been possible without this extensive effort by so many of us.

The culmination of all the hard work of so many people can be seen by visiting the Search Our Collections initial webpage (oi.uchicago.edu/idb). Here you will find the public entranceway to the wealth of information pertaining to the ancient Middle East that has been collected by the Oriental Institute over its more than ninety year existence. While not all of

Figure 2. The results of a search for "Tyre" from the Search Our Collections webpage yields a list of resulting records containing both bibliographic citations (blue) and museum objects (red)

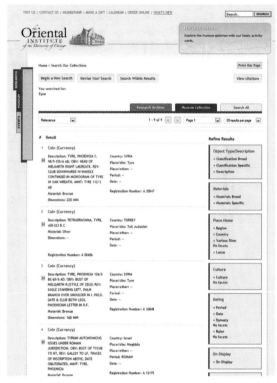

Figure 3. Clicking on the Museum Collection tab narrows down the list of results for "Tyre" to just those which are museum objects. Facets to the right of the page allow these results to be further refined by factors such as materials or dating

the millions of items are yet available, over 450,000 bibliographic records and 207,000 object records are now available through this webpage. Take a look and see! Typing in "Merneptah" as a search across all collections will provide you with books and articles written about the life and times of the Nineteenth Dynasty pharaoh as well as objects from his time at the Oriental Institute. Typing in a more complex search like "Schmidt AND Hissar" will yield the bibliographic citation to Erich Schmidt's publication of his excavations at Tepe Hissar, as well as reviews of that publication, and will show some of the sherds he excavated at the site and brought back to Chicago. Typing in "Guterbock" or "Güterbock" will yield bibliographic records pertaining to publications by Hans Güterbock. While typing in "grit" will yield just museum objects, mostly sherds and vessels with grit inclusions or temper. You can view all the results together in one list or see only the museum objects or only the bibliographic records in separate lists. Both of the separate lists can then be further refined and bibliographic records can be exported into a working bibliography.

The Search Our Collections webpage launched on January 31 of this year. Since that time it has become an indispensable resource for scholars, students, and people around the world. However, it is only a start to bringing online all the millions of items connected with the Oriental Institute. It is also only a start in the form that access to the collections will take in the years ahead. We welcome more feedback as you use this expanding resource, and encourage you to submit it to us through the feedback button on the webpages. Your feedback can help to shape how future versions of the Search Our Collections webpages look and work.

With Phase One of the project brought to a successful conclusion, work has already turned to Phase Two. We have been very fortunate to acquire generous financial support for Phase One from a combination of the Institute of Museum and Library Services (IMLS), the University of Chicago, and Aimee Drolet Rossi. The success of Phase One helped lay the groundwork for a second grant submission to IMLS to help fund Phase Two. We were extremely pleased to subsequently find out that we were awarded this second IMLS grant. Without all our ongoing support this work would soon grind to a halt.

The focus of Phase Two is to start to bring online the wealth of scans of the photographic records held by the Oriental Institute as well as to integrate data pertaining to the conservation and care of objects. Currently, you will notice that there are very few images attached to any of the records in the database. This will change with Phase Two thanks to the hard work of Mónica Vélez, who has been working with us on developing fields within the database to hold the images' metadata as well as the front-end layout. Images will be increasingly more common within the records that you already see, as photographs of objects are added. But there will soon be a separate tab in the results window that will show you all the new images that your searches uncover. These may be images of objects or they could be images taken in decades past by prior generations of Oriental Institute researchers. At the same

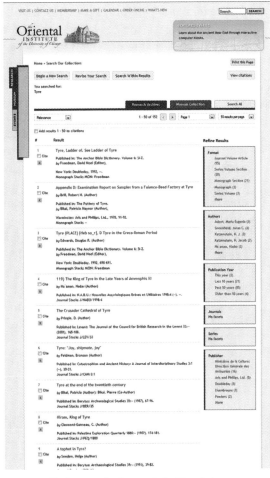

Figure 4. Clicking on the Research Archives tab narrows down the list of results for "Tyre" to just those which are bibliographic records. Facets to the right of the page allow these results to be further refined by factors such as publication year or author. Citations can also be selected and then exported into a variety of formats by checking the box next to the record and pressing the "View citations" button

time, the Oriental Institute conservators, led by Laura D'Alessandro, have been hard at work developing the backend database to convert the variety of recording systems they currently use into KE EMu. While their work will be less obvious to most users, behind the scenes it will help to coordinate communication and information management regarding each object's care.

Phase Two has also seen some changes in the core project team. Jack Green has taken on a much larger role in helping to oversee the implementation of Phase Two. At the same time, John Sanders, the visionary who has been pressing for just this sort of an integrated system since the early 1990s, retired shortly after the launch of Phase One. While no one could possibly replace his experience and vision in regards to the Integrated Database, Paul Ruffin, has filled in more than ably on the more technical portions of the project over the past several months. John's presence is still very often missed. Together Jack and Paul have joined me, Angela, and Foy in overseeing the operations of both Phase Two and the ongoing everyday work that builds upon the success of Phase One.

As can be seen above, there have been numerous people who have given time and effort to bring Phase One to a successful conclusion and to begin the work of Phase Two. Beyond the various people listed above, a number of individuals should be credited for their efforts this past year. Volunteer George Sundell, as has been the case over the past eight years, provided invaluable expertise and assistance to various aspects of the project this past year. John Larson and volunteer Justin Seppi have played key roles in assisting Monica with her work on the photographic collections. Likewise, Alison Whyte and Simona Cristanetti have worked closely with Laura on the conservation templates. Volunteers Roberta Schaffner, Andrea Dudek, Stephen Adamcik, Paula Pergament, Amanda el-Khoury, and Su Hyeon Bok have assisted in testing changes to the database and website and in the herculean task of cleaning up large amounts of data. They were joined in that effort by student assistants Melissa Bellah, Taylor Coplen, Laura Holzweg, Nicola Kanmany John, and Min Won Song. Magnus Widell, Chuck Jones, Tate Paulette, and Miller Prosser have also provided very useful guidance and suggestions throughout this past year. This project would not be the success that it has become without everyone's efforts and the funding of IMLS, the University of Chicago, the Oriental Institute, and Aimee Drolet Rossi.

OCHRE DATA SERVICE

Sandra R. Schloen

This report comes from the windy, rooftop patio of a rented apartment on the hillside of Fevzipaşa, southern Turkey, where shoes stacked outside the front door enumerate the local children gathered with the landlady for their Ramadan lesson around the Koran. This small, rural community hosts Professor David Schloen and the Neubauer Expedition to Zincirli, which has conscripted the help of the OCHRE Data Service's research database specialists Sandra Schloen and Miller Prosser to support the use of high-tech gadgetry throughout the summer's field season. Data captured in the field by dig supervisors using 7-inch Samsung tablets is downloaded via Bluetooth to the master computer at the end of each day at the Internet-equipped municipal building housing the dig office. Long before anyone is awake in Chicago the next morning, the data is uploaded directly into the OCHRE database maintained by the University of Chicago's Digital Library Development Center (DLDC). Photos taken by the dig supervisors using their tablet cameras complement the official photographs taken by traditional methods. A time-lapse sequence of aerial photographs, snapped by a tablet-enabled Nikon Coolpix strapped to the belly of a Phantom quadcopter being piloted systematically around the site, rounds out the daily photographic record (fig. 1). All data is collected and integrated within the database environment known as OCHRE: the Online Cultural and Historical Research Environment.

The Zincirli expedition is but one of several projects at the Oriental Institute and elsewhere that use OCHRE as the platform of choice for integrating, analyzing, and preserving scholarly research data and for which the OCHRE Data Service (ODS) provides technical consulting and support. In fact, OCHRE is the technological linchpin of a recent five-year, $2 million initiative that has brought together an international, multi-institutional team based at the University of Toronto (Prof. Timothy Harrison) to focus on "Computational Research on the Ancient Near East" (CRANE). On behalf of the CRANE project, the OCHRE Data Service specialists coordinate the large-scale data management and cross-project integration of diverse archaeological and scientific data sets from the participating institutions. Planned collaboration with computer scientists studying data visualization at the University of Toronto, and with (University of Chicago-affiliated) simulation expert Dr. John Christiansen at Argonne National Laboratories, promises an appropriately high-tech conclusion to the successful high-tech beginnings in Turkey's Orontes valley.

Closer to home, support of two long-term projects — the extensive collection of data from the Persepolis Fortification Archive (PFA) Project and the online edition of the Chicago Hittite Dictionary (eCHD) — has been an ongoing priority. As the number of texts being studied by the PFA Project and represented in OCHRE reaches the 8,000 mark, and with ten-fold PTM (Polynomial Texture Map) images and high-quality (BetterLight) scans thereof needing to be managed, the Ochre Data Service is busy supporting this team of scholars and students, under the direction of photographer and database specialist Miller Prosser. Other projects took advantage of these imaging services on an ad hoc basis. All images are managed by the

Figure 1. View of the Neubauer Expedition to Zincirli project team, as seen from the Phantom quadcopter

OCHRE database system, which integrates the images with other project data, makes them available for downloading as needed, delivers them via a public interface, and archives them for long-term preservation.

The OCHRE Data Service has also committed to assisting the Hittite Dictionary team, long plagued (for valid, historical reasons) by the dependency on non-Unicode-based fonts, by providing some tools to convert thousands of dictionary article documents into documents ready for the modern age of computing. These documents will be transformed into database content, which will allow the Š volume to be added to the L, M, N, and P volumes already available online via OCHRE, thereby enhancing the scope of the searchable, interactive edition of the electronic Chicago Hittite Dictionary.

Two new philology projects at the Oriental Institute were also pilot-tested in anticipation of large-scale development: an interactive, online edition of the Chicago Demotic Dictionary (eCDD), in consultation with Janet H. Johnson and Brian Muhs; and the Ras Shamra Text Inventory (RSTI) project featuring description, analysis, and the photographic record of Ugaritic texts, in consultation with Dennis Pardee.

The OCHRE Data Service was represented at a variety of conferences and special events throughout this past year, including:

- Demotic Roundtable Discussion, University of Chicago, August 29, 2012.

- Paper given jointly by David Schloen and Miller Prosser, "Using Computers to Help Scholars Have Good Arguments," at Humanities Day, University of Chicago, October 20, 2012.

- Exhibitor's booth featuring demonstrations of the Oriental Institute's OCHRE projects at the American Schools of Oriental Research's (ASOR) annual meeting, held in Chicago, November 14–17, 2012; plus a six-paper program session entitled "Innovations in Integrative Research Using the Online Cultural and Historical Research Environment (OCHRE)."

- Paper given by Miller Prosser, "The OCHRE Database: A Warehouse for Big Data Generated by Archaeological and Philological Projects at the Oriental Institute," Colloquium on Digital Humanities and Computer Science, University of Chicago, November 18, 2012.

- Paper given jointly by David Schloen and Sandra Schloen, "Organizing and Integrating Archaeological Data," annual meeting of the Society for American Archaeology (SAA), Honolulu, April 6, 2013.

For more information about the services of the OCHRE Data Service, and for links to the supported projects, visit http://ochre.uchicago.edu.

————————————

PUBLICATIONS OFFICE

Thomas G. Urban and Leslie Schramer

The full-time staff of the Publications Office remains Leslie Schramer (ninth year) and Thomas G. Urban (twenty-fifth year). Part-time staff includes Assistant Editor Rebecca Cain (fourth year) and Editorial Assistant Brian Keenan (since May 2012). Dennis Campbell worked in the office from May to June. Editorial Assistants Zuhal Kuru and Tate Paulette resigned to take on full-time employment elsewhere.

Sales

Casemate Publishers, the David Brown Book Company, and Oxbow Books handle the bulk of book distribution for the Oriental Institute. Although a limited number of titles are available for in-house sales in the Suq museum gift shop, please note that all external orders for Institute publications should be addressed to: The David Brown Book Company, P.O. Box 511, Oakville, CT 06779; telephone toll free: 1-800-791-9354; fax: 1-860-945-9468; e-mail: david.brown.bk.co@snet.net; website: www.oxbowbooks.com.

Information related to the sales and distribution of Oriental Institute titles may be obtained via e-mail: oi-publications@uchicago.edu

Electronic Publications

During the year the scanning of older titles was completed — all titles published by the Oriental Institute since its inception have been uploaded to the Publications webpages as PDF files. At present, more than 450 titles are available for complimentary download.

The older titles not-scanned-in-office were scanned by Northern MicroGraphics (NMT Corporation, http://normicro.com), located in LaCrosse, Wisconsin.

The Electronic Initiative is very successful. The uploaded PDFs are available wherever the Internet reaches, and our older titles — all our titles, old and new — are especially appreciated in the countries from where data were gathered and library shelves do not hold Oriental Institute titles.

To access the complete catalog of Oriental Institute titles, which includes *Annual Reports*, *News & Notes*, and *Chicago House Bulletins*, please visit:

https://oi.uchicago.edu/research/pubs/

Volumes Published (In Print and Online)

1. *The Demotic Dictionary of the Oriental Institute of the University of Chicago*, Volume T. Edited by Janet H. Johnson. CDD T
2. *The Oriental Institute Annual Report 2011–2012*. Edited by Gil J. Stein. AR 2011–2012
3. *Chicago House Bulletin 23*. Edited by W. Ray Johnson. CHB 23
4. *Language and Nature: Papers Presented to John Huehnergard on the Occasion of this 60th Birthday*. Edited by Rebecca Hasselbach and Naʿama Pat-El. SAOC 67
5. *Iconoclasm and Text Destruction in the Ancient Near East and Beyond*. Edited by Natalie N. May. OIS 8

6. *Between Heaven & Earth: Birds in Ancient Egypt.* Edited by Rozenn Bailleul-LeSuer. OIMP 35
7. *Heaven on Earth: Temples, Ritual, and Cosmic Symbolism in the Ancient World.* Edited by Deena Ragavan. OIS 9
8. *The Hittite Dictionary of the Oriental Institute of the University of Chicago,* Volume Š, Fascicle 3. Edited by Hans G. Güterbock†, Harry A. Hoffner, and Theo van den Hout. CHD Š/3
9. *Our Work: Modern Jobs — Ancient Origins.* Edited by Jack Green and Emily Teeter. OIMP 36
10–13. *Oriental Institute News & Notes.* Edited by Amy Weber. NN 215–218

Volumes in Preparation

1. *The Demotic Dictionary of the Oriental Institute of the University of Chicago,* Volume S. Edited by Janet H. Johnson. CDD S
2. *Early Megiddo on the East Slope (The "Megiddo Stages"): A Report on the Early Occupation of the East Slope of Megiddo; Results of the Oriental Institute's Excavations, 1925-1933.* Eliot Braun, with contributions by David Ilan, Ofer Marder, Yael Braun, and Sariel Shalev
3. *Ancient Settlement Patterns and Cultures in the Ram Hormuz Plain, Southwestern Iran: Excavations at Tall-e Geser and Regional Survey in the Ram Hormuz Area.* Abbas Alizadeh, with contributions by Loghman Ahmadzadeh and Mehdi Omidfar
4. Great Hypostyle Hall in the Temple of Amun at Karnak, Volume 2. *Translation and Commentary.* Peter J. Brand and William J. Murnane
5. *Extraction and Control: Studies in Honor of Matthew W. Stolper.* Edited by Wouter Henkelman, Charles Jones, Michael Kozuh, and Christopher Woods
6. *Barda Balka.* Bruce Howe, with contribution by Yorke Rowan

Volumes in Backlog

1. *Bir Umm Fawakhir 3: Excavations 1999-2001.* Carol Meyer, with contributions by Lisa Heidorn, Salima Ikram, Richard Jaeschke, Thomas Roby, and Wendy Smith
2. *Theban Symposium: Creativity and Innovation in the Reign of Hatshepsut.* Edited by José M. Galán, Betsy M. Bryan, and Peter F. Dorman
3. *Where Kingship Descended from Heaven: New Light on Ancient Kish.* Karen L. Wilson
4. *Ancient Mesopotamia: Highlights from the Collections of the Oriental Institute.* Karen L. Wilson
5. *The Monumental Complex of King Ahmose at Abydos,* Volume 1: *The Pyramid Temple of Ahmose and Its Environs: Architecture and Decoration.* Stephen P. Harvey

---

RESEARCH ARCHIVES

Foy Scalf

Introduction

There is an inherent contradiction in our work at the Research Archives of the Oriental Institute. On the one hand, we are the custodians, stewards, and facilitators of 60,000 print volumes representing the collective research conducted in the fields of ancient Near East studies over the past 200 years. On the other hand, we have worked tirelessly and diligently to create and refine a host of digital tools for navigating our esoteric branch of humanities academia. While many institutions and critics are touting the rapid move toward exclusively digital libraries, we have resisted, and continue to maintain a collection based primarily on the printed word. Yet, electronic tools have revolutionized the organization of information and the retrieval of data, both of which have become absolute necessities to a world drowning in information. With the close of another year for the Research Archives, it is an appropriate time to reflect on our mission, current practices, and future goals. The relationship between print and digital media is fundamentally intertwined within these concerns.

The digital age has opened up a wealth of resources and made access to research far more democratic. In many ways, it has been a boon for the study of the ancient Near East. If this development has been so positive, why do we continue to increase our print holdings? I can say unequivocally that it is not the result of any backward-leaning perspectives of traditionalism. There are real concerns to consider. The proliferation of born digital publications presents a number of problems to the archivist, first and foremost in the realm of preservation and access. Although electronic publications on the World Wide Web offer access to anyone with an Internet connection, it also means there is no access without that connection. This raises issues of connectivity, but as a librarian I am more concerned with long-term preservation of scholarly work. A brief tour of our journal stacks will reveal dozens of journals that were born with good intentions, but that quickly died, some after only a few issues. For digital publications without long-term and institutional support, digital death means that the fruits of this research will essentially disappear. As soon as a server fee is not paid, or there is an electricity crisis, or a major connectivity issue, users will not be able to access this material. If a journal's website goes under and their server disappears, the only remaining copies of that research in existence will be paper copies (if they were published) or randomly saved digital copies squirrelled away in private individuals' digital collections. Paper copies will last until physically destroyed; around the Institute, the joke is that if you want your information to last, record it on clay tablets. Once baked, they're nearly indestructible

Figure 1. Cuneiform tablets, once fired, can preserve information for millennia (University of Chicago Library, Special Collections Research Center apf2-05368)

and last for millennia (fig. 1). Without adequate policies in place, the information of the Information Age may not be so safe. For these reasons, we have maintained our print collections of journals for which digital access does not have secure preservation policies in place with backing from major institutions.

In the realm of research tools, however, the digital revolution has been a blessing to librarians and researchers alike. Overwhelming amounts of data, from object information about primary sources to bibliographic data on secondary literature, can be cataloged, indexed, sorted, searched, filtered, and mined for amazing scientific results. The Research Archives online catalog remains an incredibly important resource for scholarship within ancient Near East studies. The 460,000 records in our catalog represent a veritable index of our fields. With the developments offered through the Integrated Database Project, users can now find new and exciting ways to find, sort, sift, store, and share this information. Producing such an index by hand without the use of digital resources (an attempt was made by the Oriental Institute under the Archaeological Corpus project) is nearly unimaginable. We continue to catalog each and every book, article, and book review received. Now we can connect this data together so that for every book, all the book reviews are displayed; for every author, an author biography, degrees completed, and work history are shown; for every open-source digital document, a PDF is attached. Such projects allow us to marry our print media and digital media in unexpected and exhilarating ways. The future for the Research Archives of the Oriental Institute is certainly bright and the rest of us will benefit immensely from it.

Acquisitions

Acquisition efforts remained at the forefront of our priorities for 2012–2013. Our move to the EMu (Electronic Museum) database as part of the Integrated Database Project has given us more flexible and robust methods of organizing our data. One change from last year is reflected in table 1: the number of accession lots we received through the year (numbers for July and August 2012 are not available because the database was not in use at that time). We are also tracking the growing costs paid toward shipping and look to reduce those costs as much as possible in the coming years in order to efficiently apply the budget toward the acquisition of research materials. Although the numbers in table 1 are slightly below our historical average of 1,000 volumes, we actually exceeded the historical average, yet time commitments devoted to the Integrated Database Project forced us into a backlog from which we are still recovering. Several significant donations remain to be cataloged and the acquisition of several large encyclopedia volumes has required many hours to analyze fully in the database. We were able this year to acquire the majority of the back issues from two journals: *Égypte, Afrique et Orient* and *Sokar*. These represent important additions to the collection as they are not held in any other libraries in the Chicago region. In these ways, we continue to strive to fulfill our mission as a premier library of ancient Near East studies of providing for the research needs of scholars, students, and the public.

Table 1. Research Archives acquisitions, July 2012–June 2013

Month	Number of Accession Lots	Monographs, Series, Pamphlets	Journals	Total Volumes
July 2012	?	66	25	91
August 2012	?	43	13	56
September 2012	21	20	13	33
October 2012	54	43	51	94
November 2012	40	50	24	74
December 2012	20	35	12	47
January 2013	41	54	21	75
February 2013	17	25	3	28
March 2013	24	28	40	68
April 2013	34	58	45	103
May 2013	64	56	52	108
June 2013	33	45	19	64
Totals		523	318	841
		Total Volumes		**841**

Online Catalog

One of the major developments over the past year is the design and implementation of a new online catalog for the Research Archives as part of the Oriental Institute's Integrated Database Project. The web version of the new catalog went live to the public in February 2013 (oi.uchicago.edu/idb). The advances over the old catalog are tremendous. Foremost among these changes is that bibliographic data from the Research Archives can now be searched simultaneously with data from Museum Registration. If the user desires, they can also search only the Research Archives catalog separately. The interface is intuitive and aesthetically pleasing. Searches can be built from very simple to exceedingly complex depending upon the user's knowledge and experience. Searches can be quickly and easily audited or augmented through the "Revise Your Search" and "Search Within Results" features. Results can be sorted according to user-defined criteria and refined through a series of facets displayed on the right-hand side of the screen to demystify bibliographic research. These features ease the notoriously difficult challenge of finding what you want in a vast sea of information. A citation tool allows users to select records of their choice and download them for use in their own databases (e.g., Zotero, EndNote) or to build bibliographies in their text documents. All these developments are just the beginning of what we believe will be a long and incredibly interesting project through which the way we conduct research will change, become more efficient, and lead to increasing insights. We have many surprises in store for the future.

From July 1, 2012, to June 30, 2013, the Research Archives online catalog has grown by 40,000 records, from 420,000 to 460,000 analytic records (see table 2). These records include complete analytical entries for the back issues of *Égypte, Afrique et Orient* and *Sokar*. Roberta

Schaffner and Andrea Dudek have also begun an inventory of our serial holdings and they have worked diligently to catalog large sections of this collection and add PDF copies where appropriate to the catalog records.

Table 2. Catalog records

Year	Number of Catalog Records Added	Total Number of Catalog Records
2012–2013	40,000	460,000
2011–2012	30,000	420,000
2010–2011	30,000	390,000
2009–2010	40,000	360,000
2008–2009	63,000	320,000
2007–2008	62,000	257,000
2006–2007	28,000	195,000
—	—	—
2003–2004	10,000	130,000

We continue to add links to online material, both new and old. Currently, there are over 105,000 links (only 103,987 recorded in table 3, below) to online material in the Research Archives catalog (roughly 25% of all catalog records). We have begun the process of adding PDF files directly to the new EMu database and we look forward to developing access to these files via the online catalog during the coming year.

Table 3. Links to online journal articles

Call Number	Journal	Links	Access
JAOS	Journal of the American Oriental Society	14,818	JSTOR
CBQ	Catholic Biblical Quarterly	11,610	Ebsco
ANT	Antiquity	11,094	Antiquity
AJA	American Journal of Archaeology	11,019	JSTOR/AJA
ZPE	Zeitschrift für Papyrologie und Epigraphik	7,205	JSTOR
Syria	Syria	5,689	JSTOR
JNES	Journal of Near Eastern Studies	4,873	JSTOR/JNES
JEA	Journal of Egyptian Archaeology	4,143	JSTOR
Bib	Biblica	3,574	Open
BASOR	Bulletin of the American School of Oriental Research	3,336	JSTOR
ZDMG	Zeitschrift der Deutschen Morgenländischen Gesellschaft	3,360	Open
PEQ	Palestine Exploration Quarterly	3,286	Ebsco
ZA	Zeitschrift für Assyriologie	3,061	Open
CRAIBL	Académie des inscriptions et belles-lettres. Comptes rendus	2,255	Open

Call Number	Journal	Links	Access
BIAR	Near Eastern Archaeology (formerly Biblical Archaeologist)	2,072	JSTOR
JESHO	Journal of the Economic and Social History of the Orient	1,446	JSTOR
BIFAO	Bulletin de l'Institut Français d'Archéologie Orientale	1,688	Open
JARCE	Journal of the American Research Center in Egypt	1,180	JSTOR
RBL	Review of Biblical Literature	1,084	Open
JCS	Journal of Cuneiform Studies	1,004	JSTOR
IRQ	Iraq	993	JSTOR
BiOr	Bibliotheca Orientalis	845	Peeters
ANS	Anatolian Studies	732	JSTOR
FUB	Forschungen und Berichte	673	JSTOR
IRN	Iran	685	JSTOR
PAM	Polish Archaeology in the Mediterranean	495	Open
JANES	Journal of the Ancient Near Eastern Society	435	Open
Orj	Orient: Report of the Society for Near Eastern Studies in Japan	380	Open
ARO	Ars Orientalis	317	JSTOR
BSEG	Bulletin: Société d'Égyptologie Genève	270	Open
KAR	Cahiers de Karnak	89	
BMSEAS	British Museum Studies in Ancient Egypt and Sudan	64	Open
LingAeg	Lingua Aegyptia	47	Open
ARTA	Achaemenid Research on Texts and Archaeology	34	Open
StOr	Studia Orontica	32	Open
CDLJ	Cuneiform Digital Library Journal	32	Open
ENiM	Égypte Nilotique et Méditerranéenne	28	Open
CDLB	Cuneiform Digital Library Bulletin	20	Open
CDLN	Cuneiform Digital Library Notes	19	Open
	Total	103,987	

Resources on the Web

In addition to the online catalog, the Research Archives maintains a series of open-access online resources.

Introduction & Guide

http://oi.uchicago.edu/pdf/research_archives_introduction&guide.pdf

An updated introduction and guide to the Research Archives contains a brief history, a guide to the Research Archives collection, and instructions for using the online catalog.

Dissertations

http://oi.uchicago.edu/research/library/dissertation/

With the permission of the authors, the Research Archives provides access to PDF copies of dissertations completed in the Department of Near Eastern Languages and Civilizations of the University of Chicago.

Dissertation Proposals

http://oi.uchicago.edu/research/library/dissertation/proposals/

With the permission of the authors, the Research Archives provides access to PDF copies of dissertation proposals completed in the Department of Near Eastern Languages and Civilizations of the University of Chicago.

Acquisitions Lists

http://oi.uchicago.edu/research/library/acquisitions.html

The acquisitions reports of the Research Archives are distributed as PDFs on a monthly basis. This process has been active and continuative since September 2007.

Annual Reports

http://oi.uchicago.edu/research/library/annualreports.html

Annual Reports for the Research Archives are available from 1969 to 2012.

Networking Sites

https://www.facebook.com/pages/Research-Archives-of-the-Oriental-Institute/153645450792

The Research Archives now maintains an official page on Facebook. Information about recent publications of Oriental Institute scholars or reviews of recent Oriental Institute publications is distributed through this page. Currently, 1,961 individuals follow the Research Archives through this presence on Facebook.

Monographs

http://oilib.uchicago.edu

Copies of out-of-copyright monographs have been scanned and are made available as PDFs through links in the online catalog of the Research Archives. As of June 2013, the Research Archives provides access to over 225 volumes.

Adopt-a-Journal

http://oi.uchicago.edu/research/library/adopt-a-journal.html

The Research Archives has launched an "Adopt-a-Journal" campaign in order to increase support for the Research Archives. Donors are recognized through personalized book plates made in their honor and placed in volumes of their choosing.

Visitors

The Research Archives continues to be a place of international collaboration among the community of scholars studying the ancient Near East. Over the past year, we had research visits from the following individuals (in alphabetical order), and I apologize for anyone I may have missed: Jan Bremmer, Ed Castle, Eva von Dassow, Peter Dorman, Grant Frame, James Hoffmeier, Alexis Jankowski, Jackie Jay, Cindy Jurisson and her class for the University of Chicago Lab Schools, Isaac Kalimi, Massimo Maiocchi, Lina Meerchyad, Adam Miglio, Miriam Müller, Maggie Paddock, Elaine Fetyko Page with Jacob Hill and the Great Chicago Libraries class of Elmhurst College, Stephanie Rost, Seth Sanders, JoAnn Scurlock, Philip Venticinque, Matteo Vigo, John Wee, Jennifer Westerfeld, and Avi Winitzer.

Acknowledgments

As always, running a research library is not a solitary endeavor. I have had the privilege to work with incredibly gracious and devoted colleagues, who continue to help support the Research Archives in a variety of ways. I would like to thank the following individuals for their time, effort, and donations over the past year: Tom Urban, Leslie Schramer, Chris Woods, Seth Richardson, Jason Barcus, John Sanders, Paul Ruffin, Scott Branting, Angela Spinazze, Bruce Williams, Andrea Dudek, Catherine Mardikes, and Emily Teeter.

Our student employees continue to be responsible for a lion's share of the data entry in the Research Archives. Laura Holzweg, Taylor Coplen, Melissa Bellah, Nicola Kammany John, and Min Won Song have been instrumental in the strides we have made over the past year. I would like to take this opportunity to thank them for all their hard work and their exceptionally cheerful attitudes that make working in our office such a delight.

The work of our volunteers and the relationships I have established with them have been the most surprising and gratifying experiences of my tenure in the Research Archives. We have a tremendous group of people who have given their time and effort to our projects. No gesture made here could approximate the appreciation we have for them. Roberta Shaffner, Andrea Dudek, Ray Broms, Su Hyeon Bok, Paula Pergament, Amanda el-Khouri, and Stephen Adamcik spent countless hours cataloging, reshelving, scanning, and just all around making the Research Archives a better place. I cannot stress enough my admiration and gratitude for their generous service.

TABLET COLLECTION

Andrew Dix

The fiscal year 2012–2013 was another active one for the Tablet Collection and the Tablet Room. In July, Lance Allred of the Cuneiform Digital Library Initiative, based at the University of California, Los Angeles, returned for his annual trip to scan published tablets in the Oriental Institute for the project's website (http://cdli.ucla.edu/). Their continued collaboration has allowed scholars around the world to remotely consult tablets in the Tablet Collection. Ran Zadok of Tel Aviv University spent two weeks in the Tablet Room in August and September working on Neo-Babylonian tablets from the Oriental Institute's excavations at Nippur. In November Sara Brumfield of the University of California, Los Angeles, and Jay Crisostomo of the University of California, Berkeley, both doctoral candidates in cuneiform studies, each visited the Oriental Institute for a week to study tablets related to their dissertations. Clemens Reichel and Maynard Maidman, both of the University of Toronto, each came to the

Tablet Room in December for research visits. Reichel continued his work on tablets excavated by the Oriental Institute at Tell Asmar and Maidman documented unpublished tablets from Nuzi in the Tablet Collection.

From February to May the assistant curator of the Tablet Collection, Andrew Dix, traveled to Berlin to work on tablets in the tablet collection of the Vorderasiatisches Museum related to his dissertation. Paul Gauthier, another doctoral candidate in cuneiform studies here at the University of Chicago, stepped in as temporary assistant curator during this time and hosted two visitors to the Tablet Room. Nils Heeßel of the University of Heidelberg studied literary texts for a week in February, and Véronique Pataï, a graduate student at the University of Lyon, spent two months inspecting tablets from Nuzi. Finally, Grant Frame of the University of Pennsylvania returned for two weeks in June to continue his work on the inscriptions of Sargon II from Khorsabad.

———————————

MUSEUM

Jack Green

It was an incredibly active year for the Oriental Institute Museum on multiple fronts, continuing with our highly successful schedule of special exhibits, work behind-the-scenes continued with the launch of the Oriental Institute's Integrated Database online, an extensive program of loans, and new work on overseas cultural heritage projects. It has also been a year of considering ways that we can increase Museum visitor numbers with more targeted marketing, surveys, and gathering of visitor statistics.

The total number of Museum visitors thankfully rose in the past financial year (July 1, 2012–June 30, 2013) by just over 7.5 percent, to 52,207. In particular, the Museum witnessed increased attendance at special events, programs, and tours in 2012. In addition, our suggested donation on entry to the Museum was increased in October 2012 from $7 and $3, to $10 and $5, respectively, for adults and children over 12. This simplification has reduced the scramble for dollar bills and requests for change by visitors in our lobby and the Suq, and increased the overall level of visitor donations to around $2.50 per non-tour visitor (from less than $2.00 prior to the rise). The Oriental Institute Museum continues to be free at the point of entry, a feature that is extremely rare in Chicago today. Suq sales remained healthy over the past year with increased success with Oriental Institute Museum Publication sales now beginning to form a sustaining contribution.

Figure 1. Installation of the new Oriental Institute banners on the east side of the building (facing Woodlawn Avenue) in February. Photo by Anna Ressman

The past year's increase in donations is being used in part to contribute to a newly established general Museum marketing budget, as well as contributing to the running of our special exhibits. Creation of external banners for the Oriental Institute building, supported through the James Henry Breasted Society (fig. 1), and a new Oriental Institute Museum rack card (the first in a series; fig. 2), are just two of the ways we are making ourselves more visible to the public. Special exhibits, coordinated by Emily Teeter, continue to be a major driver in bringing visitors to (and back to) the Museum. In our marketing efforts, we have been greatly assisted in the past several months by Wahied Helmy Girgs, Oriental Institute docent and former curator of the Children's Museum at the Egyptian Museum, Cairo. As a marketing and outreach consultant, he has helped to build contacts, network, widely distribute our rack cards to new locations, and interpret our visitor demographics (for more information, see the *Museum Publicity* section below).

Our special exhibit Between Heaven and Earth: Birds in Ancient Egypt, which opened in September 2012, was a great highlight for the Museum this year (see *Special Exhibits*, below), with a wonderful set of associated events and programs. Our gratitude to guest curator Rozenn Bailleul-LeSuer cannot be emphasized enough. These thanks extend to her wonderfully edited and well-illustrated exhibit catalog which serves as the most up-to-date and comprehensive publication to date on the role of birds in visual imagery, religion, economy, and environment for ancient Egypt. Progress has

Figure 2. The eye-catching new rack card featuring the colossal bull's head from Persepolis, Iran, ca. 485–424 BC (OIM A24065). Photo and card design by Brian Zimerle

continued in the past year on several other Museum publications, including a new volume that will feature "100 Highlights" of the Oriental Institute Museum. Another book in preparation is the Ancient Mesopotamia Highlights book, and outlines and new photography for the other gallery highlights volumes

Figure 3. Poet Haki Madhubuti and Oriental Institute chief curator Jack Green studying objects in preparation for the Our Work portrait photography. Photo by Jason Reblando

have been worked on this year. Emily Teeter and I co-edited the forthcoming catalog featuring the photographs of Jason Reblando for our August 2013 special exhibit entitled Our Work: Modern Jobs — Ancient Origins (formerly known as "Connections"), which will appeal to visitors to the forthcoming exhibit and a broad readership. The preparation and photoshoots (fig. 3) for "Our Work" from January 2013 were one of our most fulfilling, enjoyable, and logistically challenging experiences, and I thank co-curator Emily Teeter as well as photographer Jason Reblando and videographer Matthew Cunningham for easing us through the twenty-four portraits that make up this exhibit.

There were some unexpected and short-notice additions to the special exhibits schedule in the past year, including our collaboration with the Renaissance Society of the University of Chicago in the exhibition We the People, by Vietnamese-Danish artist Danh Vo (fig. 4), and a mini-exhibit on the mysterious journal of Indiana Jones that turned up at the University's Office of College Admissions. The Oriental Institute's involvement in these exhibits attracted new visitors to the Museum and garnered significant media coverage. We the People also provided a fresh way to appreciate the Oriental Institute at a time when the University of Chicago is engaging more with contemporary arts. I thank Suzanne Ghez and Hamza Walker of the Renaissance Society for this excellent working collaboration. We have also had success with traveling exhibits, in the updated display of the updated Catastrophe! Ten Years Later: the Looting and Destruction of Iraq's Past, which opened at the Royal Ontario Museum, Toronto, Canada, in June 2013, and our summary updated version in the lower level of the Oriental Institute in April 2013, which prompted renewed interest in this exhibit. We hope that this is the first of many exhibits that the Oriental Institute develops for travel. Special thanks go to exhibit co-curators McGuire Gibson and Katharyn Hanson for text reviews and changes, and to Mónica Vélez for the complex work in securing image rights. I extend special thanks to Clemens Reichel, associate curator at the ROM and research associate at the

Figure 4. Danh Vo's We the People, seen here installed in the Oriental Institute Museum, included a replica fragment from the face of the Statue of Liberty. Photo by Anna Ressman

Oriental Institute, as well as exhibits coordinator Mary Montgomery, for their encouragement and enthusiasm that led to the Toronto version of the exhibit.

On April 16, in conjunction with the redisplay of the updated Catastrophe! Ten Years Later exhibit, the Oriental Institute hosted a seminar in Breasted Hall to commemorate the tenth anniversary of the looting of the Iraq Museum, and to reflect on the state of cultural heritage protection in Iraq and more widely across the Middle East. This was an important event, as it provided an opportunity not only to remember those past tragedies, but also to review and discuss the current situation, including improvements in terms of funding and support for archaeology, new excavations, lessons learned, and continued challenges. The event was coordinated and chaired by myself and Katharyn Hanson, and speakers included Abdulamir Hamdani, former director of antiquities in Nasiriya Province in southern Iraq, currently at SUNY Stonybrook; Patty Gerstenblith, professor of law at DePaul University and director of DePaul's Cultural Heritage Law program; Katharyn Hanson, co-curator of the Catastrophe! exhibit for the Oriental Institute Museum; and Gil Stein, director of the Oriental Institute (for more details, see *News & Notes* 218 [Summer 2013], pp. 18–19).

We continued to enhance and develop our permanent galleries, firstly with some much needed long-term conservation treatment (by Alison Whyte) for our cast of the Hammurabi Stele in the Edgar and Deborah Jannotta Mesopotamia Gallery. Another change was a restoration and redisplay of our cast of the Moabite Stone, previously displayed on the Oriental Institute's third floor and reinstalled in the Haas and Schwartz Megiddo Gallery, as well as a new display case for the El and Baal figurines within the introduction area of the gallery (fig. 5), prepared by Erik Lindahl and Brian Zimerle, with the kind assistance of Professor Dennis Pardee of the Oriental Institute, and Joseph Lam of the University of North Carolina at Chapel Hill. Preparations for future gallery enhancements are underway. We thank several of our docents, including, Margaret Foorman, Jean Nye, Sue Geshwender, Semra Prescott,

Figure 5. Recent changes to the Haas and Schwartz Megiddo Gallery included the installation of the Mesha Stele cast (OIM C2) and a new display for the statues of El and Baal (OIM A18316, A22467). Photo by Anna Ressman

Correa da Silva, Toni Smith, amongst others, for their donations to facilitate this display, and especially Stuart Kleven for his initial suggestion to redisplay the Mesha Stele.

In the area of gallery enhancements, particularly of the digital variety, a significant amount of planning and research went into the writing of a grant application to the Institute of Museum and Library Services in January for the Oriental Institute's Gallery Enhancements Project. Working closely with Catherine Kenyon, head of public education and outreach, and Chris Reidel and Oren Sreebny of IT Services, the proposal for improvements includes the doubling of the orientation/introduction space in the Mesopotamian gallery, a large touchtable for family or small group visits, and the integration of iPads throughout the galleries that will carry additional interpretative content to better integrate the collections and rich archaeological and historical data, allowing visitors to "dig deeper" during their visit. As part of our project research and development, I approached the Kilts Center for Marketing at the Booth School of Business of the University of Chicago with a proposal for a Marketing Lab Project to be conducted by Booth Business School graduate students. The project involved market research surveys to ascertain the receptiveness of digital enhancements in the Oriental Institute Museum. We intend to develop enhancements that benefit all our visitors, as part of this research. There was a special interest in gaining responses from families and under 35s, who are key target groups we hope to reach. Special thanks to Booth students Bryan Horvath, Gil Schwartz, Sarah Freeman, Chia Kung, and Vagesh Kumar, who did a fantastic job in their high-quality research and presentation of results.

We continue to work closely with vibration consultants and engineers Wiss, Janney, Elstner Associates, Inc. (WJE; contracted by the University of Chicago's Capital Projects), who are working as part of the project to develop the new Becker Friedman Institute for Research in Economics (5757 University Avenue), and the extension of the 58th Street pedestrian walkway to Woodlawn Avenue. Vibrations have been kept to a minimum in the vicinity of the Oriental Institute and Museum galleries. June 2013 saw the closure of 58th Street between Woodlawn and University avenues, with temporary signage installed around the building to redirect pedestrian and vehicular traffic to the public entrance via University Avenue. We eagerly await the completion of this project in summer 2014, the opening of the new pedestrian walkway, and a return to relative normality. Thanks especially to head conservator Laura D'Alessandro and head of visitor services and security Jason Barcus for attending project meetings and assessing changes and events as they happen.

One physical development that benefited the Museum this year was the refurbishment of the office space between the room being used for the Persepolis Fortification Archive project and the Photography Department Office in our lower level. This is now a more usable project room with computers for data entry for the Integrated Database Project, as well as dedicated space for Photography Department assistants to process images. The improvements were coordinated by curatorial assistant Mónica Vélez with the support of the Oriental Institute central office.

The past year saw one staff change in the Museum — Robyn Haynie, who had been working in the Conservation Laboratory as part of Professor Matthew Stolper's Persepolis Fortification Archive Project, left the Oriental Institute in November to take up the post of conservator at the Utah Museum of Fine Arts in Salt Lake City. We thank Robyn for her contributions and wish her every success in her new position.

A large number of interns, volunteers, and short-term contracted assistants worked with us over the past year. Most of these individuals are mentioned in subsequent reports from other sections of the Museum. We are extremely grateful to the volunteers and work-study interns who come to us through the Master of Arts Program in the Social Sciences (MAPSS). Thanks to Morris Fred (Anthropology), Wendy Ennes, and Moriah Grooms-Garcia for their help in finding candidates and promoting the program.

Volunteers who assisted curatorial assistant Mónica Vélez in the Museum Office included volunteer Lucy Adler and MAPSS work-study intern Justin Seppi. They helped add over 3,000 new records into the Photographic Archives database. These are among the thousands of records that will be migrated in the coming year in to the Integrated Database (IDB).

This past fiscal year the Museum continued to receive requests for Oriental Institute images for reproduction or copyright usage in books, exhibits and online, and for research. Mónica Vélez assisted and processed 223 requests for 251 images, the majority for copyright and scholarly use, with a smaller number for commercial use. We have also successfully licensed out our first video with a request from the Royal Ontario Museum to use segments from the Oriental Institute's 1935 film *The Human Adventure* in their exhibit Mesopotamia: Inventing Our World. The Museum is experiencing a slight increase in the number of image requests in comparison with previous years, but the nature of those requests is changing slightly, with more images being requested for e-books and online portals than previous years.

Interns who assisted the Museum this past year are too many to mention and are listed in the appropriate sections below. I personally thank Brendan Mackie for his assistance with highlights publication work, and photography assistant Austin Kramer for his assistance in transcribing the Catastrophe! Ten Years Later seminar at the Oriental Institute in April, and for generally stepping in where needed.

We also took on two interns in the summer of 2013, who will continue into the new financial year: Petra Creamer, an undergraduate student from Ohio State University, and Sam Butler, who is studying Classics at the College of the University of Chicago. They are both focused on a series of special projects in Registration and attending a number of Museum and special-exhibits meetings, and are making significant contributions to the Museum.

Events and outreach activities were numerous, and particularly vibrant and engaging. During the period when the Oriental Institute's Education and Public Outreach Department was going through its own staff transitions in summer and fall of 2012, the Museum staff played a more active role than usual in initiating and facilitating some key public events. In October, with the assistance of the Public Education Department and a small army of volunteers, the Oriental Institute participated for the first time in Open House Chicago. The event, organized by the Chicago Architecture Foundation, provides listings of participating public venues offering behind-the-scenes tours of interesting, historic, or unusual buildings or architectural spaces. The Oriental Institute's participation, within its Neo-Gothic building featuring Orientalizing painted and sculpted motifs from ancient Egypt and Assyria, was a huge hit, leading to near overwhelming numbers of visiting public. The behind-the-scenes tour of the director's wood-paneled suite proved extremely popular. As a result, this event will be a likely fixture in future years. Thanks to Museum staff, including Emily Teeter for docent training, and Mónica Vélez for coordinating volunteers during this event, and staff and volunteers of the Education Department for all their hard work.

Another event we helped facilitate in October was the premiere for Latino Art Beat's short film *Visiting the Museum*, shown alongside the classic 1930s film *The Mummy*, starring Boris Karloff, during the atmospherically stormy week preceding Halloween. Special thanks to Don Rossi Nuccio of Latino Art Beat for all his work in promoting the film, partnering with us on the event, and for highlighting the collections of the Oriental Institute Museum to young audiences through film viewings (see *Public Education Report* for pics).

Mariam Qaryaqos, a former employee of the Iraq Museum, Baghdad, and graduate student in museum studies at the University of Western Illinois, continued to work with the Museum and the Public Education Department in July and August during her summer internship supported by the Fulbright Foreign Student Program and America-Mideast Educational and Training Services, Inc. (AMIDEAST). Her role was as the Oriental Institute's "ambassador" to Arab-American and Iraqi communities in the Chicago area. Mariam's role continued after her internship ended, with the help of Oriental Institute docent and Middle East outreach consultant Wahied Helmy Girgs. Mariam and Wahied built contacts for diverse Middle Eastern groups in the Chicago area and developed an online survey that helped us learn more about how we can reach out to these communities. We decided to explore and experiment with our first Middle East outreach brainstorming event at the Oriental Institute. Working closely with Catherine Kenyon (head of public education and outreach) and Brittany Mullins (assistant director of development), in April we invited members of Chicago's Assyrian community to the Oriental Institute to discuss and explore the kind of programing and outreach activities we would like to develop in the future (see *Public Education* section). If the first event, aimed at both youth and adult audiences, is successful, we plan to develop similar outreach programs and museum activities adapted for other Middle Eastern communities in the Chicago area. Working with the Rohr Chabad Center in Hyde Park, facilitated by Rabbi Yossi Brackman and Miriam Jaffe, we initiated tours focused on archaeology and biblical history this year. In addition, we recently assisted the Nile Restaurant in Hyde Park, managed by Rashad Moughrabi, with images from our photographic archives for its new restaurant location. McGuire Gibson and I hosted a visit to the Oriental Institute by members and friends of the Iraqi Mutual Aid Society to commemorate the tenth anniversary of the looting of the Iraq Museum. Many other tours and events involved the Museum, including the hosting of a reception for the American Schools of Oriental Research annual meeting in November, attended by several hundred people.

As detailed in Helen McDonald's report for Museum Registration, the Museum continues to facilitate research and publication projects of the Oriental Institute, as well as those of outside researchers. A few of the projects include the Nubia Expedition publication series, headed by Bruce Williams. Bruce has obtained funding to complete four volumes over the next few years, generating a considerable amount of access to collections and new photography, particularly for the Nubian sites of Dorginarti and Serra East. Tasha Vorderstrasse has continued in her study of our Islamic collections, including the identification of important unpublished materials. For the Khorsabad Reliefs Publication Project, the sad news reached us in July that Eleanor Guralnick had passed away. Her work up until the time of her death included the near completion of a catalog of large fragments of reliefs and photography and conservation cleaning of most of the reliefs in storage. Preparations are currently being made for the completion of the project and the final publication of the relief fragments. Led by our Head Conservator Laura D'Alessandro, conservation staff continued with their analysis and research on the Khorsabad pigments project, with further trips to the Argonne Laboratory. Benedetta Bellucci worked on a report of unpublished cylinder and stamp seals of the Muriel K. Newman Collection. She also organized and identified the modern seal impressions from the Helene Kantor Teaching Collection. Both reports are on file with the Registration Department.

Major achievements in the Registration Department over the past year included the registration of over 25,000 objects within the collections (mostly from previously unprocessed material from excavations). In addition, the Metals Room project, funded with a grant from the National Endowment for the Humanities, has moved ahead steadily and is nearing completion. New cabinets arrived and were fitted into the metals stores, with approximately 11,000 objects, including the Oriental Institute's coin collections being rehoused over the past year. There were also a small number of acquisitions through donation, including packing trunks belonging to James Henry Breasted and Frances Hart Breasted that were part of the Estate of Margaret (Peggy) Richmond. Harland J. Berk donated a stone mace-head from the estate of Yondorf (OIM A17939). The mace-head, which came from the Diyala Expedition, had been given in the 1930s as a gift from the Oriental Institute to Mr. Yondorf, who was a supporter of Oriental Institute Expeditions. We also received a pair of gold earrings from the Parthian era, donated by the Moffett family (OIM A154498 A-B).

The Integrated Database project (IDB) loomed large in the behind-the-scenes projects for the Museum staff. In fulfillment of Phase 1 of the project, the Registration Department staff had significantly scaled back outside research visits and volunteers to accommodate the patient work needed to prepare collections data and its associated fields for migration to the new KE EMu (Electronic Museum) database, which took place in October 2012. In addition, work was conducted to prepare the web "front end" of the Integrated Database, which was officially launched online in February 2013. A major achievement, pushed through diligently by Helen McDonald and Susan Allison, was the inclusion of the bulk of our collections in the database — a total of 207,000 objects (out of an estimated 300,000). These are now searchable online, providing an important resource for researchers.

In July 2012, we were pleased to learn that the Oriental Institute's latest grant application to the Institute of Museum and Library Services (IMLS) was successful, allowing us to progress with this long-term project. Phase 2 of the IDB project began in October 2012, its aim to incorporate records and images from the Photographic Archives database and to build the template for the Conservation Department's treatment records. Mónica Vélez, John Larson, Laura D'Alessandro, Alison Whyte, and Simona Cristanetti have been involved in template-building and preparation in advance of our data migration next year.

The Oriental Institute Museum has recently facilitated a number of loan requests, including to some prominent international "blockbuster" exhibitions. We lent seventeen objects from our Mesopotamian collections to CaixaForum (Barcelona and Madrid, Spain), our Arabian Nights fragment, the earliest known, to the Institut du Monde Arabe (Paris, France), and the Bismaya head (fig. 6) to the Royal Ontario Museum (Toronto, Canada). Another major loan was to the Art Institute of Chicago, to coincide with the opening of the Mary and Michael Jaharis Galleries of Greek, Roman, and Byzantine Art, which opened in October. Objects provided include a selection of Hellenistic gold

Figure 6. The "Bismaya head" traveled to the Royal Ontario Museum, Toronto, for the special exhibit Mesopotamia: Inventing Our World. Bismaya, Iraq, ca. 2100–2000 BC (OIM A173). Photo by Anna Ressman

jewelry, a Coptic censer, and a large section of a Byzantine mosaic floor from Khirbet al-Kerak/Bet Yerah, Israel. The latter required extensive treatment by our conservation staff, but the effort was well worth it. Our program of lending, as highlighted in the Spring 2013 edition of *News & Notes* (no. 217, pp. 3–6), provides an excellent opportunity for us to display objects that would otherwise not be shown within our own museum, and to build institutional relations and encourage professional interaction between museum professionals. The fact that the Oriental Institute is active in its ability to lend its collections can truly help to put the Oriental Institute and its collection on to a global footing. Yet it is acknowledged that loans are complex and labor intensive for our staff, often involving periods of time away for installation and deinstallation. I acknowledge here, in particular, the support, patience, and hard work of our registration, conservation, and photography staff in making our loans possible.

This year also saw significant participation from the Oriental Institute Museum staff on the National Museum of Afghanistan-Oriental Institute Partnership Project (see Gil Stein's report). During the course of the last financial year, following Erik Lindahl's return from his participation on the project in Kabul, there were visits by Jack Green and Laura D'Alessandro to provide support and oversight in project staffing, workflow, and conservation needs as the project developed. September 2012 corresponded with the official start of the inventory process, and by the end of June, over 13,000 objects, an estimated 15–20 percent of the National Museum's collections, had been entered into the database.

In January 2013, Erik Lindahl and I visited the site of Hisham's Palace, also known as Khirbet al-Mafjar, in Jericho, in the West Bank (Palestinian Territories). This was the third season of excavations at the site, under the supervision of Dr. Hamdan Taha, director of the Palestinian Department of Antiquities and Cultural Heritage, and Donald Whitcomb, associate professor of Islamic archaeology at the Oriental Institute. The Oriental Institute's visit was intended to provide assistance and guidance to the Department of Antiquities and Cultural Heritage (DACH) and the Ministry of Tourism by conducting a review of the Hisham's Palace Museum and artifacts housed at the site. This small archaeological site museum, which is currently closed to the public, covers roughly the size of the Oriental Institute Museum's special exhibits gallery. It has great potential in being able to complement the interpretation of this important early Islamic palace and bathhouse famed for its stucco work and elaborate mosaics. It is hoped that in the course of the coming year, alongside Donald Whitcomb, Oriental Institute Museum staff will assist with the development of interpretative text and graphic content for the Hisham's Palace site and museum.

In summary, I am extremely grateful for the work of the Museum staff and other colleagues at the Oriental Institute in helping to deliver our extensive Museum program and to fit in all the additional projects we are currently engaged in. I wish to thank Oriental Institute director Gil Stein and executive director Steve Camp for all their support, assistance, and advice over the past year. In 2012–13, we have seen the Museum play an increased role in expanding and delivering its collections through loans and the online database, as well as the provision of expertise and content well beyond the confines of Chicago and the United States. While not losing sight of our collections and exhibit objectives at home in Chicago, there has also been a significant positive expansion in the scope of our work within the areas of cultural-heritage management. We look forward eagerly to the next twelve months.

SPECIAL EXHIBITS

Emily Teeter

This has been an especially busy year for special exhibits because in addition to producing the major exhibits for the Marshall and Doris Holleb Family Special Exhibits Gallery, we also presented a number of other smaller temporary shows.

The big shows over the last year were Picturing the Past: Imaging and Imagining the Ancient Middle East, which opened on February 7, 2012, and ran through September 2, 2012, and Between Heaven & Earth: Birds in Ancient Egypt, from October 15, 2012, to July 28, 2013. (For a report on Picturing the Past, see the *2011–2012 Annual Report*, pp. 225–29.)

Between Heaven & Earth was curated by doctoral candidate in Egyptology Rozenn Bailleul-LeSuer. Rozenn did a marvelous job and showed a lot of innate talent for museum work. She included objects from the Art Institute of Chicago (a bronze statuette of Re Horakhty, an artist's trial piece of a quail chick, and a cosmetic vessel decorated with ducks), a stele from the Field Museum, and a spectacular ibis coffin from the Brooklyn Museum. Helen McDonald, our senior registrar, did her usual magic arranging the endless paperwork for the loans, insurance, and the couriers. Exhibit designers Erik Lindahl and Brian Zimerle, assisted by Matt Federico, recreated the atmosphere of a bird-filled marsh in the gallery (figs. 1–2). The walls were painted dark green and the text panels were printed on fabric framed by slender wood uprights topped with lotus finials. Brian has assumed all the graphic design duties for the special exhibits, from the handsome graphics on the special exhibits gallery (fig. 3), to the text panels, labels, catalog cover, rack cards, posters, and banners. Mónica Vélez worked closely with Rozenn to track down footage of Egyptian birds — a task that turned out to be much more complicated than any one of us anticipated. Erik cleverly installed a projection system to show videos of birds in flight on the upper part of the east wall and a sound system to play recordings of birdcalls.

A "kiosk committee" consisting of Rozenn, Moriah Grooms-Garcia of Public Programs, and Emily designed the content for an interactive kiosk for the gallery. We came up with three activities. "The Bird is the Word" challenged the visitor to match a bird hieroglyph to a photo of a real bird that can be seen in the Chicago area. This was fun and it also had a nice component of comparing ecosystems. "Birds in Ancient Egyptian Art" presented eight an-

Figures 1–2. Two views of the special exhibit Between Heaven & Earth: Birds in Ancient Egypt in the Marshall and Doris Holleb Family Special Exhibits Gallery. Photos by Anna Ressman

Figure 3. Entrance to the special exhibits gallery. Graphics by Brian Zimerle. Photo by Emily Teeter

cient representations of birds with a photo of the same bird to give an appreciation of how accurate the ancient artists were. The final activity was "Learn More," which gave more detailed information about ten artifacts in the exhibit. Joshua Day did a wonderful job designing the pages and the computer interface. It was a fun and fruitful collaboration. The members' preview on October 15 was a huge success with 179 people attending (fig. 4).

Other special exhibits for the year included the reworking of Catastrophe! The Looting and Destruction of Iraq's Past, which was originally presented at the Oriental Institute in 2008. Last year, Erik rehung a selection of the original panels in the lower level of the Institute, and we quickly recognized how interested our visitors continued to be in the topic. Jack Green, working with Katharyn Hansen and Professor McGuire Gibson, updated some of the information to reflect events in the ten years since the looting of the museum. It was always our hope and intention that the show would travel again (see the *Annual Report* for 2007–2008, p. 179, and 2008–2009, p. 194). The incentive to thoroughly revise the show was provided by Clemens Reichel, a research associate at the Oriental Institute, now associate curator (ancient Near East) at the Royal Ontario Museum (ROM) in Toronto. That museum was hosting a major exhibit of Mesopotamian material from the British Museum, and Clemens suggested that the updated Catastrophe show in its entirety would be an ideal adjunct. This entailed a

huge amount of work on the part of Jack and Brian Zimerle to prepare files, and especially for curatorial assistant Mónica Vélez, who was responsible for the complicated task of re-licensing all the images. The show opened to acclaim on June 22, 2013, at the ROM, located in a very prominent location off the main stairway. It will be on view until January 5, 2014. As a result of all the effort to update the show, we can now offer it to other museums in the United States and abroad.

Figure 4. Guest curator Rozenn Bailleul-LeSuer at the members' preview for the Between Heaven & Earth special exhibit. Photo by Anna Ressman

Some of the other special exhibits dropped in our lap. Hamza Walker of the University of Chicago's Renaissance Society approached us about collaborating with them on the presentation of *We the People* by Danh Vo, a full-size, disassembled, copper replica of the Statue of Liberty. Hamza wanted to distribute sections of the statue across campus. Jack and I were enthusiastic because of the resonance that the fragmentary statue would have with some of our artifacts that are also fragmentary, their pieces dispersed among different museum collections. A further relevance was that an early version of the Statue of Liberty was designed to stand at the entrance to the Suez Canal. Hamza generously offered us one of the most dramatic pieces — a fragment of the face of Lady Liberty — as well as a section of her draped garment (see fig. 4 in the *Museum* section). The timing was fortuitous because the temporary rearrangement of the Mesopotamian gallery to protect artifacts from vibrations created by the heavy construction on 58th Street created free areas in the center north side of the gallery. As the pieces were delivered and the face fragment was rolled into the Khorsabad Court, we all fell silent seeing it juxtaposed to the Khorsabad reliefs. A bold decision was made to exhibit that section in the center of the court rather than against the north wall. Exhibiting modern art alongside our collection is new to us, and in truth, not everyone appreciated it, although the majority of our visitors did, and Vo's pieces attracted enthusiasts of contemporary art to the Oriental Institute, people who may have never considered visiting us before. The show received a lot of media attention, again bringing us to the attention of a new audience. *We the People* was shown at the Oriental Institute from September 23 to December 16, 2012. We thank Professor Robert Ritner for contributing label copy about the historical background of the Statue of Liberty, including the Colossus of Rhodes and the statue's connection with the Ptolemies of Egypt.

A minor mystery provided the incentive for another small special exhibit. In December 2012, the University of Chicago's Office of College Admissions received a damaged parcel with antique Egyptian postage addressed to Henry Walton Jones, Jr. No professor of that name works for the University, but a mailroom worker eventually realized that the package was addressed to Henry Walton "Indiana" Jones. Inside the envelope was a replica of the journal of fictional University of Chicago professor Abner Ravenswood, Indy's mentor. Finally, the mystery was solved. The notebook was created by an artist on Guam and it was being shipped to a client in Italy, but it somehow fell out of its original outer package, and the postal service forwarded it to the University of Chicago. What better place than the Oriental Institute for such an "artifact"? Jack, Mónica, Brian, and Erik designed a small display in the lobby, adding photos and background about Breasted and the "real Indiana Jones," Robert Braidwood (fig. 5). The enduring attraction of the Indiana Jones persona was apparent by the wave of publicity about the notebook on television, in print, and on the web. The notebook was donated to the Institute by the artist who created it, and has been added to the Museum Archives.

Our next show, Our Work: Modern Jobs — Ancient Origins, is moving along well toward its members' opening on August 19. The exhibit makes connections between the ancient world and today by revealing how many jobs originated, or were documented, very early in the ancient Middle East. To make that point, we selected artifacts that refer to a particular profession and then paired that object with a modern "face" of that profession. The jobs include, among others, banker, mathematician, brewer, real-estate broker, manicurist, policeman, farmer, and physician. These pairings were captured by Chicago photographer Jason Reblando in a series of twenty-four tintypes. Emily contacted the participants, a group of people who reflect the face of Chicago, ranging from the president of the University of

Figure 5. Exhibit of the replica of the Indiana Jones notebook in the lobby of the Oriental Institute. Photo by Austin Kramer

Chicago, to a taxi driver, to a makeup artist. At the core of the show is the commentary of the participants themselves, who remarked on the unexpected antiquity of their jobs. The exhibit includes six videos by Chicago videographer Matthew Cunningham, who shadowed some of the participants at their workplace to give additional voice to their professions.

As usual, we are constantly working on upcoming exhibits, and are soliciting new ideas from faculty, staff, and students. We continue to work with our museum advisory group consisting of Nathan Mason (Chicago Cultural Center), Angela Adams (South Shore Cultural Center), Matt Matcuk (Field Museum), Molly Woulfe (journalist), Jacqueline Dace (DuSable Museum), Dianne Hanau-Strain (exhibit designer), and Beverly Serrell and Patty McNamara (exhibit evaluators).

Below is the tentative schedule for our special-exhibits program (dates of members' previews and titles are subject to change):

Our Work: Modern Jobs — Ancient Origins
August 19, 2013–February 23, 2014

In Remembrance of Me:
Feasting with the Dead in the Ancient Middle East
April 7, 2014–January 4, 2015

PUBLICITY AND MARKETING

Emily Teeter

We are so sorry to say farewell to our longtime media guru Williams Harms, of the University's News Office, who retired at the end of June after twenty-nine years of assisting the Oriental Institute with media coverage. We hosted a small reception in his honor on June 13 in the Director's Study. During the event, we displayed one of the Oriental Institute's clipping scrapbooks to remind him of some of the results his hard work. At Bill's larger, official retirement party on June 26, a video tribute from *New York Times* science writer John Noble Wilford included many references to the work of the Oriental Institute.

As usual, most of the press coverage over the past fiscal year was related to our special exhibits, another reason why the program is so valuable for raising awareness of the Institute, its mission, and its activities.

Rozenn Bailleul-LeSuer, guest curator for Between Heaven & Earth: Birds in Ancient Egypt, was tireless in promoting the show, giving special talks and tours throughout the run of the show at venues such as the Women's Athletic Club, the South Suburban Archaeological Society, the Joel Oppenheimer Gallery, and for special-interest groups such as the International Women's Association and University of Chicago alumni. She worked closely with press on campus, resulting in a cover story on her forensic work on the bird mummies in the *University of Chicago Magazine*, and in *At the Forefront* and *Medicine on the Midway*, the latter two through the help of our friend Molly Woulfe, a staff writer for the medical center who is on our museum advisory group. Our efforts to reach people and groups interested in birds resulted in a nice feature on the show in the magazine *Birdwatching Daily*. The show was also featured in the *Chicago Tribune* (October 25, "All Aflutter: Chicago has Birds on the Brain ...") and on WTTW's *Cultural Connections* show. Rozenn and Jack Green also appeared on *Chicago Tonight*. Brian Zimerle designed a whole range of publicity materials, including a rack card, invitations to events, posters, and banners (fig. 1).

The presentation of *We the People* by Danh Vo (September 23 to December 16, 2012; see *Special Exhibits* report) received a lot of publicity, including color images of the installation in *Time Out Chicago*. The show was included in "10 Must-See Art Shows" in the *New York Times* and featured in *Chicago Magazine*, while the *Chicago Tribune* referred to it in "Ten Things to Get Excited about in Chicago's Bountiful Art Scene." It was also featured on ABC News.

The completion of the Demotic Dictionary garnered a flood of media attention. Coverage appeared in a wide variety of both print and electronic media, ranging from the *Hindo Times* to *Al Jazeera*. Professor Janet H. Johnson, the editor of the Dictionary, was kept busy giving interviews to *Al Jazeera*, the BBC, Australian radio, and many other outlets.

Another event that created a flurry of publicity was the University's receipt of a replica of the journal related to Indiana Jones (see more under *Special Exhibits*).

The Museum was included in "Top 30 Most Beautiful College Art Galleries in the World Ranked by Top 10 Online Colleges" on KNOE.com, and in "Chicago Travel Tips: 5 Things You Shouldn't Miss," which was syndicated and appeared in many outlets. The public programs department earned the "2012 Time Out Chicago Hipsqueak Award" for "Mummy-Spotting Critics' Award." In

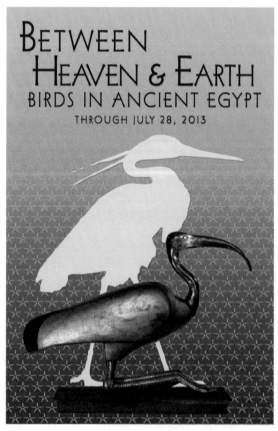

Figure 1. Poster for the special exhibit, featuring the ibis coffin from the Brooklyn Museum. Design by Brian Zimerle

June, the *New York Times* ran a story about the collaboration between Oriental Institute scholars and Pat Conway of Great Lakes Brewing Co. to recreate Sumerian beer. A very clever comment on the poor performance of two local sports figures in the *Chicago Tribune* involved the Oriental Institute. The article, entitled "Chicago Busts," featured photographs of the two athletes along with six busts of figures such as Shakespeare, Harry Caray, and Jean Baptiste du Sable. The sixth was "Nefertiti at the Oriental Institute. " It was a nice acknowledgment that, even in that context, people think of us as a local cultural asset.

The annual Hyde Park Art Fair was held on June 20, and we had a table offering kid's activities and distributing information about our exhibits and programs; the table was manned by Wahied Girgs, Carole Yoshida, Laura Alagna, Rebecca Binkley-Albright, Petra Creamer, Fred Eskra, Jack Green, Akemi Horii, Marilyn Murray, Dee Spiech, and Agnes Zellner (figs. 2–3).

Paid advertising this last year included ads in the *Hyde Park Herald*, *Footlights* (the program for the Court Theatre), *New City*, and in *Concierge Key*, an electronic newsletter for Chicago-area hotel concierges. We have identified concierges as a priority and target audience because they are often on the front line of engagement with visitors to Chicago, and their recommendations are perceived as being very trustworthy. Focusing on concierges is a cost-effective means of promoting the Museum. We also hosted a small reception for Chicago concierges on May 13. We continue to promote our activities through sponsorship of WBEZ public radio. We also maintain good relations with Choose Chicago, the official tourism authority for Chicago, and on May 6, we received a group of their visitor center staff members and walked them through the museum, showing them what we can offer people who ask them for recommendations of what to do and where to go.

We have been very fortunate this year to have Wahied Helmy Girgs as a part-time marketing assistant. He has been absolutely tireless in doing essential but time-consuming jobs that had fallen by the wayside, especially ensuring that our rack cards, both for the special exhibit and a general one for the Museum, are widely and thoroughly distributed to airports, visitors' centers, restaurants, and shops around Chicago. He has shaken the hand of dozens of hotel concierges as he dropped off our material. Another of his major initiatives has been to systematically follow the electronic visitors' book. His monthly reports are very helpful

Figures 2–3. The Oriental Institute booth at the Hyde Park Art Fair. Left: Wahied Girgs and his son Richard man the booth; right: children working on art projects. Photographs by Elisabeth Helmy

in trying to quantify the effectiveness of our paid advertising and overall visitor satisfaction. He has taken the analysis one step further by correlating his statistics with our paid ads and events, working closely with Jason Barcus, our manager of visitor services and security, who compiles weekly annotated reports on Museum attendance.

Wahied's reports continue to show that most of our visitors (of whom only a small percentage use the electronic visitor's book) hear about us through "friends and family." We still have a very high number of first-time visitors, an amazing 85 percent in February, with about 70 percent being the average. In this calendar year, of the people who responded, only between 3.7 and 7 percent of them were members of the Institute, a figure that assured us that we are successfully reaching new audiences. Fifty-one percent of the visitors were from Chicago, with only 7 percent of that number being from the immediate neighborhood, suggesting that we need to reach out to our neighbors more effectively (or perhaps that they don't use the comment book). Over half of the respondents said that they visited "just for fun," while about a fifth were part of a family outing. Of 185 responses, the exhibits ranked the most popular were Egypt (30 percent); Mesopotamia (19 percent), Persia (16 percent), and the special exhibit on birds (21 percent). A big surprise was the growing popularity of the Haas and Schwartz Megiddo Gallery, which previously only barely registered but is now judged the favorite by 12 percent of our visitors, a gain perhaps related to Jack Green's recent modifications of that exhibit space. The majority of our visitors come in small groups; about half being parties of two, and a quarter being three people. These are very interesting statistics, but of course, it is likely that people in large groups are less likely to stop and engage with the comment book.

Emily has been working with the new Hyatt Inn Hyde Park and the Museum Campus South group to have the cultural groups in Hyde Park represented in the hotel's lobby. The project is still being finalized, but we hope to have the Oriental Institute's name and image displayed prominently before guests in the hotel. In a related effort, prints of historic photographs of the Middle East from our archive are now being exhibited at the Nile Restaurant in its new location on 55th Street.

We continue to get great response from our visitors. One posting on *Yelp* (April 15, 2013) reads:

> Wow. That is just one word that came to mind when I walked through and saw the big Babylonian sculptures. This museum took me about two hours to walk through, though you could easily spend a whole day here. There are countless artifacts relating to Babylonia, Assyria, Egypt, and the Hittites, as well as a small section about Megiddo (in present-day Israel). This is one of the few places in the United States to see part of the Dead Sea Scrolls, as well. The temporary exhibit on bird mummies was also interesting. I joined a group tour that was in progress when I was here. The tour guide was very informative and enhanced the experience. This museum deserves to be in company with the Art Institute and the Field Museum as one of the great museums in Chicago. The free admission (with suggested donation) was just icing on the cake. 5 stars out of 5!

We are delighted to hear that what we do is appreciated by the public.

REGISTRATION

Helen McDonald and Susan Allison

Once again much of our time in the last fiscal year has been taken up with the migration of our data from dbase 3 to the new museum-specific software program KE EMu (Electronic Museum), thanks to the Museums for America grant from the Institute of Museum and Library Services (IMLS). At this time last year, we had just submitted our data to be loaded into the new KE EMu database for the second time. Over the summer we went through a further three data loads, each followed by a round of testing, before we finally went live in October. Since then we have been settling in and using the new system, discovering more of its possibilities and continuing with the process of data cleanup. Although we did as much cleanup as possible before the data migration, there is still a great deal to do. In particular, we ran out of time and had to move our chronological terms into the thesaurus as a flat list without a hierarchy. We are now looking to build that hierarchy, and after some discussion with the head of the Research Archives, Foy Scalf, we will see if between us we can build one hierarchy of terms that will serve both Museum Registration and the Research Archives and perhaps other departments going forward (to which end we also plan to consult with the tablet curator and the Tablet Collection staff to see about incorporating the terms that the tablet collection might need). This is exactly the kind of integration that the IDB was set up to do. In May, it was a pleasure to be involved in the visit of museum professionals and others from the University of Michigan at Ann Arbor, as they contemplate moving several museums and other collections over to KE EMu.

The assistant registrar Susan Allison was instrumental in both testing the website front end of the database and preparing those of our collection records that we are sharing through it with the general public. Registration's database reports, which are the most efficient way to export information from KE EMu, were designed by Susan and written by J. P. Brown of the Field Museum. Susan has continued to fulfill the registration component in the National Endowment for the Humanities (NEH) Metals Room re-housing grant: keeping track of object locations and printing labels. She has managed object lists and has also kept track of all object movement for special exhibits, including the deinstallation of Picturing the Past as well as the installation of Between Heaven & Earth: Birds in Ancient Egypt. For the latter show, we also received incoming loans from the Field Museum of Natural History, the Art Institute of Chicago, and the Brooklyn Museum (a splendid ibis coffin). Work for the upcoming exhibit In Remembrance of Me: Feasting with the Dead in the Ancient Middle East has begun and Susan has also been working with the Photography Department, pulling objects for inclusion in upcoming gallery highlight publications.

With regard to outgoing loans, we lent sixteen Mesoptamian objects to the "la Caixa" Foundation for an exhibit at CaixaForum (Barcelona and Madrid) entitled Before the Flood: Mesopotamia 3500–2100 BC. Registrar Helen McDonald accompanied the objects back from Madrid at the close of the exhibition. The Art Institute of Chicago's new Mary and Michael Jaharis Galleries of Greek, Roman, and Byzantine Art now includes a few of our objects on a three-year renewable loan; these include a floor mosaic from the Byzantine church excavated at Khirbet el-Kerak, in modern Israel (OIM A30490 A–E), a Coptic censer (OIM E16735), an alabastron (E9408), and Hellenistic gold jewelry (OIM A29786–A29790). We lent the earliest known manuscript fragment of the Arabian Nights (OIM E17618) to the Institut du Monde Arabe (Paris) for an exhibit on the One Thousand and One Nights. The process of renewing loans to the University of Pennsylvania Museum of Archaeology and Anthropology (pots from the embalmers cache of Tutankhamun) and the Michael C. Carlos Museum at Emory University, in Atlanta, Georgia (Diyala material), was completed this year. Both renewals required visits by our conservation staff to re-assess and record the condition of the objects. The Bismaya head of a ruler (OIM A173; see fig. 6 in Jack Green's *Museum* report) has just gone to the Royal Ontario Museum to join a British Museum touring exhibit entitled Mesopotamia: Inventing Our World.

The Registration Department has moved or inventoried over 25,000 objects this year (a total of almost 37,000 object movements). Almost 4,000 objects were registered and nearly 1,500 had new labels printed and applied to bags or containers. Nearly 5,700 were the subject of research of all kinds. Just over 600 had their locations updated, checked, or corrected. Around 130 objects were moved for photography, including for forthcoming gallery guides. Twenty-five objects were moved due to loans or while being considered for loans of various sorts. Around 115 objects were moved for temporary exhibits that were installed, dismantled, or in preparation. We had a particularly large number of in-house projects this year, from the various Nubian Expedition publications in preparation (over 6,700 objects either registered or moved), to research on our Islamic collection (over 3,900 objects studied) and Diyala objects (around 520 items studied). With regard to expanding our storage space, a study has been commissioned from storage specialists at Bradford Systems on the feasibility of installing a compact storage system into the area of the sherd cabinets.

Visiting researchers:

- Federico Zaina (PhD candidate, Sapienza University of Rome) came to study a variety of Diyala objects in July 2012.
- William and Hannah Nutt (PhD students, University of Texas at Arlington) came to study Alishar and Tell Fakhariyah material, also in July.
- Lynn Swartz Dodd (University of Southern California), who is working on a publication of the Middle Bronze and later levels at the Amuq site of Judaidah, visited to study objects in August and November.
- Debbie Schorsch (Metropolitan Museum of Art, New York) came to study Medinet Habu bronzes with Emily Teeter, also in August.
- Shannon Martino (Field Museum of Natural History) came over in October to study Alishar Bronze Age ceramics with a view to submitting an application for x-ray fluorescence (XRF) analysis, which was carried out in December with our conservation staff. A further application for inductively coupled plasma mass spectrometry (ICP-MS) analysis on a small number of the sherds has been received and those have now gone out to the Field Museum.
- Lidija McKnight and Stephanie Atherton (University of Manchester, UK) came to study animal mummies as part of their work with the the Ancient Egyptian Animal Bio Bank Project based at the University of Manchester, UK. The Oriental Institute Museum animal mummies have now been included in the online database of the Animal Bio Bank (http://www.knhcentre.manchester.ac.uk/research/animalbio-bank/).
- Kiersten Neumann (graduate student, University of California, Berkeley) studied objects from the Khorsabad temples for her PhD dissertation in October and November.

- Bettina Bader (Marie Curie Research Fellow, University of Cambridge, UK, and the Institute for Egyptology at the University of Vienna) visited to look at some of the Serra and Dorginarti material with Bruce Williams.
- Niv Allon (Andrew W. Mellon Fellow, Metropolitan Museum of Art and Yale University) studied Egyptian statue fragments in November.
- Professor Sabahattin Ezer (Adiyaman University, Department of Archaeology) came in January to look at a ceramic vessel type called the depas cup, of which we have examples from the Amuq valley and Alishar Hüyük.
- Susan Allen (Metropolitan Museum of Art [Met]) studied fish plates from the MET excavations at Lisht in February.
- Charlotte Maxwell-Jones (graduate student, University of Michigan at Ann Arbor) has visited a couple of times to look at Achaemenid ceramics from Persepolis, Iran, with a view to comparing them to material of similar date from Afghanistan.
- Sarah Clegg (University of Cambridge, UK) came in February to carry out a study on vessel capacities for pots from the Diyala region and Nippur.
- Katarzyna Danys-Lasek (Polish Centre of Mediterranean Archaeology, University of Warsaw), the ceramics specialist for the Qasr el-Wizz publication, visited in March to work on the pottery from that site.
- Laurel Poolman (George Washington University) came in May to study the unregistered but recently rehoused human bone from Megiddo. She has also been studying the Megiddo human bone housed in the Smithsonian Institution.
- Caroline Roberts (J. Paul Getty Museum) visited in June to research objects containing Egyptian green pigment.
- Travis Saul has been to photograph and scan the mold of the Katumuwa stele in order to produce a digital version to be used in the forthcoming special exhibit. The mold has now been sent out for a cast to be made from it.

Oriental Institute faculty, staff, researchers, and students:

- Artur Obluski (Oriental Institute research associate; Polish Centre of Mediterranean Archaeology at the University of Warsaw; visiting scholar) has been working all year on the Qasr el-Wizz publication. A quantity of organic material has been rehoused by Conservation staff and registered by the assistant registrar.
- Joanna Then-Obluska (Oriental Institute research associate and the University of Warsaw) has continued to work throughout this year on the Nubian beads in our collection.
- Tasha Vorderstrasse has continued with the study all of the Islamic material in our collections in preparation for a book on Islamic archaeology on which she and Donald Whitcomb are working. Also planned is a publication of the highlights of the Islamic collection. She recently joined us as a volunteer, registering sherd material.
- Lisa Heidorn has studied crucibles and fragments of slag from the Nubian site of Dorginarti and has submitted a proposal for the analysis of this material.
- Karen Wilson has continued working on the publication of the Inanna temple sounding at Nippur with McGuire Gibson, Jean Evans, and others. She has also been unpacking sherds received from the Institute of Fine Arts in New York.
- Angela Altenhofen has continued to draw seal impressions from Semna South, among other projects.

- Robert Ritner used stele OIM E10511 for a class in May.
- Yorke Rowan examined flint from Barda Balka that is to appear in a forthcoming publication of that site by the late Bruce Howe.
- Vincent van Excel studied a variety of objects from Megiddo and Egypt for a forthcoming special exhibit on the stele of Katumuwa, which was found during the Neubauer Expedition to Zincirli, Turkey, led by David Schloen.
- In the first half of 2013, Lise Truex (graduate student, NELC) studied a variety of Diyala objects from domestic contexts for her PhD dissertation.
- Carol Meyer (Oriental Institute research associate) came in to look at fragments of glass vessels from Quseir (that she has already published) as part of a proposal for analysis from Laure Dussubieux of the Field Museum. Joanna Then-Obluska made a selection of glass beads also from Quseir for this project.
- Bruce Williams has continued to work on Serra material for a forthcoming publication. Recently he has been joined by NELC graduate students Kathryn Bandy, Elise MacArthur, and Susan Penacho to re-examine the large number of clay sealings from the site.
- Benedetta Bellucci (University of Pavia, Italy) has been examining a small group of seals gifted to us some years ago and a collection of modern seal rollings that were once part of Helene Kantor's teaching collection with a view to providing us with information that will assist in their registration.
- Alexander Sollee (visiting scholar, funded by the DAAD or German Academic Exchange Service, PhD candidate at Ludwig Maximilian University, Munich) has studied a variety of objects from Khorsabad, in particular some of the royal sealings.
- David Calabro (NELC graduate student) spent a few days looking at some of our bronze smiting-god figures to include in his PhD dissertation on ritual hand gestures in a variety of media, mostly from the Middle Bronze Age through Iron Age II.
- Joshua Cannon (NELC graduate student) has been familiarizing himself with Hittite ceramic material from Alishar Höyuk in preparation for a season at Çadir Hüyük.

Although we had to call a halt to our volunteer activity early in 2012 due to the pressure of work on the KE EMu transition, we are now in the process of getting our regular volunteers back and would like to thank all of them for their efforts. Daila Shefner rejoined us in January to assist with inventory and labeling, and Toni Smith has just rejoined us to continue with the registration of Nubian sherds. Janet Helman has continued to register Tall i-Geser sherds (Iran) as part of assisting Abbas Alizadeh with the publication of that site. Museum Registration had the assistance of two MAPSS students this year: Rebekah Planto registered Islamic sherds from Istakhr (among other tasks) and Lauren Nareau registered Palaeolithic flint tools from Tabun Cave in Israel (on which she also wrote a paper). In January we were joined by high-school student Naomi Rubinstein (Roycemore School), who registered a variety of material that was included in various proposals for analysis or in publication (for

Figure 1. IDB registration at work. Photo by Austin Kramer

example, glass fragments from Quseir, Egypt; crucible and slag fragments from Dorginarti, Egypt; Alishar Bronze Age sherds from Alishar Hüyük, Turkey; and flints from Barda Balka, Iraq). Recently we were joined by summer intern Petra Creamer (Ohio State University), who is engaged in a variety of registration tasks, including the registration of clay sealings from the site of Semna South, Sudan, and Chalcolithic sherds from Tepe Sohz, Iran. Sam Butler (University of Chicago undergraduate) has also joined us for the summer and is busy inventorying the tablet collection and registering tablet casts. Tasha Vorderstrasse is registering sherds from Erich Schmidt's aerial survey of Iran. We would also like to thank George Sundell for doing all of the comma-separated value (csv) exports of our dbase 3 and Excel files for each time we reloaded our data into KE EMu. All in all it has been a busy and productive year.

ARCHIVES

John A. Larson

As of December 2012, John Larson has served as head of the Archives for thirty-two years.

Scholars visiting the Archives during fiscal year 2012–2013 included Wayne Pitard of the University of Illinois Urbana-Champaign, who came on July 19, 2012, to study A. T. Olmstead in 1922/1923; Sarah Symons of McMaster University, who visited on August 1 and 2, 2012, to look at photographs of Egyptian astronomical ceilings; James F. Goode of Grand Valley State University, author of *Negotiating for the Past: Archaeology, Nationalism, and Diplomacy in the Middle East, 1919–1941*, who came on August 21 and 22, 2012, to do research on James Henry Breasted; David Burnham, who visited on September 7, 2012, to look at photographs of Egyptian monuments for a project; Manu P. Sobti and Sahar Hossein of the University of Wisconsin, Milwaukee, who came on September 18, 2012, to look at photographs from Erich F. Schmidt's aerial survey of Iran; Jason Thompson of Bates College, author of several books on Egypt, who visited on October 5, 2012, to discuss a forthcoming book on the history of Egyptology; Daniele Morandi Bonacossi of the University of Udine, who came on November 16, 2012, to look at the field records of Sennacherib's aqueduct at Jerwan; Alexander Sollee of Ludwig Maximilian University of Munich, who came on February 5, 2013, to examine the field records of Khorsabad for his dissertation, Neo-Assyrian Fortifications within Their Topographical Context; Joanna Then-Obluska of the University of Warsaw, who visited on May 2, 2013, to look at the field registers of objects from Nubia; and Laurel Poolman of the George Washington University, who came on May 30, 2013, to consult field records from Megiddo for a project on human remains from Megiddo. From within our own Oriental Institute community, Jean Evans, Jack Green, Emily Teeter, Bruce Williams, and Karen L. Wilson have conducted research using Archives materials.

Several acquisitions were made by the Archives during this fiscal year. In the summer of 2012, Margaret Richmond of Tucson, Arizona, gave to the Archives two traveling trunks that had belonged to James Henry Breasted and his family. On December 12, 2012, a mysterious package addressed to "Henry Walton Jones, Jr." arrived at the University of Chicago's Office of College Admissions. Inside the parcel was a journal of Abner Ravenwood, the fictional University of Chicago professor who trained "Indiana" Jones of *Raiders of the Lost Ark* fame, and an assortment of other replica props from the film. The package had been purchased online and shipped by its maker, Paul Charfauros, from Guam to Italy. In transit in Hawaii, the parcel lost its original packaging, leaving only the envelope addressed to Henry Walton Jones, Jr., at the University of Chicago. The parcel and its contents were exhibited at the Oriental Institute Museum from December 20, 2012, until March 31, 2013, and Mr. Charfauros donated it to the Oriental Institute Archives. On January 16, 2013, the field records of the late Bruce Howe's excavations at the site of Barda Balka in northern Iraq arrived at the Oriental Institute. This prehistoric site was excavated by Bruce Howe and Herbert E. Wright in 1951. The manuscript is being prepared for publication by Yorke Rowan.

The following people have contributed their time as Archives volunteers during fiscal year 2012–2013 and have made it possible for us to continue a number of projects in the Oriental Institute Archives that would not have been possible without their generous assistance: Peggy Grant, Robert Wagner, and Carole Yoshida. We are grateful to have benefited from the help of these dedicated volunteers, and we thank them here for all of their efforts on behalf of the Archives. In addition to the regular volunteers in the Archives, Jim Sopranos and George Sundell scanned the Diyala plans and drawings for the Diyala Project. John has been assisted in the Oriental Institute Archives during this academic year by MAPSS graduate students Solomon Hursey, John Li, Rebecca Pamela Suhr, and Mara Zocco. John, Rebecca, and Mara scanned lantern slides from the collections for the Integrated Database project, and Solomon scanned letters of Harold Haydon Nelson from the Director's Office Correspondence for Peggy Grant's transcription project. We would like to thank all four of these students for their work.

During the past fiscal year, John Larson has continued the re-organization of the Archives, which was made possible by the successful application to the University of Chicago's Capital Projects Program by Gil Stein and Steve Camp in 2010. We are transferring the flat files (contents of the old map-cases) into the new map-cases, re-housing the collections generally, and updating the shelf-list accordingly. John was involved in the planning for improved storage of oversize framed works of art in the Archives collections. In addition to the routine of running the Archives, we have scanned 10,000 additional existing images for the online photographic database, for Phase Two of the Integrated Database project, and contributed to the IDB project in a variety of ways, including participation in meetings and planning to web front end of the database.

Figure 1. "Farmers Deliver their Quota of Geese," Catalog no. 14 from Between Heaven & Earth: Birds in Ancient Egypt. Photo by Anna Ressman

The special exhibit Between Heaven & Earth: Birds in Ancient Egypt opened on October 16, 2012, and runs through July 28, 2013. Among the items exhibited are four tempera paintings by Nina de Garis Davies from the Archives: "Birds in an Acacia Tree," "Fowling in the Marshes," "Farmers Deliver their Quota of Geese," and "Three Vignettes." We also provided a number of archival digital images for the decoration of the Nile Restaurant, which recently moved near 55th Street and Woodlawn Avenue.

CONSERVATION

Laura D'Alessandro

The Conservation Laboratory entered a new phase of its existence this year with our entry into the world of integrated databases. We joined the Oriental Institute's KE EMu integrated database project this past winter, otherwise known as the IDB Project (*see Integrated Database Project report*). Our work began with assessing the laboratory's files and images in order to understand how best to integrate our work into the Institute's newly developed IDB. The first six months consisted of a series of meetings and working groups to assess our data and customize the ways in which we will access the information with the goal of making our work easier and more efficient. It is a multi-year project that will require considerable effort on our part, but it is a necessary step to ensure that the Conservation Laboratory stays current with technology. We look forward to joining the IDB and expanding our collaboration with our colleagues here at the Oriental Institute.

Alison Whyte, associate conservator, had another very busy and productive year handling loans and exhibits activities as well as a myriad of other responsibilities. As the year started, Alison was completing her work on the special exhibit Between Heaven & Earth: Birds in Ancient Egypt, which involved the assessment and treatment of objects and providing advice on the safest way to display the delicate and fragile objects. She then moved on to the next special exhibit, Our Work: Modern Jobs — Ancient Origins, and provided conservation input during the photography of the collection with the subjects of the exhibit (fig. 1). As of this writing, she is already busy working on next year's exhibit, In Remembrance of Me: Feasting with the Dead in the Ancient Middle East, assessing and treating the objects that will be installed for this display.

One of the more interesting projects that Alison undertook this past year was the stabilization and aesthetic improvement of five of the sixth-century AD mosaic fragments from the Byzantine church at Khirbet al-Kerak (Israel), currently on loan to the Art Institute of Chicago in their new exhibition, Of Gods and Glamour: The Mary and Michael Jaharis Galleries of Greek, Roman, and Byzantine Art (fig. 2). These mosaic fragments have not been on public display for several decades and this was a wonderful opportunity to showcase the five of them in a beautiful new setting.

Alison was also responsible for the treatment of the Oriental Institute's plaster cast of the Mesha Stela in preparation for its installation in the Haas and Schwartz Megiddo Gallery. After decades of display on the third floor of the Institute, it required the repair of cracks, cleaning, and delicate retouching of the inscription before it was ready to be unveiled in the gallery. Alison also treated the plaster cast of the Code of Hammurabi Stela located in the Edgar and Deborah Jannotta Mesopotamian Gallery (fig. 3). This object is very popular with visitors and despite all precautions it tends to show the obvious effects of this devotion over time. Alison's article on the treatment of the stela, "Conservation Close-up: Plaster Cast of the Code of Hammurabi Stela," appeared in the Winter 2013 *News & Notes* (no. 216).

Figure 1. Senior registrar Helen McDonald (on left) and associate conservator Alison Whyte move the Sennacherib Prism onto a temporary mount for photography for the upcoming special exhibit, Our Work: Modern Jobs – Ancient Origins. Photo by Jason Reblando

A significant portion of Conservation's time was spent dealing with loan requests. The Oriental Institute contributes to a variety of exhibits in other institutions over the course of a year. Conservation's responsibilities include the initial assessment of the objects under consideration, conducting a condition assessment of the artifacts, preparing the objects for travel, and the packing of the fragile artifacts. This past year the Museum loaned objects from

Figure 2 (Left). Alison Whyte (in back) and Art Institute conservator Emily Heye carry out a condition assessment of the Oriental Institute's mosaic fragments from Khirbet al-Kerak during their installation in the Mary and Michael Jaharis Galleries of Greek, Roman, and Byzantine Art at the Art Institute of Chicago

Figure 3. Alison Whyte cleans the plaster cast of the Code of Hammurabi in the Oriental Institute Conservation Laboratory

its collections to CaixaForum in Barcelona and Madrid, Spain; the Royal Ontario Museum in Toronto, Canada; and the Institut du Monde Arabe in Paris, France.

Simona Cristanetti, National Endowment for the Humanities (NEH)–funded Metals Room conservator, also had a very productive year as she continued the painstaking and detailed work on this critical project to assess and re-house our metals collection. Simona and her team of interns completed the re-housing of the entire coin collection (over 3,000 in number) as well as the metals collections from Medinet Habu, Bahnasa, Abu Ghurab, and Naucratis (weights) (fig. 4). This grant award from NEH Preservation and Access: Sustaining Cultural Heritage Collections is in its final months and soon the metals room will have completed its transformation. Simona led a cadre of dedicated volunteer conservation pre-program interns who devoted their time and energies to this project: Kate Aquirre, Marissa Bartz, Magdalyne Christakis, Jacob Engelman, Anna Kosters, Ryan Lavery, Hannah Lee, Laura Moeller, Mary Wilcop, and Evelina Zielinski. We thank them all for their invaluable contribution to the project.

In June, Simona completed her responsibilities on the Metals' Room project and segued into the position of conservator for the Persepolis Fortification Archive Project, supported by a grant from the PARSA Community Foundation. She looks forward to this opportunity to work on a valuable and important research collection with its very special needs and welcomes the chance to contribute to this important project. Simona's new position was made possible as the former incumbent, Robyn Haynie, left the Oriental Institute to take up a permanent conservation position at the Utah Museum of Fine Arts in Salt Lake City. We were very sorry to see Robyn leave but we were very pleased for her on a professional level and sent her on her way with warm wishes. She contributed to the work of the Lab in an understated way and undertook many small tasks in her own time to help make our jobs easier. We thank Robyn for her generosity of spirit and team attitude. She is missed by all but we are glad that she is doing well in her new position.

In addition to the ongoing work of a busy conservation laboratory within a museum setting, there were several ongoing projects that continued over the course of the year. The most notable of these was the Oriental Institute-National Museum of Afghanistan Partnership. The goal of this ongoing cultural-heritage project is to assist the National Museum of Afghanistan with completing the inventory and registration of their collections. The project contains a conservation component that necessitated several trips to Kabul to work with our Afghan colleagues and ensure that they had the materials they required to re-house their collections, and to provide advice, where needed. We were ably assisted in this undertaking by two conservation colleagues, Natalie Firnhaber, recently retired from the Smithsonian Institution's National Museum

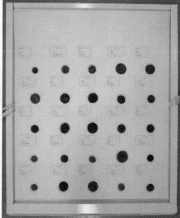

Figure 4. Newly re-housed coins in the Oriental Institute's collection in custom cabinets purchased with funding from NEH Division of Preservation and Access

of Natural History, and Noel Siver, a conservator in private practice with decades of experience working in the Middle East. We thank Natalie and Noel for their dedication and assistance and for lending their expertise to this project that is so vital to preserving the cultural heritage of Afghanistan.

And the report about the year's activities would not be complete without mentioning the ongoing pigment project that is taking on a life of its own. The Conservation staff is continuing to study the ancient pigments on the eighth-century BC reliefs from Sargon's Palace at Khorsabad in the Museum's collection. The results of this study will contribute to future publications on the collections and future exhibitions. Work on the pigment project also continued at Argonne National Laboratory, under the direction of Dr. Steve Heald, director of Sector 20. Dr. Heald's continuing interest and support of the project is very appreciated. We were also fortunate to receive support from Dr. Kenneth Shull, professor of materials science and engineering at Northwestern University, who made it possible for two of his graduate students, Chya Yan Liaw and Lauren Sturdy, to work with us on-site at Argonne. Their participation and contributions were very welcome. We were very pleased to learn that on the basis of preliminary tests carried out earlier in the year, the team was granted beamtime in December to carry out more advanced, targeted analyses on a range of samples, both ancient and modern.

In conjunction with the work at Argonne, the collaborative portion of the project moved forward with a two-day visit to the Louvre Museum in May. While there, I met with chief conservator Elisabeth Fontan in the Department of Near Eastern Antiquities to formalize the next steps. Elisabeth and I had the opportunity to examine pigmented objects in the collections in

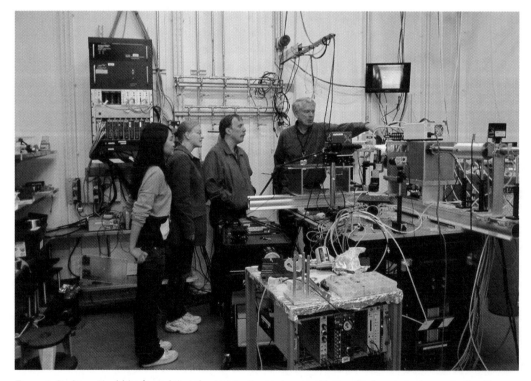

Figure 5. Dr. Steve Heald (at far right) at the APS Sector 20 Argonne National Laboratory, demonstrating the equipment set-up to the Northwestern University group: (from right to left) Dr. Ken Shull, Lauren Sturdy, and Chya Yan Liaw

storage as well as those on display and begin to draw up lists of future work for both teams. After two days of discussion we came up with a plan of action and timelines that will allow the project to move forward in a structured manner. We anticipate additional collaborations with other specialists over the course of the next year. The Conservation staff is excited to be part of this ongoing project that allows us to expand our professional capabilities, and keeps us energized and highly motivated!

PREP SHOP

Erik Lindahl

The 2012–2013 fiscal year at the Oriental Institute has been a busy one. The Prep Shop has continued to produce temporary exhibits, maintain the galleries, assist with collections management, assist with research projects, and generally advance the mission of the Oriental Institute.

The special exhibits program has continued with success. Picturing the Past finished up smoothly and Between Heaven & Earth, which is running into the next fiscal year, has been well received. Currently we are working with Jason Reblando and Matthew Cunningham on a portrait exhibit titled Our Work: Modern Jobs — Ancient Origins, which opens in August of 2013. For the photography of this exhibit we turned the laundry room into a darkroom for the processing of tintypes and prepared mounts for photography. Brian Zimerle was also one of the portrait subjects. The Museum has been meeting with the curators of the upcoming exhibit In Remembrance of Me: Feasting with the Dead in the Ancient Middle East. From these meetings a basic design and layout has been developed.

There where quite a few small exhibits and changes to the permanent galleries this year. Some of these were the Danh Vo We the People sculpture exhibit in the Edgar and Deborah Jonnotta Mesopotamian Gallery. The Haas and Schwartz Megiddo Gallery was enhanced with the addition of the Moabite Stone, and the El and Baal figurines were moved to a more prominent location. A cast of a relief of Tuthaliya IV from Yazılıkaya was installed in the Hittite Dictionary office on the third floor of the Institute (fig. 3; see also fig. 1 of the Chicago Hittite Dictionary report). With much publicity, a reproduction of the fictitious Indiana Jones's diary was put on display in the lobby along with some information about famous Oriental Institute archeologists (see fig. 5 in Emily Teeter's Special Exhibits report).

The Prep Shop was heavily involved with Institute publicity this year. Large outdoor banners where designed by Brian Zimerle and installed on the east face of the building (see fig. 1 in Jack Green's Museum report). Zimerle also designed and produced new rack cards (see fig. 2 of the Museum report), newspaper advertisements, street banners, and other publicity-related signage. Brass lettering for the Oriental Institute was designed and commissioned this year, and will be installed on the west side of the building later in the year.

Erik Lindahl and Brian Zimerle where also involved in several addition projects. For his part in an Oriental Institute–Great Lakes Brewing Co. collaboration to produce an ancient Sumerian brew, Zimerle produced replicas of large, ancient Sumerian brewing vessels. Lindahl returned from Afghanistan at the beginning of this year and continues to be involved with the purchasing of equipment for the Oriental Institute's partnership project with the National Museum of Afghanistan. For several years Donald Whitcomb has been discussing the possibility of the Museum helping with a site museum at his excavation of Khirbat al-Mafjar (Hisham's Palace) outside Jericho in the West Bank; this year Erik Lindahl and Jack Green made a trip to the site and worked with Don and the Palestinian Department of Antiquities and Cultural Heritage to produce a brief of recommendations on how to improve the site museum. It looks as if this project will continue into the next year.

The infrastructure of the Oriental Institute is something that the Prep Shop is heavily involved in improving and maintaining. This year the Institute's surveillance system needed to be updated, and the Prep Shop was involved in choosing locations for new cameras and in the supervision of the collections during installation. Due to water damage in years past the west wall in the Robert and Deborah Aliber Persian Gallery was repaired and painted. After much debate it was decided this year to purchase a powered personnel lift for the Institute. The Prep Shop did the comparison shopping and negotiated the price of our new used Genie GR-15. It will allow Museum staff to better maintain the galleries and the collection by making it easier for the monumental sculpture to be cleaned more regularly.

As in years past the Prep Shop was heavily involved in the biennial Oriental Institute Gala. For the 2013 Gala, held in May, we brought four casts of Assyrian reliefs, the copy of the Nefertiti bust, and the Morton Tent to the J.W. Marriott Hotel in downtown Chicago for the festivities.

Activities related to collections management and research kept the Prep Shop quite busy this year. Due to the large amount of photography-related projects this year, a lot of time was spent making mounts for, moving, and handling objects for photography. The Jannotta

Figure 1. Brian and Erik install the Moabite Stone in the Haas and Schwartz Megiddo Gallery

Figure 2. The El and Baal figurines in their new location in the Megiddo Gallery. The Moabite Stone can be seen in the background

Figure 3. Brian Zimerle (left) and Erik Lindahl installing the cast of Tuthaliya IV from Yazılıkaya in the office of the Hittite Dictionary

Mesopotamian Gallery was rearranged as a safety precaution related to possible vibrations from large-scale and long-term construction activities across the street at the site of the future Becker Friedman Institute for Research in Economics. To accommodate a strong interest in bones, this year hundreds of pounds of faunal remains have been moved around the basement for research purposes. The volume of loans from the Oriental Institute collection increased this fiscal year. This affects the Prep Shop in many ways, including display-mount design and production and the construction of crates.

There is never a shortage of moving and storage projects at the Institute. This year was no exception, with the Prep Shop assisting with the Research Archives compact-storage project, the Metals Room project, and with dealing with an ever-increasing demand for space. As a space-saving- and collections-management- related decision, the Prep Shop and registration decided to install sixteen feet of pallet racking in the basement of the new wing this year. This resulted in freeing up a substantial amount of space while making the collection more accessible.

The Prep Shop would like to thank our assistants and student workers. Matt Federico did an outstanding job helping with the Between Heaven & Earth production and install, as well as the cleaning of the Kipper Family Archaeology Discovery Center collapsible tell. Justin Skye Malichowski did a wonderful job assisting the Prep Shop with various tasks while pursuing his MA. Caitlin Jewell, who completed her MA while assisting the Prep Shop, was an exceptionally reliable assistant with a strong eye for detail.

The next year looks to be another exciting one. We are looking forward to more exhibits and continuing to work with wonderful people.

SUQ

Denise Browning

This was a very exciting year for us. The very popular special exhibit Between Heaven & Earth: Birds of Ancient Egypt gave us the opportunity to spread our wings and bring in 161 new items to the Suq, including twelve that we developed in house, including the trivet, pictured here (fig. 1).

It was an honor to work with the Oriental Institute's Gala this year, which was held at the J. W. Marriott Hotel in downtown Chicago. We designed the upper lobby to be a Middle Eastern Suq, covering the floor with top-line Oriental rugs priced up to $33,000, and brought in new merchandise that we don't usually carry in the Suq, including one-of-a-kind jewelry and collectables.

Figure 1. Birds in Ancient Egypt trivet

The first week of June, during the University's alumni weekend and our own annual inventory sale, we repeated and expanded our Oriental rug sale, now in its second year. We set up a huge tent in the parking lot east of the Oriental Institute and filled it with rugs, so many that they even spilled out onto the sidewalk. Special thanks to our wonderful volunteers: Judy Bell-Qualls, Ray Broms, Norma van der Meulen, and Jane Meloy, who we were excited to welcome back. Lab School student Clea Bruener was an excellent help during the summer. The Suq volunteers are our connection with the public on a day-to-day basis and give excellent service to our visitors.

We sold 199 pieces of jewelry designed and created by Norma van der Meulen. What would we ever do without her?

Three of our dependable student workers graduated this year. They all worked with the customers in the Suq but also worked independently: Dylan Genest, merchandise manager, Mark Lambert, mail-order expert; and Iman Naim, accountant. Congratulations! Thankfully, Dylan will be returning as she works on her master's degree, and Evan Bernard will also be returning.

PHOTOGRAPHY

Anna R. Ressman

The fiscal year from 2012 through 2013 has been a busy and productive time for the Photography Department. My work on the catalog, display, and publicity materials for the special exhibit Between Heaven & Earth: Birds in Ancient Egypt was completed. I began work on the upcoming highlights book of the Henrietta Herbolsheimer, M.D. Syro-Anatolian Gallery. I completed photography for a new publication of Barda Balka material as well as new photography for the catalog, display, and publicity materials for the special exhibit Our Work: Modern Jobs — Ancient Origins. I have almost completed new photography for an upcoming book that will highlight objects from all the Oriental Institute Museum galleries. In the last fiscal year a total of 219 objects have been photographed for publication, resulting in a total of 618 new photographs; 42 of the objects were photographed for requests for publicity materials, outside publications, internal and external researchers. As a result of these many projects, many important artifacts have had new photography done, some for the first time in color. Images resulting from my work this year have been published in numerous national and international books, exhibit catalogs (fig. 1), news outlets, and periodicals (fig. 2), in print and online. Photographs of the mummy Meresamun (OIM E10797) and one of the Sumerian worshipper figurines (OIM A12332) were printed on large external banners to help identify the building from the east and southeast sides.

I have added Reflectance Transformation Imaging (RTI) to the Photography Department's offerings for researchers. This equipment allows for a great range of objects sized from very small to extra-large to be studied with this research-focused form of digital imaging. RTI complements current in-house reflectance imaging methods used in the Persepolis Fortification Archive Project, Polynomial Texture Maps (PTM), which are created using a dome technique generally used on small objects. I have also been developing a method of macro High-Definition dSLR video imaging that meets archival and cultural heritage imaging standards. This will be an engaging way for Museum and website visitors to see highly detailed, 360-degree views of Museum artifacts as well as a new, accessible, and useful form of technology for researchers. Work on the Metals Rehousing Project has been ongoing thanks to the efforts of Bryce Lowry

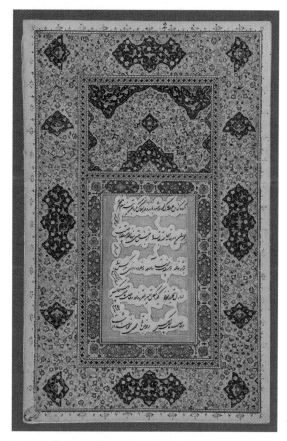

Figure 1. Illustrated Persian Calligraphy Manuscript, OIM A12100A, published on the cover of the Journal of Near Eastern Studies 17/2 (2012). Photo by Anna Ressman

Figure 2. Fragment of 1001 Arabian Nights, Arabic. OIM E17618, published in "Les Mille et une Nuits," Institut du Monde Arabe, p. 37. Photo by Anna Ressman

and John Whitcomb. Austin Kramer has been organizing and analyzing the digital materials created from the Khorsabad Relief Project.

I was helped in many aspects of my work this year by digital photography assistant Bryce Lowry, a PhD candidate in anthropology at the University of Chicago, who has now been with the Photography Department for four years. I hired a new digital photography assistant, Austin Kramer, a MAPSS student and photographer in his own right, for the 2012–2013 academic year and for the 2013 summer quarter. Continuing from the last fiscal year, John Whitcomb volunteered many hours to the Photography Department through June of 2013. I am very grateful to all of them for their excellent work and dedication.

PUBLIC EDUCATION

Overleaf: Model of a female offering bearer. Wood, stucco, and pigment. Height: 41.8 cm. Late First Intermediate Period–Middle Kingdom, ca. 2050–1760 BC. Purchased in Cairo, 1919. OIM E10744. Between Heaven & Earth Catalog No. 39

PUBLIC EDUCATION AND OUTREACH

Catherine Kenyon

Introduction

In my first year taking the helm of the Public Education and Outreach Department it was my great pleasure to spend the first several months observing and getting to know the amazingly dedicated and talented group of staff, docents, and volunteers. Meeting with faculty, staff, and volunteers in my first months allowed me to see our strengths and look for opportunities to develop new programs and audiences for the Oriental Institute. The department and staff have been reorganized to maximize our resources and strengths.

All department staff were assigned to an audience type — youth and family, adults, K–12 teacher and students, volunteers — allowing the staff to become "expert" with their group, to build collaborations and outreach initiatives, and to understand the specific needs of each audience in order to refine our limited human and marketing resources. Each of our public programs is designed for one of these specific audiences in mind. Moriah Grooms-Garcia serves as the youth and family program coordinator, Carol Ng-He joined the team in November as the K–12 and continuing education program developer, Terry Friedman is the department's volunteer manager, and Sue Geshwender is the education associate and assists Terry with managing volunteers and docents on Thursdays and Fridays. In addition to managing the department, I hold responsibility for developing programs for the adult audience.

To create and facilitate this new "team-ness" we meet on a weekly basis to understand each other's workload, share ideas, and look for ways to pitch in and help our colleagues on projects. We have instigated an annual staff retreat (our first was held in March at the Garfield Park Conservatory) focused on outreach and marketing strategies. Volunteer Shel Newman participated during the last half of the workshop. He facilitated an activity that focused us to look deeper at our roles in the department. Education staff has spent time this year cross-training our positions so that we can fill in for each other when one of us is out of the office. The Education Department's room 221 received a facelift with a redesign to create a professional, organized space that is more conducive to working. We now have an integrated phone system that connects the volunteer and education lines on all department phones.

The department has grown in many ways this year with new staff members Carol Ng-He and myself, while we also said goodbye to three long-time department staff, Carole Krucoff, Wendy Ennes, and Cathy Dueñas. We have begun to lay the groundwork for new programs, refinements to current initiatives, and are continuing to reform how we do business. I am thrilled to present below our accomplishments for the past year and give you a sneak peek of what is on the horizon for the coming year.

Youth and Family Programs. *Moriah Grooms-Garcia*

Nearly 800 people took advantage of our youth and family programs in fiscal year 2012–2013, a significant increase from the year prior. Contributing to this progress were a host of inventive bird-themed events, created in conjunction with our special exhibit Between Heaven

& Earth: Birds in Ancient Egypt, and the offering of long-time favorite programs (for example, Secret of the Mummy and Junior Archaeologists) on a regular basis. In addition, two large collaborative family festivals brought in both old friends and new visitors (fig. 1).

Art and Archaeology

The year started off with the Oriental Institute co-hosting, with the Lillstreet Art Center, the annual Be an Ancient Egyptian Artist Camp. Youngsters between the ages of 5 and 11 attended the week-long camp, which was offered for two sessions during the summer of 2012. For half the camp's duration our own Kipper Family Archaeology Discovery Center (KADC) facilitators filled the role of "artist-in-residence," facilitating the making of Egyptian-themed crafts. The camp culminated in a trip to the Oriental Institute and its simulated archaeology dig site, the KADC.

Two other family archaeology programs saw growth this year: Junior Archaeologists and the Boy Scout Archaeology Merit Badge Workshop. Previously offered on an annual basis, the Institute began offering the programs at regular intervals this year, running a total of ten programs and helping more than 160 Scouts earn their archaeology badges (fig. 2).

Literacy

This year saw the inception of a storytime series hosted by the Museum's biggest bird of all, Lamassu. This program, called LamaSeuss, pairs one of the Institute's most iconic pieces with one of the most well-known American children's book authors — Dr. Seuss — for a fun and educational opportunity that teaches children about the ancient world. The lamassu, with his cuneiform inscription and colossal stature, makes the perfect entry point to learn about ancient writing, animals, and other themes (fig. 3).

Figure 1. Jeannette Louis, from Sand Ridge Nature Center, explains the abilities and importance of hawks and other birds in the LaSalle Banks Education Center at the Oriental Institute during the Birds of a Feather program

Figure 2. Boy Scouts work on their archaeology merit badge using the Oriental Institute's Kipper Family Archaeology Discovery Center

Figure 3. The LamaSeuss series gets kids interested in the ancient Near East

This spring the program Super Birds invited participants ages 8–14 to use a comic book-style storytelling technique to make the bird-headed and bird-bodied deities of the ancient Egyptian pantheon defeat the evil Egyptian god Seth and his cohorts (fig. 4). The program was positively received and we hope to develop it further in the future.

Mummies' Night, which takes place around Halloween and attracts an average of 300 participants every year, has been one of Public Education's feature annual programs. At the end of last year we developed a pared-down version of Mummies' Night called Secret of the Mummy. This smaller-scale program showcases our reproduction mummy activity and a mummy-themed tour of the Joseph and Mary Grimshaw Egyptian Gallery, without the costumes and other activities present at the larger annual Halloween event. Offering this smaller version of the Oriental Institute classic on select Sundays has exposed an additional 160 museum-goers to our reproduction mummy, including alumni during this year's University of Chicago Alumni Weekend.

Figure 4. Intern Jenna Chapman helped us create a "super" version of the ancient Egyptian god Horus for the Super Birds program. Kids created stories of Horus triumphing over Seth

Along with special programs for parents and children, every day is family day at the Oriental Institute. Our interactive computers are regularly in use and this past year our full-color Family Activity Cards, which can be found in nearly every gallery, proved to be as popular as ever; more than 12,000 of these cards were taken home by visitors compared to the nearly 9,000 taken the previous year.

Family Festivals

The Oriental Institute became a feature for Latino Art Beat (a national not-for-profit arts organization that engages Latinos in the visual and performing arts) in their first-ever independent film, titled *Visiting the Museum*. The film, based on a short story written by young Latino author Manny Reyes III as part of a series of short, scary stories for young teens, was shot onsite and premiered at the Oriental Institute this past fall. In the film, two boys visit the Oriental Institute Museum and accidentally bring a mummy back to life. The film was paired with the classic Boris Karloff movie *The Mummy* and a costume contest. This opportunity to work with Latino Art Beat introduced a new audience to the Oriental Institute (fig. 5).

One of the most successful new family events this year, with 120 participants, was a program entitled Women and Girls in the Ancient World: Their Story, Our

Figure 5. Oriental Institute Museum chief curator Jack Green dressed up as an "archaeologist just out of the tomb" for the Latino Art Beat event

Story. This program told the stories of the mothers and daughters of ancient Nubia, Egypt, Anatolia, and Mesopotamia through the Oriental Institute's collection. Artifacts and topics were presented by four female archaeologists in short demonstrations throughout the galleries. The Education staff worked with University of Chicago Lab School teacher Cindy Jurisson to conceptualize this program, and Bonnie DeShong from the DuSable Museum helped to advertise the program (fig. 6).

Offsite Programs

This year we focused on two highly successful offsite programs with area partners. The Children's Book Fair (formerly known as the 57th Street Children's Book Fair) has been an annual Hyde Park celebration of books and reading since its start twenty-six years ago. The Oriental Institute has the distinction of being the only community institution that has taken part in the fair since its inception. Families enjoyed the Oriental Institute's booth at both the fall Children's Book Fair and the spring 57th Street Art

Figure 6. Benedetta Bellucci demonstrates the workings of a spindle whorl at Women and Girls in the Ancient World: Their Story, Our Story

Fair. Parents and children were eager to make rubbing imprints of ancient Egyptian reliefs, stamp ancient Egyptian symbols on their hands, and touch 2,500-year-old potsherds (fig. 7). As in the past, the fairs let us introduce the Oriental Institute to families from around the city.

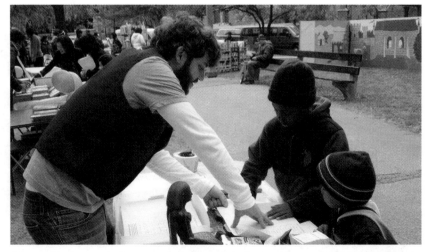

Figure 7. Facilitator Matthew Amyx helps a youth create a rubbing imprint of one of our relief replicas at the Children's Book Fair in Hyde Park

On the Horizon

The coming year will see a number of exciting youth-and-family–centered projects and programs. A major priority to growing these programs will include developing programs for the homeschool audience; the Institute looks forward to building a deeper relationship with these special family groups. Other new offerings include Little Scribe, an interactive gallery program that teaches the history of writing. A fuller offering for area Scouts, and a summer camp for youth in the summer of 2014, are also being planned. These and other programs will be highly influenced by the department's new relationship with Project Archaeology, a national heritage education program that develops curriculum to enable educators to teach archaeology to youth through inquiry-based learning. The Oriental Institute intends to become the fulcrum for building an Illinois state chapter of Project Archaeology and to both disseminate its curriculum to teachers as well as use its materials to build and offer programs to youth. The Project Archaeology curriculum will become a centerpiece of the Oriental Institute's offerings. Project Archaeology curriculum and concepts may also become a facet of the gallery tours offered to school groups and the Kipper Family Archaeology Discovery Center program. This partnership will enable the Oriental Institute to work more closely with the teachers who use its resources as part of their class curriculum, and to develop enriching professional development and outreach opportunities.

K-12 Teacher and Student Programs. *Carol Ng-He*

We are proud to report the development of new K–12 education initiatives and continuing education programs to engage teachers, students, and adult learners in meaningful ways.

On Saturday, November 17, 2012, we partnered with the American Schools of Oriental Research (ASOR) to host a free full-day professional development program for K–12 educators called Beyond Indiana Jones: Middle Eastern Archaeology in the Classroom (fig. 8). The program included presentations of curriculum ideas and activities by five ASOR members and our education staff. The topics and presenters were:

- "Why Is the Past important?" by Ellen Bedell, PhD in Egyptology and teacher at the Ellis School, in Pittsburgh, Pennsylvania

- "Archaeological Artifacts and Interpretation through Context," by Stefanie Elkins, MAEd, teacher of art history at Andrews University, in Berrien Springs, Michigan

- "Pottery Lesson," by Jeanne DelColle, teacher in American and world history at the Burlington County Institute of Technology and a recipient of New Jersey State Teacher of the Year in 2011 (fig. 9)

- "Daily Life in Bible Times," by Pamela Gaber, professor of archaeology and Judaic studies at Lycoming College,

Figure 8. Teachers collaborate on a hands-on activity for Jeanne DelColle's pottery lesson during the Beyond Indiana Jones professional development workshop (photo by Carol Ng-He)

Pennsylvania, and director of the Lycoming College excavations and field school at Idalion, Cyprus

- "Virtual Tour of Petra and Qumran," by Neal Bierling, secondary education teacher and archaeology workshop

- "Fun Ideas for Teaching Ancient Egypt," by Kristine Huffman, a secondary education teacher, archaeology workshop leader, and supervisor at excavations in Israel, Jordan, and Cyprus

- A presentation of the Oriental Institute's online resources, the Kipper Family Archaeology Discovery Center, and a guided tour of the Oriental Institute Museum by youth and family program coordinator Moriah Grooms-Garcia

The program drew nearly thirty educators from all over the Chicago area. The program offered Illinois teachers nine CPDUs for re-certification.

Figure 9. Jeanne DelColle, a presenting teacher, talked about her curriculum design that engaged students in learning about cultural heritage preservation (photo by Carol Ng-He)

Online Outreach

Beginning in January, we developed a new internal collaboration with eight other area-studies centers on campus to launch a cross-campus micro-website, called UChicago K–12 Outreach (https://k12outreach.uchicago.edu/) (fig. 10). Our collaborators are the Center for East Asian Studies, the Center for East European and Russian/Eurasian Studies, the Center for International Studies, the Center for Middle Eastern Studies, Neighborhood Schools Program, the Smart Museum of Art, and Southern Asia at Chicago. This new online platform increases online visibility of all participating affiliates among our K–12 audiences and facilitates cross-promotion of University-developed education programs.

To engage educators and their affiliated schools beyond the Museum, a new blog, titled From Ground to Gallery, was created in February. The blog provides a dynamic space where educators can share curriculum and new ideas for

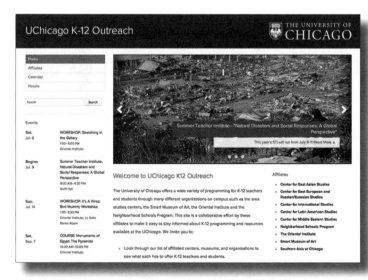

Figure 10. Screenshot of the UChicago K-12 Outreach micro-site

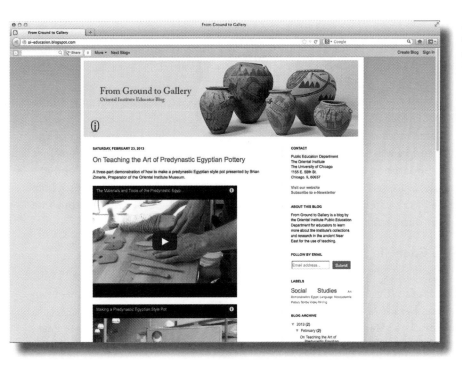

Figure 11. Screenshot of the new educator blog, From Ground to Gallery

Figure 12. Screenshot of e-Scribe, the new monthly educator newsletter

teaching about ancient civilizations in the classrooms and how they are utilizing the Oriental Institute's valuable collections and resources (fig. 11). Since its inception, the blog has attracted over 350 views from the United States, Germany, Russia, Italy, Sweden, Spain, the United Kingdom, El Salvador, and South Africa.

In conjunction with the From Ground to Gallery blog, the e-Scribe is another new online communication tool targeting K–12 educators (fig. 12). This monthly electronic newsletter serves to keep educators apprised of current research in the field of archaeology of the ancient Near East and how to use this information in the classroom. The e-Scribe offers teachers the latest updates on the Institute's upcoming teacher professional development opportunities, student programs, reading recommendations, and related resources. Since March, the e-Scribe has reached over 850 people from all over the country and will continue to grow through our outreach efforts.

Teacher Advisory Council

To further engage educators throughout the academic year a Teacher Advisory Council (TAC) was inaugurated in March (fig. 13). The Council is composed of eight practicing teachers from various disciplines and grade levels throughout the Chicago metropolitan area, ranging from West Town, Jefferson Park, McKinley Park, Hyde Park, Humboldt Park, Avondale, Oak Park, and Arlington Heights. The Council forms a group of ambassadors for the Oriental Institute in the Chicago area and serves as consultants to advise the Institute on the development of its educator resources and future K–12 programs. These members include:

- Cory Schiffern, social studies teacher at Mitchell Elementary School
- Christine Gray-Rodriguez, art teacher at Garvy Elementary School
- Kayla Vigil, social studies teacher at Namaste Charter School
- John Turek, social studies and language arts teacher at Percy Julian Middle School
- Nashwa Mekky, fifth-grade teacher at Ivy Hill Elementary School
- Jimini Ofori-Amoah, advanced-placement world history teacher at Rowe-Clark Math & Science Academy
- Nissa Applequist, social studies teacher at Lane Tech College Prep High School
- Cindy Jurisson, history teacher at the University of Chicago Laboratory School

This year's Council will serve a one-and-a-half–year term, from the school year of 2012/2013 to 2014; future councils will serve a two-year term. During their term of service, the Council members are also expected to bring their students to the Oriental Institute for a field trip at least once a year.

Figure 13. The newly established Teacher Advisory Council (photo by Carol Ng-He)

Student Programs

In April we hosted the second annual student symposium, entitled Looting and the Cultural Repatriation of Artifacts, co-organized by Cindy Jurisson, a high-school history teacher at the University of Chicago Laboratory School. Students studying early world history were stationed throughout the galleries in the Oriental Institute Museum to present an artifact they selected for their research project. Prior to their gallery presentation, the class visited the Research Archives and took self-guided tours of the galleries. Immediately following was a presentation on local and legal issues of cultural-heritage preservation by Beth Harris, a Lab School parent and the vice president and general counsel of the University of Chicago. A panel discussion with five of the participating students shared their perspectives on the cultural-heritage preservation efforts they learned about through this project. The program attracted 120 people including students and their parents (fig. 14).

Figure 14. Laboratory School students and families participated in the second annual student symposium, this year on the topic of Looting and the Cultural Repatriation of Artifacts (photo by Carol Ng-He)

In June, the Public Education Department joined the school days of the Windy City ThunderBolts, a professional Minor League baseball team located in Crestwood, a suburb southwest of Chicago. Over the course of two days we reached out to hundreds of attending middle-school students and their chaperons through a variety of hands-on activities, including rubbing and coloring activities (fig. 15). Students and teachers received a free copy of the Oriental Institute's interactive DVD game "Ancient Artifacts of the Middle East" to enjoy at home and in their classrooms.

In addition to offering school groups guided tours of the galleries, the Oriental Institute offers schools the option to participate in the Kipper Family Archaeology Discovery Center and the Artifact Analysis programs. In its first full year of operation the Artifact Analysis program has had over 1,000 participants.

Figure 15. Youth and family programs coordinator Moriah Grooms-Garcia manned the Oriental Institute table at the Windy City ThunderBolts School Days (photo by Carol Ng-He)

The Kipper Family Archaeology Discovery Center (KADC) is a simulated archaeological site based on Tel Megiddo, a major trading hub of the ancient Near East. School groups had the chance to explore the science of archaeology in a hands-on way, using the real tools and systematic methods of the pros to uncover replicas of ancient objects, many of which are on display in the Oriental Institute Museum galleries.

The Artifact Analysis program puts students in the position of an archaeologist post-dig. Each group of three to four students is given a box of replica artifacts that have been found in a particular "locus" of a dig site. Engaging their deductive-reasoning skills, students draw conclusions about the people who created the artifacts and how the artifacts were used. The second half of this two-hour program includes a tour of the Museum galleries. This program has both expanded the age range of students we can accommodate on school field trips as well as the number of students that can engage in an interactive activity while on their field trip to the Oriental Institute.

Special thanks to our 2012–2013 facilitators who taught both the KADC and Artifact Analysis Program:

- Lauren Nareau, MAPSS program
- Jenna Chapman, MAPSS program
- Hannah VanVels, University of Chicago Divinity School
- Matthew Amyx, MAPSS program
- Caitlin Jones, MAPSS program
- Leila Makdisi, MAPSS program

On the Horizon

In an effort to improve the onsite tour experience for our K–12 teachers and students, we are developing new pre- and post-visit materials to better prepare students and their teachers, as well as to extend the learning when students return to the classroom. We anticipate these new materials will be ready for spring 2014.

We will work in response to the Chicago Public School (CPS) Arts Education Plan and its Arts Liaisons program to host a series of welcome events for CPS Art Liaison teachers in partnership with the Smart Museum of Art. The events will provide free group tours based on ancient art themes found in our collections. This outreach initiative will strengthen our communications with educators, and encourage them to book a tour and use our resources. The Welcome Event will take place quarterly from July 2013 through April 2014.

In recognition of Cathy Dueñas, who served the Institute for twenty-nine years as a volunteer and volunteer coordinator, in the fall of 2013 we will launch the Catherine J. Dueñas Transportation Scholarship Fund. The fund will offer local schools assistance in securing bus transportation to make field trips to the Oriental Institute possible. A scholarship of $150 will underwrite the cost of one school bus for most districts, making it possible for fifty students to visit the Museum. We will continue to grow this fund for this important cause. Individuals who are interested in making a contribution can go to our website or contact the Development Office for more information.

Adult Programs. *Catherine Kenyon*

The adult public programs are, like the department, undergoing a re-organization and re-juvenation. The department successfully offered sixty-four programs to 3,062 participants last year for the adult life-long learner, and we intend to build on our wonderful tradition of offering adult programs. These programs represent the Institute's interest in providing compelling activities in conjunction with the Museum's collection, special exhibitions, and research and scholarship. Last year's programs were developed with community partners, enabling us to reach the widest of audiences, attract new patrons to the Institute, and use our resources wisely.

This year the department has begun offering a few new programs and is planning exciting new programs for the coming year. The adult public programs are organized around seven new program categories. In the coming year look for this new organization to show up on the website and in our printed program materials.

O. I. Creates

O. I. Creates is a new program that engages adults in the content and collections of the Museum in hands-on ways. Programs in this category include the It's a Wrap Bird Mummy Workshop that took place in February and was facilitated by docent Wahied Helmy Girgis. The participants learned to create a bird-shaped mummy using repurposed materials, such as cardboard (fig. 16). We are proud to be the only cultural organization in the country that presents this unique hands-on workshop where students learn about how ancient Egyptians mummified birds and some of the theories of why birds might have been mummified. Students also learned how to create some of the unique and beautiful wrapping designs seen on the artifacts in the Museum's collection.

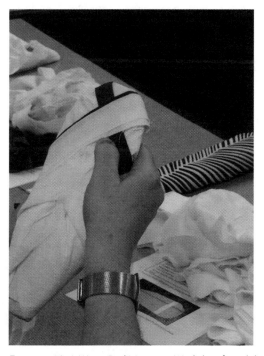 

Figure 16. It's A Wrap: Bird Mummies Workshop for adults (photos by Catherine Kenyon)

Sketching in the Gallery

A new regular Sketching in the Gallery program brought Chicago visual artists to the Oriental Institute to teach students (fig. 17). The program engaged small groups of students under the guidance of local practicing artists to experiment with different sketching techniques. The goal of this intimate class was to give participants a deeper personal connection to the artifacts in the gallery, to help them learn to use and refine observation skills, and to acquire visual-arts skills and vocabulary, all from using our collections as a springboard.

O. I. Films

O. I. Films is a favorite Sunday program showing documentary and feature films about the ancient Near East and Egypt. Last year we showed a total of thirty films to an audience of 562. Plans are underway to grow and rejuvenate this program within the next year.

Figure 17. A participant in the May session of the Sketching in the Gallery workshop shares her work (photo by Carol Ng-He)

O. I. Talks

O. I. Talks include both formal and informal programs focused on the ancient world and the Institute's research and disciplines. Last year we hosted a fall symposium entitled Birds in Ancient Egypt (fig. 18), bringing together five speakers from the Oriental Institute, Emory University, the Field Museum of Natural History, and Nature Conservation Egypt. Last year, fall lectures abounded — lectures we offered through the support of the Institute's members and the Volunteer Program's fall mini-series. In the spring we launched a new monthly informal gallery talk entitled the Lunchtime Traveler Series. Combined, the total number of participants in these talks was 1,313.

O.I. Learns

O.I. Learns are continuing adult-education courses taught by exceptional University of Chicago graduate students, research associates, and visiting scholars. Last year we taught two

Figure 18. Birds in Ancient Egypt symposium participants. Left to right: Rozenn Bailleul-LeSuer, Foy Scalf, Gay Robins, Douglas Stotz, and Sherif Baha El-Din

online courses, three onsite courses, and three correspondence courses to a total of 158 students.

On the Horizon

On the horizon for adult education are O. I. Reads, a new literacy-based program gathering interested readers for a quarterly book club based around works of historic fiction or fiction that are expressly written for the general public. Authors may be from the Middle East and/or write about, or set their works within the context of these regions. Members interested in this book club should contact Catherine Kenyon for more information.

Epic Wednesday is a new after-hours program aimed at the young professional audience. The program is being designed exclusively for adults 21 and over as an evening event that offers visitors open access to the Museum with unique entertainment and engaging hands-on activities that connect visitors with the content and scholarship of the Oriental Institute. With themes that change every month, Epic Wednesday will never be the same event twice. Visitors can reinvent their Oriental Institute Museum experience every month with friends, family, or a special date.

As an outgrowth of the Volunteer Program's exceptional tour program for the K–12 audience, in the fall of 2013 the department will begin reaching out to over 100 Chicago-area senior centers, Rhodes Scholars programs, and other organizations within the senior community to encourage booking a guided docent tour or attend other programs.

We have established a new partnership with the Chicago Mosaic School, the first and only mosaic art school in North America, to offer adult students a program to learn about this art form that originated in the ancient world. We will offer two hands-on mosaic workshops, one in July and one in September. The class utilizes design motifs from the Museum collection and students will create beautiful mosaics using these motifs to take home.

VOLUNTEER PROGRAM

Terry Friedman

Volunteers and docents are the lifeblood of the Oriental Institute. Last fiscal year a total of 7,310 hours were clocked by volunteers and docents who led tours; contributed to research for faculty and staff; helped collections, Archives, and Registration keep track of objects and stay organized; and staffed public programs and events.

This is the forty-sixth year of the Oriental Institute's Volunteer Program and it has been a time of reflection and reassessment. We have embarked on a number of new initiatives that are already helping the program achieve more, communicate better, and conduct our work with more ease and efficiency.

Online Initiatives

Online initiatives helped the Volunteer Program streamline many of its policies and procedures. One of these new initiatives was the introduction of Volgistics, an online tour-scheduling program (fig. 19). After months of testing the program's functionality, this user-friendly web-based system was introduced to the volunteers during the January Volunteer Day program. The move from the traditional pen-and-paper scheduling system to Volgistics has provided greater flexibility with tour staffing, allowing staff, docents, and captains to monitor tour coverage online. Volunteers can now easily manage their time commitments and get a bird's-eye view of where and when help is needed. Sue Geshwender was instrumental in setting up this new system and assisted the department with training all volunteers on how to use the program. Sue also sets up each new volunteer on Volgistics as part of their orientation.

Figure 19. Screenshot of Volgistics

We also redesigned our web page to attract new potential volunteers and provide them with a clear overview of the various ways the Oriental Institute uses the help of volunteers. Job descriptions were developed and posted for docents and volunteers who work at public programs and events, in the Research Archives, and at the Suq. A new online application form was also developed to help potential volunteers apply, and for department staff to manage and easily review the volumes of applications received monthly. This year alone we reviewed over thirty-two volunteer applications.

The monthly newsletter the Volunteer Voice continues to be an important communication tool between the volunteer staff and our volunteer and docent corps. In June, we updated the Volunteer Voice to a new online e-newsletter format that enables us to include images and make the information more engaging and user friendly (fig. 20).

Docents

This year, from our new group of volunteers, six were selected to become docents and train to give tours. Docent captains continue to play an active role in guiding and training new docents, giving them the support they need

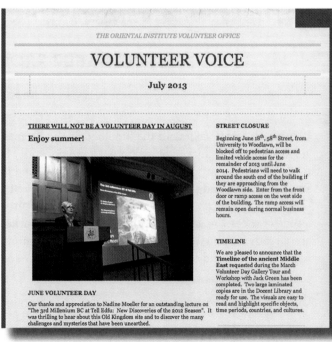

Figure 20. Screenshot of the online Volunteer Voice

to become successful and confident museum tour leaders. Monthly captain meetings were reinstated to help strengthen lines of communication and to provide an important forum to gather feedback with program refinements and changes. A formal job description was developed to standardize their responsibilities.

We extend our thanks and appreciation to the following captains and co-captains for their hard work and dedication throughout this past year: Myllicent Buchanan, Gabriele DaSilva, Wahied Helmy Girgis, Dennis Kelley, Stuart Kleven, Larry Lissak, Demetria Nanos, Jean Nye, Stephen Ritzel, Deloris Sanders, Hilda Schlatter, and Carole Yoshida. After five years of serving as Thursday co-captain, Hilda Schlatter has decided to step down from her duties. We are pleased to announce that Margaret Schmid has begun assuming the Thursday captain responsibilities.

Tour Program

Education associate Sue Geshwender took over the role of marketing and booking guided tours as well as becoming the staff contact for Thursday and Friday docents and volunteers. This past year Sue helped the department create a new online tour request form (with Moriah Grooms-Garcia's help) that works with the newly completed interactive tour database that Sue developed with the assistance of volunteer Kate Lieber. This new change has allowed the department to continue to collect accurate data about who is coming on tours and what months they are coming (see chart, below). By having access to this tour information we will be able to look for opportunities to market our tours to different groups and fill in tours around the times that school tours drop off. We are keenly aware that schools in the Chicago area are following a national trend in reducing the number of off-campus trips allowed. The financial pressures, increasing class sizes, and labor-force upheaval in the Chicago Public Schools are being felt by a reduction of school visits and we are looking for new ways to fill the gap — these new systems are an important tool in helping us achieve that goal. The tour program's hard-working docent corps conducted 212 guided tours through the Museum this year.

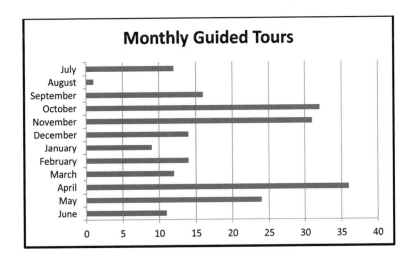

Monthly Guided Tours

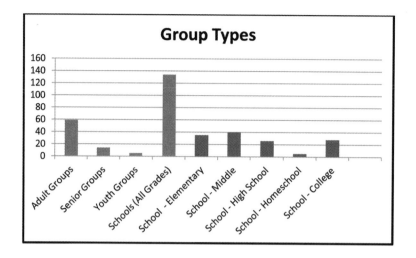

Volunteer Days

Monthly Volunteer Days offer educational programming and gallery-related activities, giving docents ongoing training for conducting high-quality tours. Volunteer Days also provide continuing education for everyone who attends. Last year these programs highlighted the research and projects of Institute faculty and staff. This season we want to thank the following speakers: Jason Barcus, John Brinkman, Wahied Girgis, Jack Green, Ray Johnson, Nadine Moeller, Gil Stein, Emily Teeter, Susan van der Meulen, and Karen Wilson (fig. 21).

Figure 21. The March Volunteer Day featured chief curator Jack Green, who discussed conducting tours for the adult learner and gave a tour highlighting tour techniques for this audience (photo by Carol Ng-He)

Docent Library

This year we made the first fundamental renovation to the docent library in over ten years. The room was repainted and reorganized to make it brighter, easier to navigate, and more open. Corkboards were added for staff to communicate information about various exhibitions, programs, and lectures that may be of interest to our docents. The hospitality area was relocated to the library creating a comfortable area for volunteers to socialize and study.

Figure 22. Margaret Foorman (right) and Marilyn Murray in the renovated docent library (photo by Terry Friedman)

Margaret Foorman, docent librarian, has continued her work organizing and curating the docent library collection. The annual book sale, which is part of the December Volunteer Day program, raised over $232 to help keep books in the docent library current. Margaret and Catherine Kenyon have spent time this year reorganizing and asking faculty to review and cull the books in the library to ensure we are offering the best scholarship and resources for our docents and volunteers. Our thanks go to McGuire Gibson, Jack Green, Theo van den Hout, Abbas Alizadeh, Jan Johnson, and Don Whitcomb for helping with this effort. We are pleased to announce that Marilyn Murray has stepped into the role of assistant librarian to help Margaret with library duties (fig. 22). Our thanks to the following volunteers for their support throughout the year with maintaining this valuable resource: Rebecca Binkley-Albright, Ginny Clark, Fred Eskra, Wahied Helmy Girgis, Sandy Jacobsohn, Marilyn Murray, Stephen Ritzel, and Carole Yoshida. We wish to thank everyone for their generous donations of books and materials that have significantly expanded our library's collection, with a special note of appreciation to the estates of Debbie Aliber Nina Longley, and Mari Terman and to the generosity of Barbara Baird.

Interns

This year the Volunteer Program officially began fielding internship applications from students around the country and placing them in departments throughout the Institute. In total we placed five interns this year:

- Petra Creamer, Museum
- Rebecca Mae Cuscaden, Education
- Alison Hundertmark, Education
- Brendan Mackie, Volunteer Office
- Lauren van Nest, Education

Fall 2012 Mini-Series

In autumn, the mini-series Medicine and Magic in the Ancient World: A Search for the Cure built on the success of prior fall mini-series. This year's programs brought together faculty members from the Oriental Institute and the University of Chicago Department of Classics and broke all attendance records with an increase of 51 percent in total attendance to the series. The four-part series featured six lectures on medical and magical practices in ancient Egypt, Greece, and Mesopotamia. The lectures offered a rare opportunity to study what ancient Egyptians, Greeks, and Mesopotamians thought about their bodies, disease, and medicine, illustrating how ancient people frequently interpreted their world through a combination of religious and magical elements. Our thanks to participants Elizabeth Asmis, Robert Biggs, Christopher Faraone, Walter Farber, Robert Ritner, and John Wee for their thought-provoking lectures and discussions. Moving forward, the fall mini-series will be

Figure 23. The final session of the four-part Medicine and Magic in the Ancient World mini-series featured a panel discussion with (from left to right) Walter Farber, John Wee, Christopher Faraone, and Robert Biggs. Not pictured are Elizabeth Asmis and Robert Ritner (photo by Terry Friedman)

incorporated into the fall lectures sponsored by Oriental Institute Membership. We hope this new collaboration will increase our target audience and give more patrons the chance to attend all the lectures offered in the fall (fig. 23).

Volunteer Recognition

December Volunteer Day remains a time when faculty, staff, and volunteers come together to recognize the contributions of the Oriental Institute's volunteers. The event has become an annual celebration, when new volunteers are introduced to the corps and awards for years of service are conferred. This year's program took place on December 3 in Breasted Hall with a presentation by Gil Stein followed by the induction of eleven new volunteers and a recognition ceremony for volunteers with over five years of service. The event culminated with a luncheon at the University Quadrangle Club (figs. 24–25).

New Volunteer Class

*Denotes new volunteers who are leading tours
and working on projects and events*

Laura Alagna

Craig Bean, docent in training

Lauren Bisio

Maeve Carpenter, docent in training

Amanda el-Khoury

Fred Eskra*

Shirlee Hoffman

Su Kang

Ralph Klein, docent in training

Paula Pergament

Stephen Scott, docent in training

Peter Rickert, docent in training

Margaret Schmid*

Figure 24. Volunteer Recognition Award recipients in Breasted Hall. Pictured, from left to right: volunteer coordinator Terry Friedman, volunteers Hilda Schlatter, Larry Lissak, Susan Bazargan, and Roberta Buchanan (all recognized for five years of service), Director Stein, and volunteer coordinator Cathy Dueñas. Not pictured: Anne Schumacher (20 years) and Kitty Picken (35 years) (photo by Craig Tews)

Figure 25. On December 3, faculty, staff, and volunteers gathered together to enjoy the annual volunteer luncheon at the University of Chicago Quadrangle Club to celebrate the year's achievements (photos by Craig Tews, compiled by Brendan Hackie)

This year, six people were recognized for their years of loyal service to the Oriental Institute. The Volunteer Program's effectiveness and resilience is built on the long-term dedication of its volunteers and we are proud that they each have reached this milestone.

Retirement of Cathy Dueñas

This year marked the end of an era for the Volunteer Program. For the past twenty years Cathy Dueñas and Terry Friedman have shared the position of volunteer services coordinator. On February 11, 2013, Cathy retired and began a new phase of her life (fig. 26). Cathy came to the Institute as a volunteer in 1984 and joined the Thursday docent team. In 1993, Cathy and Terry replaced Janet Helman as volunteer coordinators, sharing the position for the next twenty years.

Figure 26. Cathy Dueñas (photo by Randy Adamsick)

Figure 27. Head of Public Education Catherine Kenyon (left) honoring Cathy Dueñas with a plaque and scholarship in her name

In honor of Cathy's years of service, the Catherine J. Dueñas Transportation Scholarship Fund was established to help underwrite the cost of bringing school children to the Oriental Institute Museum. The fund will give priority to schools with a majority Latino student demographic — a student population that is near and dear to Cathy's heart (fig. 27).

In Memoriam

The Volunteer Program lost seven loyal friends and supporters this past year: Debbie Aliber, Ira Hardman, Nina Longley, Janet Russell, Elizabeth Spiegel, Mari Terman, and Jane Thain. These individuals exemplified the true spirit of volunteerism by devoting their time, unique talents, and generous financial support to help further the goals and mission of the Oriental Institute. We will greatly miss them and we are thankful that they chose to spend a portion of their lives with us.

On the Horizon

There are many exciting new initiatives and refinements planned for next year that will help the program develop new approaches to docent training as well as to broaden the scope of educational opportunities offered to all volunteers.

We are proud of the new collaboration with the Membership Department that will incorporate the fall mini-series into the Member's Lectures. The topic presented this fall is Why Civilizations Collapse: Internal Decay or External Forces? Look for the program dates in October through January.

In October the Volunteer Program will launch an eight-week docent-training session that marries content with tour-technique training. By the fall, new incoming volunteers and docents will have refreshed training and orientation materials, and we will introduce a concerted effort to recruit University of Chicago students for public-program volunteer positions and graduate students of ancient history to apply for docent positions.

Beginning in January 2014, Volunteer Days will be planned around an annual theme. To get things started, 2014 will be the Year of Archaeology.

On behalf of the department we are all looking forward to a dynamic and thought provoking new year.

Museum Docents

Denotes docents who are also project or event volunteers

John Aldrin	Erica Griffin*	Mary O'Connell
Dennis Bailey	Ira Hardman (deceased)	Mary O'Shea
Douglas Baldwin	Janet Helman*	Nancy Patterson
Nancy Baum*	Lee Herbst	Kitty Picken
Susan Bazargan	Mark Hirsch*	Semra Prescott*
Christel Betz	Dennis Kelley	Stephen Ritzel*
Rebecca Binkley-Albright*	Stuart Kleven	Lucie Sandel*
Daniel Bloom	Panagiotis Koutsouris	Deloris Sanders
Myllicent Buchanan	Alfia Lambert	Hilda Schlatter*
Roberta Buchanan*	Larry Lissak*	Joy Schochet
Ginny Clark*	Debra Mack*	Mary Shea
Gabriella Cohen	Paul Mallory*	Mae Simon
Gabriele DaSilva*	Margaret Manteufel	Toni Smith*
John DeWerd	Sherry McGuire	Dee Spiech*
Joe Diamond*	Donald McVicker	Mari Terman (deceased)
Margaret Foorman*	Marilyn Murray*	Craig Tews*
Barbara Heller Freidell	Demetria Nanos*	Ronald Wideman*
Dario Giacomoni	Jean Nye*	Steve Wolfgang
Wahied Helmy Girgis*	Daniel O'Connell	Carole Yoshida*

Volunteers

Benedetta Bellucci
Ray Broms
Josh Cannon
Robyn Dubicz
Andrea Dudek
Alexander Elwyn
Bill Gillespie
Terry Gillespie
Kristen Gillette
Irene Glasner
Theodore Gold
Debby Halpern

Abigail Harms
Akemi Horii
Jen Johnson
Dake Kang
Su Hyeon Kim
John D. Lawrence
Katherine R. Lieber
Amy Lukas
Carlotta Maher
Alice Mulberry
Shel Newman
Giulia De Nobili
Ila Patlogan

Paige Paulsen
Paula Pergament
Nicole Pizzini
O. J. Sopranos
Roberta Schaffner
Daila Shefner
George Sundell
Tasha Vorderstrasse
Robert Wagner
David Westergaard
John Whitcomb
Agnes Zellner

Suq Volunteers

Barbara Storms-Baird
Ray Broms

Judy Bell-Qualls
Peggy Grant

Jane Meloy
Norma van der Meulen

Volunteers Emeritus

Debbie Aliber (deceased)
Barbara Baird
Joan Barghusen
Jane Belcher
Gretel Braidwood
Noel Brusman
Andrew Buncis
Charlotte Collier
Bob Cantou
Hazel Cramer
Joan Curry
Erl Dordal
Mary Finn
Joan Friedmann

Anita Greenberg
Mary Harter
Teresa Hintzke
Patricia Hume
Sandra Jacobsohn
Alice James
Morton Jaffee
Betsy Kremers
Nina Longley (deceased)
Jo Lucas
Masako Matsumoto
Patricia McLaughllin
Roy Miller
Kathleen Mineck
Alice Mulberry

Muriel Nerad
JoAnn Putz
Agnethe Rattenborg
Patrick Regnery
Alice Rubash
Norman Rubash
Janet Russell (deceased)
Anne Schumacher
Lillian Schwartz
Elizabeth Spiegel (deceased)
Jane Thain (deceased)
Ray Tindel
Madi Trosman
Inge Winer

DEVELOPMENT
AND
MEMBERSHIP

DEVELOPMENT AND MEMBERSHIP

DEVELOPMENT

Tracy Tajbl

Oriental Institute donors continue to make new discoveries possible and this year was no exception. Generous contributions from 1,624 individual donors totaled more than $1.8 million to support a wide variety of Oriental Institute projects, ranging from special exhibition and museum education programming to fieldwork in Egypt, Israel, the Palestinian Territories, and Turkey as well as the Oriental Institute's current dictionary projects focused on Demotic and Hittite. Combined with ongoing support from foundations including the National Endowment for the Humanities (NEH), the Andrew Mellon Foundation, and the Roshan Cultural Heritage Institute, among others, philanthropic support ensures that the Oriental Institute remains in the vanguard of research institutions dedicated to the study of the ancient Near East.

Being remembered beyond one's lifetime was important to our ancient forbears, and as noted in the chart below, bequests from our most loyal donors have an enormous impact for the Oriental Institute. This year, the Oriental Institute was honored to receive gifts from the estates of longtime volunteer Janet Russell and loyal Oriental Institute member Chester D. Tripp. We are especially grateful for the visionary gift created by Alwin Clemens Carus, which provides income for the Oriental Institute over a twenty-year period through a mineral trust. In addition, the Oriental Institute was honored to receive hundreds of gifts in memory of two very special former volunteers, Deborah G. Aliber and Mari Terman. We thank their families for honoring the special relationship between these two remarkable women and the Oriental Institute.

This year, we welcomed Brittany Mullins as our new assistant director of Development. Brittany brings a strong background to the Oriental Institute, with experience in fundraising from the School of the Art Institute of Chicago. Trained as a classical archaeologist, Brittany earned an M.A. from Tufts University and a B.A. from the University of Michigan. She worked at the Boston Museum of Fine Arts on their Giza Archives Project, participated in archaeological fieldwork in Italy and England, and served as a teaching assistant for Roman history, Greek history, introductory archaeology, and Egyptian archaeology. We are honored to have Brittany join the Oriental Institute.

All of us at the Oriental Institute hope that our supporters throughout the world will take pride and pleasure in knowing that your gifts make a difference. Thank you for being our partners in discovery.

Oriental Institute Annual Fundraising Totals

	2013	2012	2011
Outright Gifts	$831,086.92	$739,020.84	$1,046,818.55
Realized Bequests	$368,382.06	$557,585.92	$133,485.60
Payments on Multi-year Pledges	$637,130.00	$510,050.00	$53,150.00
Totals	$1,836,598.98	$1,806,656.76	$1,233,454.15

* Figures above do not include foundation and federal/non-federal grants.

VISITING COMMITTEE

The Oriental Institute Visiting Committee 2012–2013

Harvey Plotnick, Chairman

Marilynn Alsdorf

Kathleen G. Beavis

Guity N. Becker

Gretel Braidwood*

Catherine A. Novotny Brehm

Aimee Drolet Rossi

Andrea Dudek

Emily H. Fine

Marjorie M. Fisher

Margaret E. Foorman

Joan Fortune

Isak V. Gerson

Nancy Gerson

Peggy Grant

Lewis Gruber

Misty Gruber

Howard G. Haas

Deborah Halpern

Thomas C. Heagy*

Janet W. Helman*

Arthur Lee Herbst*

Doris B. Holleb*

Neil J. King

Carlotta Maher*

John W. McCarter Jr.

Kitty Picken

Crennan M. Ray

John W. Rowe

Roberta Schaffner

Robert G. Schloerb

Lois M. Schwartz*

O. J. Sopranos*

Walter Vandaele

Anna M. White

Nicole S. Williams

* Denotes Life Member

MEMBERSHIP

Amy Weber

Publications

With the assistance of the Publications Office, the Membership Office continues to publish *News & Notes*, the quarterly members' magazine. The Fall 2012 edition (no. 215) featured the Living Legacy of Donald Oster and volunteer Robert Wagener. Winter 2012 (no. 216) highlighted Visiting Committee members John and Jeanne Rowe and volunteer Norma Van Der Meulen. Spring 2013 (no. 217) introduced us to the Oriental Institute number-one traveler and active volunteer Andrea Dudek. Finally, Summer 2013 (no. 218) presented us with volunteer Deloris Sanders. The Membership Office is greatly appreciative of the Publications Office for their hard work and guidance in producing *News & Notes*, as well as to all of the authors and staff contributors who provide exciting and engaging articles and program notices each quarter for our members.

Student Memberships

As part of the University of Chicago's Art Pass program the Oriental Institute began offering free membership to all University students in May 2010. As of June 2012, the Institute had over 1,000 University of Chicago student members, more than any other campus organization. Megan Anderluh and graduate student Maya Festinger were brought on to manage this program. Through partnerships with the Office of Publication and the Museum, the Membership Office was able to host several successful student member events throughout the year:

- Bulls and Buns (September 2012) — a tour of the Museum for new college students as part of O Week activities (co-sponsored by Public Education, the Oriental Institute Museum, and the Volunteer Program)
- Study at the OI (December 2012, March and June 2013) — quarterly, late-night study hall hosted in the Museum galleries

In total, we hosted over 1,000 University students at the Institute during the academic year through these special events and programs. The student membership program aims to increase student awareness of the Oriental Institute, make the Oriental Institute an integral part of the student and campus experience at the University, and become active participant in student events.

Events

Members enjoyed a wide variety of events in 2012–2013:

- Members' Preview — Between Heaven & Earth: Birds in Ancient Egypt Exhibition Preview (October 15, 2012)
- 2013 Oriental Institute Gala: An Evening of Discovery (May 11, 2013)

- James Henry Breasted Society Event — Joel Oppenheimer Gallery (June 19, 2012)

For in-depth information on the above mentioned events, please see the *Special Events* section of this annual report.

In addition to Members' events, Oriental Institute members enjoyed a comprehensive Members' Lecture Series in 2012–2013 with topics ranging from "Sex in Babylonia" to "A New Look at James Henry Breasted":

- "James Henry Breasted: A New Appreciation," by Emily Teeter (November 7, 2012)
- "Feasting on the High Road: The Median Palace at Godin Tepe," by Hilary Gopnik (December 5, 2012)
- "The Origins and Development of Mosaic Art in the Ancient Middle East from Eighth Century BC to AD," by Konstantinos D. Politis (January 9, 2013)
- "City and Hinterland in Ancient Mesopotamia: An Examination of Continuities and Developments in the Fabric of Urban and Rural Settlement from 5000 BC until the Time of Christ," by Elizabeth Stone (February 6, 2013)
- "Canals, Kings, and Hydraulic Landscapes in the Ancient Near East: An Archaeological Perspective," by Tony J. Wilkinson (March 6, 2013)
- "Death and Taxes in Ancient Egypt," by Brian Muhs (April 3, 2013)
- "Everything You've Always Wanted to Know about Sex in Babylonia ...," by Jerry Cooper (May 1, 2013)
- "'Awake in Peace!': Interpreting, Seeking, and Combating Dreams in Ancient Egypt," by Robert Ritner (June 5, 2013)

A very special thank-you is in order for all of our lecturers, co-sponsors, and members for participating the 2012–2013 Members' Lecture Series. The Oriental Institute Members' Lecture Series aims to bring a varied selection of the most recent work and scholarship on the ancient Middle East to our members and the local community. We look forward to an exciting and dynamic lecture line-up for the 2013–2014 series, which will begin in September 2013.

Members' Events would not be possible without the hard work of many dedicated Oriental Institute staff members and volunteers, and the Membership Office is thankful for all of their assistance with a very successful 2012–2013 events season.

Travel

The Oriental Institute offered four international travel programs to the Middle East in 2012–2013.

In September, seven Oriental Institute Members, led by Abbas Alizadeh, toured Persian Splendor: Journey to Ancient Iran. In October, a handful of Oriental Institute members participated in the tour of Legendary Empires: Giza, Baalbek, Byblos, Petra, and Luxor, led by Oriental Institute research associate Emily Teeter along with other expert lecturers, and explored an astounding array of archaeological sites along the Red Sea. Our sold-out Wonders of Ancient Egypt tour departed in March 2013, led by Lanny Bell. Seventeen packed days of travel from Cairo to Abu Simbel and back gave the twenty participates a wide breadth and scope of ancient Egypt. To wrap up the season in May 2013, Gil Stein, director of the Oriental Institute, led twelve members through the Archaeological Treasures of Eastern Turkey.

Oriental Institute travel programs are unique in that our passengers experience exclusive site visits and on-site learning privileges not enjoyed by other institutions or travel groups. Our members learn directly from some of the most eminent scholars in the world, at sites the Oriental Institute has been working on and researching for almost a century. For more information on Oriental Institute travel programs, contact the Membership Office at oi-membership@uchicago.edu or visit our website at oi.uchicago.edu/travel. You can also visit our Facebook OI Members Travel page at www.facebook.com/OIMemberTravel.

SOCIAL MEDIA

Moriah Grooms-Garcia, Mónica Vélez, and Amy Weber

Recognizing the importance of social media as a mainstream information source and global communication tool, the Oriental Institute has established a cross-departmental working committee to create an active presence in the major online channels. This past year the social media committee, consisting of Moriah Grooms-Garcia, Mónica Vélez, and Amy Weber, who come from the Public Education, Museum, and Membership departments respectively, have brought standards of management and measurement to the Institute's social media communications, which has produced clear results of its ability to reach a broad and diverse audience.

The Oriental Institute currently holds a place on the major social media networks including Twitter, YouTube, and Facebook, with the most significant growth seen in the latter venue. On Twitter, @Orientalinst has over 4,100 followers. The Oriental Institute's YouTube channel has a subscription base of 512, with a host of new content from the Member's Lecture Series and other programs to be posted in the near future. The Oriental Institute's Facebook fan base has increased by 47 percent in the past year, bringing it to over 8,100 fans from across the globe and putting its page among the top ten Facebook pages for cultural institutes in Chicago.

In addition, the social media committee manages the use of the Oriental Institute's social media tools such as the event-management service Eventbrite, which we use for some of our events to keep track of RSVPs, and the e-mail marketing tool myEmma, used to create and deliver the Institute's monthly e-newsletter, event reminders, and more. The use of the online traffic statistic tool Google Analytics has helped the social media committee to measure results and set future goals for the Institute's online presence.

In the next year the social media committee would like to focus on advocating and marketing the Oriental Institute to current and new patrons and to keep them abreast of the Institute's endeavors. Field projects, publications, development, and research projects will receive a greater emphasis in the coming year, bringing the valuable offerings of the Institute to an ever-larger social media community.

SPECIAL EVENTS

Brittany F. Mullins

During the 2012–2013 academic year, a variety of events were hosted at the Oriental Institute and offsite, including two new endowed lectureships, a members' preview of our special exhibit, the welcome reception for the American Schools of Oriental Research, our annual post-doctoral seminar, a service in memory of Deborah Aliber, an evening at the Joel Oppenheimer Gallery, and our biennial gala, among many others. Several of these events are described below. We would like to thank our generous donors and members, whose continued support makes these programs and events possible.

Between Heaven & Earth: Birds in Ancient Egypt Exhibition Preview

On October 15, 2012, Rozenn Bailleul-LeSuer, Egyptology PhD candidate in the Department of Near Eastern Languages and Civilizations and curator of Between Heaven & Earth: Birds in Ancient Egypt, introduced this special exhibit by presenting a lecture on the importance of birds in ancient Egyptian society as religious symbols, their use in hieroglyphic writing, the decorative arts, and as a food source. Rozenn became interested in the topic of birds in ancient Egypt not only through her work as an Egyptologist, but also as an ornithologist.

During her lecture, Rozenn shared her newest research developments in which she worked with the University of Chicago Medical Center to scan and better understand the bird mummies in the Oriental Institute collection. Following the lecture, Rozenn answered questions during a tour of the Birds exhibit in the Marshall and Doris Holleb Family Special Exhibits Gallery and during a reception in the Edgar and Deborah Jannotta Mesopotamian Gallery.

This exhibition was made possible by the generous support of Kitty Picken, Misty and Lewis Gruber, Joan Fortune, Carlotta and David Maher, Anna White, and our members and donors. A special thank-you goes to Emily Teeter, Rozenn Bailleul-LeSuer, Amy Weber, and Tracy Tajbl for organizing this preview and reception.

Braidwood Visiting Scholar Program

On March 4, 2013, former Oriental Institute professor and founder of the CAMEL lab Tony J. Wilkinson was invited to speak as the first Braidwood Visiting Scholar. Tony is currently a professor in the Department of Archaeology at Durham University. He delivered a lecture titled "Canals, Kings, and Hydraulic Landscapes in the Ancient Near East," and two graduate workshops on geoarchaeology, archaeological survey and remote sensing, and on modelling methods for ancient Near Eastern communities. Professor Wilkinson's research interests include landscapes of dry lands (deserts) and wetlands. He has undertaken fieldwork on ancient landscapes in Oman, Yemen, Saudi Arabia, Iraq, Syria, Turkey, and Iran as well as various places in the United Kingdom.

The Braidwood Visiting Scholar program was established with generous gifts from Mrs. Marjorie Webster and others in memory of Robert and Linda Braidwood. The Braidwood Visiting Scholar program aims to encourage and perpetuate the educational values of the

Braidwoods, particularly their commitment to the mentorship and training of graduate students specializing in the archaeology of the ancient Near East.

2013 Post-Doctoral Conference: Household Studies in Complex Societies

Postdoctoral Fellow Miriam Müller organized the ninth annual Oriental Institute Post-doctoral Seminar, which was held from March 14 to March 16, 2013, at the Oriental Institute. Fifteen international and domestic speakers convened to present their understanding of ancient societal structures advanced through the study of household archaeology. Household archaeology is the analysis of household architecture, artifact assemblages, the production and consumption of goods, and the interactions of individuals and families, which can be integrated with contemporaneous textual sources. Speakers cited evidence from ancient societies of Egypt, Syria, Mesopotamia, Assyria, Greece and pre-Aztec Mexico.

Those who arrived on Thursday evening were treated to a special dinner in our Robert and Deborah Aliber Persian Gallery so they could meet with Oriental Institute faculty and staff participating in the conference as well as with their fellow speakers. This dinner, along with a reception hosted in the Edgar and Deborah Jannotta Mesopotamian Gallery the following evening, gave conference speakers the opportunity to learn more about their colleague's research on and approaches to household archaeology.

The post-doctoral seminar is supported by a gift from Dr. and Mrs. Arthur Lee Herbst. A publication of the conference is currently in production. A special thank-you to Mariana Perlinac and Brittany Mullins for their assistance in organizing the conference.

Deborah Aliber Memorial Service

This past December, the Oriental Institute lost one our most beloved volunteers and supporters, Deborah Aliber. The Persian Gallery is named after Deborah and her husband Robert and was thus a fitting venue for the March 30, 2013, service in honor of Deborah's many gifts to our faculty, staff, students, visitors, and the Oriental Institute. Guests arrived as the Spektral Quartet, in residence at the University of Chicago, performed some of Debbie's favorite pieces of music. Several speakers reflected upon Debbie's role as a grandmother, faculty wife, an Oriental Institute docent and Visiting Committee member, and her years growing up in Hyde Park. Friend and colleague Emily Teeter highlighted Debbie's volunteer activities and shared stories of her time traveling with Debbie as part of the Oriental Institute travel program. Debbie will be greatly missed by those who had the opportunity to know and work with her.

Inaugural David Kipper Ancient Israel Lecture Series

On April 29, 2013, the Oriental Institute welcomed Dr. Oded Lipschits as the inaugural speaker for the David Kipper Ancient Israel Lecture Series. Dr. Lipschits delivered his lecture, titled "The Myth of the Empty Land and the Myth of the Mass Return: A New Look on the History of Judah under Babylonian and Persian Rule," to 162 members, donors, and public attendees The following day, Dr. Lipschits met with graduate students from the Department of Near Eastern Languages and Civilizations, the Divinity School, and the Department of Anthropology for lunch and to conduct a workshop on "The Royal Persian Garden and the Answer to the 'Riddle of Ramat Rahel.'"

Dr. Lipschits is a professor of Jewish history at Tel Aviv University and his research focuses on the history and administration of Judah and Judeans under Assyrian, Babylonian, and Persian rule. In addition, he has directed archaeological excavations at Ramat Rahel, the Ellah Valley Regional Project, and the Lautenschläger Azekah Expedition.

Jeanne Rowe and her husband John after receiving the 2013 Breasted Medallions (all Gala photos by Keri Wiginton)

Jay Heidel, left, greets 1997 Breasted Medallion recipient Carlotta Maher at the Oriental Institute Gala

Nan Ray, from left, Will Kellogg, and 1997 Breasted Medallion recipient Carlotta Maher are pictured at the 2013 Gala

The Kalyan Pathak Quartet perform during the cocktail hour in front of the Oriental Institute's Morton Tent

Michelle Trojan and Rowe-Clark Math & Science Academy students Keonte Griggs and Marcellus Nichols attend the Gala to honor Jeanne and John Rowe

Nancy Bergner tries on jewelry while shopping at the Suq

Visiting Committee Chair Harvey Plotnick runs the live auction during the Oriental Institute Gala

Director Gil Stein and John Lawrence talk with guests following the live auction

The David Kipper Ancient Israel Lecture Series, which focuses on the history and archaeology of ancient Israel, was established through a gift from Barbara Kipper and the Kipper Family and includes an annual public lecture as well as a lecture or workshop for faculty, graduate, and undergraduate scholars at the Oriental Institute. The Kipper Family, longtime supporters of the Oriental Institute, also established the Kipper Family Archaeology Discovery Center in 2008 to encourage children and families to learn about the archaeological method through simulated excavations.

2013 Oriental Institute Gala: An Evening of Discovery

This year for our biennial Gala, the Oriental Institute returned to the tradition of hosting offsite in order to accommodate our growing number of attendees. On May 11, 2013, the J. W. Marriott Hotel in downtown Chicago was transformed into a Middle Eastern Suq with Persian carpets covering the floor of the lobby as the Kalyan Pathak Quartet played traditional Egyptian music with the Oriental Institute's Morton Tent as the backdrop. Guests shopped for items selected especially for the Gala and not traditionally carried in the Oriental Institute's own Suq as the bust of Nefertiti gazed on from the entryway.

Following the cocktail hour, guests dined in the Burnham Ballroom, which was decorated with palm trees, lotus flowers, casts of Assyrian reliefs fresh from their crates, and photographs from the Oriental Institute's excavations, each representing the moment of discovery.

Prior to the presentation portion of the evening, a video of students from the Rowe-Clark Math & Science Academy was shown, in which the students, together with Yorke Rowan, recounted their once-in-a-lifetime experience of excavating at Marj Rabba, Israel. Oriental Institute Director Gil Stein then presented Breasted Medallions to John and Jeanne Rowe for their many contributions to the Oriental Institute, philanthropy, and education in Chicago.

A special thanks goes to our corporate sponsors for this event: Exelon, Northern Trust, and Allstate.

HONOR ROLL OF DONORS AND MEMBERS

The Oriental Institute recognizes the many donors who have furthered the mission and impact of the museum with a gift of $100 or more from July 1, 2012, to June 30, 2013. The following pages list the many donors whose gifts help to inspire excellency at the Oriental Institute. We celebrate your commitment and are please to recognize publicly the impact of your generosity on the Institute and our community. We appreciate you!

$50,000 and Above

Alwin Clemens Carus Mineral Trust, Dickinson, North Dakota
Mr. Joseph Neubauer & Ms. Jeanette Lerman-Neubauer, Philadelphia, Pennsylvania
The Neubauer Family Foundation, Philadelphia, Pennsylvania
Ms. Kathleen Picken, Chicago, Illinois
Trust Estate of Janet Russell, Pleasanton, California

$25,000–$49,000

Community Foundation for Southeast Michigan, Detroit, Michigan
Dr. Marjorie M. Fisher, Bloomfield Hills, Michigan
Mr. Daniel A. Lindley Jr. & Mrs. Lucia Woods Lindley, Evanston, Illinois
Roshan Cultural Heritage Institute, Washington, DC
Mr. & Mrs. John W. Rowe, Chicago, Illinois

$10,000–$24,999

Mr. & Mrs. Ronald R. Baade, Winnetka, Illinois
Commonwealth Edison Co., Chicago, Illinois
Ms. Aimee L. Drolet Rossi & Mr. Peter E. Rossi, Beverly Hills, California
Fidelity Charitable Gift Fund, Boston, Massachusetts
Ms. Virginia Hudson Rimmer Herrmann & Mr. Jason Thomas Herrmann, West Lebanon, New Hampshire
Mrs. Malda S. Liventals & Mr. Aldis V. Liventals, Wilton, Connecticut
Mr. & Mrs. Harvey B. Plotnick, Chicago, Illinois
Mrs. Maurice D. Schwartz, Los Angeles, California
Dr. & Mrs. Francis H. Straus II, Chicago, Illinois
The Estate of Chester D. Tripp, Chicago, Illinois

$5,000–$9,999

Allstate Foundation, Northbrook, Illinois
Ms. Hazel W. Bertz & Mr. Oscar Muscarella, New York, New York
Ms. Catherine Novotny Brehm, Chicago, Illinois
Domah Fund, Chicago, Illinois
Ms. Andrea M. Dudek, Orland Park, Illinois
Florence O. Hopkins Charitable Fund, Inc., Chicago, Illinois
Ms. Joan S. Fortune, New York, New York
Mrs. Nancy H. Gerson & Mr. Isak V. Gerson, Chicago, Illinois
Mr. & Mrs. Robert M. Grant, Chicago, Illinois
Mr. Howard E. Hallengren, Chicago, Illinois
Mrs. Deborah G. Halpern & Mr. Philip Halpern, Chicago, Illinois

$5,000–$9,999 (cont.)

Mr. Thomas C. Heagy & Ms. Linda H. Heagy, Chicago, Illinois
Mr. & Mrs. Robert A. Helman, Chicago, Illinois
Ms. Doris B. Holleb, Chicago, Illinois
Mr. & Mrs. Edgar D. Jannotta, Chicago, Illinois
Ms. Penelope Kane, Novato, California
Mrs. Barbara Kipper, Chicago, Illinois
Mr. Michael L. Klowden & Ms. Patricia D. Klowden, Santa Monica, California
Mr. Julius Lewis, Chicago, Illinois
Mrs. Jill Carlotta Maher & Mr. David W. Maher, Chicago, Illinois
Manaaki Foundation, Chicago, Illinois
Mrs. Barbara Mertz, Frederick, Maryland
Northern Trust, Chicago, Illinois
Mrs. Carol E. Randel & Mr. Don Michael Randel, New York, New York
Ms. Roberta Schaffner, Chicago, Illinois
Mr. & Mrs. Robert G. Schloerb, Chicago, Illinois
Dr. Coleman R. Seskind, Chicago, Illinois
Mr. & Mrs. H. Warren Siegel, San Juan Capistrano, California
The Chicago Community Foundation, Chicago, Illinois
The Rhoades Foundation, Chicago, Illinois
Mr. & Mrs. Robert Wagner, Chicago, Illinois
Ms. Helen Wentz, Lansing, Michigan

$2,500–$4,999

Mr. & Mrs. Gary S. Becker, Chicago, Illinois
Mr. & Mrs. Norman R. Bobins, Chicago, Illinois
Mr. Manu Chhabra & Ms. Pooja Bagga, Chicago, Illinois
Mrs. Anita Dulak & Mr. James Dulak, Mohawk, New York
Exxon Mobil Foundation, Houston, Texas
Mr. & Mrs. James L. Foorman, Chicago, Illinois
Dr. Francois P. Gaudard, Chicago, Illinois
Mr. Byron Gregory & Mrs. Sue Gregory, Wilmette, Illinois
Mr. & Mrs. Walter M. Guterbock, Anacortes, Washington
Mr. & Mrs. Howard G. Haas, Glencoe, Illinois
Mr. Roger David Isaacs & Mrs. Joyce R. Isaacs, Glencoe, Illinois
Dr. Morag M. Kersel & Dr. Yorke M. Rowan, Chicago, Illinois
Mr. Jack A. Koefoot, Evanston, Illinois
Mr. & Mrs. Robert M. Levy, Chicago, Illinois
National Philanthropic Trust DAF, Jenkintown, Pennsylvania
Mr. & Mrs. Roger R. Nelson, Chicago, Illinois
Nuveen Benevolent Trust, Chicago, Illinois
Ms. Virginia O'Neill, Littleton, Colorado
Miss M. Kate Pitcairn, Kempton, Pennsylvania
Mrs. Crennan M. Ray, Santa Fe, New Mexico
Dr. Miriam Reitz, Chicago, Illinois
Professor Stuart A. Rice & Ms. Ruth M. O'Brien, Chicago, Illinois
Dr. & Mrs. Thomas J. Schnitzer, Chicago, Illinois
Mr. O. J. Sopranos & Mrs. Angeline Buches Sopranos, Winnetka, Illinois
Mr. David Stremmel, Winnetka, Illinois
Ms. Jean P. Stremmel, Winnetka, Illinois
The Robert Thomas Bobins Foundation, Chicago, Illinois
Mr. Raymond D. Tindel & Ms. Gretel Braidwood, Earlysville, Virginia

$1,000–$2,499

Mr. William H. Alger III & Ms. Judith N. Alger, Santa Fe, New Mexico
Ms. Lisa Alther, Piney Flats, Tennessee
Mr. Arthur H. Anderson Jr. & Mrs. Rebecca E. Anderson, Chicago, Illinois
Ms. Priscilla Bath, Trenton, New Jersey
Mr. Robert Bauer & Mr. John Coble, Galesburg, Michigan
Ms. Judith Baxter & Mr. Stephen Smith, Oak Park, Illinois
Mr. Bruce L. Beavis & Dr. Kathleen G. Beavis, Chicago, Illinois
Mrs. Jean Frances Burns Bell & Mr. Max S. Bell, Pacific Grove, California
Mr. Frederick N. Bates & Dr. Ellen J. Benjamin, Chicago, Illinois
Mr. & Mrs. Cameron Brown, Lake Forest, Illinois
Mr. Quigley Bruning, New York, New York
Mr. Steven Burakoff & Mrs. Suzanne Burakoff, New York, New York
Ms. Heidi Camp & Mr. Steven H. Camp, Winnetka, Illinois
Ms. Gail Cowgill & Mr. David Cowgill, Munster, Indiana
Mr. Charles F. Custer, Chicago, Illinois
Ms. Katharine P. Darrow & Mr. Peter H. Darrow, Brooklyn, New York
Mr. Donald Davis & Ms. Peggy Wilk, Raleigh, North Carolina
Mr. Craig J. Duchossois & Mrs. Janet J. Duchossois, Elmhurst, Illinois
Mr. & Mrs. E. Bruce Dunn, Chicago, Illinois
Mr. Frederick Elghanayan, New York, New York
Mrs. Ann Gearen & Mr. John A. Gearen, Oak Park, Illinois
Mr. & Mrs. James J. Glasser, Chicago, Illinois
Mrs. Mary L. Gray & Mr. Richard Gray, Chicago, Illinois
Ms. Sandra L. Greenberg & Mr. Stephen M. Greenberg, Livingston, New Jersey
Dr. Petra Maria Blix & Dr. Benjamin Gruber, Chicago, Illinois
Ms. Louise Grunwald, New York, New York
Mr. Andrew Nourse & Ms. Patty A. Hardy, Redwood City, California
Ms. Lynn E. Hauser & Mr. Neil L. Ross, Chicago, Illinois
Ms. Sabrina Y. Hsieh, Chicago, Illinois
Mr. Richard Wetherill Hutton & Mr. John Cogswell, Northampton, Massachusetts
Ms. Capucine M. Jacob, Chicago, Illinois
Dr. Joseph W. Jarabak & Dr. Rebecca R. Jarabak, Hinsdale, Illinois
Dr. Donald S. Whitcomb & Dr. Janet H. Johnson, Chicago, Illinois
Mrs. Christine S. Kamil & Mr. Waheeb N. Kamil, Westfield, New Jersey
Mr. & Mrs. Michael L. Keiser, Chicago, Illinois
Mr. William K. Kellogg III, Wilmette, Illinois
Mr. & Mrs. Neil J. King, Chicago, Illinois
Mr. Richard Kron & Mrs. Deborah A. Bekken, Chicago, Illinois
Dr. Joseph T. Lach, PhD, & Ms. Carol C. Albertson, Evanston, Illinois
Mr. Stephen S. Lash, New York, New York
Mr. John D. Lawrence & Mr. Timothy Marchetti, Chicago, Illinois
Mr. Marcus Lok Hay Lee, Oxford, Canada
Mr. James Keith Lichtenstein, Chicago, Illinois
Mr. & Mrs. Michael D. Lockhart, Lancaster, Pennsylvania
Louis Leibowitz Charitable Trust, Coral Gables, Florida
Mr. & Mrs. John W. McCarter Jr., Northfield, Illinois
Mr. Douglas McDonough & Ms. Barbara McDonough, Homewood, Illinois
MetroPro Realty, Chicago, Illinois
Dr. Carol Meyer & Mr. Robert K. Smither, Hinsdale, Illinois
Mr. & Mrs. Kenneth Edward Mifflin, Greenwich, Connecticut
Mostafa Family Charitable Lead Trust, Pasadena, California
Muchnic Foundation, Atchison, Kansas
North Star Investment Services, Inc., Chicago, Illinois

$1,000–$2,499 (*cont.*)

Mrs. Janis W. Notz & Mr. John K. Notz Jr., Chicago, Illinois
Mr. David & Anne Patterson, APO, Military - A.E.
Dr. & Mrs. Harlan R. Peterjohn, Bay Village, Ohio
Dr. Audrius Vaclovas Plioplys & Dr. Sigita Plioplys, Chicago, Illinois
Mr. Marion Robus & Ms. Jane Voeste, San Francisco, California
Mr. Thomas F. Rosenbaum & Ms. Katherine Faber, Wilmette, Illinois
Ms. Frances F. Rowan, Reston, Virginia
Dr. Bonnie M. Sampsell, Chapel Hill, North Carolina
Mr. & Mrs. Harold Sanders, Chicago, Illinois
Mr. Lee A. Caplan & Ms. Linda A. Sawczyn, Chapel Hill, North Carolina
Schwab Charitable Fund, San Francisco, California
Mr. Richard Henry Beal & Ms. JoAnn Scurlock, Chicago, Illinois
Secchia Family Foundation, Grand Rapids, Michigan
Mr. & Mrs. Charles M. Shea, Wilmette, Illinois
Mrs. Charlotte Mailliard Shultz & The Honorable George P. Shultz, San Francisco, California
Ms. Toni S. Smith, Chicago, Illinois
Mr. & Mrs. Solon A. Stone, Portland, Oregon
Thomas Dower Foundation, Kenilworth, Illinois
Vanguard Charitable Endowment, Southeastern, Pennsylvania
Mr. John Walker & Ms. Mary Bea Walker, Urbana, Illinois
Ms. Anna M. White, Terre Haute, Indiana
Mr. George M. Whitesides & Ms. Barbara Breasted Whitesides, Newton, Massachusetts
Mr. Charles Mack Wills Jr., East Palatka, Florida
Mr. Federico Zangani, Oxford, Canada
Ms. Carol Zuiches & Mr. James Zuiches, Chicago, Illinois
Mr. & Mrs. Howard O. Zumsteg Jr., San Francisco, California

$500–$999

Abbott Laboratories Employee Giving, Princeton, New Jersey
Mr. Matthew J. Adams, State College, Pennsylvania
Mr. James L. Alexander, Chicago, Illinois
American Schools of Oriental Research, Bala Cynwyd, Pennsylvania
Mr. & Mrs. Edward Anders, Burlingame, California
Mr. Gregory Anthony, Minneapolis, Minnesota
Archaeological Tours, New York, New York
Mr. Roger Atkinson & Ms. Janet Arey, Sebastopol, California
Ms. Sharon Avery-Fahlstrom, Barcelona, Spain
Miss Janice V. Bacchi, San Diego, California
Berglund Construction, Chicago, Illinois
Mr. & Mrs. Mark Bergner, Chicago, Illinois
Mr. Greg Cavitt, Chicago, Illinois
Mr. & Mrs. E. Eric Clark, Sierra Madre, California
Mr. Steven Anthony Clark & Ms. Janet L. Raymond, Oak Lawn, Illinois
Mr. Timothy John Crowhurst & Ms. Cecila Crowhurst, New York, New York
The Honorable Kenneth W. Dam & Mrs. Marcia Dam, Chicago, Illinois
Mr. John Drake & Ms. Margaret Drake, Austin, Texas
Ms. Delores J. Eckrich & Mr. Richard Eckrich, Denver, Colorado
Mr. & Mrs. Eugene F. Fama, Chicago, Illinois
Ms. Linda Gail Feinstone, New York, New York
Ferniehirst Trading, LLC, Fort Myers, Florida
Dr. Samuel Ethan Fox, Chicago, Illinois
Mr. Wolfgang Frye, Phoenix, Arizona

$500–$999 (*cont.*)

Ms. Patty Gerstenblith & Rabbi Samuel Gordon, Wilmette, Illinois
Mr. & Mrs. Gene B. Gragg, Chicago, Illinois
Mr. Jan M. Grayson, Chicago, Illinois
Mr. & Mrs. Lewis S. Gruber, Chicago, Illinois
Dr. Clifford W. Gurney & Mrs. Doris A. Gurney, Gainesville, Florida
Mr. & Mrs. M. Hill Hammock, Chicago, Illinois
Mr. Collier Hands, Lovell, Maine
Dr. & Mrs. Arthur L. Herbst, Tucson, Arizona
Mr. & Mrs. Scott E. Hertenstein, Cary, North Carolina
Mr. Kurt Peters & Ms. Elizabeth Hopp-Peters, Evanston, Illinois
Mr. Paul Houdek & Ms. Linda Houdek, Berwyn, Illinois
Ms. Mariye C. Inouye, New York, New York
Professor Gerald E. Kadish, Binghamton, New York
Mr. Stuart Kleven & Ms. Andrea Pogwizd, Bensenville, Illinois
Mr. Gregory Gene Knight & Ms. Constance Gordon, Eagle, Idaho
Mr. & Mrs. Martin J. Kozak, Wilmette, Illinois
Mr. John D. Lewis & Ms. Phoebe R. Lewis, Milwaukee, Wisconsin
Dr. John C. Michael & Mrs. Christine G. Michael, Wilmette, Illinois
Mr. Dean Miller & Ms. Martha H. Swift, Chicago, Illinois
Mr. Richard A. Miller, Oak Lawn, Illinois
Ms. Catherine Moore, Gurnee, Illinois
Mrs. Alicia Morse & Mr. Robert Morse, Annapolis, Maryland
Mr. & Mrs. John P. Nielsen, Lombard, Illinois
Mr. & Mrs. Khalil Noujaim, Granville, Massachusetts
Dr. Arthur E. Ostergard, MD, Lake Oswego, Oregon
Ms. Joan Hunt Parks, Chicago, Illinois
Phoebe & John D. Lewis Foundation, Milwaukee, Wisconsin
Dr. Erl Dordal & Ms. Dorothy K. Powers, Atlanta, Georgia
Ms. Sandy Davis Rau, Winnetka, Illinois
Raymond James Charitable Endowment Fund, Saint Petersburg, Florida
Ms. Louise Reed, Chicago, Illinois
Mr. Percy Mwanzia Wegmann & Ms. Karen M. Rexford, Austin, Texas
Dr. Stanley Rosenblatt, MD, Huntington Beach, California
Mr. & Mrs. Norman J. Rubash, Evanston, Illinois
Saint Lucas Charitable Fund, Burr Ridge, Illinois
Professor Dr. Esther Segel & Professor Dr. Ralph Segel, Wilmette, Illinois
Ms. Alice Sgourakis, Oakland, California
Mr. Peter Shellko & Ms. Phyllis Shellko, Chesterland, Ohio
Dr. Clyde C. Smith, PhD, & Mrs. Ellen Marie Smith, River Falls, Wisconsin
Dr. Benjamin A. Smith-Donald & Mrs. Radiah A. Smith-Donald, Chicago, Illinois
Mr. Kent D. Sternitzke, Fort Worth, Texas
Mr. James & Ms. Pamela Stola, Chicago, Illinois
Ms. Gwenda Blair & Mr. Matthew W. Stolper, Chicago, Illinois
Ms. Tracy Tajbl & Mr. Neil Kent Jones, Chicago, Illinois
Mrs. Mari D. Terman & Dr. David M. Terman, Wilmette, Illinois
The Chicago Community Trust, Chicago, Illinois
Ms. Carrie Elizabeth Thomas, Chicago, Illinois
Mr. Stewart D. White, Abu Dhabi, United Arab Emirates
Ms. Deborah Williams, Evanston, Illinois
Mr. Robert I. Wilson, Peoria, Illinois
Dr. & Mrs. Jerome A. Winer, Chicago, Illinois
Ms. Debra F. Yates, Chicago, Illinois
Ms. Annette Youngberg & Mr. Daniel W. Youngberg, Albany, Oregon

$250–$499

Mr. Abudul-Hameed Al-Nassar, Bend, Oregon

Dr. Thomas W. Andrews, Hinsdale, Illinois

Mr. Barry Atkinson & Mrs. Carol E. Atkinson, Port St. Lucie, Florida

Mrs. Susan Baird, Winnetka, Illinois

Mr. Anthony J. Barrett & Ms. Marguerite Kelly, Harpswell, Maine

Mr. Kevin Francis Rock & Ms. Cynthia A. Bates, Evanston, Illinois

Mr. & Mrs. Charles E. Bidwell, Chicago, Illinois

Biff Ruttenberg Foundation, Chicago, Illinois

Mr. & Mrs. Merill Blau, Highland Park, Illinois

Mr. Bob Brier, Bronx, New York

Mr. Michael L. Brody & Ms. Anne Webber Brody, Chicago, Illinois

Mr. Bruce P. Burbage, Venice, Florida

Children's Concierge, LLC, Gaithersburg, Maryland

The Honorable Barbara F. Currie, Chicago, Illinois

Mrs. Gwendolyn P. Dhesi & Mr. Nirmal Singh Dhesi, Santa Rosa, California

Mr. Irving L. Diamond & Ms. Dorothy J. Speidel, Wilmette, Illinois

Ms. Patricia Dihel & Mr. Glen Wilson, Third Lake, Illinois

Mr. Michael Dorner, St. Paul, Minnesota

Mr. Stephen P. Duffy & Dr. Kathryn P. Duffy, Ankeny, Iowa

Mr. S. Cody Engle & Ms. Deborah Engle, Chicago, Illinois

Ms. Elizabeth A. Byrnes & Mr. Barton L. Faber, Paradise Valley, Arizona

Ms. Rosemary Ferrand, West Sussex, United Kingdom

Ms. Mary G. Finn, Chicago, Illinois

Mr. Barry Fitzpatrick, West Midlands, United Kingdom

Mr. Mark Douglas Fleming & Mrs. Madeleine Fleming, Morristown, New Jersey

Dr. Michael S. Flom, Boynton Beach, Florida

Mr. & Mrs. Charles Barry Friedman, Chicago, Illinois

Mr. Matthew W. Dickie & Ms. Elizabeth R. Gebhard, Perthshire, United Kingdom

Mr. Kevin S. Geshwender & Ms. Susan Geshwender, Barrington, Illinois

Mr. & Mrs. Jerome Gilson, Wilmette, Illinois

Mr. & Mrs. Samuel D. Golden, Chicago, Illinois

Mrs. Betty Goldiamond, Chicago, Illinois

Dr. & Mrs. Nathaniel D. Greenberg, Wilmette, Illinois

Ms. Dianne S. Haines, Naperville, Illinois

Ms. Katherine Haramundanis, Westford, Massachusetts

Mr. Richard S. Harwood, Colorado Springs, Colorado

Mr. Robert F. Hendrickson, Princeton, New Jersey

Mr. & Mrs. David C. Hilliard, Chicago, Illinois

Ms. Patricia A. Holst & Mr. Stephen L. Holst, Westport, Massachusetts

Mrs. Angela C. Jacobi & Mr. George Thomas Jacobi, Milwaukee, Wisconsin

Mr. Doug Hinckley & Ms. Jennifer Janes, Chicago, Illinois

Mr. Richard E. & Ms. Marie T. Jones, Wilmette, Illinois

Ms. Cindy Jonsson, Chicago, Illinois

Mr. David Katz & Ms. Karie Katz, Chicago, Illinois

Dr. John Sobolski & Dr. Zara Khodjasteh, Chicago, Illinois

Mr. Timothy King, Chicago, Illinois

Mr. Joe Klug, Chesterton, Indiana

Ms. Deborah C. Kobezak, Yorktown, Virginia

Dr. Irmgard K. Koehler, MD, Chicago, Illinois

Mrs. Jennifer A. Korynski, Chicago, Illinois

Mr. Bernard L. Krawczyk, Chicago, Illinois

Mr. Peter Lacovara, Albany, New York

Mr. & Mrs. Charles Larmore, Providence, Rhode Island

Mr. & Mrs. William J. Lawlor III, Chicago, Illinois

$250–$499 (*cont.*)

Mr. George MacDonald, Largo, Florida
Mr. Daniel R. Malecki, Kensington, California
Mr. Ronald Roy Malmquist, Spotsylvania, Virginia
Dr. Glennda S. Marsh-Letts, Springwood, Australia
Mr. Raymond McBride, Chicago, Illinois
Mr. & Mrs. John Robert McNeill, Chevy Chase, Maryland
Mr. Mark Christopher Mitera & Mr. Edwin Wald, Forest Park, Illinois
Mr. Robert Ralph Moeller & Ms. Lois Patricia Moeller, Evanston, Illinois
Ms. Vivian B. Morales, Saint Paul, Minnesota
Mr. Arthur H. Muir Jr., Thousand Oaks, California
Ms. Holly J. Mulvey, Evanston, Illinois
Mr. Charles R. Nelson, Seattle, Washington
Mr. Nazario Paragano, Basking Ridge, New Jersey
Mr. Valentin Parks Jr. & Ms. Michele Flynn, Gansevoort, New York
Mrs. Semra Prescott, Chicago, Illinois
Ms. Anne N. Rorimer, Chicago, Illinois
Mr. Ronald G. Lindenberg & Ljubica Sarenac, Chicago, Illinois
Mr. Nicholas Sargen & Mrs. Susan Sargen, Cincinnati, Ohio
Mr. & Mrs. John Eric Schaal, Burr Ridge, Illinois
Ms. Lynne F. Schatz & Mr. Ralph Arthur Schatz, Chicago, Illinois
Ms. Mary Ellen Sheridan, Levering, Michigan
Dr. Henry D. Slosser, Pasadena, California
Mr. Paul E. Zimansky & Ms. Elizabeth C. Stone, Stony Brook, New York
Ms. Kathleen Sumner, Columbus, Ohio
Ms. Betsy Teeter, San Francisco, California
Mr. & Mrs. Randolph Frank Thomas, Chicago, Illinois
Trans Union Corporation, Chicago, Illinois
Dr. Robert Y. Turner, Haverford, Pennsylvania
Ms. Mary Valsa & Mr. Warren Valsa, Chicago, Illinois
Vintage Radio Control Society, Endicott, New York
Ms. Tasha Karina Vorderstrasse & Mr. Brian P. Muhs, Chicago, Illinois
Ms. Nancy E. Warner, MD, Pasadena, California
Ms. Janet Rotter Wilson & Mr. Jeffrey Andrew Wilson, Chicago, Illinois
Ms. Margaret Wright, Victoria, Australia
Mr. Thomas K. Yoder, Chicago, Illinois
Mr. Sam & Mrs. Helen Zell, Chicago, Illinois
Mrs. Agnes Zellner, Chicago, Illinois

$100–$249

Ms. Margery Al-Chalabi & Mr. Suhail Al-Chalabi, Chicago, Illinois
Mr. & Mrs. John C. Aldrin, Gurnee, Illinois
Mr. & Mrs. Walter Alexander, Geneva, Illinois
Mr. & Mrs. James P. Allen, Providence, Rhode Island
Ms. Salwa Alwattar, Bannockburn, Illinois
Mr. & Mrs. John L. Anderson, Chicago, Illinois
Mr. & Mrs. Richard J. Anderson, Chicago, Illinois
Mr. Robert Andresen, Chicago, Illinois
Ms. Mary A. Anton & Mr. Paul M. Barron, Chicago, Illinois
Mr. & Mrs. David Arditi, Chicago, Illinois
Ms. Luna Arditi, Chicago, Illinois
Ms. Janice Armstrong, Milford, New Jersey
Dr. & Mrs. Barry Arnason, Chicago, Illinois

$100–$249 (*cont.*)

Art Experts, Inc., Daytona Beach, Florida
Ms. Laura Ashlock, Anchorage, Alaska
Mr. Edward H. Ashment, Manteca, California
Ayco Charitable Foundation, Albany, New York
Ayres Interiors, LTD, Chicago, Illinois
Ms. Doris Ayres, Chicago, Illinois
Dr. Eugene L. Balter & Mrs. Judith R. Phillips, Chicago, Illinois
Barclays Capital, New York, New York
Dr. & Mrs. Herbert R. Barghusen, Portage, Indiana
Mrs. Lewis R. Baron, Evanston, Illinois
Mr. Douglas Baum & Mrs. Lynne M. Wait, Homewood, Illinois
Mr. & Mrs. Richard W. Baum, Chicago, Illinois
Ms. Norma Baxa, Twin Lakes, Wisconsin
Ms. Mary Beach Prudence, Oak Park, Illinois
Mr. John M. Beal, Chicago, Illinois
Ms. Susan Bedingham, Covington, Washington
Mrs. Olya E. Benbow & Mr. Peter K. Benbow, Santa Barbara, California
Mr. Roy Benedek, Western Springs, Illinois
Benjamin Foundation, Inc., Jupiter, Florida
Mr. & Mrs. John F. Benjamin, Jupiter, Florida
Dr. & Mrs. Richard W. Benjamin, North Augusta, South Carolina
Ms. Catherine Bennett, Des Moines, Iowa
Mr. & Mrs. Thomas H. Bennett, New York, New York
Mr. Larry Bergmann & Ms. Zaida Bergmann, Fairfax, Virginia
Mr. R. Stephen Berry & Ms. Carla F. Berry, Chicago, Illinois
Mr. Roger J. Bialcik, Downers Grove, Illinois
Mrs. Helaine A. Billings, Chicago, Illinois
Ms. Rebecca L. Binkley, Chicago, Illinois
Dr. Sidney J. Blair & Ms. LaMoyne C. Blair, Oak Park, Illinois
Mr. Joost Blasweiler, Arnhem, Netherlands
Mr. Edward C. Blau, Alexandria, Virginia
Mr. James Borg, Lake Forest, Illinois
Mrs. Ann Bowar & Mr. Joe Bowar, Littleton, Colorado
Dr. John W. Boyer, PhD, & Mrs. Barbara A. Boyer, Chicago, Illinois
Mr. Norman P. Boyer, Oak Lawn, Illinois
Mr. Addison Braendel & Ms. Catherine Braendel, Chicago, Illinois
Mr. John Bremen & Mrs. Lara S. Frohlich, Chicago, Illinois
Mr. John A. Bross & Ms. Judy Carmack Bross, Chicago, Illinois
Ms. Mary Sue Brown & Mr. Jim Cherry, Glen Ellyn, Illinois
Ms. Marilyn A. Brusherd, Sugar Grove, Illinois
Mr. & Mrs. John Buchanan, Evanston, Illinois
Ms. M. Kennedy Buchanan, Chicago, Illinois
Ms. Romie Bullock & Mr. T. J. Bullock, Chicago, Illinois
Dr. Stuart S. Burstein, MD, Pittsburgh, Pennsylvania
Ms. Suzy Burstein, New York, New York
Mr. Richard Butler, Spring Grove, Illinois
Mrs. Patricia B. Carlson & Mr. Stephen C. Carlson, Chicago, Illinois
Ms. Cinthya S. Carrillo, Chicago, Illinois
Ms. Jane Gallagher Cates, Maplewood, New Jersey
Ms. A. J. Cave, San Mateo, California
Mr. John L. Cella Jr. & Ms. Laura Prail, Chicago, Illinois
Mrs. Bonnie Chajet & Mr. Clive Chajet, New York, New York
Charitable Flex Fund, Paramus, New Jersey

$100–$249 (*cont.*)

Ms. Elsa Charlston, Chicago, Illinois
Mr. Charles A. Chesbro, Missoula, Montana
Chicago Detours, Inc., Chicago, Illinois
Mr. Peter Chulick, St. Louis, Missouri
Dr. Charles M. Chuman & Dr. Mary A. Chuman, Chesterton, Indiana
CNA Foundation, Chicago, Illinois
Mr. Brian L. Cochran, Tucson, Arizona
Mr. & Mrs. Douglas E. Cohen, Highland Park, Illinois
Dr. Roger B. Cole, MD, & Ms. Ann S. Cole, Winnetka, Illinois
Mrs. Zdzislawa Coleman, Chicago, Illinois
Ms. Cynthia Green Colin, New York, New York
Comquest Corporation, Algonquin, Illinois
Mr. Richard L. Cook & Ms. Sally W. Cook, Sherman Oaks, California
Mr. Jason Cordero, South Australia, Australia
Dr. Eugene D. Cruz-Uribe & Dr. Kathryn Cruz-Uribe, Richmond, Indiana
Mr. Edwin L. Currey, Jr., Napa, California
Ms. Joan Curry, Lansing, Illinois
Mr. Michael H. Baniak & Ms. Mary Daly-Baniak, Munster, Indiana
Ms. Susan Dardar, Chicago, Illinois
Mr. Robert A. Koos & Ms. Diane L. Dau-Koos, Kenosha, Wisconsin
Mr. Claude Davis & Mrs. Linda Davis, Hillsborough, North Carolina
Dr. John M. Davis, MD, & Ms. Deborah J. Davis, Chicago, Illinois
Mr. & Mrs. Mark D. Dawson, Chicago, Illinois
Ms. Maybrit S. De Miranda, Rancho Palos Verdes, California
Mr. Leoti de Vries-Mostert, Waalre, Netherlands
Mr. Robert O. Delaney, Winnetka, Illinois
Mr. Kevin M. Dent, Columbus, Georgia
Mr. William E. Derrah & Mrs. Alicia E. Derrah, Western Springs, Illinois
Ms. Jeananne Digan, Wilmette, Illinois
Mr. Tom Digman & Ursula Digman, Elgin, Illinois
Ms. Mary E. Dimperio, Washington, DC
Mr. Henry S. Dixon & Ms. Linda Giesen, Dixon, Illinois
Mr. John J. Dombek, Jr. & Ms. Priscilla W. Dombek, Chicago, Illinois
Ms. Paula Douglass, Chicago, Illinois
Ms. Elizabeth Zenick Dudley, East Boothbay, Maine
Mrs. Rose B. Dyrud, Chicago, Illinois
Mr. Robert Eager, Washington, DC
Mr. Christopher Boebel & Ms. Glenna Eaves, Chicago, Illinois
Mr. David Eckert, Chicago, Illinois
Mr. Donald Patrick Eckler, Chicago, Illinois
Egypt Exploration Organization of Southern California, Los Angeles, California
Mr. Peter Ehrenstrom, O'Fallon, Missouri
Mr. & Mrs. Lawrence R. Eicher, Charlottesville, Virginia
Mr. Alexander Elwyn & Mrs. Sheila Elwyn, Chicago, Illinois
Engle Family Foundation, Chicago, Illinois
Ms. Ann R. Esse, Sioux Falls, South Dakota
Dr. & Mrs. Richard Evans, Chicago, Illinois
Ms. Hazel S. Fackler, Chicago, Illinois
Mr. & Mrs. Robert Feitler, Chicago, Illinois
First United Church of Oak Park, Oak Park, Illinois
Mr. James L. Padgett & Ms. Rosanne Fitko, Lake Forest, Illinois
Ms. Carol L. Forsythe & Mr. Scott M. Forsythe, Forest Park, Illinois
Mr. & Mrs. Charles J. Fraas Jr., Jefferson City, Missouri

$100–$249 (*cont.*)

Dr. Michael Frampton & Ms. Deborah Reynolds, Chicago, Illinois
Mr. & Mrs. Jay B. Frankel, Chicago, Illinois
Mrs. Susan S. Freehling & Mr. Paul E. Freehling, Chicago, Illinois
Dr. Lee A. Freeman & Ms. Kirsten R. Moline, Canton, Michigan
Ms. Elisabeth R. French, Washington, DC
Mr. Kere Frey, Chicago, Illinois
Mr. & Mrs. Stephen S. Fried, Kingston, Massachusetts
Mr. & Mrs. Peter E. Friedell, Chicago, Illinois
Dr. Gary D. Friedman & Ms. Ruth Helen Friedman, San Rafael, California
Mr. Robert C. Gaffaney, Algonquin, Illinois
Mr. Gregory J. Gajda, Mount Prospect, Illinois
Mr. John Samuel Gallop & Ms. Caryn J. Gallop, Chicago, Illinois
Mr. James Gaynor & Mrs. Jill W. Gaynor, Henrico, Virginia
Mr. Ted Geiger & Ms. Hildegard H. Geiger, Lake Villa, Illinois
Ms. Dona Gerson, Evanston, Illinois
Mrs. Terry Gillespie & Mr. William H. Gillespie, Flossmoor, Illinois
Mr. & Mrs. Thomas J. Gillespie, Chicago, Illinois
Mr. Lyle Gillman, Bloomingdale, Illinois
Ms. Irene Dorotea Glasner, Chicago, Illinois
Mr. & Mrs. Robert Dunn Glick, Chicago, Illinois
Mr. Jerome Godinich Jr., Houston, Texas
Reverend Raymond Goehring, Lansing, Michigan
Mr. Karan Goel, Chicago, Illinois
Mr. & Mrs. William H. Gofen, Chicago, Illinois
Mr. & Mrs. Howard Goldberg, Chicago, Illinois
Dr. Helen T. Goldstein, Iowa City, Iowa
Mr. John Goldstein, Chicago, Illinois
Mr. & Mrs. Frederick J. Graboske, Rockville, Maryland
Mr. & Mrs. David Gratner, Sulphur Springs, Indiana
Ms. Jessica Graybill, Quincy, Washington
Mr. Donald M. Green, Coral Gables, Florida
Ms. Francis P. Green, Bloomington, Illinois
Dr. Joseph Adams Greene & Mrs. Eileen Caves, Belmont, Massachusetts
Ms. Roberta Greenspan, Highland Park, Illinois
Ms. Ann Marie Gromme, Edina, Minnesota
Mr. Alvin Gross & Mrs. Lois S. Gross, Wilmette, Illinois
Mr. Kenneth Gross & Mrs. Margaret Gross, Downers Grove, Illinois
Mr. Greg Gross & Mrs. Wendy Gross, Wilmette, Illinois
Ms. Carolyn Guhin & John P. Guhin, Pierre, South Dakota
Ms. Gail Guralnick & Mr. Robert Guralnick, Boulder, Colorado
Mr. & Mrs. Richard C. Haines, Atlanta, Georgia
Ms. Barbara J. Hall, Chicago, Illinois
Mr. Chalkley Hambleton, Winnetka, Illinois
Mr. Joel L. Handelman & Ms. Sarah R. Wolff, Chicago, Illinois
Dr. Lowell Kent Handy & Ms. Erica Lynn Treesh, Des Plaines, Illinois
Mr. Bill Harms & Mrs. Myra Harms, Grayslake, Illinois
Dr. Thomas C. Harper, Paso Robles, California
Mr. & Mrs. Richard G. Harter, Chicago, Illinois
Ms. Mary Jo Hartle & Mr. James B. Hartle, Santa Barbara, California
Dr. & Mrs. Robert Haselkorn, Chicago, Illinois
Dr. Theresa He & Dr. Jonathan Blake Strauss, Chicago, Illinois
Ms. Lynne Pettler Heckman & Mr. James J. Heckman, Chicago, Illinois
Dr. & Mrs. H. Lawrence Helfer, Pittsford, New York

$100–$249 (*cont.*)

Mr. Gilbert B. Heller & Ms. Laura N. Heller, Denver, Colorado
Mrs. Marjorie H. Henshaw & Reverend Richard A. Henshaw, Rochester, New York
Mr. & Mrs. John A. Herschkorn Jr., San Jose, California
Ms. Hedda Hess, Chicago, Illinois
Mrs. Mary P. Hines, Winnetka, Illinois
Dr. Paul C. Holinger, MD, Hinsdale, Illinois
Mrs. Jacquelyn Holland & Mr. James Holland, Wilmette, Illinois
Mr. David Holz & Ms. Kay Holz, Iola, Wisconsin
M. K. Horne, Monee, Illinois
Mrs. Leonard J. Horwich, Chicago, Illinois
Mr. Herbert B. Huffmon, Madison, New Jersey
Ms. Lyric M. Hughes-Hale & Mr. David D. Hale, Winnetka, Illinois
Mr. Arthur T. Hurley & Mrs. Susan L. Hurley, Napa, California
Mr. Jack David Hurwitz & Ms. Penelope Ingalls, Oak Park, Illinois
Mr. Michael S. Hyman & Ms. Stephanie Young, Chicago, Illinois
Ms. Mary L. Jackowicz, Chicago, Illinois
Mrs. Sandra Jacobsohn, Chicago, Illinois
Mr. Alvin James, Irving, Texas
Ms. Jan Janowitz, Gibsonia, Pennsylvania
Ms. Caroline C. January, New York, New York
Mr. Richard Lewis Jasnow, Baltimore, Maryland
Mr. Erwin Jaumann, Gaithersburg, Maryland
Ms. Kristin Jeffries, Verona, Wisconsin
Mr. James Jenkins, Chicago, Illinois
Mr. Chris Jensen, Downers Grove, Illinois
Jewish Federation of Metro Chicago, Chicago, Illinois
Johnson Controls Foundation, Milwaukee, Wisconsin
Mr. Mark E. Johnson & Ms. Kelly Johnson, Tinley Park, Illinois
Ms. Mary Ellen Johnson, Warrenville, Illinois
Ms. Samantha W. Johnson, Colorado Springs, Colorado
Mr. Charles E. Jones & Alexandra A. O'Brien, PhD, New York, New York
Mr. Justin J. Tedrowe, Downers Grove, Illinois
Ms. Loretta A. Kahn, Evanston, Illinois
Mrs. Joanne M. Keefe & Mr. John B. Keefe, Riverside, Illinois
Mr. John A. Kelly, Jr. & Mrs. Joyce J. Kelly, Naples, Florida
Dr. John Kern & Dr. Lauren Kern, Flossmoor, Illinois
Mrs. Norma Kershaw, Mission Viejo, California
Mr. & Mrs. Jerome C. Kindred, Arlington, Virginia
Mr. & Mrs. H. David Kirby, West Linn, Oregon
Ms. Henriette Klawans, Chicago, Illinois
Ms. Blue Balliett & Mr. William Klein, Chicago, Illinois
Mr. & Mrs. William J. Knight, South Bend, Indiana
Mrs. Annie A. Kohl, Media, Pennsylvania
Dr. & Mrs. Anthony Kossiakoff, Chicago, Illinois
Mr. Christian Kourkoumelis, Bolingbrook, Illinois
Ms. Barbara A. Kovel, Evanston, Illinois
Ms. Susan G. Lacoste, Montreal, Canada
Mr. & Mrs. Alvin W. Ladd, Rancho Palos Verdes, California
Mr. Robert C. Ladendorf & Ms. Jean I. Ladendorf, Springfield, Illinois
Mrs. Marietta Land & Mr. Peter Land, Chicago, Illinois
Mr. Richard Lann, Colorado Springs, Colorado
Mrs. Elisabeth F. Lanzl, Chicago, Illinois
Ms. Laura L. Larner-Farnum, Yorba Linda, California

$100–$249 (*cont.*)

Mr. Marshall Lavin, Chicago, Illinois
Mrs. Jody LaVoie & Mr. Steven G. LaVoie, La Grange, Illinois
Mr. John K. Lawrence, Ann Arbor, Michigan
Mr. Bill Lawton, Sutton, Massachusetts
Mr. Richard Lee, Holland, Pennsylvania
Mr. Clayton Miles Lehmann, Vermillion, South Dakota
Dr. & Mrs. Mark Levey, Wilmette, Illinois
Mr. John Levi & Mrs. Jill Levi, Chicago, Illinois
Mr. & Mrs. Josef B. Levi, Chicago, Illinois
Professor Saul Levmore & Ms. Julie A. Roin, Chicago, Illinois
Mr. Thaddeus Walczak & Mrs. Carole J. Lewis, Ketchum, Idaho
Mr. Robert B. Lifton & Mrs. Carol Rosofsky, Chicago, Illinois
Mr. Robert A. Lindquist, Jr., Arlington Heights, Illinois
Mr. Charles Lindsey & Mrs. Zikri Yusof, Des Plaines, Illinois
Ms. Lynn Simon Lipman & Mr. Robert Lipman, Evanston, Illinois
Ms. Janet Lissak & Mr. Laurence Lissak, Lombard, Illinois
Lockheed Martin Corporation, Bethesda, Maryland
Mr. Robert Loman, Chicago, Illinois
Mrs. Helen Lowell, Chesh, United Kingdom
Mr. & Mrs. Philip R. Luhmann, Chicago, Illinois
Mrs. Denise C. Macey & Mr. Eric Macey, Winnetka, Illinois
Dr. Carole Mangrem, MD, Clarksdale, Mississippi
Mr. & Mrs. George Mann, Highland Park, Illinois
Ms. Karen L. Marshall, New York, New York
Ms. Masako I. Matsumoto, Napa, California
Mr. Gerald Mattingly, Knoxville, Tennessee
Mr. Howard McCue & Mrs. Judith McCue, Evanston, Illinois
Ms. Helen McDonald, Chicago, Illinois
Ms. Paddy H. McNamara, Chicago, Illinois
Ms. Betty D. Meador, Ramona, California
Mr. Richard H. Meadow, Canton, Massachusetts
Mr. R. Darrell Bock & Ms. Renee Marie Menegaz-Bock, Chicago, Illinois
Dr. Ronald Michael, Bourbonnais, Illinois
Dr. Jimmy W. Milan, Knoxville, Tennessee
Ms. Florence Kate Millar & Ms. Emma Shelton, Bethesda, Maryland
Mr. Gene A. Miller & Dr. Jenny T. Hackforth-Jones, Madison, Wisconsin
Mr. A. Patrick Papas & The Honorable Martha A. Mills, Chicago, Illinois
Mr. Edward Harris Mogul, Chicago, Illinois
Ms. April Molloy, Las Vegas, Nevada
Mrs. Vivian Mosby, Woodland, Washington
Mrs. George Moulton & Mr. George E. Moulton, Overland Park, Kansas
Mr. & Mrs. Anthony John Mourek, Chicago, Illinois
Mr. Henry Moy, Idabel, Oklahoma
Mr. & Mrs. Jay F. Mulberry, Chicago, Illinois
Ms. Maureen Mullen, Greenfield, Wisconsin
Mr. Brian Murphy, Chicago, Illinois
Mr. Douglas G. Murray & Mrs. Isobel M. Murray, Santa Barbara, California
Mr. David E. Muschler & Ms. Ann L. Becker, Chicago, Illinois
Mr. & Mrs. Stanley F. Myers, Hanover, New Hampshire
Mr. & Mrs. David Nagel, Houston, Texas
Mr. Wisam E. Naoum, Chicago, Illinois
Naperville Community Unit School District 203, Naperville, Illinois
Ms. Dawn Clark Netsch, Chicago, Illinois

$100–$249 (*cont.*)

New Trier Extension, Northfield, Illinois
Niewoehner Funeral Home, Rugby, North Dakota
Mr. Dale George Niewoehner, Rugby, North Dakota
Mr. & Mrs. Timothy Michael Nolan, Palos Park, Illinois
Ms. Karen Nordheim, Chicago, Illinois
Mr. Gerry Norman, Highland Park, Illinois
North Shore Village, Evanston, Illinois
Mr. Walter E. North & Mrs. Judy Ryon, Dulles, Virginia
Mr. Dennis O'Connor, Chicago, Illinois
Ms. Dorinda J. Oliver, New York, New York
Mr. & Mrs. Mark M. Osgood, Burr Ridge, Illinois
Mrs. China Ibsen Oughton, Dwight, Illinois
Ms. Carol E. Owen & Mr. Clinton W. Owen, Chula Vista, California
Ms. Martha Padilla, Sunland, California
Mr. Kisoon Park & Mrs. Moonyoung Park, Chicago, Illinois
Mr. Mark R. Pattis, Highland Park, Illinois
Mr. Fred Pawlak & Ms. Marianne Pawlak, Orland Park, Illinois
Mr. Gregory Pearl & Ms. Laura Preble Pearl, Glenview, Illinois
Ms. Janet Pegoraro, Gurnee, Illinois
Ms. Carolyn Perelmuter, Needham Heights, Massachusetts
Ms. Paula Pergament, Chicago, Illinois
Ms. Betty L. Perkins, Los Alamos, New Mexico
Mr. & Mrs. Norman Perman, Chicago, Illinois
Mr. Jeffrey Peters, Saint Paul, Minnesota
Ms. Anita Petty, Santa Fe, New Mexico
Ms. Gloria C. Phares & Mr. Richard Dannay, New York, New York
Mr. Andrew I. Philipsborn, Chicago, Illinois
Ms. Anne Philipsborn, Troutdale, Oregon
Mr. Peter Phillips, Manchester, United Kingdom
Mr. Jeffrey C. Pommerville & Mrs. Yvonne L. Pommervile, Scottsdale, Arizona
Mrs. Charlene H. Posner & The Honorable Richard A. Posner, Chicago, Illinois
Mr. Richard H. Prins & Mrs. Marion L. Prins, Chicago, Illinois
Mr. & Mrs. James M. Ratcliffe, Chicago, Illinois
Raytheon Foundation, Princeton, New Jersey
Ms. Xue Y. Fung & Mr. David E. Reese, Chicago, Illinois
Dr. Clemens D. Reichel, PhD, Toronto, Canada
Ms. Louise Lee Reid, Chicago, Illinois
Mrs. Janet Reimer & Mr. Thomas Reimer, Wilmette, Illinois
Mr. William C. S. Remsen, Dover, Massachusetts
Dr. Kenneth Resnick & Dr. Raiselle Resnick, Chicago, Illinois
Mr. David R. Reynolds & Mrs. Pamela C. Reynolds, Oak Park, Illinois
Mr. Dean F. Richardson, Pittsburgh, Pennsylvania
Ms. Pat Richardson, Vista, California
Mr. & Mrs. Burton R. Rissman, Chicago, Illinois
Mr. William M. Backs & Ms. Janet Rizner, Evanston, Illinois
Dr. Ronald Allan Ferguson & Ms. Agnes Ann Roach, Gurnee, Illinois
Professor John F. Robertson, Mount Pleasant, Michigan
Ms. Karen Robinson, Saint Paul, Minnesota
Miss Katherine J. Rosich, Washington, DC
Mrs. Laila Rothstein & Dr. David A. Rothstein, Chicago, Illinois
Ms. Susan Rowe, Escondido, California
Dr. & Mrs. Myron E. Rubnitz, Winnetka, Illinois
Dr. Randi Rubovits-Seitz, Washington, DC

$100–$249 (cont.)

Mr. & Mrs. Patrick G. Ryan, Chicago, Illinois
Mrs. Nancy Sachs, Bethesda, Maryland
Mr. Mazin Fuad Safar & Mrs. Michal Safar, Chicago, Illinois
Mr. Frank R. Safford & Mrs. Joan B. Safford, Evanston, Illinois
Ms. Hilda Schlatter & Mr. Paul Sakol, Oak Park, Illinois
Dr. Peter Sargon, Chicago, Illinois
Mr. Paul Benjamin Schechter & Ms Naomi Reshotko, Denver, Colorado
Mr. Martin L. Scheckner, Miami, Florida
Mrs. Lawrence J. Scheff, Chicago, Illinois
Mr. David M. Schiffman & Ms. Judith Feigon Schiffman, Evanston, Illinois
Mrs. Barbara H. Kenar-Schilling & Mr. Timothy J. Schilling, Hammond, Indiana
Mr. Stephen Oliver Schlosser & Ms. Lori Schlosser, Brooklyn, New York
Mr. Kirk Lee Schmink, San Francisco, California
Mr. Jonathan Green & Ms. Joy Schochet, Chicago, Illinois
Dr. Hans Schreiber & Ms. Karin Schreiber, Chicago, Illinois
Ms. Lillian H. Schwartz, Chicago, Illinois
Mr. Brian F. Sullivan & Ms. Kathleen Scullion, Winnetka, Illinois
Mr. Jack Segal, Chicago, Illinois
Dr. Michael Sha, Carmel, Indiana
Mr. & Mrs. Robert Eliot Shapiro, Chicago, Illinois
Mr. & Mrs. R. Chelsa Sharp, Limestone, Tennessee
Ms. Roberta L. Shaw, Toronto, Canada
Mrs. Daila Shefner, Chicago, Illinois
Mr. Robert M. Shelbourne & Mrs. Tatiana A. Shelbourne, Washington, DC
Mr. Kent Sheppard, Lake Forest, Illinois
Mrs. Junia Shlaustas, Chicago, Illinois
Mrs. Shirley Shostack, Dayton, Ohio
Ms. Annemie Sinka, Lombard, Illinois
Mr. Michael A. Sisinger & Ms. Judith E. Waggoner, Columbus, Ohio
Mr. & Mrs. Kenneth Small, Irvine, California
Ms. Amelia Smithers, Gentilino, Switzerland
Mr. & Mrs. Hugo F. Sonnenschein, Chicago, Illinois
South Suburban Archaeological Society, Homewood, Illinois
Mr. Stephen C. Sperry, Maple Grove, Minnesota
Mr. David A. Spetrino, Wilmington, North Carolina
Mr. & Mrs. Ronald W. Steele, Fairfax, Virginia
Stephen & Susan M. Baird Foundation, Winnetka, Illinois
Mrs. Phyllis Mazer Sternau, New York, New York
Mr. Stephen M. Stigler & Mrs. Virginia Stigler, Chicago, Illinois
Mr. Gary David Strandlund, Batavia, Illinois
Ms. Patricia Strenkert, New City, New York
Mrs. Patricia C. Study, Chicago, Illinois
Mr. Gerald Sufrin, Snyder, New York
Mr. George R. Sundell, Wheaton, Illinois
Mrs. Janet Rassenfoss & Mr. Alan Swanson, Wilmette, Illinois
Mrs. Peggy Lewis Sweesy, San Diego, California
Mrs. Faye E. Takeuchi, Vancouver, Canada
Mr. Michael Tausch, Vancouver, Washington
Mr. Joseph Daniel Cain & Ms. Emily Teeter, Chicago, Illinois
Mrs. Patricia T. Terman & Mr. William J. Terman, Highland Park, Illinois
The Malcolm Gibbs Foundation, Inc., New York, New York
The Pattis Family Foundation, Highland Park, Illinois
Mr. Roger Thornton & Mrs. Christine H. Thornton, Santa Monica, California

$100–$249 (*cont.*)

Ms. Leeann Thorton, Chicago, Illinois
Mr. Timothy M. Nolan, Chicago, Illinois
Mrs. Ann C. Tomlinson & Mr. Richard Tomlinson, Chicago, Illinois
Mrs. Harriet M. Turk, Joliet, Illinois
Mr. & Mrs. Russell H. Tuttle, Chicago, Illinois
Mr. Charles Ward Upton, Hudson, Ohio
Valparaiso University, Valparaiso, Indiana
Mr. Theo van den Hout & Ms. Lidwina van den Hout-Huijben, Chicago, Illinois
Ms. Annelize van der Ryst, Johannesburg, South Africa
Mr. James W. Vice Jr., Wabash, Indiana
Mr. John Vinci, Chicago, Illinois
Mr. Nicholas Vlamakis, Chicago, Illinois
Wabash College, Crawfordsville, Indiana
Mr. & Mrs. William R. Wallin, Wilmette, Illinois
Mr. Johannes Weertman & Ms. Julia R. Weertman, Evanston, Illinois
Mr. Matthew Weidman, Galesburg, Illinois
Mr. & Mrs. Stanley R. Weinberger, Evanston, Illinois
Dr. & Mrs. David B. Weisberg, Cincinnati, Ohio
Mr. & Mrs. J. Marshall Wellborn, New York, New York
Mr. & Mrs. Edward F. Wente, Chicago, Illinois
Mrs. Ellen Werner, Chicago, Illinois
Mr. Michael Weston, Evanston, Illinois
Mr. Arthur P. Wheatley, East Chicago, Indiana
Mr. & Mrs. Douglas R. White, Taneytown, Maryland
Dr. Willard E. White, Oak Park, Illinois
Mr. Jonathan D. Williams, Chicago, Illinois
Mr. Frederick Wilson, Evanston, Illinois
Ms. Debra Wingfield, Lenexa, Kansas
Mr. Mark Winter, Daytona Beach, Florida
Mrs. Molly Romer Witten & Mr. Thomas Adams Witten, Chicago, Illinois
Mrs. Grace W. Wolf, Chicago, Illinois
Ms. Ann S. Wolff, Winnetka, Illinois
Ms. Bette Wolfgang & Mr. James Wolfgang, Naperville, Illinois
Mr. Lawrence D. Wolin & Ms. Stacey Wolin, Chicago, Illinois
Mr. & Mrs. Fredrick Wright, Kingman, Arizona
Mr. Steven Wunderink, Henderson, Nevada
Ms. Carole Y. Yoshida, Orland Park, Illinois
Ms. Robin Young, La Habra, California
Ms. Mary L. Zimerle, Wheaton, Illinois

Every effort has been made by the Oriental Institute Development Office staff to ensure the accuracy of the donor list. We sincerely apologize for any inaccuracy in the names or the contributions. If your name has been listed incorrectly or you believe your name has been omitted, please accept our apologies and notify our office at 773-834-9775.

FACULTY AND STAFF

Overleaf: Model knife and goose head. Limestone and pigment. 13.6 x 7.0 x 2.4 cm. Old Kingdom, Dynasties 5-6, ca. 2435-2118 BC. Purchased in Cairo, 1920. OIM E10644. Between Heaven & Earth Catalog No. 38

FACULTY AND STAFF OF THE ORIENTAL INSTITUTE

July 1, 2012–June 30, 2013

EMERITUS FACULTY

Lanny Bell, Associate Professor Emeritus of Egyptology

Robert D. Biggs, Professor Emeritus of Assyriology
r-biggs@uchicago.edu, 702-9540

John A. Brinkman, Charles H. Swift Distinguished Service Professor Emeritus of Mesopotamian History
j-brinkman@uchicago.edu, 702-9545

Miguel Civil, Professor Emeritus of Sumerology
m-civil@uchicago.edu, 702-9542

Peter F. Dorman, Professor Emeritus of Egyptology
p-dorman@uchicago.edu

Gene B. Gragg, Professor Emeritus of Near Eastern Languages
g-gragg@uchicago.edu, 702-9511

Harry A. Hoffner Jr., John A. Wilson Professor Emeritus of Hittitology; Co-editor, Chicago Hittite Dictionary Project
hitt@uchicago.edu, 702-9527

Edward F. Wente, Professor Emeritus of Egyptology
e-wente@uchicago.edu, 702-9539

FACULTY

Fred M. Donner, Professor of Near Eastern History
f-donner@uchicago.edu, 702-9544

Walter T. Farber, Professor of Assyriology
w-farber@uchicago.edu, 702-9546

McGuire Gibson, Professor of Mesopotamian Archaeology
m-gibson@uchicago.edu, 702-9525

Petra Goedegebuure, Assistant Professor of Hittitology; Junior Editor, Chicago Hittite Dictionary Project
pgoedegebuure@uchicago.edu, 702-9550

Norman Golb, Ludwig Rosenberger Professor of Jewish History and Civilization
n-golb@uchicago.edu, 702-9526

Rebecca Hasselbach, Associate Professor of Comparative Semitics
hasselb@uchicago.edu, 834-3290

Janet H. Johnson, Morton D. Hull Distinguished Service Professor of Egyptology; Editor, Chicago Demotic Dictionary Project
j-johnson@uchicago.edu, 702-9530

Walter E. Kaegi, Professor of Byzantine-Islamic Studies
kwal@uchicago.edu, 702-8346, 702-8397

Nadine Moeller, Assistant Professor of Egyptian Archaeology
nmoeller@uchicago.edu, 834-9761

Brian P. Muhs, Associate Professor of Egyptology
bpmuhs@uchicago.edu, 702-9533

Dennis G. Pardee, Henry Crown Professor of Hebrew Studies
d-pardee@uchicago.edu, 702-9541

Robert K. Ritner, Professor of Egyptology
r-ritner@uchicago.edu, 702-9547

Martha T. Roth, Chauncey S. Boucher Distinguished Service Professor of Assyriology; Director and Editor-in-charge, Chicago Assyrian Dictionary Project; Dean, Division of the Humanities
mroth@uchicago.edu, 702-9551

David Schloen, Associate Professor of Syro-Palestinian Archaeology
d-schloen@uchicago.edu, 702-1382

Andrea Seri, Assistant Professor of Assyriology (until June 30, 2013)

Gil J. Stein, Professor of Near Eastern Archaeology; Director, Oriental Institute
gstein@uchicago.edu, 702-4098

Matthew W. Stolper, John A. Wilson Professor of Assyriology, Director, Persepolis Fortification Archive Project
m-stolper@uchicago.edu, 702-9553

Theo P. J. van den Hout, Professor of Hittite and Anatolian Languages; Executive Editor, Chicago Hittite Dictionary Project; Chairman, Department of Near Eastern Languages and Civilizations
tvdhout@uchicago.edu, 834-4688, 702-9527

Christopher Woods, Associate Professor of Sumerology; Editor, *Journal of Near Eastern Studies*
woods@uchicago.edu, 834-8560

K. Aslıhan Yener, Associate Professor of Archaeology
a-yener@uchicago.edu, 702-0568

RESEARCH ASSOCIATES

Abbas Alizadeh, Senior Research Associate, Iranian Prehistoric Project
a-alizadeh@uchicago.edu, 702-9531

Annalisa Azzoni, Research Associate, Persepolis Fortification Archive Project
annalisa.azzoni@vanderbilt.net

Richard H. Beal, Senior Research Associate, Chicago Hittite Dictionary Project
r-beal@uchicago.edu, 702-9527

Scott Branting, Research Associate (Assistant Professor); Director, Center for Ancient Middle
Eastern Landscapes (CAMEL)
branting@uchicago.edu, 834-1152

Stuart Creason, Research Associate, Syriac Manuscript Project (until 9/30/2012)
s-creason@uchicago.edu, 834-8348

Vanessa Davies, Meteor Project
jmevans@uchicago.edu

Jean Evans, Research Associate, Nippur Project
jmevans@uchicago.edu

Gertrud Farber, Research Associate, Sumerian Lexicon Project
g-farber@uchicago.edu, 702-9548

Mark Garrison, Research Associate, Persepolis Fortification Archive Project
mgarriso@trinity.edu

François Gaudard, Research Associate; Associate Editor, Chicago Demotic Dictionary Project;
Co-editor, Mummy Label Database Project
fgaudard@uchicago.edu, 702-9528

Ronald Gorny, Research Associate, Alishar Regional Project
rlg2@uchicago.edu, 702-8624

Yağmur Heffron, Research Associate, Zincirli Project

Lisa Heidorn, Research Associate, Oriental Institute Nubian Expedition
lheidorn@uchicago.edu

Wouter Henkelman, Research Associate, Persepolis Fortification Archive Project
wouterhenkelman@gmail.com

Carrie Hritz, Research Associate, Zeidan Project, Girsu Project

W. Raymond Johnson, Research Associate (Associate Professor); Field Director, Epigraphic
Survey
wr-johnson@uchicago.edu, 834-4355

Charles E. Jones, Research Associate, Persepolis Fortification Archive Project
cejo@uchicago.edu

Morag M. Kersel, Research Associate, Galilee Prehistory Project

Mark Lehner, Research Associate, Giza Plateau Mapping Project
MarkLehner@aol.com

Lec Maj, Research Associate, Persepolis Fortification Archive Project
lec@uchicago.edu

Gregory Marouard, Research Associate, Tell Edfu Project
marouardg@uchicago.edu, 834-4270

Greg McMahon, Research Associate, Çadır Höyük Project

J. Brett McClain, Research Associate; Senior Epigrapher, Epigraphic Survey
jbmcclai@uchicago.edu, 702-9524

Carol Meyer, Research Associate, Bir Umm Fawakhir Project
c-meyer@uchicago.edu

Rana Özbal, Research Associate, Tell Kurdu Project

Hratch Papazian, Research Associate
hratch@uchicago.edu

Marina Pucci, Research Associate, Chatal Höyük Publication Project

Clemens D. Reichel, Senior Research Associate, Diyala Project, Hamoukar
cdreiche@uchicago.edu, (416) 586-7938

Yorke Rowan, Research Associate, Ancient Studies; Director, Galilee Prehistory Project
ymrowan@uchicago.edu, 702-0086

Moain Sadeq, Research Associate, Khirbat al-Mafjar Project
msadeq@uchicago.edu

John C. Sanders, Senior Research Associate; Head, Computer Laboratory (until 1/15/2013)
jc-sanders@uchicago.edu, 702-0989

Oğuz Soysal, Senior Research Associate, Chicago Hittite Dictionary Project
o-soysal@uchicago.edu, 702-3644

Geoffrey D. Summers, Research Associate, Kerkenes Project
summers@metu.edu.tr

Emily Teeter, Research Associate; Special Exhibits Coordinator, Museum
eteeter@uchicago.edu, 702-1062

Joanna Then-Obluska, Research Associate, Oriental Institute Nubian Expedition

Raymond Tindel, Research Associate
r-tindel@uchicago.edu

Tasha Vorderstrasse, Research Associate, Islamic Archaeology Publication Project
tkvorder@uchicago.edu

John Z. Wee, Provost's Career Enhancement Postdoctoral Scholarship (from 8/1/2012)
johnwee@uchicago.edu, 702-7497

Donald Whitcomb, Research Associate (Associate Professor), Islamic and Medieval Archaeology
d-whitcomb@uchicago.edu, 702-9530

Magnus Widell, Research Associate
widell@uchicago.edu

Tony Wilkinson, Research Associate, MASS Project
t.j.wilkinson@durham.ac.uk

Bruce B. Williams, Research Associate
bbwillia@uchicago.edu, 702-3686

Karen L. Wilson, Research Associate
k-wilson@uchicago.edu

Richard Zettler, Research Associate
rzettler@sas.upenn.edu

STAFF

Mohamed Abo El Makarem, Conservator, Epigraphic Survey
702-9524

Keli Alberts, Artist, Epigraphic Survey
kelialberts@hotmail.com

Susan Allison, Assistant Registrar, Museum
srallison@uchicago.edu, 702-9518

Nahed Samir Andraus, Conservator, Epigraphic Survey

Alain Arnaudiès, Digital Archives Database, Epigraphic Survey
arnaudies@laposte.net

Emmanuelle Arnaudiès, Digital Archives Database, Epigraphic Survey
emmanuellearnaudies@free.fr

Jason Barcus, Visitor Services and Security Manager
jbarcus@uchicago.edu, 702-5112

Denise Browning, Manager, Suq
d-browning1@uchicago.edu, 702-9509

Birte Brugmann, Field Research Coordinator

Marie Bryan, Librarian, Epigraphic Survey
mebryan@usa.net, 702-9524

Rebecca Cain, Assistant Editor
rebeccacain@uchicago.edu, 702-5967

Steven Camp, Executive Director
shcamp@uchicago.edu, 702-1404

Dennis Campbell, Research Project Professional, Persepolis Fortification Archive Project
drcampbell@uchicago.edu, 702-5249

D'Ann Condes, Financial Manager
dcondes@uchicago.edu, 834-9886

Simona Cristanetti, Contract Conservator, Persepolis Fortification Archive Project (since May 2013)
cristanetti@uchicago.edu, 702-9519

Laura D'Alessandro, Head, Conservation Laboratory, Museum
lada@uchicago.edu, 702-9519

Margaret De Jong, Senior Artist, Epigraphic Survey
mdejong98ch@hotmail.com, 702-9524

Christina Di Cerbo, Epigrapher/Artist, Epigraphic Survey
tinadicerbo@hotmail.com, 702-9524

Catherine Dueñas, Volunteer Coordinator, Public Education (until 2/15/2013)
c-duenas@uchicago.edu, 702-1845

Wendy Ennes, Associate Head, Public Education (until 9/7/2012)
wennes@uchicago.edu, 834-7606

Michael T. Fisher, Field Registration Coordinator
mtf@uchicago.edu

Terry Friedman, Volunteer Manager, Public Education
et-friedman@uchicago.edu, 702-1845

Steven D. George, Research Assistant, Diyala Project
sdgeorge@uchicago.edu, 702-2589

Susan Geshwender, Program Associate, Public Education
geshwender@uchicago.edu, 702-1845

Christian Greco, Epigrapher, Epigraphic Survey
christian.greco@usa.net

Jack Green, Chief Curator, Museum
jdmgreen@uchicago.edu, 702-9863

Moriah Grooms-Garcia, Youth and Family Program Coordinator, Public Education
mggarcia@uchicago.edu, 702-9507

Samir Guindy, Administrator, Epigraphic Survey
samsgu1952@hotmail.com

Lotfi Hassan, Conservator, Epigraphic Survey
hslotfi@yahoo.it, 702-9524

Robyn Haynie, Contract Conservator, Persepolis Fortification Archive Project (until November 2012)

James B. Heidel, Architect/Artist, Epigraphic Survey
jbheidel@gmail.com, 702-9524

Anait Helmholz, Librarian, Epigraphic Survey
anaith@succeed.net

Frank Helmholz, Stonemason, Epigraphic Survey
frankhelmholz8@gmail.com, 702-9524

Jason Herrmann, Research Project Professional, Persepolis Fortification Archive Project
herrmann@uchicago.edu

Helen Jacquet†, Egyptologist Consultant, Epigraphic Survey
jean-jacquet@bluewin.ch, 702-9524

Jean Jacquet, Architect Consultant, Epigraphic Survey
jean-jacquet@bluewin.ch, 702-9524

Richard Jasnow, Epigrapher Consultant, Epigraphic Survey
rjasnow@jhu.edu, 702-9524

Hiroko Kariya, Conservator, Epigraphic Survey
hkariya@aol.com, 702-9524

Catherine Kenyon, Head, Public Education and Outreach (from 9/10/12)
ckenyon@uchicago.edu, 834-5401

Jen Kimpton, Epigrapher, Epigraphic Survey
jenkimpton@hotmail.com, 702-9524

Yarko Kobylecky, Photographer, Epigraphic Survey
museumphoto@hotmail.com, 702-9524

Carole Krucoff, Head, Public Education (until 9/1/2012)
c-krucoff@uchicago.edu, 702-9507

John A. Larson, Museum Archivist, Museum
ja-larson@uchicago.edu, 702-9924

Susan Lezon, Photo Archivist and Photographer, Epigraphic Survey
suelezon@gmail.com, 702-9524

Erik Lindahl, Gallery Preparator, Museum
lindahl@uchicago.edu, 702-9516

Adam Lubin, Financial Management Assistant
alubin@uchicago.edu, 834-0451

Jill Carlotta Maher, Assistant to the Director, Epigraphic Survey
jillcarlottamaher@yahoo.com, 702-9524

Samwell Maher, Assistant Administrator, Epigraphic Survey
samwellmaher@yahoo.com, 702-9524

Massimo Maiocchi, Mellon Postdoctoral Fellow (from 10/1/2012)
maiocchi@uchicago.edu, 702-2589

Helen McDonald, Registrar, Museum
helenmcd@uchicago.edu, 702-9518

Miriam Müller, Postdoctoral Scholar (from 9/1/2012)
mmuller@uchicago.edu, 702-7497

Brittany F. Mullins, Assistant Director of Development (from 10/15/2012)
bfmullins@uchicago.edu, 834-9775

Carol Ng-He, K–12 and Continuing Education Program Developer, Public Education (from 11/19/2012)
cnghe@uchicago.edu, 702-1158

Susan Osgood, Senior Artist, Epigraphic Survey
sittsu@sover.net, 702-9524

Mariana Perlinac, Assistant to the Director
oi-administration@uchicago.edu, 834-8098

Conor Power, Structural Engineer, Epigraphic Survey
conorpower@msn.com, 702-9524

Miller Prosser, Research Database Specialist, OCHRE Data Service
m-prosser@uchicago.edu

Anna R. Ressman, Head of Photography, Museum
annaressman@uchicago.edu, 702-9517

Seth Richardson, Managing Editor, *Journal of Near Eastern Studies*
seth1@uchicago.edu, 702-9552

Paul Ruffin, Head, Computer Laboratory (from 2/27/2013)
pruffin@uchicago.edu, 702-0989

Girgis Samwell, Chief Engineer, Epigraphic Survey
702-9524

Essam El Sayed, Senior Accountant, Epigraphic Survey
essam_nadosb@yahoo.com, 702-9524

Foy Scalf, Head, Research Archives
scalffd@uchicago.edu, 702-9537

Sandra Schloen, Manager, OCHRE Data Service
sschloen@uchicago.edu

Julia Schmied, Blockyard and Archives Assistant/Epigrapher, Epigraphic Survey
julisch@citromail.hu, 702-9524

Leslie Schramer, Editor, Publications Office
leslie@uchicago.edu, 702-5967

Elinor Smith, Photo Archives Registrar, Epigraphic Survey
elliesmith26@yahoo.com, 702-9524

Amir Sumaka'i Fink, Research Project Professional, Zincirli Project
asumakai@uchicago.edu

Tracy Tajbl, Director of Development
ttajbl@uchicago.edu, 702-5062

Oya Topçuoğlu, Assistant, Chicago Hittite Dictionary Project,
oyatopcuoglu@uchicago.edu, 702-9543

Thomas G. Urban, Managing Editor, Publications Office
turban@uchicago.edu, 702-5967

Mónica Vélez, Curatorial Assistant, Museum
    mgvelez@uchicago.edu, 702-9520

Krisztián Vértes, Artist, Epigraphic Survey
    euergetes@citromail.hu, 702-9524

Amy Weber, Membership Program Manager
    amyweber@uchicago.edu, 834-9777

Alison Whyte, Associate Conservator, Museum
    aawhyte@uchicago.edu, 702-9519

Arne Wossink, Research Project Professional, Persepolis Fortification Archive Project
    awossink@uchicago.edu

Brian Zimerle, Preparator, Museum
    zimerle@uchicago.edu, 702-9516

—————————————

INFORMATION

INFORMATION

The Oriental Institute
1155 East 58th Street
Chicago, Illinois 60637

Museum gallery hours:
    Tuesday and Thursday to Saturday 10:00 AM–6:00 PM
    Wednesday 10:00 AM–8:30 PM
    Sunday 12:00 NOON–6:00 PM

Telephone Numbers (Area Code 773) and Electronic Addresses

Administrative Office, oi-administration@uchicago.edu, 702-9514
Archaeology Laboratory, 702-1407
Assyrian Dictionary Project, 702-9551
Computer Laboratory, 702-0989
Conservation Laboratory, 702-9519
Department of Near Eastern Languages and Civilizations, 702-9512
Demotic Dictionary Project, 702-9528
Development Office, 834-9775, oi-development@uchicago.edu
Director's Office, 834-8098
Epigraphic Survey, 702-9524
Executive Director, 702-1404
Facsimile, 702-9853
Hittite Dictionary Project, 702-9543
Journal of Near Eastern Studies, 702-9592
Membership Office, oi-membership@uchicago.edu, 702-9513
Museum Archives, 702-9520
Museum Information, 702-9520
Museum Office, oi-museum@uchicago.edu, 702-9520
Museum Registration, 702-9518
Public Education, oi-education@uchicago.edu, 702-9507
Publications Editorial Office, oi-publications@uchicago.edu, 702-5967
Research Archives, 702-9537
Security, 702-9522
Suq Gift and Book Shop, 702-9510
Suq Office, 702-9509
Volunteer Guides, 702-1845

———————————

World-Wide Web Address

http://oi.uchicago.edu

———————————